Best Resumes for $100,000+ Jobs

Wendy S. Enelow, CPRW, JCTC, CCM

IMPACT PUBLICATIONS
Manassas Park, Virginia

Best Resumes For $100,000+ Jobs

Library of Congress Cataloging-in-Publication Data

Enelow, Wendy S.
    Best resumes for $100,000+ jobs / Wendy S. Enelow
      p. cm.
    Rev. ed. of: 100 winning resumes for $100,000+ jobs : resumes that can change
your life / Wendy S. Enelow. c1997.
    Includes bibliographical references and index.
    ISBN 1-57023-168-0
    1. Resumes (Employment) I. Title: Best resumes for one hundred thousand dollar
plus jobs. II. Enelow, Wendy S. 100 winning resumes for $100,000+ jobs. III. Title.

HF5383 .E479 2001
808'.06665--dc21   2001024154

Publisher: For information, including current and forthcoming publications, authors, press kits, and submission guidelines, visit Impact's Web site: *www.impactpublications.com*

Publicity/Rights: For information on publicity, author interviews, and subsidiary rights, contact Media Relations: Tel. 703-361-7300 or Fax 703-335-9486.

Sales/Distribution: For information on distribution or quantity discount rates, call (703-361-7300), fax (703-335-9486), e-mail (*resumes@impactpublications.com*) or write: Sales Department, Impact Publications, 9104 Manassas Drive, Suite N, Manassas Park, VA 20111. Bookstore orders should be directed to our trade distributor: National Book Network, 15200 NBN Way, Blue Ridge Summit, PA 17214, Tel. 1-800-462-6420.

Contents

Appendices 253

Preface

Let's get things straight right from the beginning. When I wrote this book, I wrote it for individuals, like yourself, *who are the best* or aspire *to be the best* – in their professions, their careers and their lives. This book was *not* written for the faint of heart nor faint of career. It was written for those who strive to move forward and upward in their careers, who push themselves to reach new heights, and who are energized, not intimidated, by challenge.

This book was written for Chairmen, Presidents, Chief Executive Officers (CEOs), Chief Operating Officers (COOs), Chief Financial Officers (CFOs), Chief Information Officers (CIOs) and Chief Knowledge Officers (CKOs). It was written for General Managers, Directors, Executive Vice Presidents and Vice Presidents who are already earning $100,000 a year or more.

This book was also written for mid-level professionals and managers aspiring to reach new heights, assume greater professional responsibilities and pursue new career opportunities. It was written for the Sales Representative making $65,000 a year and working toward that $100,000+ salary. It was written for the Purchasing Supervisor making $75,000 a year and applying for a position with a starting salary of $100,000. It was written for the MBA graduate who is just launching his career and knows that, in years to come, he will be making $100,000 a year or more.

In summary, this book was written for *you* – the leaders and aspiring leaders of the business world.

Best Resumes
for $100,000+ Jobs

1

Writing Your Best Resume

Over the past decade, as the U.S. economy has undergone dramatic and long-lasting changes, the business world has globalized and the employment market become more competitive, resume writing has evolved into a much more complex and more sophisticated process. No longer is it sufficient to type a brief listing of your work history and academic credentials. Remember the days when you prepared your resume in this fashion, passed it along to a few business associates and mailed a handful in response to advertisements? Within a week you were interviewing and within 2-3 weeks you were working.

If you remember that, forget it! The times have changed and the market has changed. Today, resume writing is a competition among often very well-qualified candidates vying for a limited number of opportunities. For that reason alone, resume writing has evolved into an art where, you, as the artist, must transition a blank canvas into a work of art that displays your talents, knowledge, expertise and success.

Showcase Your Talents & Strengths

A resume is the foundation for any successful search campaign and, in fact, it is virtually impossible to manage a job search without a resume. It is your calling card, your brochure, your marketing document. People look at it and are impressed with you and what you have accomplished. You mail it, you email it, you fax it, you hand-carry it, and you leave it behind after an interview so people have something to remember you by. Your resume is crucial in building market visibility and ultimately facilitating job search success.

To understand the value of your resume to your job search process, it is best to start with a clear definition of what a resume is. It is defined as:

- A "sales" document that clearly and succinctly communicates your professional skills, qualifications, knowledge, success and industry expertise.
- A tool designed to sell the high points of your career – your successes and achievements.
- A document that demonstrates the value you bring to a prospective employer.
- A visual presentation that communicates an executive image.

A resume is not:

- A biography of your entire career, every job you have ever held, every internship you have ever completed and every course you have ever attended.
- A document containing lengthy job descriptions and lists of duties and responsibilities.
- A passive, low-energy and narrative summary of your work history.

Today's Competitive $100,000+ Resume

Above is a precise outline of what a resume is and is not. Commonsense would have it that if you followed that outline, you'd know precisely what to do. However, as an executive job seeker, you face unique challenges in developing, writing and designing a resume that will position you for a $100,000+ position.

What it is that makes your resume so very different from others? What must you do to competitively position your resume and make it get noticed in the crowd of other qualified candidates? What makes your resume so special and so unique? The answers are straightforward:

- **$100,000 resumes** are marketing tools, written to "sell" a job seeker into his or her next position.
- **$100,000+ resumes** are dynamic, distinctive and hard-hitting.

- ***$100,000+ resumes*** present a clear and concise picture of "who" the job search candidate is.
- ***$100,000+ resumes*** are sharp and upscale in their visual presentation.
- ***$100,000+ resumes*** focus on success and achievement.
- ***$100,000+ resumes*** clearly communicate the value of a job seeker.
- ***$100,000+ resumes*** highlight the experiences, qualifications and knowledge that make each candidate unique.

Most significantly, the writing, tone, style and presentation of a $100,000+ resume must be superb. The wording must be aggressive and the presentation top-of-the-line. The impression it leaves the reader with must be that of an accomplished and successful executive who has delivered strong results and demonstrated outstanding leadership skills. The resume must communicate "I bring value to you and to your organization." If you are ever going to "toot your own horn," *this is the time to do it!*

Translating Your Qualifications Into Hard-Hitting Resume Content

Etch these words into your head, your heart and your soul ... *Resume writing is sales!* Say that phrase over and over until it becomes a part of you, for it is this mindset that will propel you to write a top-notch executive resume.

Your resume is a document that should be written specifically to market and merchandise *your* talents. Critical to that concept is the "sell it to me, don't tell it to me" strategy. Think about that. You do not want to tell someone what you have done. Rather, you want to *sell* what you have accomplished. How do you do that? You do that by writing powerful sentences, highlighting your achievements and qualifications, using action verbs, and creating a resume that communicates success.

To better understand the concept of selling your qualifications, here are a few examples:

Poor Example:

- Managed 12 sales regions and 82 sales associates throughout the U.S.

Good Example:

- Independently planned and directed a team of 82 sales associates marketing sophisticated networking and E-commerce products throughout the Northeastern U.S. Closed 1999 at 175% of revenue quota and 187% of profit goal.

Poor Example:

- Managed accounting, financial reporting, budgeting and MIS functions.

Good Example:

- Chief Financial Officer with full responsibility for the corporate finance organization for a $270 million industrial plastics manufacturer. Directed financial planning, accounting, tax, treasury, budgeting and MIS functions. Managed a direct reporting staff of 12.

Poor Example:

- Hired to reorganize the entire administrative function of the company.

Good Example:

- Recruited by Chief Administrative Officer to plan and direct the complete redesign and reorganization of all administrative and support functions for Dell's 2000-employee customer support network. Reduced operating costs 15% in first six months.

"Sell it to me, don't tell it to me" ... see what a difference in makes in the words, the tone, the style and the impact?

Use The Language Of Key Words

The words that you select create the tone and energy of your resume. If you use words such as "responsible for" and "duties included," your resume becomes passive, boring and repetitive. But when you use words such as ... directed, designed, created, achieved, delivered, increased, improved, launched, revitalized ... your resume comes to life and communicates energy, drive and achievement.

There are four strategies to follow that will help you determine your word choice. All except #3 are critical to every individual writing a resume. Strategy #3 is important only if your job search is focused on a particular industry or related group of industries.

✓ *Strategy #1:* Write in the active first-person (dropping the "I's"); never the third-person. What does this mean? Here's an example:

Active First-Person: Reduced annual purchasing costs
by 12%.

Third-Person: Mr. Smith reduced annual purchasing costs
by 12%.

Can you see the difference? The first example communicates "I did this." The second example communicates "Mr. Smith, the other guy, did that" and it moves ownership away from you. Your resume must be a part of who you are and not a distant third-party voice.

✓ *Strategy #2:* Use key words specific to your current professional goals. If you're looking for a job in sales, use sales, marketing and customer service words. If you're looking for a position in manufacturing, use words related to production, product management, inventory and workforce management. These key words are essential if you want to communicate you have the "right" set of skills and experience for the type of position you are seeking. What's more, key words are an essential component in the resume scanning process (when companies and recruiters use scanners to determine if you have the appropriate skills and qualifications for a particular opportunity). The computer, not a person, "reads" your resume. Therefore, word choice is critical.

✓ *Strategy #3:* Use key words specific to your current preferences for type of industry. Strategy #3 is applicable only if your job search is industry-specific. If you are looking for a position in a technology industry, use the appropriate technology acronyms. If you're looking for a position in the retail industry, talk about buying, merchandising and loss prevention. If the insurance industry is your objective, use words such as indemnity, E&O and risk assessment. These key words are essential if you want to communicate you have the "right" set of skills and experience for the industry. What's more, just as with "professional" key words, "industry" key words have become an essential component in the resume scanning process.

Here are a few sample key words for 28 different professions and industries. Use this list to get you thinking about the key words that are specific to your profession (Strategy #2) and your industry (Strategy #3).

➤ **Accounting:** Payables, Receivables, General Ledger, Financial Analysis, Reporting, Audit, Budgeting, Month-End Closings

➤ **Administration:** Executive Liaison Affairs, Board of Directors, Minutes, Recordkeeping, Scheduling, Project Administration

➤ **Association Management**: Fundraising, Corporate Sponsorships, Member Services, Outreach, Advocacy, Regulatory & Legal Affairs

➤ **Banking:** De Novo Banking, Commercial, Retail, Back Office, Lending, Cross-Border Transactions, Regulatory Compliance

➤ **Construction**: Commercial, Industrial & Residential, Project Planning, Scheduling, Contracts, Environmental Assessment

➤ **Corporate Finance**: Tax, Treasury, Mergers, Acquisitions, Budgeting, Cost Avoidance, Investment Management, Forecasting, Analysis

➤ **Education:** Curriculum Development, Instructional Systems Design, Program Administration, Testing & Placement, Training

➤ **Engineering:** Prototype Development, Project Management, Failure Analysis, Reliability, Experimental Design, Product Functionality

➤ **Government**: Regulatory Compliance & Reporting, Public/Private Sector, Competitive Bidding, Fixed Price Contracts, VIP Relations

➤ **Health Care:** Patient Management, Treatment Planning, Emergency Intervention, Invasive Therapies, Utilization Review

➤ **Hospitality:** Food & Beverage, Guest Relations, Facilities Management, Meetings & Events, Amenities, Labor & Food Cost Controls

➤ **Human Resources:** Staffing, Training & Development, Compensation, Benefits Administration, Employee Assistance, HRIS Technology

➢ **Human Services:** Diagnostic Assessment, Case Management, Inter-Agency Relations, Crisis Intervention, Treatment Planning

➢ **Information Technology:** Client/Server, Web-Enabling, Internet/Intranet, Integration, Migration, Configuration, Platform, Hardware, Software

➢ **Insurance:** Claims Administration, Risk Management, Liability, P&C, E&O, LLC, Portfolio Management, Client Development

➢ **Investment Finance:** Mergers, Acquisitions, Joint Ventures, Venture Funding, ROI, ROA, ROE, Portfolio Management, NASD, Cross-Border

➢ **Law/Legal:** Legal Research & Writing, Case Management, Judicial Proceedings, Investigations, Client Representation

➢ **Logistics:** Purchasing, Supply Chain, Inventory Planning, Warehousing, Distribution, Transportation, Resource & Asset Management

➢ **Manufacturing:** Productivity & Yield Improvement, Cost Reduction, MRP, JIT, Manufacturing Cell, Quality, Materials, Scheduling, Control

➢ **Marketing:** Multimedia Communications & Presentations, New Market Development, Product Launch, Advertising, Branding

➢ **Media**: New Media, Production, Direction, Broadcasting, On-Air Talent, Studio Engineering, E-Commerce, Press Relations

➢ **Purchasing** Supply Chain Management, Vendor Sourcing, Contract Negotiations, Fixed Price, Inventory Planning,

➢ **Quality:** Engineering, Reliability, ISO, TQM, Quality Assurance, Failure Analysis & Reporting, Product Performance, Quality Audits

➢ **Real Estate:** Residential, Commercial & Industrial Properties, Buy/Sell Negotiations, Contracts, Regulatory Compliance, Marketing

➢ **Retail:** Multi-Site Operations, Merchandising, Loss Prevention, Sales, Customer Service, Training, Facilities, Buying, In-Store Events

➢ **Sales:** Customer Presentations, Negotiations, Sales Closings, New Product Launch, Contracts, Competitive Positioning

➢ **Security:** Corporate Security, VIP Protection, Risk Assessment, Perimeter & Facilities Control, Emergency Preparedness

> **Telecommunications**: Infrastructure, Technology, Networking, Internet/Intranet, Cellular, Base Station, Voice & Data, Secure Transmissions

✓ **Strategy #4:** Write for the level of position you are pursuing – professional, managerial and executive. Use hard-hitting words and phrases that communicate the level of expertise that you bring to an organization. Do not talk about "controlling revenues"; talk about "P&L management." Do not talk about "supervising staff"; talk about "building and leading a 20-person management team." Use words and phrases such as:

- Accelerating Revenue Growth

- Aggressive Turnaround Leadership

- Best-in-Class Operations

- Capturing Cost Reductions

- Competitively Positioning Products, Services & Technologies

- Continuous Improvement

- Cross-Cultural Communications

- Cross-Culturally Sensitive

- Cross-Functional Team Leadership

- Distinguished Performance

- Driving Product Development & Innovation

- E-Commerce & E-Business

- Emerging Ventures

- Entrepreneurial Drive & Vision

- Executive Presentations & Negotiations

- Fast-Track Promotion

- Global Business Development

- High-Performance

- International Business Expansion

- Matrix Management

- Mergers & Acquisitions

- Multinational Organizations

- Negotiating Strategic Alliances

- New Media

- Organization(al) Leadership

- Outperforming Global Competition

- Outsourcing Operations

- Partnerships & Joint Ventures

- Performance Revitalization

- Pioneering Technologies

- Proactive Change Agent

- Process Redesign & Optimization

- Start-Up, Turnaround & High-Growth Organizations

- Strong & Sustainable Revenue Gains

- Technologically Sophisticated Organizations

- Visionary Leadership

2

Creating A Powerful Resume

Before you can ever begin to write your resume, you must decide the resume style and the presentation style that are right for you.

Making The Best Choices

Resume style will be dictated by your career history and your current career objectives. If you want to focus on your strong track record of employment experience, you'll want to use a Chronological Resume. If, on the other hand, you want a heavy focus on your skills and qualifications (more than on your work history), the Functional Resume would be your best choice. However, if you want to combine your strong work history with a clear focus on skills and qualifications, you may consider using a Combination Resume. The latter offers the "best of both worlds" as you will note from many, many of the samples in this book.

Presentation style will be determined by the manner in which you are planning to use your resume. If you are going to be printing and mailing copies, you'll want to use a Printed Resume. If you plan to send your resumes via email, an Electronic Resume will be right for you. And, if you want to combine the aesthetic qualities of the Printed Resume with the ease in transmission of the Electronic Resume, you may consider a Web Resume.

The sections explore each type of resume style and each type of presentation style. After reading these sections you should be able to quickly determine which styles are right for you based on your current career situation and objectives.

The Three Types of Resume Styles

For about as long as resumes have existed (particularly in their current state over the past 20 years), there has been an ongoing controversy about the use and effectiveness of chronological resumes versus functional resumes versus the more recent, combination-style resumes. To better understand the difference between each of them and to help you determine which is right for you, let's explore the plusses and minuses of all three.

The Chronological Resume

Chronological resumes provide a step-by-step path through your career. Starting with your current or most recent position, chronological resumes work backwards, allowing you to put the emphasis on your current and most recent experiences. As you progress further back in your career, job descriptions are shorter with an emphasis on achievements and not daily responsibilities.

Chronological resumes are the resume style preferred by the vast majority of employers and recruiters. They are easy to read and understand, clearly communicating where you have worked and what you have done. Unless your particular situation is unusual, a chronological resume will be your best marketing tool.

The Functional Resume

Functional resumes focus on the skills and qualifications you offer to a prospective employer. It is this type of information that is brought to the forefront and accentuated, while the employment experience is just briefly mentioned at the end. Individuals who might consider a functional resume are career changers, professionals returning to work after an extended absence, individuals who have been in the job market for a lengthy period of time, or candidates who are 55+ years of age. In these situations, the job seeker wants to focus on his specific expertise, qualifications and competencies, and not his employment experience.

Functional resumes are much less frequently used, particularly by $100,000+ candidates. Many corporate human resource professionals and recruiters look at these resumes with less interest, believing that the candidate is hiding something or attempting to "mess with reality." Be extremely careful if you decide this is the right style for you, and be sure to include your complete job history at the end.

The Combination-Style Resume

The most recent trend in resume writing is to combine the structure of the chronological resume with the skills focus of the functional resume. By starting your resume with a Career Summary, you can begin with a heavy focus on the qualifications and value you offer (functional approach), and then substantiate it with solid, well-written and accomplishment-oriented position descriptions (chronological approach). Many of the resumes in this book reflect this new Combination Style Resume.

Combination Style Resumes give you the "best of both worlds" – an intense focus on your qualifications combined with the strength of a solid employment history. They are a powerful marketing tool.

The Three Types of Presentation Styles

No resume discussion is complete these days without a dual focus on both printed resumes and electronics resumes. Chances are you will be sending just as many resumes via email as you will on paper, if not more. It is critical to understand the similarities and the differences in the visual presentation of the two.

The Traditional Printed Resume

The single most important thing to remember when you are preparing a printed resume is that you are writing a sales document. You have a product to sell – yourself – and it must be attractively packaged and presented. To compete against hundreds, if not thousands, of other qualified candidates, your resume must be sharp, distinct and dynamic.

Your resume should have an up-to-date style that is bold and attracts attention. This doesn't mean using an italic typeface, cute logos or an outrageous paper color. Instead, be *conservatively distinctive*. Choose a sharp-looking typeface such as Bookman, Soutane, Krone, Garamond or Fritz, or if your font selection is limited, the more common Times Roman, CG Omega or Arial typefaces. The samples in this book will further demonstrate how to create documents that are sharp and upscale while still remaining conservative and "to the point."

Paper color should be clean and conservative, preferably white, ivory or light gray. You can even consider a bordered paper (e.g., light gray paper with small white border around the perimeter). It is only for "creative" positions (e.g., graphic arts, theater, media) where colored papers can be appropriate and are an important part of the packaging. In these situations, your challenge is to visually demonstrate your creative talents.

If possible, adhere to these formatting guidelines when preparing your printed resume:

- Do not expect readers to struggle through 10-15 line paragraphs. Substitute 2-3 shorter paragraphs or use bullets to offset new sentences and sections.

- Do not overdo **bold** and *italics* type. Excessive use of either defeats the purpose of these enhancements. If half of the type on the page is bold, nothing will stand out.

- Use nothing smaller than 10-point type. If you want employers to read your resume, make sure they don't need a magnifying glass!

- Don't clutter your resume. Everything you have heard about "white space" is true. Let your document "breathe" so readers do not have to struggle through it.

- Use an excellent printer. Smudged, faint, heavy or otherwise poor quality print will discourage red-eyed readers.

The Electronic Resume

When discussing electronic resumes, take everything that is really important about preparing a printed resume and forget it! Electronic resumes are an entirely different creature with their own set of rules. They are "plain Jane" resumes stripped to the bone to allow for ease in file transfer, email and other technical applications. Professional resume writers, who work so hard to make each resume look good, "freak out," while engineers love how neat and clean these resumes are!

If possible, adhere to these formatting guidelines when preparing your electronic resume:

- Avoid **bold** print, <u>underlining</u>, *italics* and other type enhancements. If you want to draw attention to a specific word, heading or title, use CAPITALIZATION to make it stand out.

- Type all information starting on the left hand side of the page. Do not center or justify any of the text for it generally does not translate well electronically.

- Leave lots of white space just as you would with a printed resume. Ease in readability is a key factor in any type of communication.

- Length is not as critical a consideration with electronic resumes as it is with printed resumes. Therefore, instead of typing all your technical skills in a paragraph form, type them in a long list. Instead of putting your key words in a double-column format, type them in a list. It is a much easier read for the human eye!

Your electronic resume will automatically be presented in Courier typestyle. You have no control over this for it is the automatic default.

The Emerging Web Resume

As one would expect, a new phenomenon is emerging that allows you to merge the visual distinction of the printed resume with the ease of the electronic resume. The new web resume is hosted on your own website where you can refer recruiters, colleagues, potential employers and others. Rather than pasting your plain-looking electronic resume into an email message, include a link to your URL. With just one click, your printed resume instantly appears. It is easy, it is efficient and resume writers are breathing much easier!

With a web resume, you also have the opportunity to include more information than you would with the traditional printed resume that you mail. You can have separate sections for achieve

ments, project highlights, management competencies, technology skills and more. Everything is just a click away. For a good example of how such a website is structured, go to www.100000dollarcareers.com.

For those of you in technology industries, you can even go one step further and create a multimedia presentation. Never before have you been able to create a resume that actually demonstrates your technical expertise. Just think of the competitive advantage a web resume can give your job search.

Expert Resources

In order to give yourself the competitive job search advantage, it is often wise to consult a resume, career or job search expert. These individuals can provide you with insights and expert guidance as you plan and manage your search campaign. You have your choice of working with a professional resume writer, executive career coach, career counselor, outplacement consultant, recruiter and others who deliver job search services and support to candidates like yourself.

What's more, there are companies that will post your resume online, other companies that post position announcements on the web, and others that produce targeted email and print campaigns to prospective employers that you select. There are reference checking companies, coaches who specialize in interview training, and publications galore on executive job search and career marketing.

The list of potential resources is virtually endless, from the resume writer down the street to the global outplacement consulting firm with offices on 6 out of 7 continents. The emergence of all these firms has created a wealth of resources for job seekers, but also made the process much more difficult with so many choices. How do you determine exactly what help you need and from whom? Then, how do you find the right person?

Refer to Appendix A for a list of the professional members of the Career Masters Institute, a prestigious professional association whose members work with job seekers worldwide to help them plan and manage successful search campaigns. They are resume writers, career coaches, counselors, college development specialists, recruiters, outplacement consultants and others, ready, willing and able to provide you with expert job search and career planning assistance.

3

Building Your Best Resume

Writing the best resume would be an easy task if I could simply present you with a standard outline or template. All you would need to do is answer the questions and fill in the blanks, and your resume would be ready. Not much time, not much serious thought and no tremendous effort.

Step-By-Step Process

Unfortunately, as we already know, this is not the case. Each resume must be custom-written to sell each candidate's individual talents, skills, qualifications, experience, educational credentials, professional activities, technical proficiency and more. Resumes are *not* standardized, they are *not* prescribed and there is *no* specific formula. In fact, there are virtually no rules in resume writing. On the one hand, this gives you tremendous flexibility and the opportunity to be creative and unique in the presentation of your skills. On the other hand, it makes resume writing a much more difficult task for there is no single roadmap to follow.

Combine that with the fact that your resume is a document designed to sell you into your next position, not to simply reiterate where you have worked, what you did and what you accomplished. Rather, you are taking all of your past experiences and then "re-weighting" them to support your current objectives. This further confounds the process and requires that you give tremendous thought to what you will include in your resume, how and where. It is not a 30-minute task. Most likely, it will take days and days of thought, writing, editing and hard work to create your best resume.

Although resumes do vary dramatically in their structure, format, tone and presentation, there are certain common features. Specifically, most resumes will include Experience and Education sections. In addition, there are many other categories that you may include if they are relevant to your career, background and current objectives. These are Objective, Career Summary, Technology Qualifications, Professional Affiliations, Civic Affiliations, Honors & Awards, Publications, Public Speaking, Teaching Experience, International Experience and Personal Information. Some will be appropriate for you; others will not.

To help you better understand the structure and function of each of these sections, a short but thorough discussion of each follows. Use the information below to help you determine (1) if you need to include a particular section in your resume, and (2) what style and format to use for that particular section. Remember, the two key sections are Experience and Education, with the other categories surrounding them to strengthen the presentation of your qualifications and sell you into your next job.

Objective

One of the greatest controversies in resume writing focuses on the use or omission of an Objective. There are three questions to ask yourself that will help you decide whether or not you need an Objective on your resume.

1. Do you have a specific objective in mind? A specific position? A specific industry? If so, you can include a focused objective statement such as: "Seeking an upper-level management position in the Pharmaceutical R&D industry" or "President/CEO of an emerging telecommunications company." As you can see, each of these objective statements clearly indicates the type of position the candidate is seeking.

2. Is your objective constant? Will your objective stay the same for virtually all positions you apply for and all the resumes you submit? If so, include a focused objective such as that outlined in #1 above. If not, do not include an objective. You do not want to have to edit your resume each and every time you send it. It's a time-consuming process and stalls the flow of resumes out your door.

3. Is your objective unclear? Are you considering a number of opportunities? Are you interested in a number of different industries? If your answer is YES, do not include an objective statement, for it will be unfocused and communicate little of value. Consider an objective such as: "Seeking a senior management position where I can lead a company to improved revenues and profits." Doesn't everyone want to help a company make money? These are useless words and add no value to your resume. They do not tell your reader "who" you are or "what" you are pursuing.

Remember, every time you forward a resume you will also be sending a cover letter. If you do not include an objective statement on your resume, let your cover letter be the tool that communicates your objective in that specific situation to that specific employer or recruiter.

Here are a few Objective format samples:

PROFESSIONAL OBJECTIVE:

Challenging Sales Management Position in the Telecommunications Industry.

CAREER OBJECTIVE:

Senior-Level Executive Management position where I can apply my 15 years' experience in the Real Estate & Commercial Construction Industries.

CAREER GOAL: PURCHASING MANAGEMENT – PLASTICS INDUSTRY

Career Summary / Career Profile

Consider this. When you write an Objective, you are telling your reader what you want *from* them. When you start your resume with a Career Summary or Career Profile, you are telling your reader what you can do *for* them, what value you bring to their organization, what expertise you have and how well you have performed. In both, you are writing about the same concepts, the same professions or the same industries. However, the Career Profile is a much more upscale, more executive and more hard-hitting strategy for catching your reader's attention and making an immediate connection. And, isn't that the point of your resume? Your goal is to intrigue a prospective employer to (1) read your resume, (2) invite you for an interview and (3) offer you a position.

To simplify this concept, compare the two examples below:

Example #1:
PROFESSIONAL OBJECTIVE: Senior-Level Corporate Financial Management Position

Example #2:
CAREER PROFILE:

Top-flight financial management career with Dow Chemical, American Express and Microsoft. Expert in mergers, acquisitions, joint ventures and international corporate development. Personally transacted over $200 million in new enterprises, slashed $14 million from bottom-line operating costs and contributed to a 33% increase in corporate valuation. Astute planner and negotiator. PC and Internet proficient.

In both of these examples, is it clear that the individual is seeking a senior-level financial management position? Yes, they are both communicating the same overall message – that the candidate is a qualified finance executive.

Now, ask yourself which is a stronger presentation. Obviously, the Career Profile stronger. It is more dynamic, more substantive and clearly communicates the success of the candidate. Finally, ask yourself if you started your resume with a Career Profile as presented above, would you need an Objective that stated your goals. Probably not. The Career Profile paints a clear and concise picture of "who" you are. It is not necessary to include a statement above the Career Profile which states, "I want a job as a such-and-such."

There may be instances when your objective is not quite so clear and you want to be open to a number of different opportunities in different industries. This is precisely the reason why you would not include an Objective. However, Career Profiles can work extremely well in this situation. They allow you to present your qualifications in an aggressive style and communicate the overall value you bring to an organization.

Consider the following example for an executive who has combined expertise in both General Management and Sales and is looking at opportunities in both professions across a broad range of industries.

EXECUTIVE QUALIFICATIONS

Chief Operating Officer / Executive Vice President / Director of Sales & Marketing

MBA Degree – Northwestern University
Fifteen-year executive management career with start-up, turnaround and high-growth corporations worldwide. Offer cross-functional, cross-industry experience in:

General Management	**Sales & Marketing Management**
Strategic Planning & Leadership	New Business Development
Multi-Site Operations	Key Account Development
Corporate Finance & Budgeting	Client Relationship Management
Revenue & Profit Growth	New Product Design & Introduction.

Note in the above example that the Career Profile was renamed Executive Qualifications. Other headings you might consider include Executive Profile, Management Profile, Senior Management Summary, Career Accomplishments, Professional Profile, Professional Credentials and Qualifications Summary, Each of these headings communicates the same message, so select the one that you prefer.

Consider these two strategies used by professional resume writers worldwide. They will make writing your Career Profile faster and easier.

1. Resume writing is a condensation process. You are taking your career and consolidating it onto one or two pages. Then, take those one or two pages and consolidate into one or two inches at the top of your resume. You will then have your Profile.

2. The Career Profile is the last section written on a resume. How can you write the profile if you haven't yet written the text and determined what information you want to include, how and where to support your current objectives? You can't. When you write your Profile last, the text will come much more easily and tie directly into the text of your resume.

Professional Experience

This is the single most important section on your resume. It is your opportunity to highlight your professional experience, qualifications and achievements as they relate to your current career objectives. It is your chance to "toot your own horn," for no one else will. It is the time to sell everything that is great about you. It's why you are the best! Give careful thought and consideration to what you include under each position. *Every word counts!*

When writing your Professional Experience your challenge is to briefly, yet completely, describe your employment history with an emphasis on three important issues:

- **The company**. Is it a manufacturer, distributor, worldwide technology leader or multi-site service organization? What are the company's annual revenues? How many locations? How many employees? Give a brief summary of the company and its operations, customers, products, markets or technologies as they relate to your current objectives and ONLY as they relate. If your current employer is a technology company and you are looking to remain in the technology industry, briefly highlight who the company is and what it does for it is relevant to your current career objectives. If, however, you currently work for a plastic manufacturer and your goal is a position with a technology company, do not mention what your current employer does. Rather, refer to them as a $29 million production operation.

- **The challenge**. Is this a start-up venture, turnaround or high-growth company? Were you hired to lead an international expansion initiative? Are the company's costs out of control? Are there organizational weaknesses? If there were any particular challenges associated with the company and/or your position, be sure to clearly state them. A great introduction is, "Recruited by CEO to _____."

- **Your accountability**. Include your major areas of responsibility (e.g., functions, departments, organizations, personnel, budgets, revenue and profit objectives, facilities, operations). In just a few sentences you want to communicate the depth and range of your overall responsibilities.

- **Your achievements**. Herein lies the heart and soul of your resume. Not only do you want to "tell" your reader what you were responsible for, you want to "sell" how well you have performed and what value you have delivered. Did you contribute to revenue or profit improvements? Did you reduce costs? Design new products? Implement new technologies? Better train your staff? Improve efficiencies and productivity? Reduce liability and risk exposure? Penetrate new markets? Streamline operations? Eliminate redundant operations? Negotiate big deals? Raise money? The list of potential achievements goes on and on.

To begin writing your position descriptions, start with a brief introductory paragraph highlighting the company, challenges and overall responsibilities. Then follow with a bulleted listing of your achievements, contributions and project highlights. In essence, you are telling your reader, *"This is what I did and this is how well I did it."* The concept is simple; the impact, significant.

Here's an example of a sample position description for a Logistics Director.

Logistics Director
1998 to Present
TRIAX MANUFACTURING, Greenville, South Carolina

Directed the planning, staffing, budgeting and operations of a 6-site logistics, warehousing and distribution operation for a $500 million automotive products manufacturer. Scope of responsibility was diverse and included purchasing, vendor management, materials handling, inventory control, distribution planning and delivery operations. Led a team of 55 through six direct supervisors. Managed a $25 million annual operating budget.

- Introduced continuous improvement and quality management programs throughout the organization and at all operating locations. Results included a 35% increase in daily production yields, 22% reduction in waste and 52% improvement in customer satisfaction.
- Spearheaded cost reduction initiatives that reduced labor expense 18% and over time 34%.
- Renegotiated vendor contracts and saved $4.5 million in first year.
- Sourced and implemented $2.2 million in IT improvements to improve workflow.

Prospective employers who read that description can sense the scope (range, size and diversity) of the individual's experience as well as get a clear understanding of his specific accomplishments and successes.

Follow the same format all the way through your resume, becoming briefer and briefer as you get further back in time. Do not focus on the day-to-day responsibilities of your older positions, unless they were particularly unusual. Rather, focus on your achievements, notable company names (employers and/or clients), emerging products and technologies, international experience, or anything else distinguishing about that particular position.

Here are a few sample achievements to get you started in developing your own list of accomplishments and value-adds.

Achieved/surpassed all performance objectives. Increased sales revenues 28%, market share 14% and bottom-line profits 18%.

Increased sales by 48% across six major customer segments within an intensely competitive market.

Led development and market introduction of emerging client/server technologies and created new market that now generates $100+ million in annual sales.

Drove market share from 10% to 22% within first six months by transitioning to customer-focused sales teams.

Reengineered critical production planning, scheduling and manufacturing processes for a 12% reduction in annual operating costs.

Realigned field sales organization and reduced staffing expense by 27%.

Sourced new vendors throughout Southeast Asia, negotiated joint ventures and saved 25% in annual purchasing costs.

Spearheaded implementation of advanced robotics technologies to automate manufacturing operations, virtually eliminated competition and won a 5-year, $15 million contract.

Revitalized customer service organization, recruited qualified management team and increased customer satisfaction ratings from 76% to 98%.

Structured and negotiated 12 mergers and acquisitions as part of the corporation's aggressive growth and corporate expansion effort.

Wrote, produced and directed award-winning corporate training film.

Orchestrated the company's successful and profitable expansion throughout emerging international markets (e.g., Africa, Middle East, former Soviet Union).

Personally negotiated $2 million in capital financing transactions to support product R&D.

Education

In this section you will include your college degrees, continuing professional education, licenses and certification. Here's an example:

EDUCATION:

Executive MBA – Organizational Leadership, YALE UNIVERSITY, 1986
BS – Finance & Business Administration, YALE UNIVERSITY, 1984
Certified Financial Planner (CFA), 1992
Certified Public Accountant (CPA), 1987

Highlights of Continuing Professional Education:

- Center For Creative Leadership, 2000
- Strategic Planning & Leadership, Dow Jones & Company, 1998
- Management By Objectives, Xerox Learning Corporation, 1997
- Merger & Acquisition Transactions, World Bank, 1994

Should you date your college degrees? The answer is YES for the under-50 job search candidate. Over the past several years, job seekers have tended to exclude college graduation dates from their resumes for fear that it might date them. And, if you are over 50, this is a consideration. However, for the under-50 candidate, this is NOT the appropriate strategy. Include your dates and give your employer a good foundation from which to track your professional career. Let them see, for example, that you graduated in 1984, went to work for Xerox, then to IBM and are now the President of a successful Internet venture. Paint a clear and concise picture. For the over-50 job candidate, refer to our discussion in Chapter 1 in the Challenges section to determine whether or not you should date your education.

Should you include ALL of your continuing professional education? NO, if the list is extensive and/or unrelated to your current objectives. Just include a sampling. Refer to it as "Highlights of Continuing Professional

Education," as above, which communicates that it is not a comprehensive list.

Should you include colleges where you studied and did not get a degree? Generally, the answer is no. If you have earned your degree, the other colleges are not necessary to include unless they are notable institutions (e.g., Ivy League school, acclaimed international university such as Oxford). The only exception to this rule is for the non-degreed professional who must include colleges where he has studied, yet not earned a degree. Consider a format such as:

UNIVERSITY OF MINNESOTA, Duluth, Minnesota
Major in Architectural Engineering (1990 to 1993)

Professional & Community Activities

Include a listing of professional and community organizations to which you belong and any specific leadership roles, committee memberships or related accomplishments. You may also include volunteer experience if relevant to your current career objective. However, do use some discretion. If you hold three leadership positions with notable professional associations and non-profit organizations, it is not necessary to include the fact that you are on the board of your local condo association! Here's an example:

PROFESSIONAL AFFILIATIONS:

- Independent Manufacturers Representative Association (District President)
- American Marketing Association (Professional Member & Training Committee Chair)
- Sales Consultants of America (Professional Member)
- Junior Achievement (Volunteer Lecturer)

Technology Qualifications

Fifteen years ago, Technology Qualifications were virtually never seen on a resume, except for people working directly in the technology industry. Today, that's changed. Technology is a part of every professional's life and must be addressed on your resume. You may include just a brief mention of your PC qualifications in your Career Profile or you may have an entire section devoted to the topic, particularly if you're a programmer, hardware engineer, telecommunications engineer, technology project manager or CIO. You will have to determine the specific technology information and skills to include based on your current objectives. Here are two examples:

Include a statement in your Career Profile such as:

Proficient with Microsoft Word, Access and Excel, email and the Internet.

In a separate section titled Technology Qualifications:

TECHNOLOGY QUALIFICATIONS:

Software:	C, PLSQL, COBOL, PL1, CLIST, Lotus Notes, Word, MFS, Excel, PowerPoint, Clipper
Hardware:	RS6000, IBM Mainframe, Intel
Databases:	Oracle, DB2, IMS
Data Transfer:	Network Data Mover (NDM), File Transfer System (FTS)

Honors & Awards

Include your honors, awards, commendations and other professional recognition. This information can be integrated directly into your job descriptions, included under Education (if appropriate), or compiled into a separate category at the beginning or the end of your resume (depends on its impact and relevancy). If any of your honors or awards are significant and recognizable, you might integrate them directly into your Career Profile. Here are a few examples of how and where to include your honors and awards:

In your Career Profile:

- Winner, 2000 Honors Club Award For Outstanding Sales Performance
- Winner, 1998 Presidential Award For Exemplary Service
- Winner, 1996 SuperMAX Award For New Business Development

In your job descriptions:

- Honored for outstanding revenue and profit performance with five consecutive *"Salesman of the Year"* awards.

In a separate section titled Honors & Awards:

HONORS & AWARDS:
- Winner, 1999 Addy Award For Creative Design & Excellence
- Winner, 1998 Clio Award For Television Set Design
- Winner, 1998 Malcolm Award For Ad Campaign Design

Publications

Publications validate your expertise and impress your reader. Be sure to include your book and article publications either in a separate category at the end of your resume or in your Career Profile if particularly noteworthy or relevant to your current career objectives. Include the title of the publication, name of publisher and year of publication. Here are a few examples of how and where to include your publications:

In your Career Profile:

- Author, "*Sales Leadership 2000*," Forbes, 2000
- Author, "*Team Building & Leadership*," IMAX Magazine, July 1999
- Author, "*Winning In The Technology Wars*," Business Week, April 1997

In your job descriptions:

- Authored IBM's award-winning "Close To The Customer" book and accompanying multimedia presentation.

In a separate section titled Publications:

PUBLICATIONS:
- Author, "*Sales Leadership 2000*," Forbes, 2000
- Author, "*Team Building & Leadership*," IMAX Magazine, July 1999
- Author, "*Winning In The Technology Wars*," Business Week, April 1997

Public Speaking

List your public speaking engagements including title of presentation, audience, location and date. If the list is extensive, include only the highlights that are most notable and/or most related to your current search objectives. Here are a few examples of how and where to include your public speaking experience:

In your Career Profile:

- Keynote Presenter, American Manufacturing Association National Conference, Summer 2000
- Speaker, Wharton Leadership Symposium, 2000
- Panel Member, Logistics 2000 Presentation, American Quality Council Convention, 1998

In your job descriptions:

- Spoke at the 1999 Leadership Symposium sponsored by the Wharton School of Business in cooperation with the Fortune 500 business community.

In a separate section titled Public Speaking:

PUBLIC SPEAKING:
- Keynote Presenter, American Manufacturing Association National Conference, Summer 2000
- Speaker, Wharton Leadership Symposium, 2000
- Panel Member, Logistics 2000 Presentation, American Quality Council Convention, 1998

Teaching & Training

If you are an educator, a corporate trainer or otherwise employed in the fields of Teaching/Training/Education, this section will be your Professional Experience. However, if you are a business professional who has relevant teaching experience, be sure to include this information. Just like publications, it immediately validates your credentials and qualifications. List the name of the course that you taught, the school or organization, and the dates. Here are a few examples of how and where to include your teaching and training experience:

In your Career Profile:

- Instructor, Management Philosophies, Wharton School of Business, Spring 2000
- Instructor, Statistics & Demographics, University of Pennsylvania, Fall 1999
- Corporate Trainer, IBM – International Sales Division, 1990 -1997

In your job descriptions:

- Selected by corporate HR Director to design and deliver a corporate-wide training program on production scheduling and resource management for 2000+ employees.

In a separate section titled Teaching Experience (or Training Experience):

TEACHING EXPERIENCE:
- Instructor, Management Philosophies, Wharton School of Business, Spring 2000
- Instructor, Statistics & Demographics, University of Pennsylvania, Fall 1999
- Corporate Trainer, IBM – International Sales Division, 1990 - 1997

International Experience

We are definitely a global workforce with a global economy. And the more international experience and exposure you have, the better. Be sure to include your foreign language skills and travel experience either in your Career Profile or as a separate section if the information is detailed and directly relevant. Here are a few examples of how and where to include your international experience:

In your Career Profile:

- Fluent in English, Spanish, French and Portuguese.
- Lived and worked in Belgium, Portugal, France and the UK.
- Graduate, Oxford University's Executive Leadership Course.

In your job descriptions:

- Traveled throughout Europe, Asia and the Middle East to develop new supplier relationships and monitor supplier production controls.

In a separate section titled International Experience:

INTERNATIONAL EXPERIENCE:
- Fluent in English, Spanish, French and Portuguese.
- Lived and worked in Belgium, Portugal, France and the UK.
- Graduate, Oxford University's Executive Leadership Course.

Personal Information

Now on to the great controversy of Personal Information. Here are my recommendations. DO NOT include personal information such as birth date, marital status, health, number of children and the like. Do not include the fact that you enjoy golfing, camping with your family or reading. None of this is relevant to your job search, particularly early on when you're presenting a resume just to get your foot in the door.

There are certain times, however, when it is appropriate to include personal information:

- Required by the employer.
- Important to clarify your citizenship or residency status.
- Important to clarify your age.
- Unique information.

I've worked with executives who were past Olympians, ascended mountains on seven continents, raced as competitive triathletes and trekked through obscure regions worldwide. This type of information attracts others to you and can be the single reason someone calls for an interview. My motto is "Use what you have to get in the door."

If a Personal Information section is appropriate in your situation, consider the following format:

PERSONAL PROFILE:

US Citizen since 1988 (native of Switzerland)
Fluent in English, French, German and Dutch
Competitive Triathlete and Skier

Streamlining Your Outline

A great strategy for consolidating all of the "extra" resume categories (e.g., Affiliations, Publications, Public Speaking, Foreign Languages) is to integrate them into one consolidated category called Professional Profile. You will want to consider this if you have little bits of information to include in many different categories and/or you are having trouble comfortably fitting your resume onto 1-2 pages. Here's an example:

PROFESSIONAL PROFILE:

Affiliations:	Chairman, National Industries Association Chairman, Industry Oversight National Association
Publications:	"Business Management," <u>Business World</u>, May 1992 "Emerging Technologies," <u>Digital Design</u>, January 1991 "Strategic Marketing," <u>Fortune</u>, April 1987
Languages:	Fluent in Spanish, French and German.
PC Software:	Microsoft Word, Access, Excel, Lotus, PageMaker, WordPerfect

The Resume Writing Process

Everything in life has a process, and resume writing is no different. If you use the following structured outline, you will find that the task of writing and producing your resume is efficient, faster and much easier.

1. Open a file in your PC and select a typestyle that (1) you like and (2) is easy to read. Type your name, address, email and phone numbers (home, office, fax and cellular). Include your office number only if you are comfortable accepting calls during the day and can speak in confidence. *never* include your employer's 800 number. Your current employer should not be supporting your job search!

2. Type in all the major headings you will be using (e.g., Career Summary, Professional Experience, Education, Publications, Technology Qualifications).

3. Fill in the information for Education, Publications, Technology Qualifications, Public Speaking, Affiliations, Teaching Experience and all the other categories *except* Career Summary and Professional Experience. This information is easy to complete, requires little thought and is generally just a listing of factual information.

4. Type company names, job titles, dates and locations. Again, this information is easy to complete and will only take you a few minutes.

Now, take a look at how much of your resume you have already completed in just a few short minutes!

5. Write your job descriptions. Start with your very first position you ever held and work forward. The older jobs are easy to write. They're short and to the point, and include only highlights of your most significant responsibilities and achievements. Then, as you work forward, each position requires a bit more text and a bit more thought. Before you know it, you will be writing your most recent (or current) job description. It will take the longest to write, but once it is finished, your resume will be 90% complete.

6. Write your Career Summary. This is the trickiest part of resume writing and can be the most difficult. At this point, you may want to re-read the preceding section on writing career summaries. Be sure to highlight your most notable skills, qualifications and achievements as they relate to your current objectives and create a section that prominently communicates, "This is who I am."

7. Add bold, italics, underlining and other type enhancements to draw visual attention to notable information. This should include your name at the top of the resume, major headings, job titles and significant achievements. You may also insert lines and/or boxes to offset key information.

But be careful. Overuse of type enhancements will instantly devalue the visual presentation and cloud a prospective employer's initial reaction. If you highlight too much, the resume appears cluttered and nothing stands out, clearly defeating our purpose.

HINT: Using bold print to highlight numbers (e.g., sales growth, profit improvement) and percentages (e.g., cost savings, productivity gains) is a great strategy. Someone picks up your resume and those numbers instantly pop out and grab their attention. You can use this same strategy to highlight other key information such as major clients, major deals and transactions, product names, honors and awards, and more.

8. Carefully review the visual presentation. How does it look? If your resume is two pages, does it break well between pages? Is it easy to read? Does it look professional? Even more important, does it convey an "executive" message? At this point, you may need to adjust your spacing, change to a different typestyle or make other minor adjustments to enhance the visual presentation.

9. Proofread your resume a minimum of three times. Then have one or two other people proofread it. It must be perfect, for nothing less is acceptable. Remember, people are meeting a piece of paper, not you. It must project professionalism, performance and perfection.

Getting Started

You've read through all the preceding text of this book and now it's time for you to get started writing your own $100,000+ resume.

The first step in writing a powerful and effective resume that attracts prospective employers and opens new doors to new opportunities is to understand why you are the best.

- What is it that you have accomplished, delivered, produced, created, designed, managed, revitalized or built that demonstrates your knowledge, expertise and excellence?

- What have you done to positively impact financial performance of a company? Have you reduced operating costs, increased revenues and improved bottom-line profitability?

- What have you done that's innovative and creative? What have you done to improve overall performance?

- What value do you bring to an organization? Why would someone want to hire you? Why are you better and more qualified than other candidates?

To help you answer those questions and more, refer to Appendix B for a series of exercises that will:

1. Help you to identify your most significant skills and knowledge.
2. Help you identify your most notable career achievements.
3. Help you clearly identify your career objectives.
4. Help you link your skills, knowledge and achievements with your current objectives to create a powerful and winning resume presentation.

Your responses to these exercises are critical for they are the foundation for everything that you include in your resume, where you include it and how you include it. Just as important, these activities will help you identify information that you *do not* want to include in your resume – information that is irrelevant at this point in your career and/or totally unrelated to your current career objectives.

4

Best Resume Samples

Throughout this book we've discussed the power that you have in creating a resume designed to sell you into your next position. What information you include and how you include it is entirely up to you. Your challenge to is write a resume that focuses on your skills, qualifications and achievements as they relate to your current objectives. You have tremendous flexibility and room for creativity. That's what makes resume writing so challenging.

Painting The "Best Picture"

The first 10 resumes are a prime example of that concept – creating the presentation that you want someone to see. Look carefully as you review the following resumes – two each for five different candidates.

Thomas Riker – Corporate Finance Executive

Resume #1: Positions candidate for top-level Senior Finance position.

Resume #2: Positions candidate for broad Executive Management opportunities.

Robert Hassler – Association Executive

Resume #1: Positions candidate for Senior Association Management position.

Resume #2: Positions candidate for Corporate Management position.

William Tidwell – Attorney/Corporate Counsel

Resume #1: Positions candidate for Corporate Counsel in Business Development.

Resume #2: Positions candidate for broad Executive Management opportunities.

Norman Stephens – Corporate Finance & Tax Executive

Resume #1: Positions candidate for Senior Finance & Tax position.

Resume #2: Positions candidate for higher-level CFO / VP Finance position.

Ernest Stewart – Insurance Industry Executive

Resume #1: Positions candidate for Insurance Management position.

Resume #2: Positions candidate for diverse Sales & Marketing Management positions.

100 Best Resumes for $100,000+ Jobs

- **10 Resumes for Painting Your "Best Picture"** – pages 38-58

- **90 Resumes for $100,000+ Jobs** – pages 60-251

THOMAS RIKER
321 Brookmire Drive SE
Grand Rapids, Michigan 49512
Email: triker@earthlink.net

Residence: 616-172-8514

Office: 313-358-6912 x45

SENIOR FINANCE EXECUTIVE
Start-Up Enterprises, Turnarounds, High-Growth Ventures, Fortune 500 Companies, Mergers & Acquisitions

Dynamic Senior Management career providing strategic, financial and operating leadership across broad industries, markets, services, products and technologies. Expert qualifications across all corporate finance and treasury functions. Strong general management, technical, human resource, team building, problem solving and decision making skills. Bottom-line, results-driven orientation with consistent success in maximizing operations, expanding market penetration, and improving bottom line profitability. CPA with SEC experience.

Built and nurtured excellent working relationships with senior executive, management teams, professional staff, support personnel, customers, bankers, auditors, investors, insurance companies, and regulators.

PROFESSIONAL EXPERIENCE:

Chief Financial Officer   1997 to Present
ABC DISTRIBUTION & TRANSPORTATION, INC., Grand Rapids, Michigan

Senior Executive with full responsibility for the strategic planning, development and leadership of this $25+ million corporation's complete finance function. Lines of business include transportation division, retail chain contract division and retail store service division with a total of 3200 employees. Challenged to rebuild and revitalize the corporate accounting, budgeting and financial systems, restore credibility within and outside the organization, and develop best-in-class business processes. Scope of responsibility expanded to include human resources, credit, warehouse and fleet operations.

- Initiated turnaround with a complete restaffing of the entire finance department. Recruited qualified personnel, introduced internal training programs, redesigned core processes, enhanced technologies, and created a sophisticated and responsive organization. Provided executive team and senior operating management with meaningful financial data.
- Redesigned organizational structures and business plans for the corporation and its subsidiary operations. Introduced series of personnel and executive incentive plans to enhance performance, quality and efficiency, improving bottom-line profitability.
- Relocated corporate offices, warehouse, equipment and 150 employees within just 30 days.
- Introduced improved risk management and asset protection programs to safeguard the corporation. Managed critical relationships and negotiations with auditors, bankers, investors and attorneys for routine corporate matters and a series of special projects.
- Led due diligence for two potential acquisitions to diversify market penetration and create new revenue streams. Projects forecast a 100%+ improvement in profit margins within niche markets.

Partner   1995 to 1997
JACQUET & ASSOCIATES, Quebec, Canada

Partner in an entrepreneurial consulting practice specializing in strategic planning and financial leadership for growth companies in the US, Canada, Asia and Europe. Managed complex, long-term project cycles (averaging two years) with an emphasis on growth and expansion through acquisition. Direct interface with client and candidate senior management teams and officers to negotiate proposed acquisitions, terms, conditions and financial agreements.

- Key player in six major acquisition deals valued in excess of $1 billion each on behalf of AK-Steel, British Airways, K-Mart Canada, Kroger, and Mitsui Japan. Most complex transaction was the representation of a $250 billion company seeking to acquire $3 billion US manufacturer.
- Prepared comprehensive financial analyses, reviews and recommendations for inclusion in offering memoranda. Led sophisticated financial presentations.
- Represented Fortune 100 corporation in several $50 million sale-leaseback proposals.

Chief Financial Officer / Treasurer / Secretary   1992 to 1995
EXCEL PROMOTIONS & GAMES, Lansing, Michigan

Joined early stage company to provide financial and investment leadership to accelerate growth, expansion and diversification. Focused efforts on developing investor and banker relationships, strengthening corporate business infrastructure, introducing sound financial policies and implementing advanced information technologies. Supervised 16-person home office staff.

- Raised over $2 million in private and institutional investment funds. Personally prepared all financial documentation and led road show presentations, negotiations and deal structuring.
- Counseled CEO and Board in reviewing corporate contracts and other documentation.

Financial Consultant / Management Consultant   1982 to 1992
RIKER & ASSOCIATES, Grand Rapids, Michigan

Launched entrepreneurial venture and built a successful accounting, finance and management consulting practice. Interim CFO/Treasurer/Controller for more than 350 corporations and not-for-profit organizations. Extensive experience in business analysis, due diligence, valuation and IPO's. Ten years later, negotiated the company's profitable sale to a large regional accounting firm.

- Built customer base from virtual start-up to several hundred companies across diverse industries including advertising, chemical processing, construction, consulting, distribution, electronics, golf course, health care, insurance, investment banking, manufacturing, metal fabrication, product development, professional services, property management, real estate, resort, restaurant, retail sales, software development, transportation, travel, venture capital and warehousing.
- Evaluated opportunities, structured and negotiated over 20 successful mergers and acquisitions of companies with sales ranging from $5 million to $150 million.
- Advised CEO's, CFO's, Board Directors and other executives across a wide range of strategic and business planning, finance, accounting and corporate development/acquisition activities.
- Represented minority shareholder in corporate buy-out and netted shareholder $8 million more than initial offer. Represented another investor during a comprehensive investment analysis and negotiated $1 million more than an equivalent investor in the prior year.

Divisional Controller   1979 to 1982
ABC CAN COMPANY, Detroit, Michigan

Full accounting, financial analysis, financial reporting, budgeting and business planning responsibility for a $600 million division with 2100 employees and 26 operating locations. Guided a staff of 26 controllers, each managing different accounting, financial and reporting systems for their operations. Evaluated proposed projects to assess risk and forecast ROI. Managed $20 million annual budget.

- Facilitated several successful turnarounds, introduced standardized financial and accounting processes, upgraded technologies and enhanced bottom-line performance.
- Identified as a high potential management candidate and accepted into corporate training program for future presidents of the company's subsidiary operations.

Audit Manager / Manager – Emerging Businesses   1976 to 1979
COOPERS & LYBRAND, Grand Rapids, Michigan

Launched start-up and managed new department providing financial, audit and management consulting to high-growth ventures. Managed 15% of all audit in the region (20-30 engagements).

EDUCATION & AFFILIATIONS:

Bachelor of Business Administration Degree, University of Cincinnati
Certified Public Accountant, State of Michigan
Member – International Association of Finance Professionals and American Management Association
Advisory Board Member – Franciscan Health System
Director – Nutrition Council of Greater Lansing & Friends of Michigan Parks

THOMAS RIKER

321 Brookmire Drive SE
Grand Rapids, Michigan 49512
Email: triker@earthlink.net

Residence: 616-172-8514   Office: 313-358-6912 x45

SENIOR EXECUTIVE PROFILE

20-Year Senior Management Career Providing Strategic, Business, Financial & Operating Leadership to Start-Up Enterprises, Turnarounds, Mergers, Acquisitions, High-Growth Venture & Fortune 500 Companies

Management & Leadership Qualifications

- Strategic Planning & Corporate Development
- Corporate Finance, Treasury & Accounting
- Investment Presentations & Negotiations
- Organizational Design & Development
- Quality, Efficiency & Performance Improvement
- SEC Reporting & Regulatory Affairs

- Multi-Site Operating Management
- Profit & Loss Management
- IPO Preparation & Transactions
- Information Systems & Technologies
- Human Resource Affairs & Teaming
- Problem Solving & Decision Making

Industry Experience

- Advertising
- Distribution
- Insurance
- Product R&D
- Retail Sales

- Chemical Processing
- Electronics Technology
- Investment Banking
- Professional Services
- Software Development

- Construction
- Golf Courses
- Manufacturing
- Real Estate
- Transportation

- Consulting
- Health Care
- Metal Fabrication
- Resorts
- Warehousing

PROFESSIONAL EXPERIENCE:

Chief Financial Officer   1997 to Present
ABC DISTRIBUTION & TRANSPORTATION, INC., Grand Rapids, Michigan

Member of 9-person Senior Executive Team responsible for the strategic planning, development, operating management, financial affairs, marketing and leadership of this $25+ million distribution, transportation and services corporation. Customers include major retail companies (e.g., Kroger, Wal-Mart, Loews). Staffing responsibility for 3200 employees. Budget responsibility for $5 million.

- Key player in the successful turnaround, revitalization and accelerated growth of the organization. Introduced improved operating, financial, marketing, technology and human resource systems. Developed best-in-class business processes and restored market credibility.
- Reengineered the entire finance function, restaffed with qualified personnel, redesigned core processes, and created a sophisticated organization providing meaningful financial data.
- Redesigned organizational structures and business plans. Introduced personnel and executive incentive plans to enhance performance, quality, efficiency and bottom-line profitability.
- Led due diligence for two potential acquisitions to diversify market penetration and create new revenue streams. Projects forecast a 100%+ improvement in profit margins within niche markets.

Partner   1995 to 1997
JACQUET & ASSOCIATES, Quebec, Canada

Partner in an entrepreneurial consulting practice specializing in strategic planning and financial leadership for growth companies in the US, Canada, Asia and Europe. Managed complex, long-term project cycles (averaging two years) with an emphasis on growth and expansion through acquisition. Direct interface with client and candidate senior management teams and officers to negotiate proposed acquisitions, terms, conditions and financial agreements.

- Key player in six major acquisition deals valued in excess of $1 billion each on behalf of AK-Steel, British Airways, K-Mart Canada, Kroger, and Mitsui Japan. Most complex transaction was the representation of a $250 billion company seeking to acquire $3 billion US manufacturer.
- Represented Fortune 100 corporation in several $50 million sale-leaseback proposals.

Chief Financial Officer / Treasurer / Secretary   1992 to 1995
EXCEL PROMOTIONS & GAMES, Lansing, Michigan

Joined early stage company to provide financial and investment leadership to accelerate growth, expansion and diversification. Focused efforts on developing investor and banker relationships, strengthening corporate business infrastructure, introducing sound financial policies and implementing advanced information technologies. Supervised 16-person home office staff.

- Raised over $2 million in private and institutional investment funds. Personally prepared all financial documentation and led road show presentations, negotiations and deal structuring.
- Counseled CEO and Board in reviewing corporate contracts and other documentation.

President   1982 to 1992
RIKER & ASSOCIATES, Grand Rapids, Michigan

Launched an entrepreneurial venture and built a successful management consulting practice. Interim Executive to more than 350 corporations and not-for-profit organizations. Extensive experience in business analysis, due diligence, valuation and IPO's. Ten years later, negotiated the company's profitable sale to a large competitive organization.

- Built customer base from virtual start-up to several hundred clients in more than 25 industries.
- Evaluated opportunities, structured and negotiated over 20 successful mergers and acquisitions of companies with sales ranging from $5 million to $150 million.
- Advised CEO's, CFO's, Board Directors and other executives across a wide range of strategic and business planning, finance, accounting and corporate development/acquisition activities.
- Represented minority shareholder in corporate buy-out and netted shareholder $8 million more than initial offer. Represented another investor during a comprehensive investment analysis and negotiated $1 million more than an equivalent investor in the prior year.

Divisional Controller   1979 to 1982
ABC CAN COMPANY, Detroit, Michigan

Full accounting, financial analysis, financial reporting, budgeting and business planning responsibility for a $600 million division with 2100 employees and 26 operating locations. Guided a staff of 26 controllers. Evaluated proposed projects to assess risk and ROI. Managed $20 million annual budget.

- Identified as high potential management candidate and accepted into corporate training program for future presidents of the company's subsidiary operations.
- Facilitated several successful turnarounds, introduced standardized financial and accounting processes, upgraded technologies and enhanced bottom-line performance.

Audit Manager / Manager – Emerging Businesses   1976 to 1979
COOPERS & LYBRAND, Grand Rapids, Michigan

Launched start-up and managed new department providing financial, audit and management consulting to high-growth ventures. Managed 15% of all audit in the region (20-30 engagements).

EDUCATION & AFFILIATIONS:

Bachelor of Business Administration Degree, University of Cincinnati
Certified Public Accountant, State of Michigan

Member – International Association of Finance Professionals and American Management Association
Advisory Board Member – Franciscan Health System
Director – Nutrition Council of Greater Lansing & Friends of Michigan Parks

ROBERT M. HASSLER

Beacon Hill Court
Raleigh, North Carolina 27604
(919) 459-9688

SENIOR ASSOCIATION EXECUTIVE

Organizational Driver & Consummate Business Leader with a strong track record of performance in start-up, turnaround and high-growth organizations. Accustomed to overcoming market, technological, financial and competitive challenges to drive member growth, profitability and performance improvement. Expertise includes:

- Organizational & Association Leadership
- Team Building & Relationship Management
- Member Products, Services & Support
- New Member Development & Retention
- Board & Committee Liaison Affairs
- Training & Development

- Finance, Budgeting & Cost Management
- Information & Telecommunications Technology
- Contracts & Outsourcing Partnerships
- Public Relations & Media Affairs
- Strategy, Vision & Mission Planning
- Special Events Planning & Coordination

PROFESSIONAL EXPERIENCE:

Executive Vice President   1996 to Present
AAA ADVERTISING INSTITUTE, Raleigh, North Carolina
(International advertising association with 1700+ corporate members worldwide)

Member of 5-person Senior Executive Team challenged to revitalize and turnaround this non-performing membership organization challenged by significant financial and budgetary issues, a loss in membership and internal staffing concerns. Initiated assignment with a comprehensive analysis of existing operations to restructure financial operations, optimize strengths, eliminate weaknesses and reposition for solid growth.

Scope of responsibility is significant and includes overall managerial and budgetary leadership for Membership, Marketing/Communications & Public Relations, Advocacy, Global Relations, Information Center/Customer Service, MIS/Database Management, Education and Research. Support members worldwide with chapters in Japan, Australia, Europe, South America and Canada. Manage extensive relationships with the Board of Directors and numerous Institute committees. Supervise a staff of 20.

- Instrumental in leading the successful and profitable turnaround of the organization. Achieved/surpassed all financial objectives.
- Expanded and strengthened portfolio of member services, resulting in a 10% reduction in attrition and 10% gain in new membership.
- Restructured Information Center and Customer Service Operations, introduced value-added sales strategies and drove revenue growth from zero to $60,000 annually.
- Outsourced specific technology operations and delivered a 50% reduction in annual MIS expense.
- Introduced internal technology enhancements including common platforms and architectures, internal and external email communications, and internal technical training/support.
- Upgraded all educational, training and conference programs to more closely align with member needs and expectations. Transformed conferences from operating loss to $25,000+ net profit. Restructured awards program, increased member participation by 71% and delivered $180,000 in revenues.
- Key driver in development of organization-wide strategic planning and visioning process.
- Promoted from Vice President of Marketing to Executive Vice President within 8 months.

Vice President – Marketing & Public Relations   1983 to 1996
CITIZENS BANCORP, Raleigh, North Carolina

High-profile leadership position with a fast-track banking and financial services organization. Recruited as Assistant VP of Marketing in 1983 to build, expand and professionalize the institution's marketing and business development functions. Challenged to transition marketing from an "old school" function into a state-of-the-art, customer-driven business unit to drive corporate growth and market expansion.

Scope of responsibility included advertising, sales promotion, product development, market research and segmentation, corporate communications and public/investor relations. Budget accountability for $6 million annually. Member of the Executive Marketing Committee and Investment/Pricing Committee. Board Member providing marketing leadership to Citizens Consumer Financial Services (investment subsidiary).

- Transitioned Marketing from a 1-person function into a 23-person business organization delivering phenomenal financial results:

  -- Key contributor driving asset growth from $2.9 billion to $5 billion with annual income growth of 15%.
  -- Grew primary market share from 7.8% to 10.3%.
  -- Created telemarketing operations, contributing 70%+ in new loan growth within one year.
  -- Introduced PR initiatives that increased positive news coverage by 80%+ over previous year.
  -- Championed market positioning and launch of 12 new products/services generating $850+ million in combined annual sales revenues.

- Positioned Marketing as a value-added service supporting the entire corporation. Transformed from a cost center into a strong ROI producer.
- Instilled a sales culture to replace the traditional order-taking process, recruited top performers, created a competitive market intelligence and research function, and revitalized existing product portfolio.
- Developed fully integrated corporate communications programs, including new corporate image campaign and database marketing initiatives.

Assistant Director – Bank Marketing   1982 to 1983
NATIONAL BANKERS ASSOCIATION, Raleigh, North Carolina
(2200-member professional association)

Recruited to one of NBA's newest services division – Bank Marketing – established to provide members with expert leadership in marketing, advertising and business development within the highly competitive banking industry. Spearheaded development of a portfolio of new products and services, training programs and communication programs to foster member education and drive performance improvement.

Marketing Consultant   1982
SPRINT, Raleigh, North Carolina

Ten-month consulting position as Advisor to Sprint's Marketing Director. Focused efforts on the strategy, design and execution of innovative marketing initiatives to support new product development programs, enhance consumer image and gain market awareness. Concurrent responsibility for identifying and developing profitable strategic alliances with major corporations nationwide.

Advertising Manager   1975 to 1981
AMTRAK, Raleigh, North Carolina

Fast-track promotion through a series of increasingly responsible positions. As Advertising Manager, held full strategic and tactical responsibility for advertising, marketing, public relations, promotional and business development initiatives in 13 sales districts and 500 city markets. Heavy emphasis on consumer-perceived value and add-on services. Controlled $17 million annual operating budget.

EDUCATION:

Graduate Studies in Marketing, Northwestern University and George Washington University, 1977
BA, Magna Cum Laude Graduate, History/Business, Stetson University, DeLand, Florida, 1975
Graduate, School of Bank Marketing, Management & Strategic Planning, 1972

VOLUNTEERISM & COMMUNITY LEADERSHIP:

Chairman – Fundraising Committee, Treatment & Learning Center, Raleigh, North Carolina
Habitat for Humanity, Raleigh, North Carolina
American Diabetes Association, Raleigh, North Carolina

ROBERT M. HASSLER

Beacon Hill Court / Raleigh, North Carolina 27604 / (919) 459-9688

SENIOR EXECUTIVE PROFILE
Start-Up, Turnaround & High-Growth Organizations

Twenty-year business management career with consistent and measurable achievements in:

- Revenue & Profit Growth
- Market & Customer Expansion
- Operating Cost Reductions
- Productivity & Efficiency Improvement

Successful in overcoming demanding market, technological, financial and competitive challenges to drive growth, profitability and performance improvement. Expertise includes:

- Strategic Planning & Leadership
- Marketing, Sales & New Business Development
- New Product & New Service Launch
- Training, Development & Team Building
- Finance, Budgeting & Cost Management
- Contracts, Outsourcing & Partnerships
- Technology Implementation & Optimization
- Special Events Planning & Coordination

PROFESSIONAL EXPERIENCE:

Executive Vice President   1996 to Present
AAA ADVERTISING INSTITUTE, Raleigh, North Carolina
(International advertising association with 1700+ corporate members worldwide)

Member of 5-person Senior Executive Team challenged to revitalize and turnaround this non-performing organization challenged by significant financial and budgetary issues. Initiated assignment with a comprehensive analysis of existing operations to restructure financial operations, optimize strengths, eliminate weaknesses and reposition for solid growth.

Scope of responsibility is significant and includes overall managerial and budgetary leadership for Global Relations, Member/Customer Service, MIS/Database Management, Marketing/Communications & Public Relations, Advocacy, Education and Research. Support operations worldwide with chapters in Japan, Australia, Europe, South America and Canada. Manage extensive relationships with the Board of Directors and numerous Institute committees. Supervise a staff of 20.

Leadership & General Management Performance

- Instrumental in leading the successful and profitable turnaround of the organization. Achieved/surpassed all financial objectives.
- Key driver in development of organization-wide strategic planning and visioning process.
- Introduced best practices, streamlined business processes and accelerated productivity.
- Promoted from Vice President of Marketing to Executive Vice President within 8 months.

Financial & Technology Achievements:

- Expanded and strengthened portfolio of services, resulting in a 10% reduction in attrition and 10% gain in new membership.
- Restructured Information Center and Customer Service Operations, introduced value-added sales strategies and drove revenue growth from zero to $60,000 annually.
- Outsourced specific technology operations and delivered a 50% reduction in annual MIS expense.
- Introduced internal technology enhancements including common platforms and architectures, internal and external email communications, and internal technical training/support.
- Upgraded all educational, training and conference programs to more closely align with member needs and expectations. Transformed conferences from operating loss to $25,000+ net profit. Restructured awards program, increased member participation by 71% and delivered $180,000 in revenues.

Vice President – Marketing & Public Relations   1983 to 1996
CITIZENS BANCORP, Raleigh, North Carolina

High-profile leadership position with a fast-track banking and financial services organization. Member of the Executive Marketing Committee and Investment/Pricing Committee. Board Member providing operating, marketing and financial leadership to Citizens Consumer Financial Services (investment subsidiary).

Recruited as Assistant VP in 1983 to build and professionalize marketing and business development functions. Transitioned marketing from an "old school" function into a state-of-the-art, customer-driven business unit to drive corporate growth and market expansion. Directed planning, finance, staffing, technology and administration for advertising, sales promotion, product development, market research, corporate communications and public/investor relations. Budget accountability for $6 million annually.

- Transitioned Marketing from a 1-person function into a 23-person business organization delivering phenomenal financial results:
  -- Key contributor driving asset growth from $2.9 billion to $5 billion with annual income growth of 15%.
  -- Grew primary market share from 7.8% to 10.3%.
  -- Created telemarketing operations, contributing 70%+ in new loan growth within one year.
  -- Introduced PR initiatives that increased positive news coverage by 80%+ over previous year.
  -- Championed market positioning and launch of 12 new products/services generating $850+ million in combined annual sales revenues.

- Positioned Marketing as a value-added service for the entire corporation. Developed partnerships with key operating units and business management teams to transform marketing from a cost center into a strong ROI producer. Extensive communications regarding operations, finance and technology.
- Instilled a sales culture to replace the traditional order-taking process, recruited top performers, created a competitive market intelligence and research function, and revitalized existing product portfolio.
- Developed fully integrated corporate communications programs, including new corporate image campaign and database marketing initiatives.

Assistant Director – Bank Marketing   1982 to 1983
NATIONAL BANKERS ASSOCIATION, Raleigh, North Carolina.

Recruited to one of NBA's newest services division – Bank Marketing -- established to provide members with expert leadership in marketing, advertising and business development within the highly competitive banking industry. Spearheaded development of a portfolio of new products and services, training programs and communication programs to foster member education and drive performance improvement.

Marketing Consultant   1982
SPRINT, Raleigh, North Carolina

Ten-month consulting position as Advisor to Sprint's Marketing Director. Focused efforts on the strategy, design and execution of innovative marketing initiatives to support new product development programs, enhance consumer image and gain market awareness. Concurrent responsibility for identifying and developing profitable strategic alliances with major corporations nationwide.

Advertising Manager   1975 to 1981
AMTRAK, Raleigh, North Carolina

Fast-track promotion through a series of increasingly responsible positions. As Advertising Manager, held full strategic and tactical responsibility for advertising, marketing, public relations, promotional and business development initiatives in 13 sales districts and 500 city markets. Heavy emphasis on consumer-perceived value and add-on services. Controlled $17 million annual operating budget.

EDUCATION:

Graduate Studies in Marketing, Northwestern University and George Washington University, 1977
BA, Magna Cum Laude Graduate, History/Business, Stetson University, DeLand, Florida, 1975
Graduate, School of Bank Marketing, Management & Strategic Planning, 1972

WILLIAM TIDWELL

332 Brockwell Road
Johnstown, Pennsylvania 15907

Home (412) 589-9636   Office (412) 485-4181

EXECUTIVE PROFILE

Business Development and Legal Executive with global experience (US, Europe, Latin America, Far East and the former Soviet Union). Drove profitable growth of start-up ventures, turnarounds and high-growth corporations. Diverse industry, client and country experience. Solid team building and professional leadership skills. MBA/JD with corporate and law firm experience.

- P/L Management
- Mergers & Acquisition
- Joint Ventures

- Technology Licensing
- LBO & MBO Transactions
- Capital Markets

- Strategic Business Leadership
- Emerging Market Activity

PROFESSIONAL EXPERIENCE

THE XYZ STEEL CORPORATION, Johnstown, Pennsylvania   1997 - Present
Assistant General Counsel – Corporate Development

Recruited to focus on new ventures and corporate development projects as part of revitalization and market repositioning (following 1993 emergence from bankruptcy). Partnered with executive team to identify, develop, structure and negotiate domestic and international business transactions. Manage mergers and acquisitions, international joint ventures, emerging markets development (Latin America, Far East), and Board of Directors relations. Concurrent responsibility for corporate policy development.

- Partnered with Corporate Development to reposition XYZ for high-profile transactions to reignite business development and global market expansion/diversification.
- Negotiated favorable withdrawal from $185 million Chinese joint venture to halt XYZ's losses and market risk, retaining technology ownership while divesting financial/operational responsibilities.

MERCHANT SERVICES INC.   1993 - 1997
President/General Counsel (1993 - 1997)

Founded merchant banking business combining expertise in law, investment banking and corporate development for major US and international clients. Originated and/or participated in projects in the US, Europe, Mexico and the former Soviet Union. Total transactions valued at $500+ million.

- Represented Kazakhstan client seeking to purchase a fleet of aircraft. Partnered with Boeing, Pratt & Whitney, and ABM Amro to create a global supply resource and develop international financing.
- Structured the purchase of telecommunications technology with GTE, Alcatel and the City of Moscow.
- Negotiated $25 million transaction for the acquisition of a chain of theaters from Hollywood Theaters.

President/General Counsel – ABC Company– Moscow, Russia (1996 - 1997) *concurrent*

Led the turnaround and return to profitability of this $50 million catering and hotel services company with 15 locations in Russia, Eastern Europe, and the Central Asian Republics. Led a team of 4 senior expatriates (Marketing, Operations, Finance & Logistics) and 350 CIS-based employees.

- Provided strong organizational leadership and delivered the company's first-ever profits.
- Negotiated strategic global and local partnerships, forged profitable new alliances, expanded market channels, standardized contracts, and introduced employee cross-training programs and incentives.
- Reduced annual operating costs by $3+ million and collected $5 million in past due receivables.
- Raised $100+ million in new capital to fund regional market expansion of parent corporation.

Managing Director – ABC Beverage – Ukraine (1994 - 1996) *concurrent*

Led the start-up of an exclusive Pepsi franchise with full P&L responsibility. Directed 6-person expatriate management team, 400 local employees, and outside legal counsel, bankers, and Big 6 accounting firms.

- Led management team through successful business rollout and market development, delivering significant ROI results (better than 20% over projections).
- Identified and negotiated a $40 million private equity placement.
- Directed negotiations with PepsiCo International to establish terms of franchise agreement/operations.
- Negotiated strategic partner ventures and third party vendor contracts, established distribution and delivery system, recruited local employees and managed a sensitive government relations function.

RUE, BELL & ZIFFRA, P.C., Reading, Pennsylvania   1991 - 1993

Partner – Business Section
Recruited to represent a diverse portfolio of large corporate, emerging, high growth and institutional clients on domestic and international transactions generating substantial revenues to the firm. Developed capital sources and strategic partners for clientele. Member of Management Committee.

- Represented Eppler Guerin Turner as underwriter of secondary offering of securities of Cash America, the proceeds of which were applied toward a large UK investment.
- Counseled Brown & Root/Dillon Read consortium on numerous bid/financing transactions to support Latin American infrastructure development projects.
- Represented private investor developing international technology transfers involving Monsanto Chemical and Carnegie Mellon University.
- Represented EDS and Dell Computer on complex transactions.
- Guided J.P. Morgan on major international tax-exempt financing transactions.
- Advised Indoor Media Group on licensing matters for innovative partnership advertising program with major clients (e.g., Kroger, Wal-mart).

LOWRY HAUSER WARNOCK, Lancaster, Pennsylvania   1985 - 1991
Partner – Business Section

Recruited to innovative, entrepreneurial law firm to manage a portfolio of clients across diverse industries. Promoted to Partner one year early and appointed to Management Committee for Business Development
- Originated and closed $500+ million LBO and recapitalization financings (debt and equity) for Chemical Bank, structuring the single largest transaction and fee in the firm's history.
- Represented EDS Board of Directors during restructure of all corporate investment policies and designation of outside investment advisory team.
- Advised Employers Casualty Board of Directors during the sale, restructure and liquidation.

JEFFREY ZIMMERMAN, New York, New York   1981 - 1985
Associate

Worked for high-profile clients including Carl Icahn, Fortune 500 and leading investment banking firms.

PRICE WATERHOUSE, Boston, Massachusetts   1980 - 1981
Associate – Tax Department

EDUCATION

JD / MBA – Honors Graduate – 1980   WIDENER UNIVERSITY
BA – Political Science – Honors Graduate – 1976   PENNSYLVANIA STATE UNIVERSITY

WILLIAM TIDWELL
332 Brockwell Road
Johnstown, Pennsylvania 15907

Home (412) 589-9636   Office (412) 485-4181

SENIOR EXECUTIVE PROFILE
International Business Development / Corporate Development / Corporate Legal Affairs
Strategic Business Leadership / Operating & Profit Management / Business Transactions
Prestigious Global Corporations & US Law Firms
MBA & JD Degrees

High-profile executive management and corporate counsel career with global experience throughout the US, Europe, Latin America, Far East and the former Soviet Union. Drove profitable domestic and international growth of start-up ventures, turnarounds and high-growth corporations through combined operating, marketing, legal and financial leadership. Transactional expertise in:

- Mergers & Acquisitions
- LBO & MBO Transactions
- Joint Ventures
- Equity & Debt Placements
- Licensing
- Investments

Previous experience with three prestigious law firms in New York and Pennsylvania. Represented major clients, including Alcatel, Boeing, Brown & Root, EDS, Goldman Sachs, GTE, J.P. Morgan, Monsanto, NationsBank, PepsiCo and Pratt & Whitney, in global business development, investment financing, partnership and corporate transactions. Diverse industry experience, client and country experience.

Outstanding performance in relationship development and management, strategic planning, profit growth, deal structuring and negotiations. Solid team building and professional leadership skills.

PROFESSIONAL EXPERIENCE:

Assistant General Counsel   1997 to Present
XYZ STEEL CORPORATION, Johnstown, Pennsylvania

Senior Corporate Counsel specializing in business/corporate development as part of XYZ's revitalization and market repositioning (following 1996 bankruptcy). Challenged to identify, develop, structure and negotiate domestic and international business transactions to support growth, diversification and long-term profitability.

Scope of responsibility includes mergers and acquisitions, international joint ventures, emerging markets development (primarily Latin America and Far East), Board of Directors relations and senior advisory services to executive management team. Concurrent responsibility for corporate policy development and high-level corporate administrative affairs.

- Currently leading efforts to reposition XYZ for high-profile transactions to reignite business development and global market expansion.
- Negotiated favorable withdrawal from $185 million Chinese joint venture to halt XYZ's losses and market risk. Structured contracts to retain technology ownership while divesting all financial and operational responsibilities.
- Divested partnership in Thailand joint venture following insurmountable in-country corruption, political and economic volatility.

48

President / General Counsel   1993 to 1997

President/General Counsel – ABC Company – Moscow, Russia (1996 to 1997)
Senior Operating, Management & Legal Executive credited with the successful turnaround, revitalization and return to profitability of this $50 million catering and hotel services company with 15 locations in 7 countries throughout Russia, Eastern Europe and the Central Asian Republics. Led a team of 4 senior level expatriates (Marketing, Operations, Finance & Logistics) and 350 CIS-based employees.

- Provided strong organizational leadership through a period of massive change and reorganization. Achieved/surpassed all performance objectives and delivered the first-ever profits in the company's history.
- Restructured operating, financial and legal infrastructure. Negotiated/renegotiated strategic global and local partnerships, forged profitable new alliances, expanded market channels, standardized contracts and business documentation, and introduced employee cross-training programs and incentives.
- Reduced annual operating costs by more than $3 million and collected over $5 million in past due receivables for a tremendous surge in cash flow.
- Refinanced $80 million in European real estate assets and divested non-performing business units in South Africa and Canada on behalf of parent company.
- Raised over $72 million in new equity capital to fund regional market expansion.

Managing Director/General Counsel – ABC Beverage – Ukraine (1994 to 1996)
Two-year resident of Kiev, Ukraine as the Senior Operating Executive leading the start-up of an exclusive Pepsi franchise. Full managerial, financial, sales, marketing, legal and P&L responsibility for the venture. Directed 12-person expatriate management team, 400 local employees, and outside legal counsel, bankers and Big 6 accounting firms.

- Led management team through successful business roll-out and market development, delivering significant ROI results (better than 75% over projections).
- Identified and negotiated with institutional investors in New York and London to transact a $40 million private equity placement.
- Directed negotiations with PepsiCo International executives in New York, Vienna, London and Kiev to establish terms of franchise agreement and managing ongoing operations.
- Negotiated strategic partner ventures and third party vendor contracts, established distribution and delivery system, recruited local employees and managed a sensitive government relations function. Personally managed all corporate/tax/legal affairs.

President – Merchant Services Inc. (1993 to 1994)
Founded and directed successful merchant banking business combining personal expertise in law, investment banking and corporate development for major US and international clients. Originated and/or participated in projects in the US, Europe, Mexico and the former Soviet Union. Total transactions valued at more than $600 million.

- Represented client in Kazakhstan seeking to purchase a major fleet of aircraft. Partnered with **Boeing**, **Pratt & Whitney**, **GTE** and other major US manufacturers to create a global supply resource and develop international financing opportunities.
- Structured and negotiated transaction between **Alcatel** and the City of Moscow for the purchase of advanced telecommunications technology.
- Negotiated $25 million transaction for the acquisition of a chain of theaters from **Hollywood Theaters** for acquisition by **Bears & Goldman Sachs**.
- Managed high-profile business development, investment banking and transactions for other corporations worldwide including Aviation Genoa Ltd., Hicks Muse and ABM Amro.

Partner – Business Section   1991 to 1993
RUE, BELL & Ziffra, P.C., Reading, Pennsylvania

Recruited to one of the state's leading blue chip law firms to represent a diverse portfolio of large corporate, emerging, high growth and institutional clients on complex domestic and international transactions. Developed and managed a thriving legal practice generating substantial revenues to the firm. Successfully developed capital sources and strategic partners for clientele. Vital member of the firm's Business Development Committee.

- Represented **Eppler Guerin Turner** as underwriter of secondary offering of securities of Cash America, the proceeds of which were applied toward a significant UK investment.
- Counseled **Brown & Root/Dillon Read** consortium on numerous bid/financing transactions to support Latin American infrastructure development projects.
- Represented private investor developing international technology transfers involving **Monsanto Chemical** and **Carnegie Mellon University**.
- Guided **J.P. Morgan** on major international tax-exempt financing transactions.
- Advised **Indoor Media Group** on licensing matters for innovative partnership advertising program with major clients (e.g., Kroger, Wal-mart).
- Structured management buy-out of major business unit from **Republic Healthcorp**.
- Counseled other attorneys on complex **EDS** and **Dell Computer** transactions.

Partner – Business Section   1985 to 1991
LOWRY HAUSER WARNOCK, Lancaster, Pennsylvania

Recruited to prestigious law firm (most innovative and entrepreneurial in Pennsylvania) to manage a broad portfolio of clients across diverse industries. Promoted to Partner one year ahead of peers and appointed to Management Committee for Business Development. Earned reputation as a consistent top performer, among the highest in billable hours, profitability and new client development.

- Originated and closed $500+ million LBO and recapitalization financings (debt and equity) for **Chemical Bank**, structuring the single largest transaction and fee in the firm's history.
- Represented **EDS** Board of Directors during restructure of all corporate investment policies and designation of outside investment advisory team.
- Advised Board of Directors of **Employers Casualty** during the sale, restructure and liquidation of the corporation.

Associate   1981 to 1985
JEFFREY ZIMMERMAN, New York, New York

Worked on diverse matters for high-profile clients including Carl Icahn, major US corporations and leading investment banking firms for an eminent Manhattan law firm.

Associate – Tax Department   1980 to 1981
PRICE WATERHOUSE, Boston, Massachusetts

EDUCATION:

JD / MBA – Honors Graduate – 1980	WIDENER UNIVERSITY
BA – Political Science – Honors Graduate – 1976	UNIVERSITY OF RHODE ISLAND

NORMAN STEPHENS, CPA

29 SW Summerfield Drive
Topeka, Kansas 66610
Email: nstephens@bellatlantic.net

Home: (785) 685-2574

Fax: (408) 942-5503

SENIOR FINANCE & TAX MANAGER – PUBLIC ACCOUNTING & CONSULTING
Corporate Tax / Accounting / Audit / Controllership / Banking & Investor Relations
Financial Planning, Analysis & Reporting / Cash Management / Asset Management

Solutions-driven Financial Executive with 15+ years' experience in the design, delivery and management of comprehensive accounting and financial programs for corporate clients worldwide. Industry expertise in technology, software, manufacturing, distribution, transportation, oil & gas, distribution and construction/real estate.

Strategic business leader with strong team building, communication and presentation skills. Innovative and versatile. Success in optimizing productivity, efficiency and profitability through delivery of value-added services and programs.

Expert in Client Relationship Development, Management & Retention

---

PROFESSIONAL EXPERIENCE:

ABC FINANCIAL SERVICES, Topeka, Kansas   1996 to Present

Senior Manager – International Executive Services
(*Specialty practice providing corporate tax services for major corporations – Chevron, 3Com, Apple, Oracle*)

High-profile management position as ABC's #1 corporate tax executive supporting Chevron and its 1800 US expatriates and foreign nationals residing worldwide. Lead a team of 25 ABC professionals responsible for US income tax return preparation, tax equalization calculation, tax loan settlement, hypothetical and actual tax calculations and management/coordination of host country tax professionals. Travel worldwide.

- Facilitated a major transition in organizational culture from centralized command and control environment to individual decision making and information sharing. Efforts have resulted in dramatic gains in employee morale and retention while enabling more effective, solutions-driven decision making.
- Restaffed key positions, opened communication channels and pioneered innovative cross-training initiatives. Reduced 50% turnover to less than 15%.
- Spearheaded $150,000 client management and tracking database project, from preliminary concept and design through final implementation. Delivered measurable gains in cash flow direct to Chevron.
- Led project team in design and implementation of tax loan collection and monitoring accounting system, resulting in Chevron's decision to completely outsource the function to ABC. Created profitable and sustainable new value-added client service and revenue stream for ABC.
- Designed tax models subsequently being implemented for other key clients worldwide.
- Significantly improved client relationship and thwarted potential competitive threats. Negotiated contract renewal and upgrade from $1.9 million to $3.2 million annually for three consecutive years.

NORMAN STEPHENS, CPA, Topeka, Kansas   1992 to 1996

Principal

Founded and built a successful accounting practice specializing as ***"Interim Controller & CFO"*** for start-up, early stage and growth companies. Professional services included design/implementation/refinement of accounting and reporting systems, development of internal and external reporting processes, corporate income tax planning and preparation, corporate banking, investor communications and asset management.

51

- Managed new venture from concept to profitability. Built a solid client base through personal network and referrals with concentration in the software development, manufacturing and maritime industries.
- Led a $200,000+ technology investment project for a $12 million manufacturer/distributor. Evaluated organizational needs and software/technology systems, sourced vendors, negotiated contract and directed successful implementation.
- Focused on infrastructure, process, policy and system development for start-up corporations (including hiring professional staff). Concentrated on the redesign and enhancement of existing accounting and financial systems for established corporations.
- Designed and implemented cash management and budgeting processes that impacted positive gains in cash flow and bottom-line profitability for several key clients.
- Marketed and sold practice in 1996 for a substantial return on investment.

DEVELOP, INC., San Jose, California   1988 to 1991

Vice President of Finance

Recruited by previous ABC client (early stage technology company) to build their internal corporate finance organization. Given full leadership and decision-making responsibility for professionalizing the accounting functions. Designed financial infrastructure, developed business processes, and managed daily accounting, controls, internal and external financial reporting, cash flow, budgeting and corporate income tax.

- Partnered with each functional discipline with the corporation to understand their operational and financial needs. Leveraged information as baseline for accounting/financial systems design.
- Built organizational consensus to transition from antiquated accounting and reporting to a state-of-the-art, PC-based system. Resulted in a dramatic improvement in the accuracy and timeliness of financial data as well as strengthening relationships with corporate investors and bankers.
- Uncovered a total of $1 million in misappropriation of funds. Introduced sophisticated accounting controls, asset management processes and a risk management system to eliminate further loss.
- Resolved long-standing corporate tax and payroll tax issues, eliminated proposed penalty and interest payments, and redesigned reporting and payment processes.

ABC FINANCIAL SERVICES, Topeka, Kansas   1977 to 1988

Senior Manager (1986 to 1988)
Manager (1983 to 1986)
Supervisory Accountant (1981 to 1983)
Senior Accountant (1979 to 1981)
Staff Accountant (1977 to 1979)

Fast-track promotion through a series of increasingly responsible positions in ABC's Audit Division. Clients included mid-size public and private corporations in software/technology, manufacturing, wholesale distribution and construction/real estate. Led teams of up to 12 professionals per engagement.

- Designed and taught all Audit programs nationwide for ABC staff. Specialization in Corporate Taxation.

EDUCATION:

BS – Business & Accounting, Kansas State University, Manhattan, Kansas, 1977

Licensed CPA, State of California, 1979

NORMAN STEPHENS

29 SW Summerfield Drive
Topeka, Kansas 66610

Home: (785) 685-2574   Email: nstephens@bellatlantic.net   Fax: (408) 942-5503

CORPORATE FINANCE EXECUTIVE
Vice President of Finance / Acting CFO / Senior Manager

Innovative, versatile and solutions-driven executive with outstanding strategic planning, team building and communication skills. Industry expertise in technology, software, manufacturing, distribution, transportation, oil & gas, distribution and construction/real estate. Successful in identifying, capturing and building new opportunities.

Corporate Financial Leadership

As CFO of an early-stage technology venture, built the corporation's entire financial infrastructure including policies, procedures and business processes for accounting, accounting controls, financial reporting and analysis, cash management, asset management, audit, capital and operating budgets, and corporate tax.

Financial Information Technologies

Architected design, customization and implementation of advanced information technologies and systems to enhance the accuracy, availability and timeliness of financial data for strategic planning and reporting.

Revenue & Profit Growth

Delivered significant gains in revenues, market share and bottom-line profits through strategic financial and operational leadership. Optimized productivity, efficiency and operations to drive performance improvement.

Corporate Taxation

Expert in the entire spectrum of corporate taxation to include planning, preparation, regulatory compliance and strategic management/reduction of corporate tax liabilities.

Organizational Leadership

Top-performer in team building and leadership across broad functional disciplines. Senior advisor to CEO's, CFO's and other senior executives. Supervisory responsibility for up to 25 professionals and support staff.

Banking & Investor Relations

Developed and nurtured proactive working relationships with bankers, investors, business partners and other personnel critical to corporate growth, expansion and profitability.

PROFESSIONAL EXPERIENCE:

ABC FINANCIAL SERVICES, Topeka, Kansas   1996 to Present

Senior Manager – International Executive Services
(*Specialty practice providing corporate tax services for major corporations – Chevron, 3Com, Apple, Oracle*)

High-profile management position as ABC's #1 corporate tax executive supporting Chevron and its 1800 US expatriates and foreign nationals residing worldwide. Lead a team of 25 ABC professionals. Travel worldwide with Chevron principals to disseminate information relative to finance and human resources.

- Facilitated a major transition in organizational culture from centralized command and control environment to individual decision making and information sharing. Efforts have resulted in dramatic gains in employee morale and retention while enabling more effective, solutions-driven decision making.
- Restaffed key positions and pioneered cross-training initiatives. Reduced 50% turnover to 15%.
- Spearheaded $150,000 client management and tracking database project, from preliminary concept and design through final implementation. Delivered measurable gains in cash flow direct to Chevron.
- Led project team in design and implementation of tax loan collection and monitoring accounting system.

NORMAN STEPHENS, CPA, Topeka, Kansas   1992 to 1996

Principal

Founded and built a successful accounting practice specializing as ***"Acting Controller & CFO"*** for start-up, early stage and growth companies. Professional services included design/implementation/refinement of accounting and reporting systems, development of internal and external reporting processes, corporate income tax planning and preparation, corporate banking, investor communications and asset management.

- Managed new venture from concept to profitability. Built a solid client base through personal network and referrals with concentration in the software development, manufacturing and maritime industries.
- Led a $200,000+ technology investment project for a $12 million manufacturer/distributor. Evaluated needs and software systems, sourced vendors and directed successful implementation.
- Designed and implemented cash management and budgeting processes that impacted positive gains in cash flow and bottom-line profitability for several key clients.
- Marketed and sold practice in 1996 for a substantial return on investment.

DEVELOP, INC., San Jose, California   1988 to 1991

Vice President of Finance

Recruited by previous ABC client (early stage technology company) to build their internal corporate finance organization. Given full leadership and decision-making responsibility for professionalizing the accounting functions. Designed financial infrastructure, developed business processes, and managed daily accounting, controls, internal and external financial reporting, cash flow, budgeting and corporate income tax.

- Partnered with each functional discipline with the corporation to understand their operational and financial needs. Leveraged information as baseline for accounting/financial systems design.
- Built organizational consensus to transition from antiquated accounting and reporting to a state-of-the-art, PC-based system. Resulted in a dramatic improvement in the accuracy and timeliness of financial data as well as strengthening relationships with corporate investors and bankers.
- Uncovered a total of $1 million in misappropriation of funds. Introduced sophisticated accounting controls, asset management processes and a risk management system to eliminate further loss.
- Resolved long-standing corporate tax and payroll tax issues, eliminated proposed penalty and interest payments, and redesigned reporting and payment processes.

ABC FINANCIAL SERVICES, Topeka, Kansas   1977 to 1988

Senior Manager (1986 to 1988)
Manager (1983 to 1986)
Supervisory Accountant (1981 to 1983)
Senior Accountant (1979 to 1981)
Staff Accountant (1977 to 1979)

Fast-track promotion through a series of increasingly responsible positions in ABC's Audit Division. Clients included mid-size public and private corporations in software/technology, manufacturing, wholesale distribution and construction/real estate. Led teams of up to 12 professionals per engagement. Designed and taught all Audit programs nationwide for ABC staff. Specialization in Corporate Taxation.

EDUCATION:

BS – Business & Accounting, Kansas State University, Manhattan, Kansas, 1977
Licensed CPA, State of Kansas, 1979

ERNEST W. STEWART

439 Coolidge Street
Lexington, Kentucky 40508

Home: 606-589-2454
Email: ewstewart@aol.com

INSURANCE INDUSTRY PROFESSIONAL
SALES & MARKETING MANAGEMENT / NEW BUSINESS DEVELOPMENT
NEW PRODUCT DEVELOPMENT / PRODUCT PRICING & PROFITABILITY

Eighteen-year professional career highlighted by rapid advancement and consistent achievement in market, premium and profit growth. Outstanding qualifications in building and managing relationships with sales producers and field management teams. Strong qualifications in underwriting and policy rating. PC literate with word processing and spreadsheet applications, email and the Internet.

PROFESSIONAL DESIGNATIONS & INDUSTRY CREDENTIALS:

Certified Professional Insurance Agent (CPIA), 1998
Chartered Property and Casualty Underwriter (CPCU), 1996
Certified Insurance Counselor (CIC), 1994
Accredited Advisor in Insurance (AAI), 1994
Associate in Risk Management (ARM), 1987

PROFESSIONAL EXPERIENCE:

NATIONAL GRANGE MUTUAL, Lexington, KY   1994 to 2000

Senior District Marketing Manager – Western Virginia

Fast-paced marketing and business development position with this personal and commercial lines P&C insurance carrier. Responsible for recruiting, appointing, training, developing and managing an independent sales force that grew from 10 to 30+ agents over four years. Managed statewide meetings and led presentations to senior management teams. Conceived and implemented long-term marketing strategy to drive premium growth, improve financial performance and outpace the competition. Held bottom-line responsibility for production and profitability of the district.

- Won the **1999 Leadership Council Award**, National Grange's highest marketing honor.

- Achieved/surpassed all financial goals for the district:
  -- Increased 1996 written premium by 24% with a loss ratio of only 47%.
  -- Increased 1997 written premium by 48% with a loss ratio of only 50%.
  -- Increased 1998 written premium by 62% with a loss ratio of only 60%.

- Appointed to the Corporate Change Management Task Force to solicit feedback from customers regarding products, services and Grange's field operations (baseline data for the redesign of corporate policies and procedures to enhance market performance).

ABC INSURANCE GROUP, Shelby, OH   1989 to 1994

Territorial Marketing Manager – State of Kentucky

Recruited to accelerate ABC's market presence throughout the State of Kentucky for the sale of both P&C and life insurance products. Focused efforts on the recruitment, appointment, training, development and support of independent insurance agents marketing products to commercial and large industrial accounts. Directed policy underwriting, pricing and field sales. Concurrently, launched several new products to further enhance revenue performance and bottom-line profitability.

- Won the **1994 APEX Award** as the #1 marketing producer in the company.

- Built territory to 70+ agents with strong premium volume and below industry loss ratios.

PROFESSIONAL EXPERIENCE (*Continued*):

INDUSTRIAL INSURANCE MANAGEMENT CORPORATION, Bowling Green, KY   1988 to 1989

Risk Management Consultant – Kentucky, Indiana, Ohio, Virginia, Maryland & Washington, D.C.

Developed and managed insurance programs for 40+ colleges, universities, banks, cities, and other large municipal and industrial accounts throughout the region. Authored bid specifications, led presentations to CEO's, Boards of Trustees and Supervisors, and other key decision makers, and negotiated final insurance coverages to meet specific P&C requirements.

CONTINENTAL INSURANCE COMPANY, Lexington, KY   1986 to 1988

Commercial Underwriting Manager – Brokerage Division

Built a 4-person underwriting unit into one of the most productive and efficient in the region with 14 underwriters and insurance raters. Directed daily underwriting operations, long-range business planning, and all training and development functions for newly-hired professional staff.

HARLEYSVILLE INSURANCE, Harleysville, PA   1984 to 1986

Field Marketing Representative – State of Virginia

Sold/marketed P&C and life insurance products to insurance agencies and brokerages. Consistently ranked as one of the top producers in the Eastern U.S.

NATIONWIDE INSURANCE, Reston, VA   1980 to 1984

Lead Underwriter (1983 to 1984)
Senior Underwriter (1981 to 1983)
Commercial Underwriter (1980 to 1981)
Claims Examiner (1980)

Recruited to Nationwide's fast-track management training program. Promoted through a series of increasingly responsible assignments to final position managing a six-person P&C underwriting unit.

EDUCATION:

B.S., Business Administration, Virginia Tech University, Blacksburg, VA, 1979

PROFESSIONAL AFFILIATIONS:

Chartered Property and Casualty Underwriters Society
Society of Certified Insurance Counselors
Certified Professional Insurance Agents Society
Professional Insurance Agents Association
Independent Insurance Agents Association

References Provided Upon Request

ERNEST W. STEWART

439 Coolidge Street
Lexington, Kentucky 40508

Home: 606-589-2454
Email: ewstewart@aol.com

SALES & MARKETING MANAGEMENT PROFESSIONAL
District Sales Manager / Territory Marketing Manager

Eighteen-year professional career highlighted by rapid advancement and consistent achievement in revenue and profit growth within extremely competitive markets. Outstanding qualifications in building and managing customer relationships across diverse industries with top-level decision makers. PC literate with word processing and spreadsheet applications, email and the Internet.

- Strategic Planning & Business Development
- New Market & Territory Development
- Multi-Channel Distribution Networks
- Competitive Market Positioning

- Sales Training & Team Leadership
- New Product Development & Pricing
- Executive Presentations & Negotiations
- Productivity & Performance Improvement

PROFESSIONAL EXPERIENCE:

Senior District Marketing Manager – Western Kentucky   1994 to 2000
NATIONAL GRANGE MUTUAL, Lexington, KY

Fast-paced marketing and business development position with an emphasis on distribution channel management/expansion, new product development/introduction and sales training/team leadership. Managed statewide meetings and led presentations to senior management teams. Conceived and implemented long-term marketing strategy to drive growth, improve financial performance and outpace competition. Held bottom-line responsibility for production and profitability of the district.

- Won the **1999 Leadership Council Award**, National Grange's highest marketing honor.

- Achieved/surpassed all financial goals for the district. Increased volume 24% in 1996, 48% in 1997 and 62% in 1998. Consistently exceeded all financial goals and objectives.

- Built independent sales force from 10 to 30+ agents.

- Appointed to the Corporate Change Management Task Force to solicit feedback from customers regarding products, services and Grange's field operations (baseline data for the redesign of corporate policies and procedures to enhance market performance).

Territorial Marketing Manager – State of Kentucky   1989 to 1994
ABC INSURANCE GROUP, Shelby, OH

Recruited to accelerate ABC's market presence throughout the State of Kentucky. Focused efforts on the recruitment, appointment, training, development and support of independent sales agents marketing products to commercial and large industrial accounts. Concurrently, launched several new products to further enhance revenue performance and bottom-line profitability.

- Won the **1994 APEX Award** as the #1 marketing producer in the company.

- Built territory to 70+ agents with consistently strong volume. Closed each year over quota.

PROFESSIONAL EXPERIENCE (*Continued*):

Risk Management Consultant   1988 to 1989
INDUSTRIAL INSURANCE MANAGEMENT CORPORATION, Bowling Green, KY

Developed, marketed and managed programs for 40+ colleges, universities, banks, cities, and other large municipal and industrial accounts throughout Kentucky, Indiana, Ohio, Virginia, Maryland and Washington, D.C. Authored bid specifications, led presentations to CEO's, Boards of Trustees and Supervisors, and other key decision makers, and negotiated complex final transactions.

Commercial Underwriting Manager   1986 to 1988
CONTINENTAL INSURANCE COMPANY, Lexington, KY

Built a 4-person underwriting unit into one of the most productive and efficient in the region with 14 underwriters and insurance raters. Directed daily underwriting operations, long-range business planning, and all training and development functions for newly-hired professional staff.

Field Marketing Representative – State of Virginia   1984 to 1986
HARLEYSVILLE INSURANCE, Harleysville, PA

Independently managed field sales and marketing programs throughout the region. Consistently ranked as one of the top producers in the Eastern U.S.

Management Trainee   1980 to 1984
NATIONWIDE INSURANCE, Reston, VA

Recruited to Nationwide's fast-track management training program. Promoted through a series of increasingly responsible assignments to final position managing a six-person business unit.

EDUCATION:

B.S., Business Administration, Virginia Tech University, Blacksburg, VA, 1979

Earned several distinguished insurance industry credentials and certifications.

References Provided Upon Request

The 90 resumes that follow are all "real-life" resumes written for "real-life" job seekers, all of whom either make $100,000+ a year or are close to that mark. Each resume was written with a specific objective in mind; each was written to showcase the talents, achievements and career successes of each job seeker. Most important, each has opened doors, generated interviews and helped close top-level opportunities. Use the sample words, formats, styles, strategies and concepts as the foundation for writing your own powerful executive resume.

JOHN P. SMITH

5555 North Avenue
Los Angeles, California 92009
(619) 222-3333

CORPORATE ACCOUNTING & FINANCE PROFESSIONAL
Start-Up, Turnaround & High-Growth Corporations

Eighteen years experience in the design, development and management of comprehensive corporate accounting, budgeting, financial reporting, financial modeling, tax and MIS systems. Consistently successful in linking accounting with general operations to provide hands-on financial leadership for strategic planning, technology R&D, sales/marketing, purchasing, inventory, production and distribution.

Delivered strong and sustainable revenue and income gains. Equally effective in capturing cost reductions through process redesign and performance management.

PROFESSIONAL EXPERIENCE:

Controller   1994 to Present
NEWS, INC., Los Angeles, California
(Acquired by International Publishing in December 1995)

Recruited as an Inventory Accountant in 1994 following the acquisition of News, Inc., a $50 million multi-media and CD-ROM software publisher. Promoted to Controller with full responsibility for accounts payable, accounts receivable, general ledger, royalty and contract management, departmental budgeting, and all related MIS operations. Direct a 3-person management team and 10+ support personnel.

- Reengineered royalty and licensing agreements in cooperation with the Legal and Licensing Departments. Incorporated sophisticated financial analysis into intellectual property negotiations, designed financial models and saved over $800,000.

- Designed an Excel relational database daily revenue flash report which graphically depicted gross shipments and returns by product line. Provided senior executives with accurate data to evaluate actual sales performance versus plan in this rapidly changing commercial market.

- Launched a process-by-process redesign of key accounting functions, consolidated workflow, streamlined staffing requirements and captured over $190,000 in annual savings.

- Accelerated internal automation and full use of existing system applications. Brought inventory control module on-line, resulting in annual physical adjustment of less than 1%. Currently transitioning (via electronic transmission conversion) from AccPac to J.D. Edwards software.

- Modified amortization schedules for capitalized software development costs for the R&D Department, linked with actual units sold and integrated payroll costs to more accurately record profit margins and recapture development expenses.

NOTE: *Instrumental in positioning division for sale at twice the acquisition cost after only two years.*
             Assisted Price Waterhouse in preparation of 8K filings for the SEC.

Accounting & Financial Systems Consultant   1992 to 1994
MOVERS & SHAKERS, Boston, Massachusetts

Recruited to design, implement and manage a PC-based accounting system for this sporting events management company and producer of the annual Boston Marathon. As the only accounting and finance professional in the organization, provided daily accounting, budgeting and cash management support in addition to long-range strategic, business, market and finance planning.

MOVERS & SHAKERS *(Continued):*

- Created a comprehensive accounting and financial reporting system:
  — Prepared financial statements for fiscal years 1992, 1993 and 1994.
  — Redesigned chart of accounts to track sponsorship fees, entry fees and concession fees by multiple product classes and specific events.
  — Developed detailed job cost and profitability analysis reports as the foundation for budgeting and event planning to facilitate future growth and improved earnings.

Accounting Manager   1991 to 1992
SIERRA, Carlsbad, California

Managed accounts payable, accounts receivable, payroll, billing, credit and collections, sales and use tax filings, and financial statements for this $12 million electronics manufacturer.

- Restructured and tightened the company's cash management policy to ensure prompt recovery of all receivables to meet cash requirements of payroll and vendor commitments.

- Renegotiated payment schedule to recover $2 million from an Italian company. Personally collected first $500,000 payment and established framework for subsequent collection of all outstanding funds.

- Redesigned Bill of Materials for all products (in cooperation with Engineering Department) to facilitate development/refinement of standard cost system.

- Managed annual physical inventory in cooperation with Price Waterhouse auditors.

Director of Operations   1983 to 1991
COLORADO VIDEO, Mountain View, Colorado

Recruited as Controller for a start-up video production company servicing cable television, corporate training and expanding consumer video markets. Created all general accounting, cost accounting, budgeting, financial analysis/reporting, tax, payroll and long-range business planning systems.

Promoted to Director of Operations in 1985 with full P&L responsibility for the entire business unit. Directed sales/marketing, studio and location production, post production, technology, human resources, purchasing, and all corporate finance and administrative affairs.

- Built company from start-up to over $2 million in annual revenues.

- Evaluated emerging technology, sourced vendors and directed over $200,000 in annual technology acquisitions to develop a state-of-the-art production facility.

- Successfully marketed, negotiated and closed sales contracts with IBM, Apple, Pepsi, Department of Defense and numerous other corporate and government clients.

Previous Professional Experience:

Cost Accounting Manager, Katy Windows, Irvine, California	1981 to 1983
Cost Accountant, Anderson, Santa Monica, California	1980 to 1981
Cost & Budget Administrator, Continental Group, Boston, Massachusetts	1977 to 1980

EDUCATION:

B.S., Business Administration Management, Honors Graduate, 1979
NORTHEASTERN UNIVERSITY, Boston, Massachusetts

Certified Tax Practitioner (CTP), State of California, 1992

LAURA M. HALSEY

5555 North Avenue
Los Angeles, California 92009
(619) 592-3653

CAREER PROFILE

Accounting Professional / Accounting Department Supervisor with 13 years of progressively responsible experience with high-growth, turnaround and mature corporations. Qualifications include:

- Accounts Receivable
- Accounts Payable
- Account Reconciliation
- General Ledger

- Credit & Collection
- Customer Service
- Cash Application
- Staff Training/Development

- Billing/Invoicing
- Financial Analysis/Reporting
- Chargeback/Adjustments
- Team Building/Leadership

Delivered strong and sustainable operating, financial and service gains through expertise in systems design/implementation, standardization, workflow optimization and long-range planning. Excellent analytical, problem-solving and negotiating skills. PC proficient with IBM System 38, HP 918 Image Data, Lotus and Word.

PROFESSIONAL EXPERIENCE:

INVESTOR'S, INC., Los Angeles, CA   March 1990 to December 1996

Accounts Receivable Supervisor

Recruited as Assistant Supervisor for the Accounts Receivable Department of this rapid growth national daily newspaper. Challenged to design and implement the systems, policies, procedures and technologies to regain control of the A/R function and establish a professional business unit. Promoted to Supervisor within six months. Assumed increased responsibilities for accounting, financial planning/reporting and MIS operations.

Scope of responsibility was diverse and included all billing, credit and collection activity for 1500 active accounts. Prepared monthly financial schedules, graphs, journal entries, sales commissions, and account analyses. Reviewed and approved credit applications, advertising agency discounts and advertising contracts. Monitored cash receipts application, contract adjustments and account reconciliations.

Worked in collaboration with Advertising Sales Department to provide data relevant to account history and credit status. Personally communicated with customers nationwide to resolve billing discrepancies and expedite collections. Consulted with executive management to establish corporate policy impacting A/R and credit operations.

Achievements:

- Built an Accounts Receivable organization successful in meeting the demands of the company as it grew from $7 million to $30 million in annual advertising revenues over a five year period. Met all production requirements with no additional staff.

- Redesigned procedures to collect on past due accounts and increased cash flow by 37%.

- Consistently surpassed all credit and collection targets. Maintained DSO of 35 days or less.

- Captured a $250,000 annual cost savings through development/implementation of an Advertising Management System to integrate and consolidate billing, credit and collection information from three autonomous business units.

- Designed a series of internal reporting mechanisms to measure sales, credit and collection performance.

SANFAX, Los Angeles, CA   May 1986 to March 1990

Accounts Receivable Supervisor (1989 to 1990)
Lead Coordinator - MIS Systems (1988)
Lead Cash Processor (1987 to 1988)
Cash Processor (1986)

Fast-track promotion through a series of increasingly responsible accounting, MIS and management positions with this $150 million fax machine manufacturer and wholesaler. Advanced to a final position training and supervising a staff of 10, where we provided accounting, credit and collections support for a 75-person customer service department.

Prepared monthly sales and cash receipts reports, account analyses and journal entries. Authorized customer credit adjustments and bad debt write-offs. Acquired extensive experience in customer communications and collection negotiations.

Achievements:

- Instrumental in transitioning A/R from in-house software to a fully-integrated accounting and financial reporting system. Resulted in a significant improvement in the quality, accuracy and usefulness of financial data for daily operating management and long-range business planning.

- Realigned key accounting positions, consolidated similar functions, avoided need for increased staffing, and improved information processing and reporting.

- Designed and implemented a series of standards, policies and systems to more efficiently manage accounting/financial data collection, analysis and reporting.

PUBLISHERS INC., New York, NY   April 1984 to May 1986

Staff Accountant

Diversified accounting and financial reporting responsibilities with this nationwide book publisher and distributor. Analyzed and reconciled accounts, prepared journal entries, calculated monthly sales summary for 35 field sales representatives, and participated in month-end closing. Computed and reported monthly commission, bonus and royalties. Conducted quarterly audit of consigned products with 20 book depositories nationwide.

CAPITAL JEWELERS, INC., New York, NY   March 1983 to April 1984

Bookkeeper

Managed accounts payable, accounts receivable and billing for this NYC-based jewelry wholesaler. Prepared cash deposits, bank reconciliations and journal entries. Worked with Assistant Controller on month-end closings and month-end reporting.

EDUCATION:

B.S., Business / Major in Accounting, San Sebastian College, Manila, Philippines, 1982

Continuing Professional Development:

Graduate of numerous professional training programs, seminars and workshops on topics including management, organizational development, credit, collections and related legal affairs. Several courses were sponsored by Dun and Bradstreet.

HELEN P. GARRETT

200 Hillside Lane
Silver Spring, Maryland 20660
Home (301) 858-2278   Office (301) 595-6487

CAREER PROFILE

Over 15 years experience planning and directing executive-level administrative affairs and support to Chairmen, Boards of Directors and Senior Management. Combines strong planning, organizational and communications skills with the ability to independently plan and direct high-level business affairs. Qualifications include:

- *Shareholder Meetings & Communications*
- *Regulatory Reporting & Communications*
- *Corporate Political & Legislative Affairs*
- *Customer Communications & Liaison Affairs*
- *Confidential Correspondence & Data*

- *Executive Office Management*
- *Staff Training & Development*
- *Budgeting & General Accounting*
- *Special Events Planning*
- *Special Project Management*

Proficient in the use of WordPerfect for Windows 5.2. Experienced with Lotus 1-2-3.

PROFESSIONAL EXPERIENCE

INTERSTATE SAVINGS BANK, Silver Spring, Maryland   1989 to Present

Corporate Secretary
Executive Assistant to the Chairman and Board of Directors

High-profile, executive-level administrative position supporting the Chairman, Board of Directors and other top management personnel throughout the organization. Scope of responsibility is diverse and includes Board affairs, customer and stockholder communications, employee stock options, special events, regulatory reporting and executive administration.

- Executive Liaison between Chairman and Senior Management Committee, Business Departments, and employees to plan, schedule and facilitate a broad range of corporate initiatives, company operations and large-scale business functions.

- Handle confidential operating and financial information, maintain corporate records and minutes, and execute corporate contracts and agreements.

- Project Supervisor for annual shareholders report. Coordinate annual shareholders meetings, manage liaison affairs with outside counsel regarding proxy statements, and facilitate print production of shareholder communications.

- Maintain/update files for regulatory review, oversight and approval.

- Provide training and supervision to Executive Department's support staff.

CONSTITUTION PAPER COMPANY, Washington, D.C.   1977 to 1989
Federal Corporate Affairs Division

Secretary to Vice President & Director / Office Manager (1983 to 1989)
Assistant Administrator for Voluntary Contributors / Office Manager (1981 to 1983)
Secretary to the Vice President (1977 to 1981)

Fast-track promotion through a series of increasingly responsible administrative management positions in Constitution's government affairs and lobbying division. Worked directly with the Director to provide executive-level administrative and operating management support.

- Planned, staffed and directed all office management functions for the Department. Scope of responsibility was diverse and included A/P, A/R, budgeting, petty cash and corporate checking accounts. Recruited, trained and supervised administrative staff. Developed procedural and documentation manuals.

- Managed confidential correspondence, appointments, meetings and schedule for the Director. Personally planned and coordinated industry and inter-company meetings involving the Corporate Affairs Department.

- Independently researched, responded to and followed up on requests from Congress and company management.

- Worked cooperatively with Corporate Secretary to direct the planning/execution of the 1986 and 1988 annual shareholders meetings.

- Administered the Voluntary Contributors for a Better Government Program, nationwide employee fundraising effort to increase support for corporate lobbying and legislative initiatives. Directed all Federal Election Commission filings and State Election Committee filings for the corporation's Political Action Committee.

PREVIOUS PROFESSIONAL EXPERIENCE included several responsible administrative and customer service management positions. Completed a three-year position with Engravers of Europe, managing sales and service relationships with foreign embassy personnel, government officials and corporate VIPs.

EDUCATION

University College/University of Maryland, College Park, Maryland
Business Courses (1989 to Present)

ITT Business Institute, Bethesda, Maryland
Secretarial & Administrative Training Program (1977)

Montgomery College, Rockville, Maryland
Music Major (1969 to 1970)

References Provided Upon Request

HELEN MISKELLY

1616 Caroline Drive
Amarillo, Texas 79108
(806) 597-3791

ADMINISTRATIVE / BUSINESS MANAGER
High-Growth & Turnaround Healthcare Practices

Dynamic Management Professional with more than 10 years of increasingly responsible experience building and managing multi-site healthcare operations. Recognized for consistent success in developing the systems, processes and methodologies to reorganize/revitalize practice operations, increase revenues and enhance profit performance. Strong planning, organization development, MIS and general management qualifications. Cross-functional communications, resource allocation and project management skills.

CORE COMPETENCIES:

Practice Management & Business Administration

Internal and external consultant to both single practice and multi-site/multi-doctor operations providing expertise in operations management, administration, finance, accounting, human resources, MIS, regulatory affairs, resources/facilities management and insurance administration.

- Created innovative practice management models and methodologies to strengthen quality of care.

- Designed and implemented administrative programs to reduce redundancy, streamline processes and improve daily operations.

- Prepared regulatory manuals and led internal office training to ensure compliance with all local, state and federal health safety requirements.

Project Planning & Management

Skilled at leading cross-functional teams in the planning and execution of special projects for Marketing, Operation and Information Technology. Able to critically evaluate project requirements and coordinate the delivery of appropriate resources to meet operating demands.

- Championed the introduction of state-of-the-art PC and MIS technologies to transition from previously manual to fully-automated operating systems. Sourced vendors, negotiated contracts for equipment, coordinated installation and led user training.

- Selected by software/systems vendor to provide hands-on training and product demonstrations at potential client accounts and leading industry tradeshows.

- Built cooperative working relationships between staff and management personnel to facilitate project completion on time, within budget and as per operating requirements.

Personnel Management & Leadership

Excellent qualifications in the recruitment, selection and supervision of up to 20 professional and support staff. Skilled in staff training, development and performance management to meet operating and financial goals. Extensive experience in benefits administration, compensation structuring, and workforce diversity.

- Built work teams that consistently exceeded goals for productivity, efficiency and quality of operations.

- Resolved long-standing issues impacting employee retention and interaction. Implemented training and incentive programs which delivered measurable improvements in employee morale and satisfaction.

- Developed innovative dental hygiene/periodontal program which significantly increased productivity of the entire hygiene department.

Accounting, Billing & Collections

Expert qualifications in accounts receivable, billing, reimbursement, banking, accounting/financial analysis, financial reporting, cost/benefit analysis, insurance and claims administration. Managed up to $50,000 operating budget.

- Restructured patient accounting operations and designed/implemented policies, procedures and processes that improved collections, reduced outstanding debt and strengthened bottom-line profitability.

- Personally managed aged receivable accounts, established case presentations and coordinated financial arrangements. Represented the practice in legal proceedings. Consistently exceeded collection goals.

Customer Service & Client Relations

Independently managed relationships with up to 35,000 patients. Served as the direct liaison to maintain cooperative relationships, resolve billing and operating problems, and outperform competitive organizations. Actively involved in developing marketing programs to capture new business opportunities.

- Launched a comprehensive marketing and business development campaign to revitalize existing client relationships. Recaptured more than 60% of lost business within four months.

- Delivered strong and sustainable improvements in client service, satisfaction and retention.

CAREER PROGRESSION:

Office Administrator	Mark George, DDS	1995 to Present
Office Manager	Victor Valdez, DDS	1994 to 1995
Office Administrator	Stuart Rubin & Associates	1992 to 1994
Practice Manager / Assistant Manager	Sunset Dental Group	1990 to 1992
Practice Manager / Supervisor	Harold Nemetz & Associates	1988 to 1989
Regional Director / Office Manager	The Dental Group	1987 to 1988
Assistant Manager / Bookkeeper	The Orthodontist	1986 to 1987

EDUCATION & CERTIFICATIONS:

B.S., Business Administration *(Summa Cum Laude)*, Iowa State University, 1997

Certified Chiropractic Assistant, Los Angeles College of Chiropractic, 1994

Continuing Professional Education & Seminars sponsored by Career Track, Fred Pryor, Dunn & Bradstreet, McVey & Associates, Academy of Management Sciences, Cerritos Community College and others. Topics included:

- Practice Management
- Health Insurance & Collections
- Patient-Centered Care
- Supervision & Leadership

- Medical Terminology
- Hyperbaric Medicine
- Marketing Techniques
- Prioritizing Daily Tasks

MARSHA SMITH

943 Park Avenue
New York, New York 19436
(202) 971-6577

EXECUTIVE PROFILE

Corporate Communications / Marketing Communications / Advertising Communications

Top-flight management career building innovative marketing, communications and business development programs worldwide. Combines expert creative design, strategic and market positioning qualifications with strong general management, project management and financial accountabilities. Qualifications include:

- Print & Broadcast Media
- Market Positioning & Awareness
- Sales Promotions & Incentives
- Public Speaking & Public Relations
- Team Building & Team Leadership
- Crisis Communications

- Customer Marketing Communications
- Corporate Vision & Strategy
- Investor & Shareholder Communications
- Executive Presentations & Negotiations
- Business Process Reengineering
- Employee & Management Communications

- Awarded membership in YWCA Academy of Women Achievers, 1994
- Woman of the Year Nominee, Business-Professional Womens Club, 1980
- Member, International Association of Business Communicators and New York Junior League

PROFESSIONAL EXPERIENCE

1994 to Present
**Managing Director - Corporate Communications, Advertising & Marketing
CUSHMAN & WAKEFIELD**, New York, New York

($300 million multi-service global real estate firm with operating units in financial services, leasing, asset services, outsourcing, valuation analysis and research services. Client base includes AT&T, Ford, Kraft, IBM, Hertz and J.P. Morgan.)

Recruited as the Senior Management Executive responsible for the strategic planning, development and leadership of the entire marketing, advertising and communications function. Manage a team-based organization with both in-house and contract marketing, communications, advertising, design, graphic arts and printing personnel. Manage a $2.5 million annual operating budget.

- Authored the firm's strategic communications plan and orchestrated successful effort to update corporate vision, mission and values statement. Transitioned marketing focus to core customer types and segments.

- Architected new corporate advertising and client testimonial trade campaigns which appeared in Forbes, Business Week, Fortune and other major national publications.

- Revitalized and expanded marketing communications program throughout Manhattan (company's largest market) utilizing industry-leading initiatives. Expanded editorial and advertising penetration from the "real estate" to "business" pages to increase market visibility with CEOs, CFOs and other top operating executives of target accounts.

- Launched development of global branding strategy to establish the firm as the preferred business-to-business real estate services provider. Leveraged existing client base as key partners in the firm's worldwide marketing and business development initiatives.

1990 to 1993   **Corporate Communications, Marketing & Management Consultant**
ALLEN ASSOCIATES, San Francisco, California / New York, New York

Executive Consultant providing integrated marketing and communications advisory services to major corporate clients throughout the national market. Worked on a project-by-project basis with top operating management. Key engagements included:

ITT Corporation World Headquarters (New York)
- Consulted with ITT consumer, commercial finance and other business units on a broad range of internal/external communications, marketing and reengineering projects. Managed sensitive negotiations during union dispute, authored business plan for new operating unit, and designed process improvements for field and staff operations.

American Express (San Francisco & New York)
- Created and implemented marketing and promotional plans for Amex travel agencies throughout California, Arizona, Colorado, Illinois and Georgia. Recommended strategic and tactical action plans to increase market awareness and coordinated regional media affairs.

1984 to 1990   **Director - Corporate Communications**
ITT CORPORATION WORLD HEADQUARTERS, New York, New York

Senior Management Executive with responsibility for numerous ITT worldwide Corporate Communications Programs. Provided expertise counsel, strategic and tactical action programs for public relations, advertising, sales promotions, marketing and crisis communications for major ITT businesses, subsidiaries and operating units worldwide. Managed a $25+ million annual group operating budget.

- One of the highest ranked executive women within the ITT organization. Consistently earned highest performance ratings and several key promotions.

- Appointed Chairperson of the ITT Corporate Political Action Committee and the New York-Washington interface.

- Authored speeches for ITT Chairman, Board of Directors and executive management team. Managed various shareholder communications and annual reporting functions.

- Coordinated press, radio and television interviews during Chairman's 1989 media tour.

NOTE: Served as **Vice President of Operations / Board Member** for ITT's International Conference Center. Transitioned business from $10 million loss to $2+ million profit through a series of successful business process reengineering initiatives.

1976 to 1983   **Legislative Director / Legislative Assistant**
U.S. HOUSE OF REPRESENTATIVES, Washington, D.C.

Promoted from Legislative Assistant to Legislative Director for the Former Representative Beverly B. Byron. Served as the principal legislative policy advisor to the Member. Responsible for identifying and recommending legislative initiatives, training and supervising a team of legislative assistants and interns, and coordinating all legislative committee projects. Drafted major speeches, committee testimony and floor statements. Acquired substantial public speaking experience throughout the legislative, public interest communities and local districts.

EDUCATION

MBA in Marketing, NEW YORK UNIVERSITY / LEONARD N. STERN SCHOOL OF BUSINESS, 1993

MA in Legislative Affairs, GEORGE WASHINGTON UNIVERSITY, 1983

BA in Political Science, Honors Graduate, UNIVERSITY OF NORTH CAROLINA AT CHAPEL HILL, 1976

RALPH MARSH, CAE, CIC

54 Bellflower Road
Akron, Ohio 44307

Home: 330-584-1221   Office: 330-874-5456

SENIOR ASSOCIATION EXECUTIVE

**Profit & Loss Management / Policy & Procedure Development / Strategic Planning & Leadership
Member Development & Retention / Programs, Services & Products / Marketing, Advertising & Media
Government Relations / Budgeting & Financial Affairs / Human Resource Affairs / Information Technology**

Over 15 years of executive-level experience in the leadership of member-driven organizations. Consistently successful in increasing revenues, improving profitability, accelerating cash flow and enhancing the quality of member services. Top performance in turnaround, high-growth and well-established organizations. Combines expert leadership, communication, negotiation, team building and creative skills. Decisive and results-driven.

Consistently successful in building consensus and driving cooperative relationships with staffs, Boards of Directors, government agencies and business partners. Keen marketing and business development skills.

PROFESSIONAL EXPERIENCE:

INSURANCE AGENTS OF AMERICA, Akron, Ohio   1989 to Present
(*Association serving 22,000 insurance agents nationwide*)

CEO & Executive Vice President (1994 to Present)

Senior Management Executive with full planning, operating, marketing, financial, legislative/regulatory and administrative responsibility for the Association, its programs, services and business affairs. Direct a staff of 62 and manage a $14.5 million annual operating budget. Work in cooperation with the Board of Directors to drive strategic planning and annual budgeting processes.

- Initiated new position with a complete reorganization to reverse previous financial decline and restore stability. Outsourced non-critical functions, eliminated 40 staff positions, implemented aggressive cost reductions and redirected $2.2 million in revenues to IAA's affiliate members.

- Restored positive cash flow, eliminated all debt and built a $1.2 million reserve.

- Launched multimedia advertising, public relations and marketing campaigns to increase the visibility and market penetration of the Association.

- Negotiated business partnerships and devised new programs to further expand market reach and drive member/revenue/profit growth.

- Achieved and maintained 98% member retention (despite previous membership decline).

- Divested interest in a government coalition and leveraged resources to strengthen IAA's internal government affairs organization.

- Realigned budget process, introduced ABC models, and developed/implemented new strategic plan to achieve organizational goals through the year 2000.

- Generated a positive variance of $1.6 million on consolidated financial statements.

COO & Senior Vice President (1989 to 1994)

Full responsibility for directing all accounting, finance, technology, administrative, building services and insurance affairs for the Association and its wholly-owned for-profit subsidiary. Managed during a period of tremendous volatility throughout the industry. Challenged to provide financial control within an unstable environment through targeted reorganization, process redesign, cost reduction and technology improvements. Concurrently, managed the entire human resource function (e.g., recruitment, performance reviews, compensation, training/development) for a 110-person staff.

- Orchestrated conversion from outdated proprietary computer system to an open architecture system allowing for full integration of all hardware and software peripherals. Resulted in measurable gains in organizational productivity and efficiency.

- Designed and implemented the first Association-wide salary administration program.

- Developed and presented Strategic Planning Program and Board Orientation Program for IAA's affiliate members.

SHIP INTERNATIONAL, INC., Canton, Ohio   1987 to 1988
(*Publicly traded OTC company engaged in the "flowers by wire" industry*)

President & COO

Senior Executive with full strategic planning, operating, marketing and P&L responsibility for a company with $40 million in annual sales and 125 employees. Challenged to accelerate profitable growth through venture capital funding and an aggressive new product development program. Member of the Board of Directors, Executive Committee and Finance Committee.

- Negotiated a successful venture with FTD (industry leader) allowing company to leverage FTD's national technology and telecommunications network.

- Strengthened nationwide field sales, marketing and advertising programs to expand market penetration and drive profitable sales growth. Linked revenue goals to strategic plan.

- Spearheaded a complete redesign of all existing software programs to enhance data management competencies.

NATIONAL ASSOCIATION OF TRAVEL AGENTS, Youngstown, Ohio   1982 to 1987
(*Association representing 34,000 retail travel agents nationwide*)

Vice President – Finance, Administration & Automation

Recruited to orchestrate the Society's relocation from Washington, D.C. to Youngstown, Ohio and to build a fully-integrated financial, administrative and technology function. Transitioned from an understaffed and inefficient operation into a "best-in-class" business organization supporting a 90-person staff and a $14.5 million annual operating budget.

- Built a complete business infrastructure, all financial and accounting policies, administrative processes and a leading edge technology environment.

- Forged innovative, new income-producing programs that drove member surplus from negative $55,000 to positive $6+ million.

- Redesigned core benefit and compensation programs to improve coverages while reducing annual costs. Introduced salary administration and 401(k) programs for all employees.

- Designed and implemented cash management and investment programs to optimize returns, and expanded internal audit and financial control functions.

PREVIOUS PROFESSIONAL EXPERIENCE:

Vice President – Administration & Finance – National Association of Truck Operators (1981)

Director – Finance & Market Research – Train Passenger Association, Inc., (1979 to 1981)

Assistant Vice President – Meetings & Conventions – The Landscape Institute (1976 to 1979)

Assistant Vice President – Commercial Banking (1968 to 1976)

EDUCATION & PROFESSIONAL CREDENTIALS:

MBA – Finance & Investments – Bowling Green State University (1978)

BA – History & Political Science – University of Akron (1968)

Certified Association Executive – American Society of Association Executives (1990)

Certified Insurance Counselor – The Society of Certified Insurance Counselors (1995)

PROFESSIONAL AFFILIATIONS:

ASAE Fellow (1997)

ASAE Award of Excellence (1996)

GWSAE Board of Directors (1995 to 1998)

Chair, ASAE International Section Council (1992)

Advisory Panel, University of Arkon, University College Graduate School (1992 to Present)

MAURICE DEANGELO, CAE

214 Kenilworth Avenue
Philadelphia, Pennsylvania 19120

Home: 215-574-1441   Email: deangelo@nsba.org   Office: 267-245-7477

CERTIFIED ASSOCIATION EXECUTIVE

- Strategic Planning & Marketing Leadership
- Budgeting, Cost Control & Financial Management
- Meetings, Conventions & Special Programs
- Product Development & Revenue Generation
- Publishing, Order Fulfillment & Distribution

- Membership Development
- Member Services & Retention
- Administration & Process Design
- Change Management & Growth
- Public Relations & Liaison Affairs

PROFESSIONAL EXPERIENCE:

NATIONAL ABC ASSOCIATION, Philadelphia, Pennsylvania   1970 to Present

Associate Executive Director – Member Services, Publications & Marketing (1985 to Present)
Associate Executive Director – Finance & Administration (1973 to 1985)
State Association Liaison (1970 to 1973)

Member of the 12-person Senior Executive & Management Team providing strategic, financial, operational, programming and legislative leadership to NAA (national association serving the governance of America's 15,000 public programs). Scope of responsibility has extended throughout the entire organization of 140 employees and significantly impacted $21 million annual operating budget.

Catalyst in the conceptualization, development and marketing of innovative new products, programs and member services to drive annual revenue growth and expand NAA's operations. Equally effective as a Change Agent leading organizations through process redesign, turnaround and revitalization.

Challenges, Contributions & Achievements

- **Marketing, Product/Service Development & Revenue Growth** – Senior Executive with full marketing responsibility for all NAA For Fee Services, Products and Programs. This program contributes 90% ($19+ million) of the Association's annual operating budget and is vital to its continued success. Focus efforts on creating new revenue-generating ventures, revitalizing non-performing programs, expanding market research capabilities and strengthening member support.
  - Built 13-person marketing department managing an average of 100 concurrent projects.

- **National Affiliate Program** – Transitioned new venture from concept to a fully-staffed and self-sustaining organization providing policy writing services, publications and legislative advocacy for affiliate members. Created operating infrastructure and dedicated service organization to support marketing and fulfillment.
  - Developed a 2150-affiliate organization generating $5 million in annual gross revenue and $2.5 million in annual net revenues for the Association. Achieved and sustained a 95% annual affiliate renewal rate.

- *The American Board Journal* – Appointed Publisher in 1989 with full editorial, marketing, advertising and production responsibility for 100-year-old, independent newspaper with a paid circulation of 250,000. Introduced database technology to enhance subscriber relations and launched innovative marketing/market outreach programs.
  - Reversed revenue decline, improved market share and sustained profitability.

73

- **Technology Leadership Network** – Driving force behind the development of NAA's financially successful Technology Leadership Network (educational and mentoring program for technology innovation) and the annual Technology + Learning Conference. Partnered with InfoMart to launch a trade show devoted exclusively to educational technology, applications and transfers.
  - Created conference with 3000+ registrants annually and recognition as premier technology trade show.

- **Annual Association Conference Program** – Senior Executive directing NAA's Annual Conference Program (held in four major cities each year with 15,000+ registrants and 400+ exhibitors) for 14 years. Currently managing program in cooperation with 9 other executives. Rejuvenated conference programs, created conference newspaper, introduced revenue-generating initiatives, and attracted nationally-known speakers and entertainers (e.g., Former President George Bush, Colin Powell, Margaret Thatcher, Walter Cronkite, Bill Cosby, Tony Bennett, Johnny Carson).
  - Conference is currently generating $5.5 million in annual gross revenues and $2.2 million in annual net revenues to the Association.

- **Finance, Administration & Organizational Leadership** – Chief Financial Executive and Chief Budget Officer for various programs, projects and operations within NAA. Led development of program budget system, transitioning from departmental to product/service focus. Developed and mentored both finance and HR professionals, and created infrastructure for both functions. Led 3-person team responsible for construction of NAA's 50,000 square foot Headquarters Building.

- **External Liaison Affairs** – Champion for the development and negotiation of strategic alliances and partnerships to strengthen marketing, public outreach and public relations initiatives. Introduced outsourcing to expand creative network and improve product quality. Concurrently, manage external communications with other associations, non-profit organizations and for-profit corporations. Created programs to link state boards with the national association and its initiatives.

EDUCATION:

BALL STATE UNIVERSITY, Muncie, Indiana
Graduate Studies in Sociology

UNIVERSITY OF ILLINOIS, Chicago, Illinois
BA Degree in Sociology / Minor in Psychology

Graduate of 74+ hours of Continuing Professional Education & Association Leadership Studies.

PROFESSIONAL AFFILIATIONS:

AMERICAN SOCIETY OF ASSOCIATION EXECUTIVES
- Evaluation Committee Chair (1984-85)
- Spring Conference Committee (1995-96)
- Member, Eight Peer Review Teams

GREATER WASHINGTON SOCIETY OF ASSOCIATION EXECUTIVES
- Research Committee Chair (1983-84)

PROFESSIONAL CONVENTION MANAGEMENT ASSOCIATION
- Founding Board of Directors – Capital Chapter (1992-95)

DIRECT MARKETING ASSOCIATION
DIRECT MARKETING ASSOCIATION OF WASHINGTON
MAGAZINE PUBLISHERS ASSOCIATION
SOCIETY OF NATIONAL ASSOCIATION PUBLICATIONS

RALPH MARTINEZ, JR.

14 Echo Ridge Lane
St. Louis, Missouri 63123
Home (314) 251-1221   Office (314) 524-8547

CORPORATE AUDIT EXECUTIVE

Member of the Senior Management Team of three Fortune 500 companies and the most Senior Audit Executive. Expert in creating the systems, tools, processes and methodologies to create best-in-class, quality-driven, value-added audit organizations. Delivered consistently strong financial results and restored credibility with internal and external stakeholders. Staffing responsibility for up to 600. Budget responsibility for up to $298 million.

Certified Financial Services Auditor   *Certified Fraud Examiner*   *Certified Information Systems Auditor*

PROFESSIONAL EXPERIENCE:

THE ABC INSURANCE COMPANY   1990 to Present
($30 billion, multi-line insurance, financial services & real estate organization with market presence worldwide)

Vice President & General Auditor (1995 to Present)
Vice President & Associate Auditor (1994 to 1995)
Vice President – Internal Audit (1992 to 1994)
Director – Internal Audit (1990 to 1992)

Recruited by the Board of Directors to rebuild, revitalize and strengthen the Internal Audit function after the company had experienced several significant control and compliance issues. ABC was under Federal prosecution for product misrepresentation with the potential for $4+ billion in losses. Challenged to redefine the mission and strategy of Internal Audit, professionalize the organization and restore credibility as part of a corporate-wide, top-to-bottom restructuring.

- Delivered phenomenal performance results. Changed Internal Audit's perception from an historical "police" function into a business partner, working cooperatively with senior and operating management teams to achieve financial, regulatory and operating goals.
- Redesigned and expanded audit practice and management functions, introduced improved risk and control methodologies, and recreated core audit processes. Increased business unit experienced staff to 41% and technology experienced staff to 26%.
- Rebuilt the entire staffing function. Flattened organizational infrastructure, promoted rotational assignments within business functions, and downsized by 23% (from 375 to 220) while continuing to increase all measurable customer satisfaction rankings.
- Invested over $7 million in advanced information systems and technologies to enhance internal controls, analysis, risk assessment, project management and reporting competencies.
- Participated in development and led implementation of Quality Improvement Program.

Currently providing executive-level audit, business process and strategic leadership for transition from mutual to public company. Investigating issues relative to specific business practices, their potential risk, benefit and financial results. Participating in transformation to customer-driven organization.

MEDICORE, INC.   1987 to 1990
(Group insurance & managed care joint venture of Equitable Life Assurance Society & Medical Corporation of America)

Senior Vice President (1989 to 1990)
Vice President (1987 to 1989)

Recruited by previous CFO of Wilson Equipment to join the 18-person Senior Management Team leading Medicore through an aggressive revitalization and return to profitability ($200 million turnaround over two years). Personally credited with the development and leadership of Medicore Management Services, a new internal venture integrating Internal Audit, Over-Payment Recovery and Internal Consulting into one business unit. Directed a staff of 39. Controlled a $1.2 million budget.

75

- Assimilated the diverse cultures of venture partners to create one common vision and internal operating infrastructure for a fully integrated Internal Audit function. Built new organization from ground floor into a fully-functional, cost-effective and efficient operation within first year.
- Identified core issues impacting profitability (e.g., claims, provider fraud, quality of care, pricing, sales, benefits administration) throughout the entire organization. Provided executive-level strategic guidance and operating-level tactical leadership to enhance internal controls and business processes. Resulted in contributions of millions of dollars to the company's bottom line.
- Enhanced Over-Payment Recovery and achieved recovery ratios exceeding 5:1 of expenses.
- Directed Internal Consulting projects throughout the corporation including start-up of First Medicore Life Insurance, evaluation of new product development initiatives, and internal financial, audit, operating and process reviews to strengthen Medicore's operating infrastructure.

WILSON EQUIPMENT COMPANY   1977 to 1987
(*$359 million industrial equipment manufacturer & supplier throughout global markets*)

Vice President – WILSON Management Services Company (1984 to 1987)

Following tremendous success in professionalizing Wilson's Internal Audit function, conceived, developed and launched new venture to establish Audit as a value-added profit center. Created business plan to market services to other major corporations nationwide for expert audit, consulting and IS services to enhance clients' internal operations.

- Transitioned new venture from concept into a $2.2 million annual revenue producer generating profits of $245,000 to the parent corporation.
- Built key client base including Allied Signal, Avon, Chrysler and Price Waterhouse (domestic and internal engagements). Leveraged client relationships to market additional services and products.
- Positioned Wilson Management Services as the #1 market leader in the profession.

Manager – Internal Audit (1978 to 1984)
Supervisor – Internal Audit (1977 to 1978)

Recruited by previous manager from Pullman. Challenged to rebuild and strengthen the Internal Audit function for the company's largest operating division and all international operations. Directed an audit staff of 52. Managed a $2.2 million annual audit budget.

- Significantly improved the image of the Internal Audit function with executive and operating management, Audit Committee of the Board of Directors and company's public accounting firm.
- Pioneered several innovative new internal control programs including Warranty Audit Program and Sales Discount Audit Program. Combined cost savings exceeded $3.4 million annually.
- Appointed to Corporate Task Force established by the Board to restructure the entire inventory function. Identified critical issues impacting accountability, introduced stringent internal controls and eliminated over $10 million in annual inventory losses.
- Served on another Corporate Task Force to provide strategy, controls and process leadership for the development and successful deployment of a company-wide disaster recovery plan.

Early Professional Career as a **Financial Auditor** & **EDP Auditor** with Pullman Incorporated and Brunswick Corporation. Management responsibility for complete audit programs, staffing, budgeting and process.

PROFESSIONAL & CIVIC ACTIVITIES:

Affiliations   Institute of Internal Auditors (Chapter Board of Governors, Officer & Committee Member)
Information Systems Audit and Control Association
United Way (Corporate Chairman; National Co-Chairman; Management Development Ctr)

Training   **Presenter – Technical Seminars** – Institute of Internal Auditors, Information Systems Audit and Control Association, and MIS Training Institute

EDUCATION:
MBA – International Business, Lincoln University, Missouri, 1979
BS – Business Administration, Lewis University, Lockport, Illinois, 1972

NAWAZ BHUTTO

784 Hoffman Place
Belle Mead, New Jersey 08502
Phone: 908-574-2544 / Fax: 908-557-1544

FINANCIAL SERVICES & BANKING INDUSTRY EXECUTIVE
US & International Markets
MBA Degree – NYU Stern School of Business

Distinguished executive career working in cooperation with senior management of major banking and financial institutions worldwide – First Bank, Australia-New Zealand Bank, HongKong Bank and others. Combines sophisticated financial expertise with outstanding performance in marketing and account relationship management.

Leadership & Organizational Expertise	*Financial & Investment Expertise*
New Business & Market Development	Foreign Exchange & Treasury Operations
Strategic Planning & Development	Corporate Credit Analysis & Risk Management
Team Building & Performance Improvement	Investment Analysis & Asset Management
Cross-Border Trade & Finance Transactions	Debt & Equity Financings
Inter- & Intra-Banking Relationships	Market Trading & Analysis

---

PROFESSIONAL EXPERIENCE:

FIRST BANK, N.A. – GLOBAL CAPITAL MARKETS   1997 to Present

International Officer – Commercial Lending Division – Asia

High-profile management position as the direct liaison between Head Office and Asian Division to facilitate commercial credit transactions. Selected for this position from a group of competitive management candidates from five Asian branches based on solid growth and ROI performance in Singapore.

- Represented Asian Division in 100+ transaction approval requests to the Head Office Credit Committees (total of $2.5 billion in approved facilities with exposures in Thailand, Malaysia, Singapore, Japan, Korean, Hong Kong, Taiwan, Philippines and the PRC).
- Achieved and maintained 90% success rate for all approvals.
- Reviewed strategies for nine countries in the Asian Division as part of approval process for cross-border exposure totaling $1+ billion. Obtained approval for exposure utilization and ensured that analyses accurately assessed economic and political environment/risk.
- Led high-level presentations with an in-depth review of the facility structure, profitability, financial analysis and strategic fit with First Bank's global portfolio. Addressed core risk management issues.
- Guided asset recovery specialists throughout the Asian Division in the strategic recovery of outstanding loan and credit obligations totaling more than $2.2 million.

Assumed additional responsibility in 1998 for Global Foreign Exchange and First Bank focused on expanding FX activities worldwide. Conduct sophisticated financial and credit analyses of corporations and financial institutions targeted for new business development to evaluate creditworthiness and potential risk.

- Key player in positioning Global FX Group as a prime contributor to bank-wide profitability.

Successfully managed through several major reorganizations, providing leadership and financial expertise to both US and international operations. Instrumental in driving domestic market growth in FX, targeting the more stable and growth-driven US market.

- Demonstrated expert qualifications in building consensus and managing internal business relationships.

FIRST BANK, N.A. – SINGAPORE   1996 to 1997

Senior Treasury Credit Officer

Accepted opportunity with a major U.S. banking institution seeking to expand and strengthen their treasury operations throughout Southeast Asia. Participated in the design and market launch of new products and services to build customer base, strengthen credibility and improve competitive market positioning. Combined marketing, new business development and sophisticated financial/investment expertise.

- Key player in the successful and profitable introduction of foreign exchange operations in Singapore and Taipei. Provided foundation for expansion and new product/service development opportunities.
- Prepared complex financial and credit analyses to enhance ROI from First Bank's offshore securities.
- Identified corporate and financial institution prospects in Southeast Asia to support short-term investments of $100 million and facilitate customer-based foreign exchange revenues.

KAMBAR SECURITIES, LTD. – PAKISTAN   1994 to 1996

Partner

Member of 4-person executive team who founded and built an investment boutique to capitalize on emerging market opportunities throughout the Middle Eastern region. Created strategy for asset management, participated in corporate finance projects, and marketed firm's equity brokerage capabilities.

- Appointed to corporate finance consortium, in partnership with ABC Investment Bank, to provide high-level financial advisory services during the privatization of Habib Bank Ltd. (largest government-owned banking institution in Pakistan with assets of more than $98 billion).
- Developed and marketed closed-end mutual fund managed by Kambar. Personally raised over 50% of total equity participation from financial institutions throughout the region.
- Authored asset management policies and procedures.

ANZ BANKING GROUP – PAKISTAN   1991 to 1994

Senior Relationship Manager

Following graduation from NYU's MBA Program, joined one of the most prestigious multinational banks in Asia. Selected from a group of 16 competitive candidates for a unique opportunity to merge corporate and investment finance experience with previous success in customer/account relationship management.

- Managed daily banking relationships, capital and trade finance programs, and assets valued at more than $90 million. Clients included major multinational corporations in the consumer products, pharmaceutical and manufacturing industries (e.g., Unilever, Pfizer, Ciba-Geigy, ICI).
- Led consortium of 20 banks to expand short-term and term loan borrowing facilities for major clients.

HONGKONG BANK – MIDDLE EAST & FAR EAST   1983 to 1991

Account Manager (1987 to 1990)   **Trade Finance Analyst** (1984 to 1985)
Foreign Exchange Analyst (1985 to 1987)   **Relationship Banker** (1983 to 1984)

Fast-track promotion through a series of increasingly responsible financial analysis and account development/management positions with the world's most profitable banking institution. Acquired solid experience in all banking functions including FX, trade finance, international credit and retail banking.

- Staffed and managed a 12-person import and export trade finance operation in Pakistan.
- Increased branch US dollar deposits by 60% in Pakistan by leveraging international relationships.
- Graduate of the distinguished HongKong Bank's Global Executive Training Program.

EDUCATION: **MBA – Finance** – New York University Stern School of Business – 1991
BA – Economics & Political Science – Occidental College - 1983

AARON GIBSON

Annapolis, Maryland 21403

Phone (443) 485-1547

Fax (443) 484-2548

SENIOR OPERATIONS EXECUTIVE
Global Banking & Financial Services Industry

Dynamic leadership career, providing strategic, creative and tactical execution of bankwide initiatives to enhance productivity, quality, customer service, technology and bottom-line financial performance. Delivered millions of dollars in cost reductions and revenue/profit growth through innovative hands-on operating leadership and high-profile project management.   Multicultural background – Fluent in Chinese. MBA Degree.

Published Author (*Magazine of Bank Management*)
Public Speaker (American Banking Association, Banking Association Industry & American Institute)

PROFESSIONAL EXPERIENCE:

BANK ONE, Annapolis & Baltimore, Maryland   1982 to Present

Recruited in 1982 to spearhead the introduction of the Bank's first-ever quality, internal consulting, process and productivity improvement programs.   Promoted through a series of increasingly responsible leadership, operating management and special projects management positions as the organization has grown, diversified and reengineered core functions impacting operations worldwide.   Catalyst for the development and successful implementation of numerous technological, process and operating improvements impacting virtually the entire organization.   Direct leadership responsibility for up to 2000 employees and an $80+ million annual operating budget. Active role in due diligence reviews of prospective banks for acquisition.

Scope of responsibility has included all major Bank operations for retail and commercial business:

- Check Processing
- Lockbox Operations
- Statement Production
- Electronic Check Systems

- Customer Service
- Cash Management
- Account Processing
- Branch Support Services

- Mail Operations
- Money Centers
- Transportation
- Information Technology

Senior Vice President & Director – Imaging Technology (1996 to Present)
Development, implementation and leadership of imaging technology to increase revenues, streamline operations, reduce expenses and strengthen customer service (including Year 2000 initiatives).

Senior Vice President – Operations (1992 to 1996)
Bankwide operations leadership for 320 branches, domestic and international corporate cash management and commercial business.

Administrative Vice President & Operations Manager (1987 to 1992)
Operations management for 112 branches, corporate and commercial business.

Administrative Vice President (1984 to 1987)
Internal consulting on productivity and float/non-earning asset reductions, concurrent with leadership of all financial planning and administrative affairs for 2000-person Retail Operations Group.

Vice President (1982 to 1984)
Directed bankwide purchasing, contract administration, financial planning and personnel administration for 1700-person Retail Operations Group.

ACHIEVEMENTS:

Revenue & Profit Growth

- Increased fee income by $3 million annually through implementation of technological advances in high-speed imaging lockbox processing/operations.
- Reclassified NOW accounts, redesigned business processes and generated $7.1 million in incremental annual revenues.

Cost Reduction & Avoidance

- Reduced operating expenses by an average of $1 million per year in each of the past 15 years through leadership of innovative productivity improvements, process consolidations, paper reductions, contract renegotiations and transportation network simplification.
- Renegotiated vendor contracts for technology acquisition that saved over $400,000.

Organizational & Project Leadership

- Created project team and authored business plans which resulted in reductions of $370 million in non-earning assets.
- Led team that reduced financial risk exposure from $198 million to only $3 million.
- Introduced innovative personnel training, motivational and incentive programs to enhance quality of workforce, accelerate productivity and create a customer-driven organizational culture.

Turnaround Management

- Planned and led the successful consolidation and revitalization of Bank One's Maryland operations (320 branches with 800 employee and a $55 million annual operating budget). Achieved/surpassed all quality, service and financial objectives within eight months.
- Transitioned Check Processing from a manually-intensive operation into a state-of-the-art technology function with dramatic productivity, efficiency, quality and performance improvements.
- Restored Trade Service Operations ($20 million business unit with 150 employees) to profitable global performance.

Technological Innovation

- Developed 5-year strategic technology and business plans for the development and implementation of imaging technology and electronic check presentment systems. Projecting $10 million of incremental revenue growth and a 100% gain in ROI as a direct result of technological advances.
- Currently spearheading the Bank's global Year 2000 programs (78% complete as of 12/98).

Customer Service, Retention & Loyalty

- Enhanced customer satisfaction through creation and execution of DIRFT (Do IT Right The First Time) and total quality improvement processes throughout the entire organization.
- Created systems, processes and strategies to retain customer base during an aggressive period of bank acquisitions, integrations and consolidations.

CHEMICAL BANK, New York, New York   1978 to 1982

Assistant Vice President – Check Processing Operations (1981 to 1982)

Member of 4-person management team directing a 200-person Check Processing Operation with $8 million annual operating budget. Identified core factors impacting performance and resolved critical productivity, morale and retention issues.

- Reduced personnel turnover by 60% through internal training efforts and enhanced group productivity by 20% through innovative employee incentive programs.
- Redesigned workflow process and eliminated holdover of $2 million daily.

Assistant Vice President – Productivity Improvement (1978 to 1981)

Conceived, created and implemented a series of productivity improvement initiatives impacting 6000+ employees in more than 142 operating locations. Led a team of 22 internal consultants.

- Captured $1.2 million in annual cost savings. Trained 250 managers on productivity concepts.
- Developed a computerized productivity measurement and improvement process and computerized forecasting systems for manpower and cost management.

PEPSICO, INC., Purchase, New York   1972 to 1978

Administration Manager & Controller (1976 to 1978)
Planning Manager (1974 to 1976)
Assistant to Executive Vice President – Operations (1972 to 1974)

- Delivered over $2.75 million in annual operating cost reductions through internal process redesign, productivity/efficiency improvements and materials substitution programs for a global manufacturing organization.

EDUCATION:

Advanced Management Development	UNIVERSITY OF CHICAGO
MBA Degree	FAIRLEIGH DICKINSON UNIVERSITY
Master of Engineering Degree	NEW YORK UNIVERSITY
Bachelor of Engineering Degree	NEW YORK UNIVERSITY

SANDRA L. WORTHINGTON

5871 Helmwood Drive
Nashville, Tennessee 37216

Phone: 615-125-4785
Email: slworth@aol.com

SENIOR-LEVEL BANKING INDUSTRY EXECUTIVE
De Novo & High-Growth Banking Institutions
Strategic Planning / Multi-Site Operations / Marketing / Business Development
Acquisitions & Integrations / Loan & Deposit Growth / Customer Relationship Management

Top-Performing Executive with 15+ years' experience building and managing a major banking institution. Delivered consistently strong financial results and profitable growth within intensely competitive markets. Outstanding planning, organizational, team building, leadership and communication skills. Executive liaison to regulators, attorneys, financiers, auditors and key customer base. Excellent qualifications in PC and network technology.

PROFESSIONAL EXPERIENCE:

AAA BANK, FSB, Nashville, Tennessee   1984 to 2000
(2nd largest banking institution in Tennessee; $4 billion in assets, $187 billion in deposits & 30 branches)

Senior Vice President – Administration & Information Systems (1998 to 2000)
Senior Vice President – Administration (1997 to 1998)
Senior Vice President – Operations (1990 to 1997)
Vice President – Systems Administration (1988 to 1990)
Assistant Vice President – Systems Administration (1987 to 1988)
Assistant Vice President – Systems Administration – Corporate Office (1986 to 1987)
Branch Manager / Regional Manager / Assistant Vice President – Branch (1984 to 1986)

Member of 30-person Senior Executive Team credited with transitioning this de novo institution into the second largest bank in the State of Tennessee ($4 billion in assets, $187 billion in deposits, 30 branches and 275 employees). Promoted rapidly through a series of increasingly responsible management positions with direct leadership and P&L responsibility for core operating and business functions throughout the institution. Reported directly to President/Chairman of the Board. Career highlights included:

As Senior Vice President for 10 years, held full planning, staffing, financial, technology and operating management responsibility for back office, compliance, internal audit, training, property management, office systems and information systems. Independent loan approval for up to $500,000.

Corporate Development

- Instrumental in the successful acquisition of four banking/S&L institutions (up to $400 million in assets each) into AAA's operating organization. Extensive interface with attorneys, sellers and financiers to facilitate transaction and efficient integration of networks, systems, products, branches and personnel. Acquisitions were vital to the tremendous growth and profitability of the institution.
- Actively participated in the structuring, marketing and sale of several equity offerings including capital stock and subordinated debt. Raised over $14 million to support continued growth and expansion.
- Independently managed deconversion issues and transition for the sale of three West Coast branches.
- Participated in an extensive Investor Relations communications and outreach initiative.

Regulatory & Audit Affairs

- Directed preparation and managed annual regulatory reviews by federal bank examiners and annual external audits. Passed all exams and audits (with no exceptions) for 10 consecutive years. Instrumental in achieving regulatory approval in 1984 for the start-up of the institution.

Information Systems & Technology

- Led the institution through a series of technology installations and ugprades to keep pace with emerging hardware, software, systems and proprietary products. Successfully converted over 100,000 customer accounts to new outsourced mainframe system and upgraded 400+ PCs to new software. Achieved fully-functional installation on time and within budget, saving $2 million in third-party technology costs.
- Orchestrated successful transition from PC technology to WAN and LAN integrated systems.
- Organized and directed a massive Y2K project impacting virtually every system and employee of the institution. Won the support and participation of all bank personnel, and delivered project ahead of schedule and fully-operational.
- Led project teams responsible for hardware and software acquisitions, policy and procedure development, data integrity, contingency planning, disaster recovery and technology training/support.

Human Resources Leadership

- Directed the bank's entire HR organization for eight consecutive years, including recruitment, hiring, manpower planning, compensation and benefits administration, and employee services. Recruited over 100 new employees to the organization.
- Personally trained and directed staffs of up to 15. Direct supervisor for 8 Vice Presidents.
- Researched, sourced, designed and administered 401(k) plan.

Multi-Site Branch Operations

- Built bank's 30-site branch network. Established all operating policies and procedures, designed reporting systems and methodologies, recruited/trained personnel, and managed all site and market development activities for new locations.

New Product Development

- Identified customer demand and market opportunity, led product development teams, and rolled out 8 new products over the past 10 years. Total financial (revenue and profit) impact exceeded $2.2 million.

Committee Leadership

- As Chairperson of Cost Control Committee, delivered $1+ million in annual operating cost savings.
- Appointed Chairperson of Classified Assets Committee and managed over $875k in delinquent loan recovery and restructuring.
- Appointed Treasurer of Political Action Committee, Security Officer and Compliance Officer.
- Served as Inspector of Elections at annual Board of Directors meetings.

FEDERAL SAVINGS & LOAN ASSOCIATION, Nashville, Tennessee   1978 to 1984

Regional Residential Lending Manager (1982 to 1984)
Branch Manager (1979 to 1982)
Loan Officer (1978 to 1979)
Head Teller / Savings Counselor (1976 to 1978)

Directed mortgage lending functions throughout a 3-county region. Built annual loan volume from $1.2 million to over $2.6 million (300% greater than any other loan officer in the institution). Doubled deposit and lending goals as Branch Manager.

EDUCATION:

AMERICAN INSTITUTE OF BANKING / NOVA UNIVERSITY
Graduate - 72+ hours of professional training in Banking, Lending, Marketing

MARILYN GOLDSTEIN

Abbott Street SW, Atlanta, Georgia 30314
Phone: 406-256-6743   Fax: 406-323-6516   Email: mgold@aol.com

CAREER PROFILE:

Chief of Staff / Director of Communications with the ABC Society. Record of consistent success in furthering the goals and objectives of the organization through cross-functional management of the entire portfolio of operations, programs and services.

- Talented writer with strong experience in developing written communications and speeches to disseminate information on strategy, policy, marketing, development/fundraising, education and public information. Extensive experience in corporate/organizational communications.
- Strong organizational management, project management and leadership experience as #2 in a 4500-employee association. Efficient, productive and resourceful.
- Outstanding media/press relations, VIP relations and organizational liaison skills.
- Sharp, keen and focused. Easygoing management style. Dynamic presentation style.

PROFESSIONAL RECOGNITION / HONORS:

- Women in Communications
- Educational Press Association
- International Association of Business Communicators
- Society of National Association Professionals

PROFESSIONAL EXPERIENCE:

ABC SOCIETY, Washington, DC   1988 to Present

Chief of Staff (1999 to Present)
Senior Associate – Communications – President's Office (1997 to 1998)
Writer (1996 to 1997)
Communications Consultant (1988 to 1996)

Promoted through a series of increasingly responsible positions writing and managing communications for one of the largest non-profit organizations in the US. Provide strategic insight and analysis to favorably position communications to reflect positively upon the organization, its leadership, programs and services.

Most recently, promoted to Chief of Staff, second-in-command, working with the President to provide broad-based management support in achieving the vision and objectives of the ABC. Direct a staff of 11 and manage a $1.2 million annual operating budget.

Organizational Leadership

- Worked directly with former ABC President Elizabeth Dole for two years and now with the newly-appointed President. Instrumental in facilitating new President's transition into office and the resulting changes in the organization, management staffing and policy.
- Key advisor in establishing organizational priorities, developing strategic objectives, analyzing issues, optimizing internal resources and managing communications throughout the entire organization.
- Serve as the President's primary point of contact with senior management, field leadership, Board of Governors and organizations/individuals outside the ABC.
- Coordinate scheduling, logistics, travel/transportation and security for the President.
- Manage high-profile special events including a recent engagement at the White House.

Communications

- Served as primary speechwriter for ABC President and Chairman of the Board of Governors (James Kennedy, CEO of Lockheed Martin) for 12 years. Wrote President Dole's commencement address for the 1994 graduating class of Harvard.
- Wrote/edited thousands of documents including briefing papers, policy statements, annual reports, feature articles, marketing communications, op-eds, videoscripts, crisis communications, educational materials and high-level correspondence.
- Managed high-profile communications projects for the Development Department including case statements, funding proposals, reports and campaign materials.
- Developed and authored an International Humanitarian Law course for the general public.
- Presented up to 74 speeches and public presentations per year to introduce new ABC programs, raise community awareness and support development efforts.

ERISA INDUSTRY COMMITTEE, Washington, DC   1986 to 1987

Director of Public Affairs

Advised Executive Director on media strategy, nurtured media relationships, managed press briefings and wrote/produced newsletter. Trained/supervised support staff. Worked in cooperation with Fortune 100 member companies on core communications issues.

Writer/Editor – Time-Life Books (1984 to 1987). Best-selling series *Whole Earth* and *U.S. Wars*.
Writer – Common Cause (1977 to 1982). Communications for public interest lobbying group.
Reporter/Journalist – Miami Herald and St. Petersburg Times (1974 to 1976).

CONSULTING EXPERIENCE:

Communications Consultant (1988 to 1996). Wrote advertisements, marketing materials, annual reports, speeches, PSA's, articles and corporate communications. Clients included:

- US Holocaust Memorial Museum
- American Public Health Association
- American Institute of Architects
- Points of Light Foundation

- National Geographic
- Lockheed Martin
- Habitat For Humanity
- US Information Agency

EDUCATION:

Certificate – Public Relations Program, George Washington University, 1979
B.A. – English, University of Tampa, Florida, 1974

PUBLICATIONS:

Author	*Waterways of the World* (National Geographic Society)
Editor	*Tough Legal Decisions* – A Biography of Janet Reno (John Wiley)
Editor	*Anatomy of a Holocaust Death Camp* (Indiana University Press)

COMMUNITY LEADERSHIP:

Co-Chair, Washington Decorator Showhouse - *$500,000 budget & 1000+ volunteers* (1996)
Chair, Buildings & Grounds Committee, United Farm School - *$1 million budget* (1994 to 1996)

ROBERT HASTINGS

211 North Gateway Lane
Edison, New Jersey 07207
(856) 358-7414

CONSTRUCTION INDUSTRY EXECUTIVE

"Bottom-Line" Business Manager with over 20 years experience in Design, Engineering & Construction. Directed over 30 turnkey projects from initial planning and proposal stage throughout the entire design, engineering and construction cycle, to staffing and facilities start-up. Worldwide project, licensing and partnership experience. Strong general management, P&L management, mentoring and team leadership skills. Decisive, determined and profit-driven. Tough, but fair negotiator.

Well-respected throughout the industry for achievement in both project construction management and business management. Able to identify and implement strategies to reduce costs, increase revenues, strengthen customer relationships, improve business processes and drive profitable growth. Expert in the latest technologies, processes and systems in the hazardous materials and handling systems industry.

Industry Honors & Awards

- EPA Awards, 1996, 1988, 1985
- EnviroSource President's Award for Teamwork, 1998, 1991
- American Concrete Institute Outstanding Achievement Award, 1998
- Who's Who in the Construction Industry, 1996 (Excellence Award in 1995 and 1996)
- Sun Oil Company Excellence Award, 1982
- Anheuser Busch Outstanding Achievement Award, 1981

PROFESSIONAL EXPERIENCE:

ABC SYSTEMS, Edison, New Jersey   1979 to Present
($587 million global environmental materials handling systems company)

Vice President – Engineering & Construction / Corporate Officer (1985 to Present)
Director of Project Management (1984 to 1985)
Manager of Projects (1983 to 1984)
Senior Project Manager (1982 to 1983)
Project Manager (1981 to 1982)
Senior Project Engineer / Project Engineer (1979 to 1981)

Joined AA International (ABC's predecessor company) at the bottom of the organization and, within six years, advanced to one of the top 3 executives in the corporation. Since 1985, have held full P&L responsibility for the Engineering & Construction Division and all related operations:

- Project Proposals & Presentations
- Project Control / Management
- Start-Up Human Resources
- Contract Administration
- Subcontract Administration
- Design & Engineering
- Purchasing & Materials
- Trade Union Negotiations
- CPM Scheduling
- Field Project Management
- Estimating
- Construction
- Contracts
- Budgeting
- Licensing

Managed through a period of dramatic organizational change and transformation as the company was acquired, divested, reorganized, spun off and transitioned through several names (FIL, WOT, MET), ownership and top management changes. Concurrently, responded to changing regulatory demands impacting the industry, its technologies and its operations. Continued to achieve results and deliver strong performance despite volatility.

86

Achievements & Project Highlights:

- Directed over 20 major turnkey design, engineering and construction projects over the past 10 years. Delivered $300+ million in projects at $30.5 million under budget. Achieved/surpassed all cost, schedule, quality and performance objectives.

- Built a "best-in-class" construction and engineering organization consistently effective in controlling operating and project costs. Reduced departmental staffing from 120 to 40 over six years and maintained stable workforce through the use of both permanent and job shop personnel. Cross-trained staff to optimize performance.

- Partnered with key suppliers and reduced annual purchasing costs by up to $100,000.

- Successfully managed one of the company's first-ever international projects, a $12 million venture in the Czech Republic. Brought project from concept through design and construction to start-up in cooperation with a Czech, Japanese and US workforce. Expanded international presence with licensing agreements with companies in Japan, China, Italy, Greece, Germany, Poland and the Czech Republic.

- Introduced leading edge design and engineering technologies, including complete conversion from manual to AutoCAD systems. Reduced time requirements by 50%.

- Structured and negotiated numerous strategic partnerships and alliances with equipment manufacturers and trade contractors to deliver multi-million dollar projects. Negotiated with union representatives to develop project costs and timelines.

- Orchestrated operations design, integration and consolidation for new start-up ventures, mergers and acquisitions. Evaluated proposed business opportunities and new technologies/systems. Member of corporate M&A advisory team.

- Corporate Architect/Engineer responsible for office layout designs, lease negotiations, relocations and all office services.

SUN OIL COMPANY, Marcus Hook, Pennsylvania   1978 to 1979

Project Engineer at an industrial/chemical refinery. Completed backlog of 35 projects within first six months. Designed and built a $500,000 facility six weeks ahead of schedule and $350,000 below budget.

MP LOWRY, INC., Williamsburg, Virginia   1976 to 1978

Construction Engineer for building and start-up of $1.25 million Anheuser-Busch brewery.

EDUCATION: **MSCE – Construction Management**, Penn State University
BSCE – Structural Engineering, Penn State University
Quality Assurance Certification in Nondestructive Testing
Certification in Hazardous Waste Handling

AFFILIATIONS: American Society of Construction Engineers
American Institute of Structural Engineers
Construction Management Association of America

MILITARY: Decorated Veteran, US Army. One-year tour with the Airborne Rangers in Vietnam.

ABRAHAM KURTZ

75 Highwood Avenue
New Haven, Connecticut 06850

Phone: (203) 854-2515   Email: abekurtz@aoll.com

ORGANIZATIONAL CONSULTANT & PERFORMANCE IMPROVEMENT STRATEGIST
Expertise in Strategic Leadership, Sales, Marketing, Business Development & Technology
Cross-Functional, Cross-Industry Experience
Darden MBA / Harvard BA

Dynamic leadership career as an Executive Consultant to major US and foreign corporations to optimize performance, drive revenue growth and strengthen competitive market position. Introduce leading edge process, business, training and leadership competencies to facilitate positive change.   Expert in client relationship management, traditional and emerging sales channels/techniques, and high-level project management.   Keen negotiating, problem solving and team building skills. Innovative, creative and entrepreneurial. Fluent in Spanish.

PROFESSIONAL EXPERIENCE

WORLDWIDE CONSULTING, INC. , New Haven, Connecticut

Senior Manager (1998 to Present)
Manager (1997 to 1998)

Recruited from Darden's MBA School to join a specialized consulting group focused on strategy development versus the more traditional tactical implementation. Promoted from Manager to Senior Manager within 9 months of hire.

Consult with client companies worldwide to provide expertise across a broad cross-section of business disciplines including strategic planning, business development, organizational design, information technology and customer service. Lead high-profile Balanced Scorecard development and implementation projects. Major engagements:

- **Major Telecommunications Company.** Architected complex change management process to transform customer service organization into an integrated solutions provider. Led project team in redefining customer lifecycle processes across the entire customer management cycle. Provided executive management with critical analyses, performance delivery models and a high-level business case to identify opportunity areas.

- **Latin American Corn Processing Company.** Led Board members in defining a new business strategy to transition from family-owned operation into an international competitor with key strategic business partners. Enhanced decision making processes and guided business strategy implemented into five core operations.

- **Japanese International Wholesale Bank.** Orchestrated strategic alignment project to support global multi-phase technology project. Coordinated multinational team of US and Japanese management personnel to link business strategy to systems implementation. Strategy drove successful implementation with no restructuring.

- **Mexican Conglomerate.** Transformed group of large Mexican companies in the insurance, mining and retail industries from "operator" to "owner" leadership style focused on accelerating profits and creating organizational value.   Concurrently, facilitated implementation of advanced information technology and Internet capabilities to enhance decision making and internal/external communication capabilities.

J.P. THOMAS, INC., Atlanta, Georgia

Summer Associate (Summer 1996)

Selected from a competitive group of MBA candidates for 3-month Associate position with one of the world's preeminent consulting organizations. Complemented previous field consulting and training experience with an intense focus on analysis, problem solving and strategy development. Major projects:

- **Team Member – Eli Lilly Vendor Sourcing Project**. Evaluated company's existing purchasing organization, assessed potential impact of five major organizational initiatives and wrote business case for evaluating alternative vendor strategies.
- **Team Member – Johnson & Johnson Managed Care Strategy Development Project**. Evaluated 150 services to identify optimum product mix to strengthen J&J's market penetration and competitive position.

KURTZ, KEPLER & ASSOCIATES, Hartford, Connecticut

Partner (1991 to 1995)

Co-founded a niche consulting firm specializing in sales training and leadership development for major corporations nationwide. Worked with top executives of major US and foreign companies to identify organizational needs and develop/conduct training programs to optimize their sales, marketing and business development expertise.

- Transitioned business concept into a full-scale consulting venture generating over $300,000 in annual revenues.
- Established a firm niche market presence and captured key national accounts (e.g., Merck, Schering Plough, Rhone Poulenc, 3M, Miles, Medco).
- Won a 1994 vendor award for customer service excellence.
- Expanded into several collateral business lines including market research and competitive analysis, issues identification and analysis, and project definition.

SMITHKLINE BEECHAM PHARMACEUTICALS, Philadelphia, Pennsylvania

Senior National Accounts Manager (1987 to 1991)
Corporate Sales Trainer (1986 to 1987)
Professional Sales Representative (1984 to 1986)

Targeted as a high potential management candidate and promoted through a series of increasingly responsible sales, sales training and account management positions. Selected as one of the first eight National Account Managers in a new business unit targeting sales penetration in alternative pharmaceutical and health care distribution markets.

- Exceeded annual sales goals by $65 million while maintaining a 2% marketing/expense ratio. Honored with two consecutive outstanding performance ratings.
- Transitioned from product sales to a solutions-based account management paradigm to foster long-term client development, relationship management and retention.
- Directed sales teams in strategic account planning and management to achieve revenue and market share objectives. Led sales and account management training. Developed best practice sales process model.

ENTREPRENEURIAL EXPERIENCE

Founded **MBO Entertainment** (recording company) in 1997 to develop and mass merchandise alternative R&B music. Identified market opportunity, assembled creative and production teams, secured capital investment and built business/financial infrastructure. Currently negotiating with EMI, BMG Publishing and other major players in the entertainment industry to launch MBO recordings into the national market.

EDUCATION

MBA – General Management (1985)
DARDEN GRADUATE SCHOOL OF BUSINESS/UNIVERSITY OF VIRGINIA
Fellow, The Consortium for Graduate Study in Management

BA – Biochemistry (1982)
HARVARD UNIVERSITY

MARGARET R. JOHNSTON

101 Wabash Avenue #682
Chicago, Illinois 60606

Home (847) 315-6784   Office (847) 544-2587   Fax (847) 544-6498

SENIOR OPERATING & MANAGEMENT EXECUTIVE

Expert in Process Redesign, Performance Reengineering & Productivity/Performance Improvement

Over 15 years top-flight management experience consulting and directing manufacturing, production and industrial operations worldwide. Pioneer in the design and delivery of innovative change management programs that have generated millions of dollars in cost savings through redesign of internal operating, production and business processes. Expert in facilitating change in a workforce to support reengineering initiatives and meet organizational operating, financial and quality objectives.

PROFESSIONAL EXPERIENCE:

INTERNATIONAL CONSULTING, Chicago, Illinois   1985 to Present

Consultant / Project Manager / Site Implementation Manager

Recruited to join this global consulting group based upon expertise in the design and delivery of value-added process improvements for large scale manufacturers. Assigned to Value Chain Discipline, one of four distinct consulting disciplines, working with clients worldwide to provide expertise in operations, process redesign, productivity improvement and quality.

- Recognized as a subject matter expert on facilitating process change and implementation through training, mentoring and motivation of operating staff and management teams.

Project Highlights & Achievements:

- **U.S. Chemical Products Manufacturer**
  Three-year assignment to a Fortune 500 corporation to facilitate the introduction of process improvement initiatives. Led initial process change that delivered $15 million in cost savings in first year to demonstrate the operational and economic value of business process redesign.

  Long-term efforts impacted operations at 22 sites throughout the U.S. and Europe, and led to successful redesign of processes in maintenance, purchasing, transportation, capital project management, environmental safety & health, product management and other core business functions. Advocated and won the support of in-house operating and management teams to drive forward and maintain process changes.

  RESULTS: Instrumental in implementation of over 15 workstream process changes that cumulatively saved the corporation over $150 million in operating costs.

- **U.K. Pharmaceutical Products Manufacturer**
  Led 6-person consulting team in extensive internal reengineering and process redesign impacting key operating units of the corporation (e.g., quality, production, warehousing, distribution, staffing, manufacturing).

  RESULTS: Created innovative Crewing Allocation Map (manpower allocation model) that reduced staffing costs by 50% within the logistics function and subsequently served as the prototypeother projects. Led a packaging area capacity analysis and process redesign that reduced manpower/machine requirements by 60%.

- **Automobile Manufacturer**
  Launched a complete redesign of maintenance and tool engineering processes for company's Canadian-based operations.

  RESULTS: Delivered a 30% reduction in staffing requirements, reduced delivery lead times and maintained overtime at a rate less than in all previous years of operation.

- **International Information Management Project**
  Led development of prospect database for internal telemarketing and business development that drove International's revenue stream throughout mature and emerging markets.

  Transferred to corporate headquarters to lead the development/implementation of solutions-driven information technologies for a diversity of internal applications. Facilitated needs assessment, hardware/software selection, and implementation of customized technologies.

- **International Consulting Projects**
  Maintain an active leadership role in the design and delivery of process improvement initiatives for internal applications. Co-designed program management process for Leadership Learning Lab and creation of Market Focused Reengineering Methodology (MFR) to create global centers of excellence to support client field engagements.

  Currently operating and participating in a redesign of the staffing process utilized to allocate 350 professionals to 60+ ongoing client projects throughout North America.

NABISCO BRANDS INC., Chicago, Illinois   1980 to 1985

Maintenance Systems Manager (1984 to 1985)
Process Engineering Manager (1981 to 1983)
Process Engineer (1980 to 1981)

Pioneered innovative process development and improvement initiatives throughout the company. Controlled millions of dollars in operating and capital budgets. Led a staff of eight.

- Analyzed, designed and installed process layout including support utilities for a facility with $6.3 million in capital costs. Total capital expenditures exceeded $3.1 million.
- Researched, designed, and supervised installation and start-up of a new continuous production process that increased capacity, quality and material yield while reducing labor costs by 50% for a major product line.

KELLOGG COMPANY, Battle Creek, Michigan   1978 to 1980

Director of Manufacturing (1978 to 1980)
Engineering Manager (1978)

Recruited to direct the design and construction of a new manufacturing facility. Promoted to Director of Manufacturing leading operations at four production facilities.

- Researched, designed, and directed construction and installation of a continuous production operation which increased capacity 800%, reduced labor costs 66% and improved yield 8%.
- Reengineered operating and human resource processes to upgrade raw material yields. Efforts resulted in a 10% reduction in annual purchasing costs.

GENERAL FOODS CORPORATION, St. Paul, Minnesota   1974 to 1977

Senior Process Engineer (1977)
Maintenance Supervisor (1974 to 1977)

Designed and implemented process, quality and facility improvement projects. Designated as an "operations troubleshooter" for the division, travelling to facilities nationwide to direct plant start-ups, resolve long-standing process problems and increase production output.

- Spearheaded problem-solving team implementing process changes that extended the life of $3 million in capital equipment from three years to 20+ years.
- Increased production from 4100 units to 11,400 units per shift over a five-month period.

EDUCATION: **BS / Mechanical Engineering**, University of Illinois, 1974
               Continuing Professional Education in Information Technology and Statistics.

JAMES SALTZMAN

24 Cherry Hill Avenue
Shreveport, Louisiana 71107
Email: jimsaltzman@aol.com

Phone: 318-588-4578   Fax: 318-685-2565

EXECUTIVE PROFILE

Corporate Development Executive/Business Development Strategist with 15+ years across broad industries, products, services and technologies in US and foreign markets. Intuitive, insightful, creative and intelligent. Confidential Advisor to CEOs, CFOs, Chairmen and other senior executives. Impeccable ethics and integrity. MBA Degree. CPA.

- Growth & Development Strategy, Value Analysis, Vision & Leadership
- Mergers, Acquisitions, Joint Ventures, Strategic Alliances & Partnerships
- Capital Formation, Investment Banking & Venture Capital Funding
- Complex Financial Analysis, Modeling & Transactions Structuring
- Executive Mediation, Negotiation, Facilitation & Partner/Liaison Affairs
- Acquisition Integration & Post-Integration Leadership

CAREER PROFILE:

CORPORATE DEVELOPMENT CONSULTANT   1994 to Present
THE BAKER COMPANY, Alexandria & Shreveport, Louisiana

Strategic & Financial Advisor / Investment Banker to US and foreign corporations committed to acquisition-focused growth strategies. Provide turnkey leadership for major acquisition, strategic alliance, joint venture and refinancing programs, from initial business planning, candidate/partner selection, due diligence, deal structuring and negotiations through final execution. Project highlights include:

- **Digital International** – Developed and executed strategy to employ high market capitalization of UK biotech company for US expansion. Delivered strategy that achieved profit targets to counter R&D costs; product/service outsourcing; and roll-up consolidation. Point person for two acquisitions, driving client revenues from $2 million to $30+ million. Listed company on the London Stock Exchange.

- **Crimson & Rose** – Authored business plan for strategic alliance to establish a US consulting firm joint venture for $2 billion Dutch corporate division. Executive committee voted full funding for $750,000.

- **Technology Group** – Architected competitive strategy for Fortune 1000 client to increase market share and profitability within the changing healthcare reimbursement market.

- **Biotech Client** – Currently leading effort to acquire larger, publicly-held competitor to build critical mass, expand product line and achieve public listing with less-costly and creative, "back door" strategy.

VENTURE PROJECTS DIRECTOR   1988 to 1994
LOUISIANA GENERAL HOSPITAL (LGH), Shreveport, Louisiana

Recruited by Chairman of the Board as **Venture Projects Director** to orchestrate an aggressive expansion throughout highly competitive healthcare industries, technologies and services. Conceived, developed and led successful corporate development projects (strategic alliances, joint ventures, start-up ventures). Served as **CFO, Treasurer or Director of Finance** for new projects. Member - Corporate Strategies Committee. **Board Member** – LGH portfolio companies.

- **ICON, Inc.** – CFO tasked to either restore this medical imaging technology transfer venture to profitability or close. Sought new funding to energize company, expand operations and strengthen financial performance. Achieved/surpassed financial objectives.
  - Negotiated $2 million strategic alliance with 3M and $5 million contract with Procter & Gamble.
  - Developed capital strategy and business plan leading to acquisition by French merchant bankers.

- **Wentworth Village Partnership** – Partnered with two for-profit companies to develop a $100 million retirement community. Negotiated complex $75 million construction loan and subsequent permanent mortgage financing package. Restructured loan status when FDIC took over bank. Structured and negotiated successful buy-out of corporate partner facing bankruptcy to eliminate partnership liability.
  - Returned $7+ million profit on $2.3 million investment (despite poor regional real estate market).

VENTURE PROJECTS DIRECTOR (*Continued*):

- **Louisiana Biomedical Research Corporation** – Singlehandedly structured a complex financial model for $257 million bond financing for development of 650,000 sq. ft. of biomedical research labs. Met debt covenants, grant restrictions, market lease rates, FASB 13 and debt burden limits.
  - Created financial plan in place for six years. Co-led company's $30 million operations during tenure.

- **Alzheimer's Disease Care Center** – Authored strategic, financial and business plans approved for $22 million in new venture funding by the Board of Trustees.

- Conceived, developed and/or launched several other successful new ventures/portfolio companies:
  - **Chartwell Home Therapies** – Partnered with another hospital to enter the home infusion therapy market. Provided investment leadership to support growth to $50 million (*one of region's fastest growing firms*).
  - **ATI** – Partnered with Paris-based venture capital firm to develop international telemedicine partnership.
  - **MGHIC** – Launched diagnostic imaging venture. Increased utilization and reimbursement by $5 million.
  - **American Express** – Partnered hospital with American Express to establish profitable inhouse travel agency.

VENTURES PROJECTS CONSULTANT / INTERIM CFO   1985 to 1988

- **MGH** – Developed and implemented strategic business plan to establish innovative marketing initiative. Subsequently recruited as Venture Projects Director with this $1+ billion corporation.
- **Summit Ventures** – Developed and automated accounting and financial management systems for seven partnerships of this $160 million new venture firm (*now one of the world's largest VC firms*). Directed investor relations with corporations and pension funds. Managed $40 million cash fund.
- **Chateau Stores, Inc.** – Created and implemented financial and administrative infrastructure to lead Canadian-based retail chain into US market (18 stores in Eastern and Midwestern regions).
- **Fifth Avenue Franks** – Developed strategic business plan for retail food company that attracted majority ownership investment offer from Beatrice Foods.

CHIEF FINANCIAL OFFICER / SENIOR VICE PRESIDENT   1983 to 1985
CORNADO & JUSTIN, Alexandria, Louisiana (*22-office regional investment brokerage*)

Promoted from Vice President of Finance to CFO with full leadership responsibility for the firm's finance, investment, credit, accounting, MIS and human resource operations. Teamed with Chairman and CEO in negotiating the profitable sale of the firm in 1985 (*declined offer to remain with new corporation*).

MANAGER – INVESTOR RELATIONS   1980 to 1983
DATA GENERAL CORPORATION, Westborough, Massachusetts

Communicated financial results and strategic direction to Wall Street, strengthening Data General's market credibility (*despite negative industry press*). Authored corporate financial press releases and speeches.

ASSISTANT TO THE PRESIDENT   1977 to 1980
NORTH AMERICAN ROYALTIES, Chattanooga, Tennessee

Managed SEC affairs through two security offerings for this $100 million oil & gas and foundry company.

Early Professional Experience:
Staff CPA – Petty & Landis (*public accounting firm*)   1974 to 1977
Assistant Treasurer – Coca-Cola Bottling Company   1970 to 1974

EDUCATION:

MBA – Finance	EMORY UNIVERSITY – 1976
BA – Economics	UNIVERSITY OF VIRGINIA – 1975
CPA	STATE OF TENNESSEE – 1979

HUMANITARIAN EFFORTS:

Conceived, planned, solicited and integrated corporate partners, and spearheaded Shreveport-based Ethiopian famine relief effort in 1987. Led project in cooperation with local network television affiliate to create "*The Spirit of New England*" campaign. Raised $600,000+ in donations and relief supplies within two weeks.

NICOLE L. HARRIS

23225 George Washington Boulevard
Arlington, Virginia 22553
Home (703) 654-7773   Work (703) 843-4657

CUSTOMER SERVICE AND DISTRIBUTION MANAGER

Results-driven professional with 10 years experience managing high-volume business operations. Excellent problem-solving skills and a strong orientation in customer service/satisfaction. Able to work under pressure in fast-paced, time-sensitive environments. Experienced in analyzing and streamlining product delivery systems to increase productivity, quality and efficiency. Proven ability to manage projects from planning through execution and completion. PC proficient in Microsoft office applications with extensive knowledge of system capabilities.

- Customer Relations
- Policy/Procedure Development
- Distribution/Warehousing Management
- Order Management

- Freight & Transportation Operations
- Productivity Improvement
- Staff Training/Development
- Business Systems Implementation

PROFESSIONAL EXPERIENCE:

PILSEN, INC., Fairfax, Virginia   1986 to Present
(Largest importer of international beers in the U.S.)

> **Customer Service Manager** (August 1990 to Present)
> **Customer Service Coordinator** (January 1990 to August 1990)
> **Distribution Analyst** (1986 to 1990)

Rapidly promoted through several increasingly responsible assignments to current position as Customer Service Manager. Direct the strategic planning, development, staffing, management and financial performance of Pilsen's customer service organization. Scope of responsibility impacts product flow and distribution to 900 distributors nationwide with revenues of more than $350 million annually.

Manage the depletion of warehouse inventory (3 million cases per month) with a monthly asset value of $9 million. Effectively communicate with customers, sales representatives and carriers to facilitate expedient and cost-effective product delivery. Liaison between breweries, warehouses and distributors.

Train, direct and motivate a staff of six. Manage and coordinate action plans for daily operation of the Customer Service Department, establish work priorities, and assist staff with problem resolution.

Project team member for the implementation of a new inventory management system to support the business and improve customer service. The system comprises applications from American Software, runs on an IBM AS400 platform, supports remote warehouses and is linked to major vendors. Worked extensively with MIS staff as client representative to develop user requirements, work flow procedures and user documentation. Trained staff at both corporate headquarters and warehouse facilities during implementation phase. Post-implementation responsibilities involved a series of improvement projects.

PILSEN, INC. *(Continued):*

- Successfully maintained exemplary customer service levels during the introduction and explosive growth of Pilsen Ice, the largest imported product launch in the industry.

- Coordinated the implementation of new packaging affecting the entire Pilsen brand family. Worked cooperatively with wholesalers and sales staff in placing orders and converting existing orders to ensure proper timing of inventory runouts at the distributor level.

- Reorganized customer service organization and improved customer service levels from 70% to over 95%.

- Created and initiated procedures and reporting to facilitate the sale of excess stock, partial pallets and over-age stock to avoid product obsolescence.

- Managed all customer service activities associated with the conversion of 300 wholesalers (30% of customer base) from Pilsen to Coors as part of the 1997 acquisition.

- Selected from among 85 employees to receive the prestigious President's Award for consistent excellence in performance, productivity and attitude in 1993 and 1995.

BENEFITS ADMINISTRATION, Centerport, New York   1984 to 1986

Account Supervisor

Processed millions of dollars in major medical and dental claims for member groups. Consulted with clients regarding coverage, claims and payment. Researched and resolved complex issues.

NATIONAL INSURANCE COMPANY, Hackensack, New Jersey   1978 to 1984

Dental Claims Supervisor

Supervised a staff of five in a dental claims unit. Audited processed claims and maintained production reports. Designed and implemented new office procedures to increase productivity and facilitate greater efficiency.

PROFESSIONAL TRAINING AND EDUCATION:

Management Training & Development
Customer Service Management
Computer Technology

Diploma, Westbury High School, New York, 1977

References Available Upon Request

KENNETH R. THOMPSON, M.Ed.

3593 Ivy League Hill
Springfield, Massachusetts 08251

Home   (801) 336-5978
Office   (801) 853-4476

HIGHER EDUCATION EXECUTIVE / SENIOR MANAGER / VICE PRESIDENT

Twenty-year collegiate and university management career with three distinguished institutions. Consistently successful in introducing strategic marketing and operational plans, athletic programs and student services to increase enrollment, enhance the student experience and strengthen competitive market position. Strong leadership, communication, and student and institutional advocacy skills. Committed to holistic student development and learning experience. Core competencies include:

- Departmental/Divisional Leadership
- Admissions & Recruitment
- Enrollment Management
- Financial Aid
- Strategic Planning
- Budgeting & Financial Planning

- Intercollegiate Athletic Operations
- Alumni Relations & Fundraising
- Career Development & Placement
- Campus & Residence Life
- Student Activities & Services
- Analytical & Statistical Methodologies

PROFESSIONAL EXPERIENCE:

MORRISON COLLEGE, Springfield, Massachusetts   1979 to Present

Recruited to this small private college in 1979 and promoted through a series of increasingly responsible management positions. Instrumental in transitioning from a regionally-based college into a nationally-recognized institution. Pioneered innovative marketing, recruitment, financial aid, student service, alumni development and technology programs. Career highlights include:

Vice President of Enrollment & Student Life / Dean of Campus Life (1989 to Present)

Senior Executive with full responsibility for the strategic planning, development, budgeting and operating leadership of Admissions, Financial Aid, Intercollegiate Athletics & Recreation, Alumni Relations and Career Development Departments. In partnership with Dean of Students, oversee Greek Affairs, Student Activities, Community Service, Social Judicial Board and Residence Life. Manage $900,000 in annual operating/administrative budgets. Teach wellness curriculum.

Admissions & Enrollment

- Innovated high-profile student recruitment and retention programs that have increased enrollment 10% and five-year graduation rates 8%.

- Created an integrated recruitment, admissions and financial aid program that delivered for five consecutive years a freshman class which exceeded enrollment targets and remained at or below budgeted financial aid. Currently award $9 million annually in financial aid to 900+ students.

- Expanded print communications to extend marketing, advertising and promotional programs.

- Directed design of application review grid methodology and implementation of LAN data management system.

Financial Aid

- Orchestrated development of a predictive methodology to project financial aid funding requirements based on historical trends.

- Facilitated introduction of leading edge software program (Micro/PowerFaids) to enhance forecasting, analysis and reporting capabilities.

Athletics

- Spearheaded the design and implementation of a student-focused program of intercollegiate and intramural athletics. Focused department's mission and reallocated resources to enhance program quality and increase student participation.

- Currently leading comprehensive capital campaign to raise $3.3 million for construction of all-weather track and renovation of athletic playing fields.

- Upgraded student employment program in athletic facilities to reduce staffing costs to the College while increasing career training and development opportunities for the student population.

- Launched complete reorganization of Athletic Department management team, restructured core processes and procedures, and produced comprehensive operations manual.

Alumni Relations

- Appointed for two-year tenure as Director of Alumni Relations, leading a number of innovative alumni development and management programs.

- Developed plan to organize 15,000 alumni by geographic regions to accelerate support for admissions, careers, volunteerism and fundraising.

- Established on-campus, lifelong learning program for alumni to increase alumni involvement and further strengthen partnerships.

- Developed leadership program targeted to recent graduates and dedicated to long-term support.

Dean of Admissions & Financial Aid (1983 to 1989)

Promoted to plan and direct the reorganization and refinement of the Admissions and Financial Aid Departments. Redesigned core processes, streamlined operations and accelerated program growth. Directed a staff of 14 and managed a $300,000 annual operating budget.

- Created and launched a multi-faceted recruitment program including high school visitations, open house visitations, targeted direct mail, guidance counselor cultivation and alumni admissions networking. Results included 185% increase in admissions inquiries, 53% increase in applications and 10% increase in matriculants.

- Appointed to senior management team which developed and implemented the College's strategic planning processes for enrollment, facilities, curriculum, personnel, finances and public relations.

Associate Dean / Assistant Dean of Admissions & Freshmen (1979 to 1983)

High-profile position building market presence nationwide to increase enrollment. Directed freshman orientation and advisement programs with a team of 30 faculty/staff advisors and 100 student volunteers. Directly supervised 10 professional and support staff in Admissions Department.

Highlights of Committee Participation & Leadership:

- Member, Middle States Accreditation Committee, Subcommittee on Campus Climate (1995 to 1996)
- Member, College Committee on Athletics, Recreation & Intramurals (1993 to Present)
- Member, Centennial Athletic Conference (1993 to Present)
- Co-Chair, Athletic Facility Task Force (1992 to 1993)
- Member, Middle States Five-Year Review Committee (1990 to 1991)
- Chair (5 years) & Member, College Retention Committee (1989 to Present)
- Member, Budget Advisory Committee (1989 to 1993)
- Chair, College Center Renovation Committee (1989 to 1990)
- Member, College Marketing Task Force (1986 to 1990)

UNIVERSITY OF TENNESSEE, Knoxville, Tennessee   1977 to 1979

Graduate Advisor to Dean of Students

Broad administrative, organizational and special projects responsibilities in the Office of the Dean of Students for this 7000-student university.

- Appointed to the University's Risk Management Committee and as Coordinator of In-State Residency Committee.

- Planned and directed a large-scale research project on competitive strategies for student retention.

BURLINGTON COLLEGE, Burlington, North Carolina   1975 to 1977

Associate Dean of Admissions

Led a team of two professional and three support staff in directing student recruitment and admissions programs for this 500-student institution.

EDUCATION:

HARVARD UNIVERSITY GRADUATE SCHOOL OF EDUCATION
Institute of Educational Management, 1995

UNIVERSITY OF TENNESSEE
M.Ed., Higher Education Administration, 1979

BURLINGTON COLLEGE
B.A., Interdisciplinary Philosophy, summa cum laude, 1975

PROFESSIONAL AFFILIATIONS:

Member, MA Department of Education Visiting Team, Harcum Junior College
Member, National Collegiate Athletic Association
Member, The College Board
Past Member, MA Association of School & College Admissions Counselors
Past Member, MASCAC Executive Committee
Past Member, National Association of College Admissions Counselors

COMMUNITY ACTIVITIES:

Board of Directors, Morrison College Habitat for Humanity
Co-Founder, Morrison College/Jefferson Elementary School Partnership
Member, Church Adult Christian Education Committee
Coach, South Parkland Youth Association
Past Member, Board of Directors, Springfield YMCA
Past Member, Big Brothers/Big Sisters of Springfield
Past Member, Selection Committee, Mack Truck Scholarship Program
Past Member, Selection Committee, Sponsored Scholarship Program (ETS)

LOUIS M. ROBINSON

5778 Cypress Manor Lane
Athens, Georgia 30606

Home: 706.457.1475   Email: lourobinson@yahoo.com   Cell: 706.125.5161

CAREER PROFILE:

Fourteen years' progressively responsible experience in the sales, marketing, installation and technical training/support of state-of-the-art mobile electronic systems and technologies. Combines outstanding skills in sales, customer relationship management, product demonstration and product management with excellent technical qualifications. Solid presentation, negotiation, public speaking and communication skills. Extensive store, shop and plant management experience. PC proficient with Word, Excel, PowerPoint, Photoshop Pro, S.B.S., Term-Pro Bass-Rox.

Certified Sony ES Installer. Sold, installed and supported Sony systems for more than 10 years.

PROFESSIONAL & TECHNICAL QUALIFICATIONS:

- Mobile Electronics Technology
- Electronics Systems Design & Installation
- Technology Product Sales & Service
- Customer Service, Support & Communications
- Recruiting, Training & Team Leadership
- Operations Planning, Scheduling & Management

- Multimedia Analog & Digital Technologies
- CAD Systems & Technologies
- Systems Production & Fabrication
- Trade Shows, Seminars & Special Events
- Purchasing & Supply Chain Management
- Revenue, Cost & Profit/Loss Management

PROFESSIONAL EXPERIENCE:

General Manager – Sales, Service & Product Training   1995 to Present
HIGHTECH AUDIO, INC., Athens, Georgia

Senior Business Manager with full planning, sales, marketing, technology, training, product design/engineering, product fabrication and P&L responsibility for this leading-edge designer/installer of mobile electronics, security and multimedia systems/networks. Direct a staff of up to 45. Scope of management responsibility includes the entire business operation, all accounting and financial affairs, the complete human resource function, purchasing and vendor selection, inventory and supply chain management, and general administrative affairs. Concurrently, manage sales, marketing, new business development and a high-quality customer service, training and support function.

- Positioned HighTech Audio as a leader in the mobile electronics and multimedia technology industry with state-of-the-art design and applications. Honored for product innovation and design/installation efficiency with four product features in "*Low Rider*" magazine.

  -- Honored as the #1 Kicker System Design Specialist (factory contest) in the US in 1998.
  -- Winner of the HOPI National Pro Hop (East Coast) and HOPI Outlaw SPL in 1996.
  -- Built vehicles for Sony's Rollin' Thunder Representative in South Florida.

- Achieved/surpassed all sales and profit objectives with a better than 2000% increase in revenues over four years. Closed 1999 with sales of $400,000 and $800,000 projected by year-end 2000.
- Led product teams in the design and fabrication of custom enclosures, fluid transfer systems, intricate low voltage circuits and other unique products/applications. Redesigned/remodeled shop work stations to increase efficiency on specific installations.
- Orchestrated design and technical development of company website to expand marketing and market penetration efforts. Negotiated strategic alliances with area retailers to increase customer base.

99

HIGHTECH AUDIO, INC. (Continued)

- Implemented commission and incentive programs to boost employee productivity and performance.
- Designed and built award-winning product display. Rebuilt another display to increase sales.
- Planned logistics and managed technology displays for a variety of sponsored entertainment events.

Sales Manager / Technical Shop Foreman   1991 to 1994
A+ AUTOS & TRUCKS, INC., Athens, Georgia

Promoted from Installer to Sales & Shop Manager responsible for training, scheduling and supervision of a team of five sales representatives and six technicians. Coordinated liaison affairs between manufacturers and distributors for custom orders and product expediting to meet customer specifications.

- Designed and installed mobile multimedia systems and mobile electronic kiosks.
- Independently managed all high-end product fabrication and custom woodworking projects for large-dollar sales and installation contracts.

Sales Representative   1989 to 1991
BLACK INFINITY, Athens, Georgia

Sold/marketed mobile electronics systems and technologies to an affluent consumer market. Designed innovative product displays and merchandising schemes, including portable display used at the Computer Electronics Show (CES) in Las Vegas.

Co-Owner / Electronics Technician   1986 to 1989
TOP SECURITY, Atlanta, Georgia

Launched part-time entrepreneurial venture specializing in the installation of audio and security systems. Independently managed product sales and customer service.

Plant Manager   1986 to 1989
CREATIVE SYSTEMS WOODWORKING, Athens, Georgia

Fast-track promotion through a series of increasingly responsible assignments to #3 management position with this designer/manufacturer of custom case goods and furniture. Scope of responsibility included the entire manufacturing operation including staffing, scheduling, materials, inventory, production planning, new product integration, safety, quality and reporting. Led a team of up to 75 employees.

- Personally managed key account relationships for contracts valued in excess of $215 million. Major clients included Athens Community College, Georgia Turnpike and Coral Springs Aquatic Complex.
- Implemented a series of business processes and technologies (including CAD) to enhance manufacturing efficiency, minimize waste and improve production yields.

EDUCATION / TECHNICAL TRAINING / CERTIFICATIONS:

Clifford Electronics Master Technician	Sony ES Certification
Rockford Technical Training Institute	Mobile Electronics Certificate
Automotive Service Excellent Training	Broward Community College

***Graduate** of the following Factory/Product Training Programs:*

Blum, Holzma, Sony, Fujitsu Ten, Mitek, Rockwell, MB Quart, Homag, SCMI, BSE, DEI, Extant, Mb Quart, Panasonic, Linear, Kicker, MTX

ANDREW R. KENNEDY
312 Saratoga Springs Road
Allentown, Pennsylvania 19344
(610) 713-9711

NUCLEAR UTILITY / ENERGY / PROCESS INDUSTRY EXECUTIVE

Strategic & Financial Planning / Finance & Budget Analysis / Engineering & Technology
Executive Marketing / MIS / Training & Development / Project Planning & Costing
Organizational Development / Productivity & Efficiency Improvement / Cost Reduction
Regulatory Affairs / Risk Analysis / Manpower Planning / Process Reengineering

Successful industry executive with an impressive record of achievement in designing the strategies, analyses, methods, processes and operations to improve financial performance. MBA Degree.

PROFESSIONAL EXPERIENCE:

PENNSYLVANIA POWER & LIGHT COMPANY, Allentown, Pennsylvania   1981 to Present

Promoted rapidly during 14-year career through a series of increasingly responsible operating and management positions to current assignment as the **Supervisor of Operating Experience Services**. Innovated state-of-the-art processes to manage large-scale utility operations with focus on cost control, safety management, personnel development and regulatory compliance. Provided technical, finance and operating leadership in complex business divisions. Delivered significant and sustainable results:

- Pioneered an innovative maintenance work observation and analysis technique that increased labor availability and captured over $500,000 in annual operating cost savings. Introduced leading edge probabilistic risk assessment methods that saved over $5 million in power generation costs.

- Identified $5 million in cost reduction of a $117 million operating budget. Launched a series of high-profile process analysis, productivity improvement and quality initiatives that saved and additional $1 million in operating costs.

- Authored comprehensive justification for Public Utilities Commission of schedule delays on construction of a $4.25 billion, 2-unit nuclear power plant. Resulted in 100% allowance for all project costs in approved rate base.

- Pioneered innovative operating processes including the first Human Performance Enhancement Program, Master Resource Planning Protocols, Regulatory Compliance Standards and a Professional Certification Program.

- Designed and managed a multi-tiered cost improvement program which reduced operating expenses and resulted in a net decrease of 2% in the customer cost of electrical utility.

- Created a maintenance backlog reduction program that reduced open work orders by 15% and average age of backlog by 20%.

- Designed standards and models for financial planning, performance analysis, manpower planning, estimating, costing, budgeting and forecasting implemented throughout the entire corporation.

- Led a series of successful MIS and networking technologies installations and system upgrades.

SUMMARY OF POSITIONS & KEY RESPONSIBILITIES:

Supervisor - Operating Experience Services (1995 to Present)
Supervisor - Nuclear Compliance (1994 to 1995)

Promoted to high-profile position directing all nuclear compliance programs for the entire organization. Scope of responsibility includes technical specifications compliance and interpretation, operability determination procedures and methods, reporting processes, deficiency and corrective action programs, root cause analysis and investigation programs, and daily interface with NRC resident inspectors.

Transferred to newly created position as Supervisor of Operating Experience Services in February 1995. Maintain all previous responsibilities with additional accountability for the analysis and trending of all nuclear operating experience events.

- Pioneered development of Human Performance Enhancement Program, a self-reporting system of non-consequential and "near miss" events, utilized to analyze trends and identify precursors to consequential events. Created solutions-driven strategies to enhance long-term performance factors.

- Restored cooperative relationships with on-site NRC inspectors and preempted escalation of potential regulatory issues.

- Orchestrated transition from obsolete mainframe-based deficiency management information system to newly-designed LAN technology incorporating Microsoft ACCESS, Oracle and other graphical software applications.

- Designed leading-edge root cause analysis methods, developed standards and criteria, and incorporated into existing training materials.

- Instituted 24-hour investigations for all new internal operating experience events (800+ per year). Program has subsequently been reviewed by other utilities nationwide and is currently pending issuance of "Industry Good Practice" designation by the Institute of Nuclear Power Operations.

Acting Supervisor - Nuclear Planning & Cost Services (1993 to 1994)

Directed 20 engineers and analysts responsible for all costing, budgeting, process redesign, financial planning and operating planning functions for this $4 million business unit. Coordinated strategic, annual operating and 5-year business planning. Managed organization-wide benchmarking initiatives.

- Replaced former financial budgeting and reporting system with an integrated on-line, real-time information system to network plant operations with headquarters and provide computerized decision making models and analyses.

- Provided technical and engineering expertise for a massive system retrofit and construction program. Brought $3 million project in under budget and ahead of schedule.

- Designed a professional certification program to upgrade technical and project management skills.

Senior Project Engineer - Susquehanna Planning & Cost Services (1985 to 1993)

Led a team of 4 engineers, 2 computer analysts and external consultants responsible for cost management and financial planning process development, analysis and reporting of $190 million O&M budget and a $60 million capital expenditure budget. Designed new computer technology for cost and planning functions, developed labor estimating standards and spearheaded productivity improvement programs.

Senior Project Engineer - General Office Planning & Scheduling Group (1981 to 1985)

Supervised a team of 6 engineers and analysts responsible for master resource plans and integrated schedules for facilities construction, start-up, operations and maintenance.

OWENS-CORNING FIBERGLAS CORPORATION, Toledo, Ohio   1970 to 1981

Project Manager (1979 to 1981)
Schedule Manager (1978 to 1979)
Project Engineer (1977 to 1978)
Project Control Supervisor (1976 to 1977).
Cost Control Engineer (1970 to 1976)

Fast-track promotion through a series of increasingly responsible capital project estimating, costing, planning and scheduling positions. Directed general and subcontractor scheduling and all manpower planning functions for the then-largest fiberglass reinforcements manufacturing facility in the U.S.

Promoted to final position as Project Manager with full responsibility for marketing and process development of state-of-the-art specialty insulation systems (primarily for the process and nuclear industries). Authored Nuclear Quality Assurance Manual for systems design and manufacture.

- Launched marketing plan for new product portfolio that delivered over $10 million in first year sales.

- Designed new thermal insulation technology for cryogenic and underground piping systems that generated over $18 million in new revenues.

- Directed on-site system installations worldwide.

EDUCATION:

MBA / Finance, Lehigh University, 1985
BS / Mechanical Engineering, University of Notre Dame, 1970

Post Graduate Studies in Industrial Engineering and Management

PROFESSIONAL PROFILE:

Licenses
- Professional Engineer (PE), Registered in Pennsylvania & Kansas
- Certified Cost Engineer (CCE), American Association of Cost Engineers
- Certified BWR Non-Licensed Operator

Publications
- Presented 12 technical papers at professional symposia and conferences, including Lehigh University, American Association of Cost Engineers, Pennsylvania Electric Association, Edison Electric Institute, American Society of Mechanical Engineers, American Nuclear Society and Institute of Industrial Engineers.

Affiliations
- Director & Past President, Eastern PA Association of Cost Engineers
- Legislative "Minuteman," National Society of Professional Engineers
- Past Fund Raising Chairperson, MATHCOUNTS, National Society of Professional Engineers
- Member, Institute of Industrial Engineers

ADAM F. EDMONDS

418 Alexander Street
Philadelphia, Pennsylvania 18969
(215) 721-0294

SENIOR ENGINEERING & PROJECT MANAGEMENT EXECUTIVE
Expert in the Design & Installation of Complex Technology Systems

---

Fifteen years of progressively responsible experience in engineering design and project management for clients in the US, Canada, Latin America, Far East and Australia. Combines excellent technical, analytical and engineering qualifications with demonstrated achievement in delivering multi-million dollar projects on time and within budget. Strong leadership, team building and problem solving expertise. Qualifications:

- Project Design & Management
- Engineering Management
- Estimating, Budgeting and P&L
- Field Installation Management
- Resource Planning & Management

- Client Presentations & Negotiations
- Cross-Functional Team Leadership
- Vendor Selection & Negotiation
- Material Selection & Management
- Product & Technology R&D

Excellent skills in client relationship management and cross-cultural communications. PC proficient with CADRA CAD, Lotus, Microsoft Projects, WordPerfect, and other spreadsheet, database and word processing applications. Experienced in PC FORTRAN and BASIC programming.

PROFESSIONAL EXPERIENCE:

ACCURATE SYSTEMS, Chester, Pennsylvania   1996 to Present
(Material Handling Systems Technology)

Project Manager / Project Director

Recruited to direct the design, development and installation of high-speed material handling equipment and related bar coding technology, designed specifically for the postal, mail handling and direct mail industries worldwide.

AMC CORPORATION, Berwyn, Pennsylvania   1982 to 1996
(Material Handling Systems Division)

Project Manager / Senior Design Engineer (1990 to 1996)
Design Engineer (1983 to 1990)
Engineer (1982 to 1983)

Fast-track promotion through a series of increasingly responsible engineering and project management positions in a $100 million business group. Responsible for the cost-effective design and management of "turnkey" automated material handling systems for clients worldwide. Held P&L responsibility for all assigned projects (from $4 million to $16 million).

Managed programs from initial concept and proposal preparation through design, specification, installation, commission, debug and final client acceptance. Provided technical and engineering assistance to marketing teams and participated in client presentations/contract negotiations. Led cross-functional teams of software, electrical and mechanical engineers throughout entire project cycle. Managed relationships with project managers, production managers and plant managers at client sites worldwide.

AMC CORPORATION *(Continued):*

Project Highlights & Achievements:

- **News Limited (Australia).** Directed completion of 6-year, $16 million project with installation at four sites in Australia. Delivered project at 10.1% over profit projections.

- **Singapore Press Holdings (Singapore).** Negotiated 60% of $3 million project as "up front" cash to finance project design, engineering and installation.

- **The Age (Australia).** Led successful turnaround of technically challenging project (first time installation of new non-wire guided vehicle system). Resolved technical issues and negotiated favorable settlement at $382,000 over initial selling price.

- **World Press (US).** Integrated all RAVEN (automated material handling systems) into one large-scale project, defined installation phases, led client presentations and returned project to "on-time, on-budget" status.

- Other major clients included **The New York Times, The Washington Post, Fruit of the Loom (US), Apotex (Canada), Reckitt & Colman (Brazil)** and **Vernon Warehouse.** Managed a mixed portfolio of projects, each with unique technical challenges and emphasis on cost-effective project delivery and customer satisfaction.

- Championed concept and spearheaded initial design of an automatic loading table (C-93) designed specifically for newspaper publishing. Revenues are projected at $15+ million.

NOTE: *Early career experience designing automatic guided vehicles and bulk handling systems.*

ALTECH INDUSTRIES, Allentown, Pennsylvania   1980 to 1982

Product Engineer

Designed, developed and facilitated manufacture of vapor recovery systems for oil storage tanks. Coordinated departmental and production scheduling, customer interface, project planning and field installations.

EDUCATION:

M.S., Mechanical Engineering, Lehigh University, Bethlehem, Pennsylvania, 1989
B.S., Mechanical Engineering, Lafayette College, Easton, Pennsylvania, 1980

References Provided Upon Request

MATTHEW R. KINARD

232 Horse Stable Road
St. Paul, Minnesota 55203
(612) 384-4652

CAREER PROFILE:

Senior R&D Professional successful in leading sophisticated product design, development and scale-up programs for diverse market and industry demands. Liaison among R&D, manufacturing and marketing to define customer demand, lead product development and facilitate cost-effective, quality-driven production. Experienced in health care, pharmacology, photo imagesetting, printing, industrial, automotive and construction products/technologies.

Excellent qualifications in cross-functional team leadership, resource management, project planning and technical documentation. Effective customer liaison with strong interpersonal and communication skills. Expertise in designed experiment and statistical analysis methodologies.

PROFESSIONAL EXPERIENCE:

3M CORPORATION, St. Paul, Minnesota   1979 to Present

Seventeen-year career leading complex R&D programs for several core 3M divisions. Recognized for outstanding research, product development and project management expertise.

- Nominated for 3M's "Technical Circle of Excellence" award in 1995.
- Finalist for 3M's "Corporate Quality Achievement" award in 1993 and 1995.

Research Specialist - Printing & Publishing Systems Division (1989 to Present)
3M, St. Paul, Minnesota / **Rochester Technical Center (RTC)**, Rochester, New York

Senior R&D Scientist for 3M's family of new Onyx™ Silver-Halide Imagesetting Products designed to increase efficiency, improve productivity and reduce the cost of commercial printing operations. Challenged to accelerate product development, introduce methods and designs to increase product functionality, and redesign and implement processes to reduce annual R&D and manufacturing costs. Function as Acting Manager of RTC in absence of manager.

Scope of responsibility includes leadership of the entire Onyx™ Program R&D function and the direct training/supervision of a cross-functional team of scientists and engineers. Guide Marketing and Technical Services teams in identifying customer/market demand and developing appropriate products, line extensions and technologies. Consult directly with key accounts nationwide.

- Technical Team Leader for scale-up and continuous improvement of Silver-Halide products. Delivered significant improvements in performance, consistency and manufacturability. **RESULTS:**

  — Directed development of new product line and line extensions that delivered $7.8 million in revenues in 1996.
  — Reduced factory unit costs by 20% ($200,000+).

- Co-Developer and Co-Team Leader for scale-up of new laser imagesetting plate (line extension). Directed a 15-person R&D, quality assurance and technical service team. **RESULTS:**

  — Increased factory emulsion productivity by 50%.
  — Reduced sensitometric speed variability by 33%.
  — Resolved key production scale-up issues using designed experiments.
  — Delivered product on time and within budget despite several critical redevelopment stages.
  — Projected volume of $6.5 million in new revenues to the corporation.

- Developer and Team Leader for delivery of reduced speed RLD/HN imagesetting plate (line extension). Redesigned core product in response to specific market/customer demands to increase product functionality, field performance and reliability.

  — Currently facilitating final product completion and field testing prior to full-scale introduction.

3M CORPORATION *(Continued):*

Medical Service Representative (1984 to 1989)
3M Riker, St. Paul, Minnesota

Recruited to 3M's pharmaceutical and transdermal drug delivery systems business unit to identify and strengthen experience in customer/market demand. Challenged to launch the introduction of new pharmaceutical products while continuing to build volume in existing product lines.

- Successfully introduced first of a new class of antiarrhythmic agents to the University of Iowa Medical Center. Worked closely with University cardiologists over a three-year period to launch product and facilitate further drug studies.

- Won 1987 "Outstanding Sales Achievement Award" and nomination for "Top Performer's Group" in 1986 and 1987.

Post-Doctoral Fellow - Chemistry & Pharmacology (1982 to 1984)
University of Minnesota / Rochester School of Medicine & Dentistry, Rochester, New York

Two-year leave of absence from 3M to complete an NIH-funded intensive post-doctoral research training fellowship. Conducted in-vitro investigation of the mechanism of activation of cyclophosphamide, a highly-effective, but toxic anti-tumor agent, to determine if more stable, less-toxic analogues could be developed.

- Conducted preliminary laboratory investigations that led to subsequent development of new analogues for pharmacological testing.

- Recipient of the competitive and prestigious Wilson Fellowship.

Senior Chemist - Industrial Specialties Division (1979 to 1982)
3M Center, St. Paul, Minnesota

Led development, introduction and successful application of new urethane foam tapes for automotive applications. Concurrent with R&D responsibilities, provided technical service/support to major customers and to 3M's nationwide sales and marketing teams.

- Guided development through the R&D cycle including pilot plant and factory production scale-up.

Previous Professional Experience:

Industrial Chemist - Eastman Kodak Company (1974 to 1975)
Quality Control Supervisor - U.S. Gypsum Co. (1971 to 1974)

EDUCATION:

Ph.D., Organic (Heterocyclic) Chemistry, University of East Anglia, Norwich, England, 1979
M.Sc., Organic Chemistry, University of East Anglia, Norwich, England, 1976
B.A., Chemistry, State University of New York, Buffalo, New York, 1971

PROFESSIONAL AFFILIATIONS:

American Institute of Chemists (Fellow)
American Chemical Society
American Association for the Advancement of Science

MICHELLE JENKINS
10 Goosedown Court
Morrestown, New Jersey 08532
Home (609)732-9705   Office (609) 296-6479

ENVIRONMENTAL ENGINEER / ENVIRONMENTAL HEALTH & SAFETY MANAGER
Wastewater, Solid, Air & Site Hazard Remediation

CAREER PROFILE

Fourteen years of increasingly responsible experience in Environmental & Safety Engineering. Directed remediation of more than 100 sites nationwide, reducing corporate exposure and liability, cutting costs and achieving regulatory compliance. MS Degree in Environmental Engineering. Qualifications include:

- Environmental Technology & Engineering
- Site Assessment & Remediation
- Resource Recovery & Conservation
- Governmental Liaison Affairs
- Acquisition & Investment Analysis
- Public Speaking & Media Affairs

- Policymaking & Process Management
- Project Budgeting & Management
- Environmental Law & Litigation
- Cross-Functional Team Leadership
- Environmental & Safety Training
- Crisis Management & Emergency Response

Regulatory Affairs

Expert knowledge of Superfund requirements and methodology (including four years direct employment with the EPA), and all RCRA, TSCA, CERCLA, SARA, UST and CWA regulations. Extensive knowledge of governmental regulations, occupational safety (OSHA), industrial hygiene standards, health and safety affairs, and permitting.

Industry Experience

Broad experience in heavy manufacturing including chemicals, polymers, electronics, advanced technology, metals, oil and gas, mechanical components and consumer products.

Project Management Experience

Directed project teams of up to 25 engineers and field managers at sites nationwide. Wrote project remediation and management plans, prepared budgets, acquired technology resources and directed field operations. Managed outside liaison affairs with consultants, regulatory agency personnel, attorneys and the press.

PROFESSIONAL EXPERIENCE

Environmental Engineer , UNITED INTERNATIONAL, Princeton, New Jersey   1994 to Present

- Directed 350+ site remediation projects in less than two years.
- Saved $1 million in remediation costs on proposed site acquisitions, foreclosures and divestitures.
- Only Environmental Engineer in the entire corporation.

Environmental Engineer, AMERICAN WATER HEATER, Johnson City, Tennessee   1993 to 1994

- Spearheaded design, development and implementation of company-wide environmental health and safety program for this large manufacturer. Achieved 100% regulatory compliance.
- Delivered $650,000 cost savings on large soil remediation project.

PROFESSIONAL EXPERIENCE *(Continued)*

Project Manager, GENERAL ELECTRIC COMPANY, Fairfield, Connecticut   1991 to 1993

- Created a comprehensive hazardous materials remediation, resource recovery and conservation program for a $10 million GE facility.
- Controlled $1.4 million in remediation funds.
- Managed technical and regulatory reviews of proposed acquisitions and divestitures.

Project Manager, AMOCO OIL COMPANY, Farmington Hills, Michigan   1989 to 1991

- Led remediation teams in the design/development of soil and groundwater remediation systems, proposed technologies for subsurface investigation and other advanced environmental engineering programs.
- Managed up to 860 ongoing projects with supervisory responsibility for both in-house and consulting engineers.

Environmental Engineer, ENVIRONMENTAL PROTECTION AGENCY, Atlanta, Georgia   1985 to 1989

- Superfund Project Manager for CERCLA, RCRA and Underground Storage Tank programs throughout the U.S. Completed more than 100 projects and regulatory reviews.

Environmental Engineer, WANG LABORATORIES, Lowell, Massachusetts   1983 to 1985

- Designed and managed environmental systems for hazardous waste, hazardous materials, air emissions and wastewater discharges.

MILITARY SERVICE

Bioenvironmental Engineer/Safety Officer, U.S. AIR FORCE RESERVE, Denver, Colorado   1984 to 1991

- Directed safety and environmental programs at large base installation. Designed and led on-site training programs on hazard recognition, documentation, handling, transportation and abatement/remediation.

EDUCATION

MS (Environmental Engineering), Tufts University, Medford, Massachusetts, 1982
BS (Biology), Morgan State University, Baltimore, Maryland, 1979
Diploma (Bioenvironmental & Safety Engineering), USAF School of Aerospace Medicine, 1984

AFFILIATIONS

National Environmental Health Association
National Association of Environmental Professionals
American Conference of Government Industrial Hygienists
National Society for Black Engineers

LAWRENCE BLAIR
22 Westerham Road
Ashford, London W5 4HR
44-457-554-362

EXECUTIVE CAREER PROFILE
US & European Business Operations

Dynamic leadership career combining both general management and financial management responsibilities within highly competitive organizations, industries and markets. Outstanding presentation, communication and cross-cultural team management skills. Entrepreneurial attitude, energy and style. Fluent in French.

General Management / Operating Management	Corporate Financial Planning & Leadership
Strategic Business Planning & Development	Financial Planning, Analysis & Reporting
New Venture & Enterprise Start-Up/Launch	Merger & Acquisition Analysis/Valuation
Strategic Marketing & New Business Development	Competitive Contract Negotiations
Worldwide Manufacturing & Distribution Operations	Cost Accounting & Cost Reduction/Avoidance
Product, Performance & Market Optimization	Financial Information Systems & Technologies

Currently pursuing Executive MBA degree to complement Wharton studies and MS degree.

PROFESSIONAL EXPERIENCE:

DOW CHEMICAL CORPORATION   1990 to Present

Fast-track promotion through a series of increasingly responsible management positions within both emerging ventures and well-established operations. Promoted rapidly based on consistent success in finance, operating management, strategic business development, business process/performance improvement and team/project leadership. Career highlights include:

Business Leader for Strategic Development – Latitude Team, London, England (1998 to Present)
Business Analyst – Latitude Team, London, England (1997 to 1998)

High-profile management position with newly-formed business team responsible for launching Dow Chemical's newest product line (Accel), the first major new product roll-out in Europe in 25 years. Directly responsible for creating strategic business development and roll-out plans based on extensive competitive, product and market intelligence. Senior Advisor to top management throughout Dow Chemical and to all field marketing and business management teams.

- Instrumental in developing business plans and strategies that have far surpassed corporate objectives. Began with initial launch in Ireland (completely sold out inventory within 6 months), on target to launch in the UK, Germany, Poland and Belgium in 2000, and in France and China in 2001. Currently projecting $66 million in additional NPV by year end 2001 with total business value of $300 million.
- Created a portfolio of new business processes for supply chain development/management, market positioning, competitive positioning, pricing and customer service. Developed improved financial planning, analysis and reporting methodologies that tied performance directly to bottom-line results.
- Pioneered the "Smart Marketing" concept, a best-in-class performance model to accelerate revenue and profit performance. Facilitated innovative benchmarking projects with BMW, Marks & Spencer and other prominent European companies.
- Designed business infrastructure and operating model for implementation throughout other Dow Chemical locations worldwide.

DOW CHEMICAL CORPORATION *(Continued)*

Financial Reporting Manager – Europe, Brussels, Belgium (1995 to 1997)

Promoted, transferred to Brussels and given full responsibility for directing all financial reporting for Dow Chemical's European Agriculture Business ($400 million in sales from 30 countries worldwide). Consulted directly with senior operating management teams on core business strategies, market penetration, supply chain management, product pricing and competitiveness, new product development and long-term revenue/profit growth. Provided strong financial and operating leadership during a period of 20%+ annual growth.

- Achieved/surpassed all budget objectives. Introduced innovative cost management strategies to spur bottom-line growth and consulted on a number of new market and product initiatives.
- Demonstrated a keen ability to transition detailed financial data into specific business strategies and actions.
- Provided high-level financial analysis and negotiations support for two key acquisitions ($525 million acquisition in the UK and $6 million acquisition in the Czech Republic).

Cost Analyst, New Orleans, Louisiana (1993 to 1995)

Complex cost analysis and financial management position at Dow Chemical's second largest manufacturing facility in the world ($1.5 billion in annual sales). Business was structured with 75% of the facility manufacturing Dow Chemical products and the remaining 25% operating through contract manufacturing agreements with Rhone Poulenc, Texaco and Oxychem. Fully responsible for determining accurate operating and billing costs for all three contract operations.

- Led an aggressive technology program to automate all financial analysis and reporting functions, streamline business processes and upgrade the quality of financial data. Reduced month-end closing cycle from 7 to 4 days.
- Designed and taught courses on cash flow management and financial reporting for non-financial managers.
- Appointed Chairman of Plant Safety Committee and spearheaded several successful improvement initiatives.
- Member of Public Relations and Community Outreach Project Team for the plant's 50th anniversary.

Internal Auditor, St. Louis, Missouri (1990 to 1993)

Traveled worldwide performing on-site financial and operational audits throughout all five of Dow Chemical's core operating divisions (chemicals, technology, pharmaceuticals, food, agriculture) in 36 countries. Led teams of up to 12 per engagement.

- Developed expertise in inventory analysis and reporting demonstrated by an $18 million write-off for Dow Chemical.
- Appointed Chairman of the Internal Audit Ethics Committee.

EDUCATION:

Currently pursuing Executive MBA, London Business School
(Concentration in New Venture Development, Entrepreneurship & Marketing)

Wharton Executive Program on Strategic Planning & Leadership, 1995
MS – Accountancy, University of Florida, 1989
BS – Accounting, University of Florida, 1987

Certified Management Accountant, 1995
Certified Public Accountant, 1993

JACOB WESTERLING
873 Shady Oak Terrace
Dunnegan, Missouri 64841

Home: 541-969-8759   Office: 541-254-3636

SENIOR EXECUTIVE PROFILE
Start-Up Ventures / Turnaround Businesses / Growth Organizations

Consummate Business Executive with 20+ years experience driving profitable growth in challenging, competitive and volatile customer markets. Strong leadership, communication, negotiation, creative and analytical skills. Decisive, solutions-focused and results-oriented. Combines cross-functional expertise in:

- Strategic Planning & Leadership
- Marketing & Business Development
- Finance, Accounting & Budgeting
- Human Resources/Team Building

- Revenue & Profit Growth
- New Product/Service Development
- Information Systems & Technologies
- Partnerships & Alliances

PROFESSIONAL EXPERIENCE:

CEO & Executive Vice President (1994 to Present)
COO & Senior Vice President (1989 to 1994)
INSURANCE ASSOCIATION OF AMERICA, Springfield, Missouri

Challenge: Lead a financially unstable organization through an aggressive turnaround, market repositioning, product/service expansion and business process reengineering initiative to restore profitability. Full P&L responsibility.

Responsibility: Senior management responsibility for strategic planning, operations, marketing, finance, regulatory affairs, administration, human resources, technology and P&L. 110 employees, $14.5 million annual budget and 22,000 clients/members.

- Outsourced non-critical functions, eliminated 40 staff positions, implemented aggressive cost reductions and redirected $2.2 million in revenues to IAA's affiliate members.
- Restored positive cash flow, eliminated all debt and built a $1.2 million reserve. Generated a positive variance of $1.6 million on consolidated financial statements.
- Launched multimedia advertising, public relations and marketing campaigns to increase the visibility and market penetration of the Association.
- Negotiated business partnerships and devised new programs to further expand market reach and drive member/revenue/profit growth.
- Achieved and maintained 98% customer/member retention (despite previous decline).
- Orchestrated conversion from outdated proprietary computer system to an open architecture system allowing for full integration of all hardware and software peripherals. Resulted in measurable gains in organizational productivity and efficiency.
- Realigned budget process, introduced ABC models, and developed/implemented new strategic plan to achieve organizational goals through the year 2000.

President & COO (1987 to 1988)
ABC INTERNATIONAL, INC., Tulsa, Oklahoma

Challenge: To accelerate profitable growth through venture capital funding and an aggressive new product development program for this publicly-traded OTC company in the "flowers by wire" industry.

Responsibility: Senior management responsibility for strategic planning, operations, marketing, finance, administration, information technology and P&L. $40 million in revenue, 125 employees. Member, Board of Directors, Executive & Finance Committees.

ABC INTERNATIONAL, INC. (*Continued*):

- Negotiated a successful venture with FTD (industry leader) allowing company to leverage FTD's national technology and telecommunications network.
- Strengthened nationwide field sales, marketing and advertising programs to expand market penetration and drive profitable sales growth. Linked revenue goals to strategic plan.
- Spearheaded a complete redesign of all existing software programs to enhance data management competencies.

Vice President – Finance, Administration & Automation (1982 to 1987)
NATIONAL ASSOCIATION OF TRAVEL AGENTS, Jackson, Mississippi

Challenge: To orchestrate the headquarters relocation from New York City to Washington, D.C. and build a fully-integrated financial, administrative and technology function.

Responsibility: Senior management responsibility for finance, accounting, administration, employee compensation and benefits, revenue growth and information technology.   90 employees; $14.5 million annual operating budget, 34,000 clients/members.

- Transitioned from an understaffed and inefficient operation into a "best-in-class" business organization.   Built a strong operating infrastructure, all financial and accounting policies, administrative processes and a leading edge technology environment.
- Forged innovative, new income-producing programs that drove surplus from negative $55,000 to positive $6+ million.
- Redesigned core benefit and compensation programs to improve coverages while reducing annual costs. Introduced salary administration and 401(k) programs for all employees.
- Designed and implemented cash management and investment programs to optimize returns, and expanded internal audit and financial control functions.

Previous Professional Experience:

Vice President – Administration & Finance – American Association of Truck Stop Operators (1980)
Director – Finance & Market Research – Airline Passenger Association, Inc., (1980 to 1982)
Assistant Vice President – Meetings & Conventions – The Fertilizer Institute (1976 to 1979)
Assistant Vice President – Commercial Banking (1968 to 1976)

EDUCATION & PROFESSIONAL CREDENTIALS:

MBA – Finance & Investments – The George Washington University (1980)

BA – History & Political Science – Northeastern University (1970)

Certified Association Executive – American Society of Association Executives (1990)

Certified Insurance Counselor – The Society of Certified Insurance Counselors (1995)

PROFESSIONAL AFFILIATIONS:

American Society of Association Executives – Fellow (1996)

American Society of Association Executives – Award of Excellence (1995)

Greater Washington Society of Association Executives – Board of Directors (1994 to 1996)

Chair, American Society of Association Executives – International Section Council (1995)

MARTIN T. FENNEWAY
Pinnacle Drive SW
Grand Rapids, Michigan 49509

Phone: 616-475-1432   Email: fenneway@aol.com   Fax: 616-587-5434

SENIOR EXECUTIVE PROFILE
President / CEO / COO / Senior Vice President / Division Vice President
Start-Up Entrepreneurial Ventures / Turnarounds / High-Growth Companies / Fortune 500 Companies
Industrial Products & Technologies / US & International Markets / MBA Degree

Twenty-year senior management career. Expertise in building, revitalizing and/or optimizing a company's organizational infrastructure, products, technologies, processes, measurement systems and sales/marketing strategies to optimize results.

EXECUTIVE LEADERSHIP COMPETENCIES

- Strategic Planning & Organizational Leadership
- Mergers, Acquisitions, Joint Ventures & Alliances
- Revenue/Market Growth & Profit Improvement
- Negotiations, Persuasion & Communications
- Executive Sales, Marketing & Business Development

- Multi-Site Manufacturing Operations
- Commercial Development & Licensing
- Supply Chain Management & Optimization
- Value-Added Products & Customer Relationships
- Corporate & Investor Relations

PROFESSIONAL EXPERIENCE:

LIQUID AIR CORPORATION, Grand Rapids, Michigan   1997 to 2000
($1.5 billion US subsidiary of $8 billion French company, the largest industrial, medical & specialty gas manufacturer/distributor serving the semiconductor, industrial, technical & medical markets worldwide)

Senior Vice President of $650 million Merchant Activities Division, a reasonably profitable business unit facing three significant challenges: (1) Optimization & Growth; (2) Organizational Realignment; and (3) FDA Regulatory Issues. Held full strategic planning, financial, operating, marketing, technology and administrative leadership responsibility for organization (4 vice presidents, 2500 employees, $2 billion in assets and $120 million annual operating budget). Member of the Executive Committee.

- Positioned the division for strong and sustainable financial results:
  - 6-8% sales increase and 12% profit improvement through cultural transition from product-driven to customer-centric business model.
  - $5 million in profit contribution through development of value-added pricing model.
  - $10 million operating cost reduction through merchant supply chain reorganization.
  - $10 million sales increase and $7 million SG&A reduction through innovative customer relationship management initiatives (e.g., e-commerce, call centers, sales force automation).
- Spearheaded several key acquisition initiatives (over $50 million in investment) as part of a strategic initiative to develop and/or acquire value-added products and technologies.
- Championed new quality initiative and implementation of ISO 9000. Effectively responded to FDA decree, protecting $60 million US business segment and $1 billion worldwide healthcare subsidiary.
- Restructured the entire sales organization, reduced sales regions from 36 to 12, segmented customer markets to optimize financial results and introduced performance-driven sales team incentives.

AZTECA CERAMICA S.A., Boulder, Colorado   1996 to 1997
(International start-up manufacturer of electronic grade components for semiconductor & ceramic markets)

Vice President recruited by investor group for 1-year executive assignment to build operating infrastructure for start-up technology venture. Challenged to create and introduce business processes, sales/marketing strategies, financial systems and complete manufacturing operations to penetrate billion dollar global market. Full operating and decision making responsibility. Reported to Chairman of the Board.

- Spearheaded the development, set-up and start-up of two operating plants in Arizona and Guadalajara, Mexico. Delivered both projects on time and within stringent budget constraints.

114

CONSOLIDATED ENGINEERING CO., Lansing, Michigan   1994 to 1996
(Privately-held $30 million manufacturer of patented industrial & environmental equipment)

Chief Operating Officer recruited by Chairman and President to transition this high-growth, family-owned manufacturer to the next level of corporate structure, business and operations. Challenged to deliver sustained growth and position for possible IPO. Full strategic planning, operating, manufacturing, sales, marketing, service, administrative, engineering and employee relations responsibility.

- Created first formal strategic and operating plans in the company's history, resulting in a 100% increase in both sales and profitability over two years.
- Achieved "Qualified Vendor" status with Ford Motor Company and Daimler-Benz following reorganization, management restaffing and implementation of a sophisticated TQM program.

AMERICAN COMBUSTION, INC., Detroit, Michigan   1990 to 1994
($10 million, pre-IPO industrial technology company with 25+ patents for environmental, metals & ceramics technologies)

President & Chief Executive Officer recruited by Heidrick & Struggles to transform this high-growth equipment manufacturer into a value-added, global-minded technology company. Concurrently, challenged to orchestrate an aggressive turnaround and return to profitability. Complete strategic, marketing, operating, product/technology and P&L responsibility. Reported to the Chairman of the Board.

- Delivered a 300% increase in sales and 1000% increase in profits over three years.
- Led development, market introduction and licensing of three major new technologies.
- Identified opportunity and negotiated global marketing alliance with $3 billion Fortune 150 company, adding $1 million per year to the bottom-line. Structured several international licensing agreements and a $1.5 million R&D grant from a major research institute.

AIR PRODUCTS & CHEMICALS, INC., Denver, Colorado   1977 to 1990
(Fortune 250, $5 billion international manufacturer/distributor of specialty chemicals & industrial gases)

General Manager – Distributed Gas Division (1988 to 1990)
Region Manager – Southern Region (1985 to 1988)
Product Manager – Specialty Gases (1984 to 1986)
District Manager – Detroit Market (1980 to 1984)
Sales Representative – Chicago Market (1977 to 1980)

Fast-track promotion through a series of increasingly responsible sales, marketing, product management and general management positions. Final promotion to General Manager following corporate-wide reorganization. Challenged to restructure and rebuild unprofitable $250 million division (1200 employees and 90 operating plants/sales offices nationwide).

- Achieved/surpassed all operating and financial objectives. Restructured virtually all operations of the Division and transitioned from lowest performance in the US to #1 (12 months after my departure).
- Achieved 50% profitable sales growth and 400% increase in contract signings in the Southern Region.
- Delivered a 71% increase in sales and restored the Detroit Market to profitability.
- Extensive experience structuring, negotiating and managing joint ventures, mergers, acquisitions and partnerships nationwide. Equally solid performance in national account contract negotiations.

UNITED STATES NAVY   1971 to 1977

Naval Officer. Vietnam Veteran. Leadership Instructor at the US Naval Academy (two years).

EDUCATION:

MBA Degree	DEPAUL UNIVERSITY / UNIVERSITY OF DETROIT	1981
BS (Mechanical Engineering)	US NAVAL ACADEMY	1971

JOSEPH QUINBY

Justin Square Circle
Burlington, Vermont 05402
(802) 254-1254

PRESIDENT & CEO - $100 Million, Multi-State Corporation

- Built emerging electronics, telecommunications, video and appliance distribution company from **$300,000 to $100,000 million in annual sales**.

- Directed purchase and resale of **$1+ billion in merchandise** over 15 years.

- Achieved and maintained **profitability for 15 consecutive years**.

- Negotiated multi-million dollar partnerships with **Sony, Sanyo, Panasonic, Tappan, Litton, BASF**, and other major US and international manufacturers.

- Created a **state-of-the-art distributed PC network** to automate and inventory all core business functions.

PRESIDENT & CEO – Executive Consulting & Management Advisory Firm

- Negotiated $500+ million in financing, lending and credit transactions. Prepared sophisticated financial documentation for M&A, IPO, franchise and lease transactions.

- Acquired substantive industry experience in consumer goods manufacturing, retail sales, wholesale distribution, commercial real estate, industrial products manufacturing and automotive. Client engagements included **North American Phillips, Polaroid, Bendix/Fram, Mazda, Chrysler** and **Bridgestone**.

- Partnered with **Prudential, John Hancock and Metropolitan Life** to market their commercial real estate portfolio. Negotiated a total of $250 million in transactions.

EXECUTIVE MANAGEMENT CONSULTANT - $3 Billion Organization

- **Delivered $3-$5 million in annual operating cost reductions** through redesign of core purchasing and supply chain management processes/systems.

- Partnered with EDS Technology to develop and implement a master health care program that **saved $5+ million** annually.

- Partnered with the US Postal Service to centralize all mail processing operations and **cut over $2.5 million from annual operating budget**.

- Conceived and currently implementing migration from checks to electronic processing with projections to **save $5 million annually**. Introduced technologies forecasted to **improve cash flow $10+ million annually**.

CORE EXECUTIVE QUALIFICATIONS

- Full P&L Responsibility
- Multi-Site Operations
- Sales & Marketing Leadership
- Productivity & Performance

- Strategic Planning
- Product Management
- Corporate Legal Affairs
- Government Relations

- Corporate & Investment Finance
- Domestic & Foreign Business
- Distribution & Warehousing
- Logistics & Supply Chain Management

Outstanding communications, interpersonal relations, negotiations and leadership skills. Extensive M&A, IPO, franchising, alliance and partnership development/transactions experience. Top-flight personnel management skills.

PROFESSIONAL EXPERIENCE:

Executive Management Consultant   1992 to Present
STATE OF VERMONT, Burlington, Vermont

Recruited by senior executive staff to introduce "corporate" business processes, infrastructure and operations into a heavily-regulated government organization. Challenged to drive major cost savings while optimizing productivity, performance and efficiency. On-site at headquarters providing strategic, operating and financial expertise to all 17 operating departments (budgets of $500 million to $1 billion each).

Reinvented virtually all major operating processes to eliminate redundancy, optimize staff performance, improve the allocation of state and federal funds, and build a best practices organization. Created strategic plans to drive future operations, growth and transformation.

President & Chief Executive Officer   1985 to 1992
JQ ENTERPRISES / LIK ASSOCIATES, Providence, RI & Boston, MA

Launched private consulting firm offering management advisory, leadership training, strategic planning, negotiating and operating management services to emerging, turnaround and high-growth organizations. Consulted with Presidents, CEOs, CFOs and other senior executives to resolve core operating issues, implement growth plans, and drive bottom-line revenue and profit growth. Established an extensive network of contacts with bankers, attorneys, accountants and other professional providers to the corporate community. Leveraged relationships to expand client base.

Engagements involved a broad range of functions with particular emphasis on P&L, strategic and marketing plans, cash flow, financial analysis, organizational needs assessment, purchasing, product management, sales, contracts, legal affairs, banking and lending, letters of credit and surplus inventory liquidations.

President & Chief Executive Officer   1970 to 1985
MOORE DISTRIBUTORS, INC., Hartford, CT & Providence, RI

Acquired small entrepreneurial electronics, appliance, telecommunications and video products wholesaler generating $300,000 in annual sales revenues. Built to $100+ million in annual sales. Challenged to drive profitable growth through an aggressive product and market expansion initiative. Held full strategic, operating and P&L responsibility. Negotiated/managed banking, lending and credit relationships. Orchestrated several acquisitions.

Scope of responsibility included all core executive leadership, operating management, sales, marketing, human resources, purchasing, finance, accounting, supply chain management, warehousing, transportation, distribution, technology, customer service and administrative functions. Led a team of up to 200 employees at two large warehouse/showroom/service centers (approx. 300,000 sq. ft.) and four satellite distribution centers throughout the Northeastern US. Managed over 5000 product lines and SKUs.

Captured key customer accounts in the retail chain, independent store, department store, catalog and fulfillment markets. Maintained long-term account relationships averaging 10+ years. Created high-performance sales team. Introduced innovative customer service, support and loyalty programs. Managed ambitious, cooperative, multi-media advertising, publicity and promotional campaigns.

EDUCATION:

BS – Business Administration – BOSTON UNIVERSITY – 1973
Graduate of 100's of hours of continuing management and leadership training.

FERNANDO QUADROS

Piracicaba, 742
Minas de Boa Vista
Sao Paulo, SP – 05843-784, Brazil
Email: fernando@quadros-agri.com

Home/Fax: 55-11-685-1452

Office: 55-11-985-1421

EXECUTIVE PROFILE

General Management / Strategic Planning & Growth / Performance Reengineering / Profit Revitalization
Marketing & New Business Development / P&L Management / Multi-Site Operations / Technology

Over 10 years of senior management experience building new markets, launching start-up ventures and revitalizing non-performing operations throughout Latin America. Combines expert planning, organizational development and leadership skills to produce consistently strong revenue, market and profit results. Decisive, analytical and driven by market trends and competition. Strong cross-cultural communications and liaison experience throughout Latin America, North America and Europe. Fluent in Spanish and Portuguese.

MA – Economics – University of California, Santa Barbara, CA – 1991
BA – Agricultural Administration – Universidad Argentina de la Empresa, Argentina – 1980

PROFESSIONAL EXPERIENCE:

ABC, Sao Paulo, Brazil   1988 to Present

President & Founder

Founded and currently direct an exclusive management consultancy providing strategic, marketing and operating expertise to Brazilian and international corporations. In addition, featured guest speaker at international conferences and symposia including the 1998 Brazilian International Trade Association and the 1998 International Agribusiness Management Association World Congress. Major projects:

- **AAADex International Ltda.** Conducted comprehensive market analysis and developed business proposal to facilitate new market entry for one of Brazil's largest import/export operations (including all General Motors product movement throughout the region).
- **ABC/Government of the State of Parana.** Led multidisciplinary study team in evaluating supply chain and identifying new business opportunities to diversify, expand product offerings and enhance profit performance.
- **The Brazil Group Financial Advisors.** Managed financial, market and operational analysis of Brazilian investment holding (with complete recommendations for economic growth and expansion).

THE XYZ COMPANIES, Brazil & Costa Rica   1991 to 1998

President – XYZ Brazil Ltda. (1996 to 1998)

Senior Executive with full strategic, marketing, operating and P&L responsibility for the start-up of the newest division of XYZ Latin America. Initiated project with a comprehensive assessment of the Brazilian market to identify specific opportunities, recruited/trained personnel, established distribution operations, developed finance and accounting systems, and led the entire marketing/business development function.

- Built new venture from concept to over $4 million in sales within first 11 months. Ranked as the third largest fruit exporter in the country after first year of operation.

Director of Strategic Planning – XYZ Fresh Fruit International, Ltd. (1995 to 1996)

Headquarters position with XYZ Latin America ($1 billion in annual revenues). Reported directly to the President of the Division. Selected for position based upon tremendous success in reorganizing/revitalizing Costa Rican operations in previous position. Initiated the same reengineering concepts throughout other Latin American regions and delivered a 20% overall cost reduction in first quarter.

Focused efforts on the conceptualization, design, development and implementation of innovative business strategies to accelerate performance in both new and existing businesses. Championed two large and successful projects with full supervisory responsibility for cross-functional project teams.

- **Distribution Center Network**. Orchestrated planning and initial development of full-service market distribution centers in Chile, Brazil, Colombia, Argentina, Uruguay, Peru, Ecuador and Venezuela in an aggressive effort to expand market penetration throughout all of Latin America.
- **Packing Conversion Project**. Partnered with a major European plastics manufacturer to develop environmentally-friendly and reusable shipping cartons to replace current packaging. Projected results include a better than 35% reduction in material costs and significant gain in logistical efficiencies.

Director of Pilot Farms – Standard Fruit Co. of Costa Rica (1993 to 1995)

Selected to plan and lead an aggressive reorganization and performance turnaround of this $4.5 million operation. Introduced TQM, SPC, participative management and a series of productivity/efficiency improvement programs. Retrained management teams and launched several technology installations.

- Delivered dramatic performance results including a 40% reduction in workforce, 35% decrease in working capital costs and 38% operating cost reduction within first year.
- Changed management philosophy from a production to market focus, the model for the subsequent reorganization and redefinition of XYZ operations worldwide.
- Co-led project teams at 33 XYZ facilities throughout Latin America to provide leadership for reorganization, management structure redesign, training and bottom-line profit improvement.

Senior Financial Analyst – Standard Fruit Co. of Costa Rica (1991 to 1993)

Intensive 2-year assignment providing in-depth analytical, cost and financial performance data as baseline for business strategy and operations. Participated in technology installation projects, field operations reengineering and initial TQM implementation.

LANUSSE CONSULTING S.H., Buenos Aires, Argentina   1986 to 1988

Management Consultant

Consulted with major production, farming and agricultural operations throughout Argentina, Brazil, Uruguay and Paraguay. Specializations in economic/financial analysis to enhance productivity and profitability, management recruitment and development, and business control systems.

- Retained for one-year assignment as **Technical Director/New Products Manager** for Coprar International Trade S.A. Co-founded "By Genetica Argentina," a business association for the country's six largest embryonic transplant centers. Leveraged global network of contacts to develop foreign markets and launched preliminary stages for project proposals in Moscow and Beijing.

FLAMEX TALAMONI S.A., Buenos Aires, Argentina   1985 to 1986

Chairman & CEO

Recruited to orchestrate the turnaround of a $16.5 million, 400-employee home appliance manufacturer operating under Chapter 11. Initiated a thorough analysis of operations, financial performance, assets, product lines and regional markets. Resolved critical union issues impacting productivity and profitability.

- Maximized real estate value and negotiated asset disposition for strong return on investment.

LAGUNA DEL MONTE S.A., Santa Fe, Argentina   1982 to 1985

General Manager

Promoted from Production Manager to General Manager within first year with full operating, sales and financial responsibility for a 61,000-acre agricultural and livestock farm. Redesigned organizational structure, revitalized process flows, introduced in-house training and strengthened market presence.

- Doubled production yields and increased company profits by an average of 25% per year.

ILDARRAZ S.A., Corrientes, Argentina (**Assistant Farm Manager**)   1981 to 1982

JUDGE R. WILLITS

4343 Macarthur Boulevard NW
Washington, D.C. 2007
Phone: 202-425-5471   Email: judgewillits@globalnet.net   Cell: 202-875-6887

SENIOR EXECUTIVE PROFILE
Senior Business Executive / Senior Corporate Counsel / Business Strategist
Pioneer in the Global Technology Revolution

ABC Executive combining expertise in Strategic Planning, Organizational Leadership, Corporate Law, Finance, Marketing, Tax, Risk Management, Technology R&D, Strategic Partnerships, New Ventures and International Business Development. Decisive and proactive leadership style driven by emerging market and business opportunities. Committed to fostering global growth while protecting the integrity of the corporation.

PROFESSIONAL EXPERIENCE:

SENIOR COUNSEL & DIRECTOR – ABC CORPORATION – US & WORLDWIDE LOCATIONS

High-profile senior management career with one of the world's largest and most prestigious technology companies. Promoted rapidly through a series of increasingly responsible leadership positions as ABC has grown, diversified and globalized. Dual responsibilities as Senior Legal Counsel to the corporation and as a Senior Management Executive with strategic planning, operating, marketing, product, service, HR and P&L responsibility.

Notable Career Achievements:

- **Strategic Planning, Vision & Leadership**. Top Advisor to ABC's Senior Executive Team, Chairman and Board of Directors to drive forward strategic initiatives and innovations in products, technologies, services, business operations and new opportunities. *Contributed to ABC's 20-year growth of better than 400% in revenues and 175% in net profits.*

- **New Venture Start-Up & Leadership**. Member of 4-person Senior Executive Committee credited with the successful and profitable start-up of ABC's in-house financing corporation. *Drove growth from $400 million in volume to over $6 billion with $225 million in annual net income.*

- **New Market & Distribution Channel Development**. Member of 12-person Senior Executive Committee that built ABC's first reseller distribution network, *now a $500 million per annual business unit generating an average 25% net profit margin.*

- **Corporate Partnerships & Public/Private Alliances**. Partnered with leading educational institutions, state and federal government agencies, and private corporations to launch joint technology development and technology training opportunities. *Currently orchestrating over $15 million in new projects and new initiatives across the US.*

- **Corporate Legal Affairs**. Well-respected expert in corporate law with specializations in anti-trust, fair competition, regulatory affairs, risk management, finance and partnership/funding agreements. *Personally structured and negotiated $287 million in corporate contracts over the past 10 years.*

- **International Business Development & Leadership**. Five-year career living in Paris and orchestrating ABC's business development activities, legal affairs and operations in France, the U.K. and other countries throughout Northern Europe. *Demonstrated outstanding cross-cultural and multinational skills in building and nurturing profitable business relationships.*

ABC Career Track & Highlights:

Director of Education Initiatives – Corporate University Relations (1996 to Present)

Senior Management Executive with full strategic planning, operating and P&L responsibility for one of ABC's most critical and most high-profile ventures, a $45 million initiative to build cooperative partnerships with leading educational institutions nationwide. Report through ABC's Strategy Operations Business Unit directly to the Chairman of the corporation.

Challenged to develop and recruit top scientific, engineering and technology talent to ABC, strengthen ABC's image as a technology and employment leader, and spearhead initiatives between ABC and other business/academic partners to further ABC's success in technology development and commercialization. Negotiate large-dollar, multi-partner funding agreements and grants to spread financial risk across all venture partners. Extensive focus on increasing educational and professional opportunities for underrepresented minorities (part of ABC's corporate diversity commitment).

- Negotiated and currently manage successful partnerships with University of Houston, University of Northern Arizona, University of Utah, State of Texas, State of Florida, Lawrence Livermore Laboratories and several other institutions. Currently projecting a pipeline of several thousand qualified scientists, engineers and technologists to join ABC over the next five years.
- Driving forward a number of new development initiatives in data mining, Internet/web-based technology, E-commerce, database structures, speech recognition technology, computer modeling and simulation, global learning, virtual learning and other emerging opportunities. Currently projecting new product commercialization efforts to generate $450 million in new revenue to ABC.
- Spearheaded development and funding for ABC Ph.D. Fellowship in Science, Engineering and Mathematics for Underrepresented Minorities and Women.
- Guest Lecturer at National Science Foundation's Centers of Research Excellence in Science & Technology and Association of Departments of Computer and Information Science & Engineering at Minority Institutions' annual meeting. Key Advisor to the Model Institutions of Excellence.

Senior Counsel – ABC Credit Corporation – Hartford, CT (1989 to 1996)

Partnered with newly-appointed President, CFO and CIO to plan and launch this new venture, transitioning ABC from a third party financing organization to development of an ABC-owned finance company. Directed all staffing, training and infrastructure development functions for new business. Developed training curriculum in UCC and risk management compliance for new legal staff. Created a structured program of credit review, analysis and decision making to guide credit authorizations and reduce ABC's financial exposure. Counseled ABC executives on A/R and risk management.

- Built venture from $400 million to $6 million in outstanding receivables in five years and market presence throughout the US, Europe and Asia. Generated $225 million in earnings after tax.
- Expanded new business model and operations to integrate the financing of non-ABC systems and technologies, further increasing A/R portfolio by more than 41%.
- Established corporate policies for legal affairs, contracts, debt management and risk management.

Senior Counsel – Antitrust & General Law – US Headquarters – Armonk, NY (1986 to 1989)

Corporate HQ position managing sensitive legal affairs, business conduct and business ethics worldwide. Authored a revised edition of ABC's conduct guidelines, partnered with IS to automate handbook and distributed worldwide. Arbitrated issues and cases in dispute. Concurrently, managed ABC's position as a GSA contractor to ensure adherence to government ethics and anti-trust guidelines.

Division Counsel – Data Systems Division HQ – Brooklyn, NY (1984 to 1986)

High-profile position directing corporate legal affairs for ABC's #1 business unit ($750 million in annual revenues). Worked with R&D, engineering, manufacturing, pricing and distribution to introduce business models and practices to reduce ABC's market exposure. Demonstrated products were designed and manufactured to optimize efficiencies and that the company was not anti-competitive.

Division Counsel – National Distribution Division HQ – Manhattan, NY (1983 to 1984)

Designed and implemented business infrastructure for new operating division supporting ABC's evolution into the reseller distribution channel. Established policies and standards for cost, pricing, distribution and transportation. Established innovative go-to-market strategies to spur channel growth and foster cooperation within this competitive marketing channel.

Division Counsel – System Supplies Division HQ – Newark, NJ (1982 to 1983)
Division Counsel – Information Records Division – Trenton, NJ (1979 to 1982)
Assistant Counsel – General Systems Division – Athens, GA (1978 to 1979)

Senior Legal Counsel, Business Advisor and Operating Executive across three of ABC's core operating divisions. Extensive focus on contracts, business issues, vendor relations, customer problem resolution, the transportation of hazardous materials and related remediation projects. Managed legal staff, budgets, policymaking and affairs with outside counsel.

Area Counsel – Northwest Europe – Paris, France (1975 to 1978)
Staff Counsel – ABC Europe – Paris, France (1974 to 1975)

Five-year European career directing ABC's legal affairs in six European countries. Extensive focus on new product development and market launch, business practices, pricing and currency fluctuation issues, and expatriate compensation. Identified local legislation that negatively impacted ABC's operations and negotiated with government officials to win exceptions and in-country concessions.

Senior Attorney – Systems Products Division HQ – Syracuse, NY (1973 to 1974)
Assistant to Vice President & General Counsel – US HQ – Rochester, NY (1972 to 1973)
Attorney – ABC World Trade Corporation – New York, NY (1970 to 1972)

Early career experience across all core businesses and operating divisions of ABC. Specializations in legal issues impacting R&D, product launch, product pricing, international technology and business transfers. Participated in high-profile antitrust suit brought by the EEC and a civil suit by Control Data.

Previous Professional Experience: **White House Fellow & Special Assistant** – **Department of Defense; Attorney** – **General Mills, Inc.**

EDUCATION:

JD Degree UNIVERSITY OF MINNESOTA LAW SCHOOL
BA Degree UNIVERSITY OF MINNESOTA
(*Varsity Football, All-American & Rose Bowl Champion; recruited by St. Louis, NY & Montreal*)

EDWARD P. STEIN

2365 Palisades Crest Drive
Lincoln, Nebraska 68321
659.654.8794

SENIOR MANAGEMENT EXECUTIVE
Start-Up Ventures / Turnarounds & Reorganizations / High-Growth Corporations

Consummate Business Leader with 15+ years operating and management experience. Significant contribution to revenue, performance and profit improvement. Outstanding organizational, team building, communications and crisis management skills.

- **Business Planning & Organizational Leadership**
  Developed business plans and built best-in-class infrastructures to meet diverse organizational, operational and market challenges. Transitioned entrepreneurial ventures into sound business organizations and revitalized non-performing companies. Achieved full consensus and buy-in by senior management team to support new initiatives and internal change.

- **Human Resources & Organizational Development**
  "Tenured" HR Executive with expert qualifications across all core HR, OD and labor relations affairs. Outstanding performance in recruiting and developing top producers, successful managers and senior executives (including CEO) to support ramp-up and accelerated growth. Leadership responsibility for up to 250 employees and 12 management reports.

- **Acquisitions & Divestitures**
  Senior member of numerous successful acquisition and divestiture teams, including current employer's recent acquisition by TYCO International. Consistently successful in facilitating the efficient transfer of personnel, technologies, capital assets and customers to achieve seamless integration. Solid experience in due diligence on "both sides of the table."

- **Downsizings, Turnarounds & Revitalizations**
  Dramatic improvements in operations, cost structures and profitability achieved through reorganization initiatives in both US and international business units. Brings a sense of urgency to drive positive organizational change, process redesign, quality improvement, benchmarking and best practices. Project leader on several high-profile engagements with Ernst & Young.

- **Corporate Financial Affairs**
  Delivered a total of more than $874 million in operating cost reductions to three major corporations. Led budgeting, financial planning, financial analysis, capital spending and cash flow programs. Prioritized expenses to match operating needs.

- **Corporate Legal Affairs**
  Executive liaison to legal counsel on a broad range of corporate, administrative, HR, real estate and contract issues impacting operations in the US and international markets. Strong negotiations, mediation and crisis management performance.

- **Marketing & New Business Development**
  Repositioned company image and services to drive aggressive marketing and new business development efforts. Credited with creating new services delivery methodology that won $15+ million contract against stiff market competition.

- **Information & Telecommunications Technology**
  Astute strategic understanding of leading-edge technologies to leverage resources and optimize productivity.

PROFESSIONAL EXPERIENCE:

Senior Vice President	**ABC INDUSTRIES, INC.** – Nebraska	1997 to Present
Vice President	**XYZ LTD.** – Washington	1993 to 1996
Manager	**AIR PRODUCTS & CHEMICALS, INC.** – Pennsylvania	1985 to 1993
Administrator	**POWER & LIGHT CO.** – Wisconsin	1980 to 1985
Assistant Manager	**NATIONAL ELECTRICAL CONTRACTORS ASSN.**	1973 to 1980

EDUCATION:

BS – Business Management – Nebraska University – Brady, Nebraska – 1973
Executive Management Training – Harvard Business School & University of Michigan

RICHARD WATKINS

587 Amelia Avenue
Dallas, Texas 75212
Email: rwatkins@bigfoot.com

Phone: 584-5755-1425

Fax: 584-548-6588

SENIOR EXECUTIVE PROFILE

**Entrepreneurial Start-Up Ventures / Turnarounds & Revitalizations / High-Growth Organizations
Organizational Leadership / Revenue & Profit Maximization / Information Technology
Strategic Marketing / Competitive Sales Negotiations / Cross-Functional Operating Management**

Results-Driven Business Strategist successful in creating vision, identifying opportunities, building organizations, and delivering strong revenues and profits despite intense market competition. Succeed through combined expertise in strategic development, technological advancement, process design and team leadership. Outstanding analytical, organizational, interpersonal and communication skills. Extensive international experience including Canada, Europe, Latin America and Australia. Expert in change management. Experience across diverse corporate cultures.

Profit Growth:	Delivered $150+ million in profits to the bottom-line over the past nine years.
Revenue Growth:	Led team that closed $100+ million in new contracts/new sales over four years.
Cost Savings:	Delivered total operating cost savings of more than $9 million over six years.

PROFESSIONAL EXPERIENCE:

EXECUTIVE MANAGEMENT CONSULTANT – Chicago, Illinois

Currently consulting with senior executives on core business strategies, organizational development initiatives, performance improvement, alliance development and emerging systems technologies.

ABC TECHNOLOGY CORPORATION – Dallas, Texas
(World leader in design/delivery of advanced IT systems, services and solutions to clients companies worldwide)

Fast-track promotion through responsible senior management positions as ABC experienced years of phenomenal growth. Advanced from early career in IT systems design/project implementation through sales and marketing to more recent executive positions managing several of the company's most critical client engagements. Worked closely with top management of client companies to drive technology development, support strategic objectives, and enable clients' business and financial success.

Held full strategic, operating, technical, staffing, customer relationship management and P&L responsibility for multi-million dollar, multi-year client engagements (averaging 3-4 years each with values up to $250 million annually). Served as both on-site senior executive/general manager as well as corporate consultant. Clients spanned diverse industries worldwide. Specialized in start-up ventures, high-growth organizations and turnaround/change management.

Division Vice President –Tech-Plus Manufacturer, New York, New York (1994 to 1998)

Challenge: *Restructure IT delivery for one of the world's top five technology companies.*

Key executive leading massive IT initiative for one of the industry's largest and most challenging service agreements. Led strategic and tactical implementation to recreate the client's technology infrastructure worldwide while guiding project teams in the redesign/optimization of existing systems and operations.

- Exceeded performance and financial targets each year. **Led team that sold $48 million** in new business to client in just one year. **Added approximately $40 million** to bottom-line over four years.
- Developed and deployed new architecture for client/server infrastructure within three years. Achieved industry standards for systems architecture and facilitated introduction of next generation technology.
- Introduced advanced technologies for Brazilian subsidiary and delivered the first profits ever.

Division President – **XYZ Financial Services Company**, Grand Rapids, Michigan (1990 to 1994)

Challenge:　_Orchestrate a massive turnaround and revitalization of global IT organization._

Accepted challenging opportunity to lead a critical turnaround of IT organization supporting over 15,000 employees throughout Europe, the Far East, Canada, Latin America and Australia. Redefined technology objectives, strategies and service delivery. Completely rebuilt leadership team to focus on core business segments and process improvement initiatives. Pioneered innovative sales, marketing and business development operations. Led a team of 1400+ employees.

- Delivered strong turnaround results and transitioned the operation into a best-in-class organization with outstanding efficiency, productivity and cost performance.
- Restored ABC's credibility with client and **added $110+ million in profits** over five years (on $250 million annual contract). **Improved IT earnings by 62%**.
- Avoided $10+ million in project penalties in Europe.

Division President – **International Wholesale Distribution**, Saginaw, Michigan (1984 to 1990)

Challenge:　_Lead start-up of new IT business for distribution segment of major automotive manufacturer._

Senior Executive challenged to create and manage new IT organization to support three large distribution operations (service parts, vehicle export, corporate QA). Established strategic IT direction, reconfigured operations and organizational structure, and enabled client to strengthen supplier/customer communications.

- Created the technology infrastructure to enable consolidation of inventory and order management for hundreds of millions of dollars in service parts and components.
- **Delivered $8.7 million (12%) in annual IT cost reduction** to client company.

Area Manager – **AAA Health Administration Company**, Killeen, Texas (1982 to 1984)

Challenge:　_Manage the start-up of a new ABC business venture._

Selected by senior management to lead the start-up of a new business unit for administering insurance coverage and cost containment services to large employee groups. Scope of responsibility was significant and included contract administration, staffing, cost containment, member enrollment, claims, medical review and IT operations. Full leadership for six contracts with over $1 billion in total premium value. Led a team of 350+ in three locations.

- Built a successful new organization insuring more than 400,000 persons. Credited with creating organizational infrastructure, operations, sales, marketing, service and support programs.
- **Reduced claims expense $24.7 million** through accurate claims and medical review processes.
- Redesigned business processes and saved one client $1.2 million in administrative costs.
- Negotiated pilot contract, trained sales force and sold two additional corporate customers.
- Developed justification and valuation model for acquisition of insurance subsidiary.

Account Manager – **Major Health Insurer**, Denver, Colorado (1979 to 1982)

Challenge:　_Redesign and enhance IT as part of corporate-wide restructuring/change initiative._

Member of client company's executive staff responsible for guiding development of a completely new IT infrastructure and operating organization.

- **Transitioned IT organization from loss to 20% profit** and surpassed all performance objectives.
- Led efforts to double productivity. Added enhanced communication and electronic interface technologies.

Sales & Marketing Manager, Dallas, Texas (1974 to 1979)

Challenge: *Optimize ABC marketing, sales and business development strategies/performance.*

"Blue Ribbon" Task Force member redesigning business, operating, sales, marketing, technology and client/engagement management processes. Led on-site evaluations of seven key operations and defined specific actions to improve organizational performance and client satisfaction. Created a portfolio of marketing communications, presentation materials and proposal guidelines. Subsequently, represented ABC in direct sales to major health insurance providers, government agencies and international companies.

- Personally negotiated and closed a **10-year, $100+ million contract**, ABC's first major private health contract in six years. Designed sales strategies used to close three other industry contracts.
- Provided technical sales leadership for ABC's initial entry into the US Government market and forged a successful alliance with the US Department of State for design of immigration systems technology.
- Developed methodologies and performance models to manage client productivity using ABC systems.

Prior to 1974:

Promoted through several responsible Computer Systems Design/Engineering and Project Management positions during the early growth stages of ABC. Managed four major IT development and implementation projects, from needs assessment through design, testing and customer implementation.

- Member of core team establishing operations for a project that doubled the size of ABC.
- Delivered a **40.6% improvement in productivity** and a **43.4% reduction in claims processing time** for a large client in upstate New York.
- Managed design team setting the industry standards for group health information systems.

EDUCATION:

BS – Mathematics, Kansas State College

Graduate Studies in Business & Mathematics, University of Missouri at Kansas City

Management Training & Development Courses in business valuation, marketing, organizational learning, process and quality management.

38 Brentwood Avenue
Lubbock, Texas 79416

Phone: 806-584-5788   Email: geneva@bellsouth.net

MANAGEMENT PROFILE

- 10+ years experience in Sales, Marketing & New Business Development.
- 15+ years experience in Product Engineering, Industrial Engineering & Manufacturing.
- 17+ years experience in Team Building, Management & Leadership.
- 17+ years responsibility for Bottom-Line Profit & Loss Performance.

PROFESSIONAL SKILLS PROFILE

- Strategic Planning, Business Planning, Goal Setting & Organizational Leadership
- New Product/Technology Design, Prototype Development, Quality & Production Management
- Presentation, Communication, Negotiation, Persuasion & Dealmaking
- Technology Sales, New Market Development & Customer Relationship Management

---

PROFESSIONAL EXPERIENCE:

Owner/General Manager   1995 to Present
GENEVA NURSERY & GROVES, Lubbock, Texas

Founded and currently operate an Oriental agricultural farm and nursery operation supplying products nationwide. Identified market demand and opportunity, negotiated with product and equipment suppliers, and developed the entire farming operation.

- Built new company from concept into a profitable business generating up to 200% in annual profit margins within a difficult commodities market.
- Structured and negotiated favorable relationships with leading brokers nationwide to advance product sales and market penetration.
- Recognized as a forerunner in the use of Internet technology and E-commerce as a viable marketing and promotional tool to further expand market reach.

Owner/General Manager/Senior Agent   1991 to 1995
HOWARD TUMMONS & ASSOCIATES, Amarillo, Tcxas

Established, built and managed a regional financial products sales organization with representation throughout Texas and Oklahoma. Built new venture from concept to over 15 agents marketing throughout the federal government, postal and military communities.

- Transitioned entrepreneurial venture from start-up to over $2.5 million in annual sales with more than 700 customers.
- Leveraged past relationships to successfully penetrate and establish credibility within intensely controlled and competitive markets.
- Created an action-driven, performance-based training and leadership program to enhance the field performance of sales/marketing team.

District Manager   1989 to 1991
ABC FINANCIAL, GmbH, Kitzingen, Germany

Built & managed German-based sales organization. Challenged to identify market opportunities, develop client relationships and drive long-term revenue growth.

- Delivered 300% increase in sales in both 1990 and 1991. Ranked #1 European producer.

Regional Manager   1985 to 1989
MILITARY MARKETING CONSULTANTS, Frankfurt, Germany

Full strategic, operating and financial responsibility for a real estate sales and marketing organization generating over $20 million annually in revenues.

- Honored as one of only two individuals to personally close $5+ million in annual sales.

Associate Manager – Custom Products   1982 to 1985
Marketing Specialist   1980 to 1982
CORDIS CORPORATION, Childress, Texas

Complete responsibility for R&D, engineering and manufacture of customized products for the Angiography Division. Interfaced with sales/marketing and physicians worldwide to develop innovative medical devices. Trained and directed a professional staff of 28.

- Increased production 300% while reducing lead-time 80% in Custom Products Manufacturing Facility. Surpassed performance, production, quality and cost objectives.
- Established Advanced Product Development Laboratory to enhance R&D. Spearheaded development of eight new products over three years and filed for 23 U.S. patents.
- Established production facilities for two new product lines. Brought projects in on time and 30 % under budget. Resulted in first year sales of $4+ million.

As a Marketing Specialist, responsible for sales and technical leadership in a 14-state region. Marketed to hospitals and rehabilitation facilities, coordinated site installations and provided medical staff training. Personally generated 67% of total EMG sales nationwide. Taught biofeedback courses at the University of Texas, Nova University and Oklahoma State University.

Project Engineer/Product Manager   1979 to 1980
HYPERION, INC., Midland, Texas

Provided sophisticated engineering and technical support for computer-based EEG, EKG and EMG product lines. Redesigned and brought to market new EMG biofeedback product lines.

Signal Officer   1973 to 1978
U.S. ARMY

Fast-track promotion throughout five-year career in high-tech communications and electronics technology. Leadership responsibility for 40 personnel. Honorably discharged.

EDUCATION:

MS – Biomedical Engineering, University of Texas, 1979
   Published abstracts and research papers in Biofluid Mechanics & Biorheology.

BS – Engineering, United States Military Academy, West Point, New York, 1973

EARL HADLEY

5389 S. Henderson Street
Seattle, Washington 98118
Phone: (206) 854-8451   Email: ehadley@bellnet.net

SENIOR EXECUTIVE PROFILE
Senior Operating Executive / Senior Management Executive / Corporate Attorney
Strategic Planning / Marketing & Business Development / Corporate & Investment Finance
Corporate Law & Litigation / Business Process Optimization / Team Building & Leadership

Successful professional career working with top executives of more than 500 companies nationwide to provide operating management and legal expertise across all core business disciplines. Successful in start-up, turnaround and high-growth organizations. Able to identify business opportunities and leverage competencies to drive growth, reduce costs, improve market positioning and strengthen bottom-line financial performance.

Astute and persuasive negotiator. Outstanding team building, mentoring and leadership skills. Analytical with sharp problem solving and analytical capabilities. Thrive in challenging, fast-paced organizations. Executive MBA Candidate.

PROFESSIONAL EXPERIENCE:

Founder / General Manager – Law Offices of Earl W. Hadley   1993 to Present
Co-Founder / General Manager – Haas & Hadley LLP   1996 to 1997

Founded two specialized legal practices providing corporate advisory services to CEO's, COO's and other senior executives across a broad range of industries and on a broad range of topics/business issues. Built new venture from start-up to three locations and 12 employees. Achieved and maintained profitability for six consecutive years. Excellent reputation for ethical performance and integrity.

Serve in the capacity of a **Senior Operating Executive/General Counsel** to client companies providing hands-on leadership in:

* Strategic Planning & Vision	* Operations Management	* Human Resources
* Policies & Procedures	* Cost Control & Avoidance	* Technology
* Growth & Expansion	* Process Design & Analysis	* Capital Assets
* Market Analysis & Positioning	* Banking & Corporate Finance	* Executive Compensation
* Acquisitions & Valuations	* Asset/Stock Purchase Agreements	* A/R & Collections
* Letter of Credit & Intent	* Licensing & Leasing Agreements	* Bankruptcy/Turnaround

Clients range from start-up ventures to $200 million corporations and represent the software development, high-tech manufacturing, industrial manufacturing, consumer products, heavy equipment, transportation, automotive and marine dealerships, services, professional trades industries.

Firm responsibilities include: As **General Manager**, direct all daily and long-term business planning and management functions, staffing, technology systems, and all business process/infrastructure affairs. As **Marketing & Business Development Executive**, lead client development, networking, marketing and client relationship management. As **Principal Attorney**, manage all legal affairs and client representation.

129

PROFESSIONAL EXPERIENCE (*Continued*):

Attorney – Hubert, Schneider & Berringer   1992 to 1993

Strategic management of complex corporate legal affairs involved corporate defense, antitrust and malpractice litigation in the construction, light manufacturing, transportation, heavy equipment, food, credit and professional services industries.   Confidential advisor to CEOs, COOs and other executives on core operating issues, staffing, financial and legal affairs.

Attorney – Dayhoff, Scanlon & Yaegar   1990 to 1992

Specialized in securities fraud and litigation. Excellent experience in critical analysis, case management, research, documentation and litigation.

Attorney – Wilson, Ward, Tyson & Chester   1989 to 1990

Early legal career specializing in construction default and bad business faith.

RELATED EXPERIENCE:

Adjunct Professor in International Business Law and Environmental Law, Western University (1995 to 1997).   Active involvement in design/development of course curricula and instructional materials. Consistently superior instructor ratings.

Supervisor with Trans World Airlines (1986 to 1987). Promoted through increasingly responsible positions to final assignment with direct leadership/supervisory responsibility for 200 personnel.

EDUCATION:

Executive MBA Degree	WASHINGTON STATE UNIVERSITY	June 2000
Juris Doctor Degree	ARIZONA STATE UNIVERSITY SCHOOL OF LAW	1990
BS – Business Administration	MARQUETTE UNIVERSITY	1984

PROFESSIONAL AFFILIATIONS:

Board of Directors, GET Engineering Corporation
Chairman/Member, Environmental Restoration Advisory Board
Honorary Sergeant, Seattle Honorary Deputy Sheriffs' Association
Association of Trial Lawyers of America; Washington Bar Association

JENNIFER A. LANGLEY

11517 Pamplona Boulevard
Boynton Beach, Florida 33437

Home: 561-740-1213
Fax: 561-740-1217

SENIOR FINANCE EXECUTIVE / SENIOR MANAGEMENT EXECUTIVE
CFO / Controller / General Manager / Vice President / Director
Multi-Media Advertising & Public Relations Agencies

Dynamic management career building top-performing organizations that have consistently outperformed revenue and profit objectives. Combines solid strategic planning and general management skills with outstanding corporate finance qualifications. Expertise and achievements include:

- Organizational Redesign & Restructuring
- Financial & Contract Negotiations
- Productivity & Efficiency Improvement
- Team Building & Team Leadership
- Process Redesign & Change Management
- Acquisition Negotiation & Integration
- Budgeting & Cash Flow Optimization
- Information Systems & Technologies
- Banking, Lending & Investment
- Client Relationship Management
- Cost Reduction & Avoidance
- Human Resource Administration

Proficient with Word, Excel, Lotus, AD/AID, Adware, Adman, Grandad, AMS, AMPS and Accpac.

PROFESSIONAL EXPERIENCE:

High-Profile Finance, Operating, HR & Information Technology Management Career with some of the nation's most exclusive advertising and public relations agencies. Recruited to each position based on substantial industry experience, strong organizational leadership and team building skills, and the ability to consistently and favorably improve bottom-line financial results. Maintained an active role in client relationship management with major corporate accounts worldwide (e.g., Land Rover, Ernst & Young, Miller Brewing Company).

Chief Financial Officer / General Manager   1996 to Present
YOUNG & YOUNG, Orlando, Florida
($143 million advertising agency with global market presence)

Senior Finance & Operating Executive with full management responsibility for all agency financial affairs, the entire HR function, daily business operations, administration and all HR/employee benefit programs. Concurrent responsibility for identifying and negotiating acquisitions to further accelerated growth and global expansion. Recruit, train and lead a staff of 121 through 12 managers. Report directly to Partners.

- Delivered strong and sustainable financial gains:
  - 300% increase in interest income following restructuring of core corporate investments.
  - $225,000 increase in agency income through redesign of billing practices.
  - $160,000 operating cost reduction in HR staffing and employee costs.
  - $1 million collected in outstanding past due receivables.
  - $95,000 savings through renegotiation of business leases and agreements.

- Orchestrated agency-wide technology conversion for a dramatic improvement in organizational efficiency, productivity and internal communications. Directed several subsequent system upgrades and enhancements.

- Designed and implemented project estimating, billing and time reporting systems that increased cash flow by better than 32% and improved revenues by $2.4 million.

- Established corporate policies and procedures for cash management, investment management, budgeting, asset management and long-range financial planning.

Director of Finance   1992 to 1996
SMITH & COMPANY, Farmington, Connecticut
($60 million advertising & public relations agency with clients nationwide)

Recruited to revitalize and enhance all internal financial, accounting, auditing, budgeting, HR and administrative affairs as agency continued to grow and expand. Challenged to introduce flexible systems and processes to accommodate growth while providing a stable business infrastructure. Trained and directed a staff of 10. Reported directly to the Chairman.

- Delivered a 39% increase in net profit through restructuring/renegotiating key client contracts.

- Redesigned employee benefit and compensation plans for a $175,000 annual cost savings.

- Restructured collection processes and reduced bad debts by 90%.

- Implemented best-in-class financial analysis, reporting and management systems.

Vice President / Chief Financial Officer / General Manager   1989 to 1992
CROSBY & ASHER, New York, New York
($40 million advertising agency)

Recruited to professionalize high-growth advertising agency, introduce strong management policies, establish operating systems, and improve bottom-line financial performance. Full financial, accounting, HR and administrative management responsibility. Reported to Chairman.

- Upgraded billing procedures and improved revenue collection by 48%. Realigned corporate investments and improved ROI by 7%.

- Redesigned and improved employee benefit programs while reducing annual costs by 32%.

Vice President / Chief Financial Officer   1984 to 1989
THE MINGO GROUP, New York, New York
($60 million advertising & public relations agency)

Planned, staffed and directed all internal business and financial affairs, IS operations, HR and acquisitions. Responsibility for corporate HQ and two subsidiaries. Reported to Chairman.

- Increased investment income returns by 50%. Expanded banking relationships and negotiated corporate lines of credit with favorable terms. Managed IS conversion and upgrade.

Vice President / Chief Financial Officer   1979 to 1984
ASH-LeDONNE, INC., New York, New York
($35 million advertising agency)

Full financial, accounting, HR and IS management responsibility for HQ operations and two subsidiaries. Delivered over $500,000 in cost savings through collection of delinquent accounts and redesign of employee benefit programs. Facilitated measurable productivity improvements.

EDUCATION:

BS – Business Administration – Cornell University

THOMAS J. AVERILL

783 E. Oakwood Terrace
Fort Worth, Texas 76132
Home (817) 542-5488   E-mail: tjaverill@ aol.com   Office (817) 811-5421

CORPORATE FINANCE & TREASURY EXECUTIVE
MBA in Finance & International Business

Hands-on Finance Executive with 20-year career with Pharmaceutical Corporation. Combines expert qualifications in both strategic business/financial leadership and complex operating management. In-depth experience across all core business functions and operations, from International Finance and Technology to HR, Purchasing and Manufacturing. Consistent contributions to bottom-line efficiency, performance, process and profit improvements. Strong leadership, communications, interpersonal relations and organizational development skills. Top-rated analyst.

PROFESSIONAL EXPERIENCE:

PHARMACEUTICAL CORPORATION, Pittsburgh, Pennsylvania   1979 to Present
(Wholly-Owned US Subsidiary of Pharmaceutical AG, German Parent Company. Previously, Pharmaceutical USA, holding company.)

Director – Treasury & Trust Services – Pharmaceutical Corporation (1995 to Present)
Treasurer – TIPCO, Inc. – US Holding Company (1994 to Present)
Director – Treasury Services – Pharmaceutical Corporation (1991 to 1995)
Manager – Treasury Operations – Pharmaceutical USA (1986 to 1990)
Manager – Treasury Operations – Medpay Chemical Corp. – Pharmaceutical Subsidiary (1984 to 1985)
Supervisor – Cash Management – Medpay Chemical Corp. – Pharmaceutical Subsidiary (1979 to 1984)

Twenty-year financial management career with one of the world's leading pharmaceutical, chemical and imaging companies ($9.3 billion in annual revenues). Promoted rapidly based upon consistent contributions to improved operating results, profits, technological advancements and positive organizational change. Member of 14-person Senior Executive Team. Report directly to US Corporate HQ and German Corporate HQ. Career highlights include:

Financial Management & Leadership. Twenty years of progressively responsible experience in operating finance, corporate treasury, cash management, debt management, risk management, foreign exchange, hedging, lease financing, corporate financing and other high-level corporate financial affairs. Currently manage a $2.7 billion defined benefit plan (pension, 401(k), VEBA) and $1.8 billion defined contribution program. Direct professional staff and manage departmental operating budget.

Corporate Financings. Directed financing projects generating over $125 million in funding over the past 10 years. Experience with a broad range of financing vehicles including committed bank back-up lines (at sub-market prices), unsecured bank lines, interest rate swaps, private placements, tax exempt bonds, Euro-currency bonds, synthetic leases, asset acquisitions and others. Pioneered innovative multi-currency netting arrangements and other hedging vehicles.

Information Systems & Technologies. Consultant to IS personnel throughout the Pharmaceutical organization to provide strategic leadership for systems development and systems redesign processes impacting virtually all core operating functions. Led/participated in more than 14 projects (e.g., treasury workstation, credit systems). Currently involved in a massive Y2K initiative.

Cost Containment & Elimination. Championed successful cost reduction initiatives contributing to more than $46 million in total cost savings. Evaluated outsourcing opportunities, introduced advanced information technologies, restructured core business/operating processes and designed performance/workflow efficiencies.

Risk Management & Debt Management. Drove forward an aggressive program to develop best-in-class risk management and debt management processes. Benchmarked against leading US and international companies to enhance internal forecasting and control systems/processes.

Cash Management. Currently working with multinational team to create a portfolio of sophisticated, fully-automated cash management tools for worldwide implementation

Mergers & Acquisitions. Performed complex valuations and performance analyses for more than seven proposed merger and acquisition transactions. Established and currently maintain strong working relationships with Pharmaceutical's investment banking community.

Corporate Leasing. Authored Pharmaceutical's proprietary Master Lease Agreement and Corporate Lease Policy. Structured, negotiated and managed over $450 million in corporate leasing agreements.

Corporate Accepting Operations. Managed $170 million A/R portfolio, A/P portfolio, daily debt and investment accounting, daily cash reporting and corporate credit operations.

Purchasing Management – Upgraded corporate purchasing technologies, expanded internal EDI capabilities, redesigned processes and created Dell's benchmark purchasing model.

Corporate Ethics. Spearheaded US/international corporate ethics and awareness process to clearly define corporate values, market credibility and standards for corporate behavior/performance.

Notable Achievements:

- Orchestrated a politically sensitive downsizing and consolidation in the US Corporate Finance function following 1990 worldwide corporate reorganization (integration of 11 companies with sales of $4.5 billion). Led project team in the automation and integration of all treasury information systems to streamline operations, eliminate redundancy and drive performance improvement. Reduced banking relationships by 70. Generated over $3.6 million in total cost savings.
- Expanded equity investment indexing from 25% to 55% of asset portfolio and improved return on $450 million in corporate investments.
- Launched the start-up of a new internal commercial paper function to more effectively manage cash for operating and acquisition activities. Worked closely with Investor Relations team, corporate bankers and financiers to design credit facilities. Built portfolio to $1.5 billion.
- Directed the start-up of PHARMCO (new US holding company) as a vehicle to reduce debt and tax obligations following 1990 reorganization and re-acquisition of Pharmaceutical corporate name.
- Guided operating finance teams across broad business functions (e.g., co-generation, natural gas, rail, corporate fleet, manufacturing) to better manage/control fixed costs and operating efficiencies.
- Senior Business Advisor to SAP Vision Development & Realization Committee and to Strategic Sourcing Team (managing $100 million in annual energy hedging). Quality Improvement Team Leader for AMEX to MasterCard conversion, delivering over $500,000 in annual cost savings.

MELLON BANK, N.A., Pittsburgh, Pennsylvania   1974 to 1979

International Officer (1978 to 1979)
Assistant International Officer (1977 to 1978)
Divisional Assistant/Credit Analyst (1974 to 1977)

- Lending Officer for trade finance, direct loans, cash management, letters of credit and foreign exchange for corporate client transactions.
- Planned and led International Finance & Service training seminars for clients and bank officers.
- Conducted economic and financial analyses of industries and companies throughout North America, Europe and Australasia.

EDUCATION:

MBA – Finance & International Business – University of Michigan
BS – Finance – Bowling Green State University
Certified Cash Manager (CCM) – Permanent Certification
Pharmaceutical's Senior Managers Development Program
Mahler Advanced Management Skills Program

ALFRED RACINE

19 Homestead Road
Tallahassee, Florida 32308
Phone: 850-588-5451 / Fax: 850-478-5788

SENIOR FINANCE & OPERATIONS EXECUTIVE

Start-Up Entrepreneurial Ventures / Turnarounds & Revitalizations / High-Growth, High-Profit Corporations
Diverse Product & Service Industries, Customer Markets & Geographies Worldwide
MBA Degree

EXECUTIVE QUALIFICATIONS PROFILE:

- Strategic Planning & Organizational Leadership
- Multi-Site Operations Management
- Sales, Marketing & New Business Development
- Budgeting, Forecasting, Reporting & Analysis
- Process Design & Productivity Improvement

- Corporate & Investment Finance
- Mergers, Acquisitions & JV's
- Team Building & Leadership
- Public Relations & Media Affairs
- Manufacturing & Distribution

Charismatic business leader with outstanding presentation, negotiation and relationship management skills. Successful in building synergy between operations, finance and marketing to support strategic business objectives and drive profitable growth. Flexible, customer-focused and driven to improve performance and results.

PROFESSIONAL EXPERIENCE:

THE BANKING GROUP *(privately-owned merchant banking group)*

Partner (1998 to Present)

Recruited to provide strategic, operational and financial leadership to private investor group seeking to acquire a portfolio of small businesses, build value through turnaround and expansion, execute future acquisitions and joint ventures, and position for eventual IPO.

- Following initial acquisition of $6.5 million graphics company, transitioned into principal role as Chief Financial Officer of this 24x7 operation. Challenged to rebuild this 50-year-old company, introduce the first-ever computer technology, and orchestrate a massive change initiative.

- Revitalized the company and currently on target to achieve all operating and financial objectives. Designed new organizational, financial, administrative and operating infrastructure. Launched a series of sales and marketing programs to expand customer base. Restaffed the entire organization.

- Developed and led start-up of two new stand-alone businesses offering technical design services and advanced CAD/CAM and graphics software packages. Currently projecting $1 million in first-year revenues. Launched additional venture offering high-tech digital and laser imaging services forecasted to general $800,000+ within first year.

- Reengineered core printing and production processes, introduced team-based work cultures, and designed incentive systems to drive quality and productivity gains.

HEALTHCARE COMMUNICATIONS, INC. *(#1 privately-held healthcare communications company)*

Senior Vice President / Sector CFO – AAA Network (1996 to 1998)
Vice President of Finance - $95 Million Business Unit (1994 to 1996)
Vice President of Finance - $71 Million Business Unit (1991 to 1994)

Promoted through several increasingly responsible corporate finance assignments to final position as #2 Finance Executive in this $120 million corporation. Instrumental in profitably transitioning company from an early-stage technology venture into a major industry player with market penetration worldwide.

- Member of 7-person Executive Management Team credited with building organization from 3 companies, 30 employees, 12 clients and $18 million in annual revenues to 28 companies, 100+ clients, 200 employees and over $120 million in annual revenues. Major clients included J&J, Marion Merrill Dow, Rhone Poulenc, Abbott and SmithKline.

- Appointed #1 Finance Executive for the largest and most profitable business division ($70 million group of 25 medical communications companies). Held full P&L responsibility for the organization.

- Led a high-profile acquisition and joint venture program to drive business growth. Managed projects from candidate identification through due diligence, financial negotiations and contract transactions.

- Spearheaded a series of internal process improvements to enhance performance and client satisfaction through accelerated growth cycle. Developed both business and financial systems impacting sales, operations, service, reporting, marketing, public relations, technology and more.

- Launched, in cooperation with COO, the start-up of company's initial market entry into several new business lines. Designed financial, budgeting, reporting, forecasting, cost accounting and administrative processes to manage operations in a fast-paced, entrepreneurial environment.

JOHNSON & JOHNSON *($16 billion diversified, global healthcare products corporation)*

Controller – Corporate Marketing Group (1988 to 1991)
Marketing Accounting Manager – Rexall Consumer Healthcare (1986 to 1988)
Financial Manager – National Operations Accounting (1979 to 1986)

Twelve-year financial and operating management career with several major divisions worldwide.

- Full budgeting, controllership and interim IT responsibility for $200+ million in television and print media expenditures. Developed allocation model by type of media and print to optimize spending, advertising, frequency and customer reach. Reduced corporate costs 10%+.

- Directed business, purchasing, administration and financial affairs for start-up, operation and cost restructuring of in-house media buying agency.

- Orchestrated a massive global analysis of all advertising agency assignments and compensation for all J&J brands (200+ brands in 50 countries with 36 agencies worldwide).

- Provided executive-level financial leadership and analysis for International Marketing Group exploring international growth, co-marketing and joint venture opportunities.

- Directed complex financial affairs during transition of core product from prescription to OTC.

- Launched the start-up of two new accounting operations for start-up manufacturing facilities in Puerto Rico and Texas. Developed accounting and workflow processes, implemented technology and recruited/trained staff. Delivered both projects on time and within budget.

MILITARY SERVICE:

Captain – U.S. Army Finance Corps, 1975 to 1979

EDUCATION:

MBA – Business Management & Finance – Temple University, 1983
BSBA – Accounting – Miami University, 1975

HAROLD W. KIDSTON
haroldkidston@hotmail.com

1492 Green Meadow Way
Reno, Nevada 89532

Voice: 832.854.8747
Fax: 841.587.5744

SENIOR CORPORATE FINANCE EXECUTIVE
Industry Roll-Ups, Start-Up Enterprises, High-Growth Ventures & Public Companies
15+ Years' CFO Experience / 10+ Years' Operating Management Experience / MBA Degree

- Corporate & Investment Finance
- Seed Funding & Cash Flow Financing
- Wall Street & Investor Communications
- Information Systems & Technologies
- Strategic Business & Market Planning

- Mergers, Acquisitions, IPOs & Private Placements
- Joint Ventures, Partnerships & Strategic Alliances
- Revenue, Profit & Market Share Growth
- Operations & Profit/Loss Responsibility
- Organizational Development & Leadership

PROFESSIONAL EXPERIENCE:

Founder & Chief Executive Officer   **Vice President**   1997 to Present
AAA DISTRIBUTORS, INC., Reno, Nevada   **STAR FINANCIAL, INC.**, Reno, Nevada

CHALLENGE: Recruited by former advisor to help manage Star Financial, a large private equity investment firm operating as an incubator for emerging, undercapitalized, rapidly growing and turnaround businesses requiring hands-on management and leadership. Challenged to identify strategic investment opportunities, develop innovative business models, conduct due diligence, structure transactions and negotiate private placements.

ACHIEVEMENTS:

- **New Venture Start-Up** – Personally founded and invested in **AAA Distributors, Inc.**, a privately-held business-to-consumer (B2C) direct marketing company focused on continuity-based direct marketing utilizing the Internet, direct mail, telemarketing and television advertising. Created a portfolio of eight consumer-based direct marketing products, orchestrated the entire go-to-market strategy, developed best-in-class financial infrastructure and all financial systems, and launched new venture in 1999.

- **Organizational & Financial Infrastructure** – Created a unique business/finance model leveraging outsourcing to deliver operating expertise in product development, manufacturing, packaging, media placement, inbound/outbound telemarketing, fulfillment and customer service. Operated AAA with only 14 employees and a team of 12 core business partners/vendors. Controlled costs at less than 12% of revenue.

- **Financial Growth Through Strategic Marketing** – Rolled out national direct marketing campaign utilizing media to drive Internet and inbound telemarketing traffic. Generated $4.3 million in sales within first six months and secured 70,000+ web-based/directed customers (majority were continuity-based).

- **Corporate Roll-Up** – Structured and negotiated sale of AAA Distributors to a large international direct marketer to achieve economies of scale, improve operating efficiencies and increase net profitability.

Chief Financial Officer / Director / Founder   1993 to 1996
TOPP, INC., Los Angeles, CA

CHALLENGE: CFO working in partnership with CEO to launch entrepreneurial venture funded with $4 million in private seed capital. Directed all finance, tax, treasury, banking, cash management, accounting, internal auditing, financial reporting, HR, technology and administrative affairs. Held joint P&L and operating management responsibility with CEO. Led a staff of 8-10 and 500+ employees.

ACHIEVEMENTS:

- **Business Strategy** – Pioneered a unique business model to develop a private satellite and Internet-based distribution network (TOPP) to deliver digitally-encoded television commercials and interactive data to broadcasters and cable systems nationwide.

- **New Business Launch** – Provided decisive financial leadership as venture grew from start-up into a publicly-traded company with $120 million market value and 500 employees in 10 US cities, Europe, Africa and Southeast Asia. Delivered $48.7 million in revenues and $4.54 million positive cash flow (EBITDA) in 1996.

- **Corporate Finance & Investor Relations** – Directed road shows with Sutro and Company and Worthheim Shroader (investment bankers), and secured 33 NASDAQ market makers and analyst coverage. Raised $22.5 million through public offering and three private placements.

- **Growth Through Acquisition & Market Expansion** – Achieved tremendous growth through a combination of internal development initiatives and five acquisitions over 18 months. Acquisitions delivered technical expertise and established base of broadcasters, cable systems and advertisers leveraged to the network. Personally directed acquisition planning, analysis, due diligence, candidate review and contract negotiations.

- **Technology Products & Service** – Oversaw the development and deployment of leading edge technologies to support new venture, including the newly-created MPEG-2 digital video standard. Created integrated network comprised of commercial library management system, digital encoders, master file server, satellite uplink, transponders, and network of remote digital video file servers and receivers.

- **Technology Partnerships** – Managed exclusive relationships with McDonalds, WalMart, FritoLay, Coca Cola and other Star 500s converting them from conventional legacy systems to the IndeNet Digital Network.

- **Operational Infrastructure** – Created a unique business, operating and "partnership-type" infrastructure to support cooperative efforts between operating subsidiaries.

- **Financial & Wall Street Performance** – Divested financial interest in the company in 1996 through stock sale and left to pursue investment and new business start-up opportunities. Stock had increased seven-fold averaging 97% per year. XYZ merged with IO Systems (NASDAQ:XZIO) in 1997, manufacturing unit was sold to a European manufacturer and broadcast management software unit sold to MEARS.

Chief Financial Officer / Director   1990 to 1993
XYZ MEDIA GROUP, INC., Los Angeles, CA

CHALLENGE: Joined NASDAQ media company to assist in raising capital and executing business plan. Independent Media was one of the largest pay-per-view program distributors (title fights, concerts, etc.) in the nation. Challenged to build a business and financial infrastructure to support the company's growth.

ACHIEVEMENTS:

- **Revenue & Market Growth** – Member of a five-person senior management team credited with increasing gross event bookings to $100 million. Structured transactions and raised $5.5 million in capital to fund business growth.

- **Financial & Operational Leadership** – Built the entire corporate strategic planning, finance and administrative functions. Established operating policies, processes, technologies and management models. Designed unique financial and revenue guarantee model to structure partnerships between company, event promoters and cable systems.

- **New Market Entry** – Spearheaded company's entry into the pay-per-call audio text business to penetrate the "new media" market which grew to $13.8 million in revenue and $290,000 in earnings in 1992. Built 24x7 service bureau operation utilizing an integrated network of micro and minicomputers to provide automated information delivery with full audio text, voice response, credit card billings, collection and merchant account settlement. Established and utilized long distance carrier status.

- **Corporate Transactions** – Structured and negotiated the profitable sale of the business in 1993.

Chief Executive Officer / Director / Founder   1986 to 1989
ABC COMMUNICATIONS, INC., Denver, CO

CHALLENGE: Excited after my experience working with XYZ and other media and communications companies, and recognizing the obvious and dramatic changes and potential within these industries, co-founded a new media company publishing "video magazines." Held P&L responsibility and directed staff of six.

ACHIEVEMENTS:

- **Seed Funding & Cash Flow Financing** – Raised $1.4 million in private equity funding to launch new venture. Managed two additional private placements and IPO, raising a total of $2.5 million in financing.

- **Strategic Marketing & Business Development** – Personally directed the entire business development and marketing function. Led company from concept through development to 12,000 subscribers and $1.2 million in annual sales revenues in first year. Achieved profitability by end of year one.

- **Strategic Partnerships & Competitive Positioning** – Built company to #1 market share as the largest supplier of "video magazines." Concurrently, structured and negotiated distribution relationships with ABC, National Geographic, ESPN, Sports Illustrated, Better Homes & Gardens and other major corporations and publishers for product sales, fulfillment and distribution functions.

- **Team Building & Cross-Functional Leadership** – Company grew to 30 employees with full in-house creative and production capabilities, inbound and outbound telemarketing, data processing, media purchasing, circulation and direct marketing services.

- **Business Divestiture** – As a result of the decline of consumer market demand, ABC Communications was taken private and eventually closed. All 29 "video magazine" market competitors have since discontinued operations as well.

Financial Consultant – Management Consulting Services Group   1984 to 1986
PRICE WATERHOUSE AND COMPANY, Denver, CO & Anchorage, AK

Recruited by Price Waterhouse's Management Consulting Services Group to help build a local consulting practice focused on emerging businesses, business modeling and capital formation. Evolved into a specialized practice with clients in the media, cable, communications, video and technology industries.

- **Process Improvement & Cost Reductions** – Built, nurtured and managed consulting relationship with U.S. West. Developed financial models and billing account processes which recovered $8.2 million through post AT&T divestiture efficiency improvements.

- **Technology Optimization** – Led major technology system requirements definition studies for both PC network operations and legacy mainframe systems.

- **Policy & Procedure Development** – Introduced policies, processes and productivity improvements for customer service and distribution functions.

Financial Consultant   1981 to 1984
EQUIVEST SECURITIES CORPORATION & TAX PLANNING CONSULTANTS, Anchorage, AK

Provided advisory services and structured tax-advantaged instruments for businesses and high net worth individuals. Specialized in financial consulting, structuring equity placements and marketing private placements. Raised a total of more than $12 million for eight different investment opportunities.

Prior to 1981:

- After college graduation, moved to Alaska for adventure and to seek my fortune. Founded Kidston Builders, a commercial construction company riding the Alaskan oil boom.

- Grew up working and managing family-owned and operated livestock ranch. Instilled a strong work ethic, desire to succeed and entrepreneurial foundation.

EDUCATION: **MBA – Finance** – University of Alaska – 1981
                 BA – Economics – The Colorado College – 1979

ROBERT J. LYONS

Finance, Administration, Information Technology & General Management
BS Degree in Accounting ... MBA Degree

3221 Camelback Avenue
Omaha, Nebraska 68136
Phone (402) 144-8451   Fax (402) 487-2554

FINANCIAL QUALIFICATIONS PROFILE:

Mergers, Acquisitions, Joint Ventures, Partnerships & IPOs. Extensive qualifications structuring, negotiating and transacting multi-party alliances to launch new ventures, expand market penetration, leverage business and financial resources, and improve bottom-line profitability.

Strategic Planning & Business Development. Led high-level strategic planning affairs for start-up ventures, business turnarounds and high-growth organizations. Equally strong experience in marketing, sales and public relations to drive business development and expansion initiatives.

Accounting, Financial Reporting & Financial Planning. Hands-on responsibility for managing broad-based accounting, billing, budgeting, collections, financial analysis, financial reporting and complete administrative support functions for multi-site organizations.

Credit, Lending & Financial Transactions. Managed commercial financing, leasing and credit transactions in the capital equipment, telecommunications and computer industries. Extensive qualifications in financial analysis, review, risk assessment and ROI/ROA/ROE performance.

Information Technology. Team Leader for numerous technology installations to automate complete financial, administrative, marketing, contracting, purchasing and related business support functions. Managed projects from initial needs assessment through vendor sourcing, acquisition and implementation.

PROFESSIONAL EXPERIENCE:

Division Manager / Business Manager   1996 to 1988
NATIONAL MEDICAL AND RESEARCH CENTER, Omaha, Nebraska

Created and led strategic planning, financial, accounting, administrative, contracting and joint venture/partnership operations for the start-up of a new entrepreneurial division launching new ventures in emerging health care markets for this world renowned medical research center. Developed business plans and directed operating budgets for eight distinct profit centers. Extensive financial analysis, financial planning, forecasting, ROI projections and risk assessment responsibility.

- Identified opportunity, structured, negotiated and closed a joint venture with Central Health, the largest non-profit hospital system in the region. Created a Limited Liability Corporation (LLC) to manage and market community-based health care programs. Appointed to Board of Managers.

- Created a portfolio of financial models, indices and analyses to monitor/evaluate performance of all new ventures, new products and new service delivery programs.

- Collaborated with business partners to create a new respiratory care company. Won 21 contracts with projections for an additional 12 contracts by end of year two ($2+ million in revenue).

- Established program to facilitate new business development opportunities in research, case management and clinical services. Delivered $4 million in first year revenue.

- Negotiated joint venture with medical technology company that included a valuable insider equity position prior to IPO.

140

PROFESSIONAL EXPERIENCE (*Continued*):

Executive Director   1994 to 1996
OMAHA HEALTH ALLIANCE, Omaha, Nebraska

Chief Executive recruited to newly-created management services company providing centralized business systems for seven regional hospitals. Fully responsible for the strategic and tactical leadership of all accounting, financial reporting, payroll, billing, banking, credit, budgeting, business development and public relations functions.

- Created the alliance's first-ever, fully-integrated regional business organization with centralized strategic planning, financial, administrative, human resources, purchasing and contracting services. Established operating policies and goals. Aligned all financial and personnel resources.

- Integrated purchasing, vendor sourcing and inventory planning/control functions, implemented JIT and projected a 50% reduction in inventory carrying costs.

Corporate Director   1989 to 1994
ALLIED MEDICAL CENTERS, Denver, Colorado

One of 6 senior business executives credited with the successful growth and profitable expansion of this multi-site service organization. Scope of responsibility was broad-based with an emphasis on marketing, new business development, information technology and all supporting financial affairs. Worked cooperatively with President/CEO to guide strategic planning and long-term market growth.

- Expanded from two sites and $3.3 million in annual revenue to six sites, 125 employees and over $10 million in annual revenue (including 40 professionals). Achieved 214% revenue growth over five years (averaged 21% annually). Recognized as the largest and most successful multi-site medical service provider in the region.

- Led the computerization of the entire business organization (e.g., accounting, finance, billing, marketing, customer management, human resources, capital equipment).

- Negotiated innovative alliances with business partners to create a first-of-a-kind business services infrastructure providing comprehensive administrative, IS, budgeting/financial and operating management expertise throughout the clinical care network.

- Key player in the successful negotiation, merger and integration of AMC with a competing organization and its subsequent IPO. Managed complex deal structuring and financial transactions.

Account Representative   1987 to 1989
AMERICAN FINANCIAL SERVICES, INC., Kansas City, Missouri

Managed over $18 million in commercial leasing transactions (emphasis in advanced information and telecommunications industries). Traveled to customer and dealer sites nationwide.

Credit Analyst   1986 to 1987
THE WESTERN GROUP / EQUIPMENT FINANCING, INC., Overland Park, Kansas

Hands-on responsibility for commercial loan processing, credit analysis, risk review and packaging.

EDUCATION:

BS Degree – Accounting	California State University, Fullerton, California	1998
MBA Degree	University of North Dakota – Grand Forks, North Dakota	1988
BS Degree – Business	Southwest Missouri State University – Springfield	1984

JASON ROBERTSON

823 W. Kentucky Avenue
Washington, D.C. 20015

Home: 202.849.5470   martin.patnick@aol.com   Office: 202.859.4154

SENIOR CORPORATE FINANCE EXECUTIVE
Technology / Insurance / Transportation / Financial Services / Entertainment Industries
MBA in Finance – Columbia University

Consummate CFO, Treasurer & Finance Executive with 15+ years experience building and directing best-in-class corporate finance organizations. Successful in partnering finance with operations to drive long-term gains in business performance, revenues, market share and bottom-line profits. Strategic analyst, planner and problem solver with keen negotiation, transaction and dealmaking skills. Consistently effective in optimizing capital, reducing risk and increasing corporate liquidity.

PROFESSIONAL EXPERIENCE:

ROCK GROUP HOLDINGS, INC., Washington, D.C.
Executive Vice President & Chief Financial Officer (1998 to Present)
Senior Vice President & Chief Financial Officer (1974 to 1998)
Vice President (1972 to 1974)
Treasurer / Assistant Treasurer (1969 to 1972)

Fast-track promotion through a series of increasingly responsible senior-level Corporate Finance and Treasury positions as Rock grew and diversified from a specialty computer and P&C insurance company into one of the nation's largest insurance corporations. Direct a professional staff of up to 20. Travel worldwide on behalf of the corporation. Report directly to CEO.

> *Key player in driving Rock's revenue growth from less than $400 million to $3.3 billion with $400 million in profit and an investment portfolio valued in excess of $10 million.*

Scope of leadership responsibility was diverse and included:

- **Treasury** – Built a best-in-class corporate treasury function where none had previously existed.

- **Cash Management** – Designed and implemented a strict cash management policy that increased operating profit of core business by 23.5%.

- **New Venture Start-Up** – Spearheaded development of new life insurance company that grew from concept to over $71.4 million in assets and new technology-based (artificial intelligence) workers compensation that delivered $95.9 million in annual revenues.

- **Credit/Deal Analysis** – Led sophisticated financial reviews and analyses to determine the potential fit and financial benefit of a portfolio of corporate development initiatives.

- **Credit & Collections** – Realigned and expanded credit organization with a solid strategic plan to ensure adequate capitalization.

- **Budgeting** – Provided strategic leadership for the development of business plan, operating budgets and capital allocations.

- **Contract Management** – Successfully negotiated contracts and resolved contract disputes for a transaction involved 30+ partners and $1+ billion in exposure.

- **Investor Relations & Communications** – Primary spokesperson to the private, bank and venture capital investment communities (including road show presentations).

Led the corporation's aggressive investment finance program which included hundreds of major transactions and raised a total of more than $5 billion in public, private and bank financings:

- **Initial Public Offering** – Led $150 million IPO of common equity to refinance approximately $1 billion in the public and bank debt markets.

- **Debt Refinancing** – Initiated capital enhancement program, issued $200 million of common equity, and refinanced $650 million in public debt and $240 million in bank debt.

- **Leveraged Buy-Out** – Led LBO to transition from public to private company (returned to public ownership through subsequent IPO).

- **Reverse Merger** – Merged the 3rd largest title insurance company (Lawyers Title) into the 6th largest (Commonwealth Land Title) and created over $400 million in asset value for Rock.

- **Divestitures** – Structured, negotiated and closed the sale of four corporate holdings, $45 billion in total transactions for over $21 million in capital gains. Transactions involved sales to GE Credit, Travelers Insurance and several other major corporations.

- **Acquisitions** – Identified market opportunity, identified candidate and led negotiations and final transaction for acquisition of title company (foundation for Rock's tremendous growth and expansion over the next 10+ years).

Represented the corporation in a series of high-profile external transactions across a broad range of industries (e.g., biotechnology, Internet and computer technology, transportation, entertainment, banking/financial services). Major deals included:

- **Corporate Buy-Out** – Analyzed and structured buy-out of the Walt Disney Company, a transaction that laid the foundation for eventual sale to Disney for $60 million cash gain.

- **Investment Funding** – Negotiated $10 million venture capital-type investment in Symbol Technologies which generated $1 billion gain over 15 years.

- **Debt Restructuring** – Restructured Tiger International's debt position and transitioned an unprofitable investment into a high-profit gain following the company's sale to Federal Express.

EDUCATION:

MBA – Finance – Columbia University
BA – Economics – New York University

BOARD OF DIRECTOR APPOINTMENTS & PROFESSIONAL AFFILIATIONS:

Current	Past
Prudential Group Holdings, Inc.	Symbol Technologies, Inc.
Global Land Financial Group	Tiger International, Inc.
AAA Institute Council	Frank B. Hall
Juilliard School Dance	Imperial Corporation of America

RONALD LOCKWOOD

47 Plymouth Avenue
Duluth, Minnesota 55811

Phone: (218) 245-4712   Email: ronlockwood@bellnet.net   Cell: (218) 845-8745

INVESTMENT MANAGEMENT & FINANCIAL SERVICES EXECUTIVE
Cross-Functional Expertise in Business Development & Investment Portfolio Management
Darden MBA Degree

Talented deal-maker, negotiator and portfolio manager with a reputation for honesty and integrity. Successful in evaluating business and investment opportunities, quickly understanding companies and their markets, and making sound and profitable investment decisions. Equally strong performance in new business development, growth and diversification. Mature business planning and leadership skills.

Licenses: Series 7, Series 63, Minnesota Real Estate Broker
Computer: Proficient in Factset, Baseline, Microsoft & Lotus Applications
Awards: Top Investment Broker, Greater Minneapolis Real Estate Board, 1991-1992

PROFESSIONAL EXPERIENCE:

LEXINGTON INVESTMENT MANAGEMENT, Duluth, MN   1998 to Present
Vice President
Equity Research Analyst – *Financial Services, REIT's, Utilities, Gaming & Lodging Sectors*

Recruited from Rockwell based on strong track record in stock selection and company valuation. Joined 6-person senior portfolio management team responsible for $6 billion in market capitalization (Lexington Small Cap Growth Fund). Directly responsible for buy/sell transactions on a sector-by-sector basis ($200 million of total portfolio). Maintain a highly-visible profile with companies, investors, fund managers, financiers and customers.

- Reconfigured stock portfolio, divested non-performers and repositioned for an immediate improve in portfolio value.
- Expanded investments in the financial services, real estate, Internet technology and other growth markets to diversify portfolio and optimize current market conditions.
- Identified and invested in several severely under-valued companies with conservative projections indicating a 15% growth rate.

ROCKWELL INVESTMENT ADVISORS, Rochester, MN   1996 to 1998
Vice President
Senior Equity Research Analyst – *Financial Services & REIT Sectors*

Senior Investment Executive directing all investment and financing activities for Rockwell's Galaxy Mutual Funds, a $2 billion financial services portfolio (including $75 million REIT). Challenged to transition the portfolio from steady to fast-track growth to accelerate long-term value.

- Maintained an active role in structuring, trading and managing stocks to yield maximum results. Worked one-on-one with portfolio managers to monitor changing trends, modify investment strategies and strengthen market value. Delivered consistently strong investment returns (up to 22% on specific M&A transactions).
- Initiated coverage and performed original, fundamental research on select financial sector names for addition or deletion to the portfolios of Rockwell's Galaxy Mutual Funds. Designed and maintained proprietary valuation/earnings models.
- Maintained a dynamic dialogue with senior management of Rockwell's top 50 holdings, including regular company, customer and marketplace visits.

MASTER SECURITIES INTERNATIONAL, Boston, MA   1994 to 1995
Senior Associate – *Real Estate Investment Banking/Mortgage Backed Sales*

Top-ranked MBA Graduate recruited by this well-established financial services corporation to participate in the start-up of a new business division (with $1 billion in internal capital funding). Gained tremendous experience across the entire business development spectrum – marketing, deal origination, price negotiations, financial modeling and deal rating. Extensive client interface.

- Designed and built preferred equity financial model for analyzing the firm's equity participation level in the restructured credit facilities of public REIT's. Concurrently, developed and managed a program for contacting and securing related financing transactions.
- Prepared presentation to the ratings agencies for a $100 million issue of secured notes.
- Completed extensive training in the fixed income analytics offered by the Bloomberg System and in the fundamentals of mortgage pass through securities and mortgage derivatives.

MONTICELLO-DARDEN FUND, Charlottesville, VA   1993 to 1994
Portfolio Manager

Selected from a competitive group of candidates to co-manage the University of Virginia's $1 million endowment fund. Worked with three other portfolio managers to define fund strategy, research securities and execute investment decisions. Presented results to University & Darden School Trustees. Managed within stringent regulatory and compliance reporting requirements.

- Achieved 10.2% annual returns, exceeding the fund's comparative bogey by 875 basis points.
- Ranked as the #1 performer in fund management and growth for five consecutive years.

THE CALDWELL COMPANY, INC., Boston, MA   1992 to 1993
Senior Investment Consultant – *Investment Brokerage Division*

Senior Executive directing all business development activities and sales transactions for the Investment Brokerage Division of this large commercial real estate services organization. Managed high-profile, high-dollar client relationships in cooperation with the firm's sales team.

- Closed over $2.1 million in transactions. Disposed of $1 million in non-performing portfolios.

THE NILES COMPANY, INC., Boston, MA   1983 to 1992
Senior Vice President (1991 to 1992)
Vice President (1988 to 1991)
Commercial Real Estate Agent (1983 to 1988)

Promoted through increasingly responsible positions to final assignment directing a team of 13 sales professionals for this commercial real estate firm. Introduced client relationship management strategies to drive market growth and expansion. Member of 7-person Management Committee.

- Led team to close over $50 million in business in 1990-1991 and $70 million in 1991-1992.
- Negotiated, structured and executed $30 million in transactions in 1991 with a leading national retailer and an international toy manufacturer.
- Transacted a $40 million joint venture, the largest land deal south of Boston.
- Launched the start-up of a successful and profitable investment brokerage division.

EDUCATION:

UNIVERSITY OF VIRGINIA / DARDEN GRADUATE SCHOOL OF BUSINESS
MBA – May 1996

TRINITY COLLEGE – Hartford, CT
BA – Economics & Political Science – 1985

MARTIN L. PATNICK

823 W. Kentucky Avenue
Washington, D.C. 20015
martin.patnick@aol.com

Home: 202.849.5470

Office: 202.859.4154

SENIOR EXECUTIVE: Public & Private Financing, Debt & Equity Financing, IPOs, M&As, LBOs

INDUSTRY EXPERIENCE: Banking, Financial Services, Insurance, Biotechnology, Computer & Internet Technology, Transportation, Entertainment

CREDENTIALS: MBA in Finance – Columbia University

Financier, Dealmaker & Transactions Specialist with more than 15 years experience structuring, negotiating and funding sophisticated, multi-party transactions totaling over $5 billion in investment. Talented negotiator able to build rapport and bring transactions to closure despite differing objectives of each partner.

Chief Financial Officer & Corporate Treasurer with excellent qualifications in all core corporate financial management functions with an emphasis on cash management and liquidity, risk management, treasury, transactions analysis, contracts and investor communications. Strong team builder and leader.

PROFESSIONAL EXPERIENCE:

Executive Vice President / Investment Officer / CFO / Treasurer
ROCK GROUP HOLDINGS, INC., Washington, D.C.

Member of a 7-person Senior Executive Team leading this corporation's growth from $400 million to $3.3 billion in annual revenues and an investment portfolio of $10+ million.

Initiated and led an aggressive **corporate development and investment finance** program which included over 500 major transactions. Raised a total of more than $5 billion in public, private and bank financings. Personally led all major road show presentations and investor relations/communications. Major transactions included:

- **Initial Public Offering** – Led $150 million IPO of common equity to refinance approximately $1 billion in the public and bank debt markets.

- **Debt Refinancing** – Initiated capital enhancement program, issued $200 million of common equity, and refinanced $650 million in public debt and $240 million in bank debt.

- **Leveraged Buy-Out** – Led LBO to transition from public to private company (returned to public ownership through subsequent IPO).

- **Reverse Merger** – Merged the 3rd largest title insurance company into the 6th largest (Commonwealth Land Title) and created over $400 million in asset value for Rock.

- **Divestitures** – Structured, negotiated and closed the sale of four corporate holdings, $45 billion in total transactions for over $21 million in capital gains. Transactions involved sales to GE Credit, Travelers Insurance and several other major corporations.

- **Acquisitions** – Identified market opportunity, identified candidate and led negotiations and final transaction for acquisition of title company (foundation for Rock's tremendous growth and expansion over the next 10+ years).

Concurrently, directed a series of **capital financing and investment** programs across numerous industries to diversify Rock's asset portfolio:

- **Corporate Buy-Out** – Analyzed and structured buy-out of the Walt Disney Company, a transaction that laid the foundation for eventual sale to Disney for $60 million cash gain.

- **Investment Funding** – Negotiated $10 million venture capital-type investment in Symbol Technologies which generated $1 billion gain over 15 years.

- **Debt Restructuring** – Restructured Tiger International's debt position and transitioned an unprofitable investment into a high-profit gain following the company's sale to Federal Express.

As CFO & Treasurer, provided strategic, business planning and financial leadership during periods of accelerated and high-profit growth, turnaround and market repositioning. Staffing responsibility for up to 20 professionals with worldwide responsibility. Report directly to CEO. Substantial experience:

- **Treasury** – Built a best-in-class corporate treasury function where none had previously existed.

- **Cash Management** – Designed and implemented a strict cash management policy that increased operating profit of core business by 23.5%.

- **New Venture Start-Up** – Spearheaded development of new life insurance company that grew from concept to over $71.4 million in assets and new technology-based (artificial intelligence) workers compensation that delivered $95.9 million in annual revenues.

- **Credit/Deal Analysis** – Led sophisticated financial reviews and analyses to determine the potential fit and financial benefit of a portfolio of corporate development initiatives.

- **Contract Management** – Successfully negotiated contracts and resolved contract disputes for a transaction involving 30+ partners and $1+ billion in exposure.

EDUCATION:

MBA – Finance – Columbia University
BA – Economics – New York University

BOARD OF DIRECTOR APPOINTMENTS & PROFESSIONAL AFFILIATIONS:

Current	Past
Prudential Group Holdings, Inc.	Symbol Technologies, Inc.
Global Land Financial Group	Tiger International, Inc.
AAA Institute Council	Frank B. Hall
Juilliard School Dance	Imperial Corporation of America

MICHAEL NAVARRO

841 Inglewood Drive
Asheville, North Carolina 28805
Phone: 828-874-4711   Email: mikenavarro@aol.com

INTERNATIONAL BUSINESS & INVESTMENT EXECUTIVE
MBA (General Management) & BS (Agricultural Economics) – Cornell University

Talented business executive, marketer and "dealmaker" with extensive experience throughout the North American and Latin American markets. Broad range of industry and investment experience, from advanced telecommunications and information technology to agricultural and forestry commodities. Strong leadership talent. Expertise includes:

- Investment Portfolio Management
- Risk & Investment Analysis
- Corporate Finance & Asset Management
- Financing & Project Funding

- Marketing & New Business Development
- Mergers, Acquisitions & Partnerships
- Strategic Business Planning & Management
- Relationship Management

Bicultural and bilingual in English and Spanish. Conversational in French and Italian. US citizen.

PROFESSIONAL EXPERIENCE:

INDUSTRIAL MATERIALS, LLC, Mt. Kisco, New York   1997 to 2000
(*InMat, a US private equity firm, founded by Michael Kearney, specializing in creating value in international commodity-related businesses.*)

Vice President – Investment Management

Recruited to leverage investment opportunities in the international agricultural and forestry commodities markets, including wood products manufacturing and distribution businesses worldwide. Teamed with other companies to create and sustain value, identified global market opportunities, and developed strategy for US marketing of Central American products. Directed entire investment oversight function. Reported to CEO.

- Increased corporate value 400% over two years.
- Directed complex financial planning and modeling effort for successful IPO of subsidiary company.

EUROPEAN PRIVATE INVESTMENT CORPORATION, Washington, DC   1995 to 1997
(*EPIC, with assets of $3 billion, sells project financing, equity funding & political risk insurance to support US private investment in 140 emerging economies worldwide.*)

Vice President for Management & Chief Information Officer

Member of 4-person Senior Executive Team reporting directly to the CEO. Responsible for the leadership of the entire administrative infrastructure and all information technology functions of the corporation.

- Turned around a massive, troubled, 2-year, $9 million technology investment. Reorganized a team of 50 professionals, evaluated issues impacting user functionality, and re-architected software into an object-oriented, multi-tier, client-server framework. Transitioned project ownership from contractor to EPIC, developed implementation plan and staffed with an effective management team to bring to completion.

VELASCO, S.A., Zamora, Ecuador   1987 to 1995

(Prestigious Eucadorian holding corporation with 45 years in the information technology business and numerous subsidiaries, including an internationally renowned software house. Distributor for Microsoft, NCR, Sybase & Motorola.)

President & CEO – InteckR, Inc. – USA (1990 to 1995)

Senior Executive leading the successful start-up of an independent US subsidiary of Velasco to serve as an early point of contact to identify trends, source technologies, and provide value-added programming and software development services. Negotiated a complex transaction with Scottish company to obtain US marketing rights for high-end document retrieval technology. In addition, negotiated reseller relationship with SUN Microsystems.

- Created and launched an integrated electronic document and workflow management solution as an initial source of revenue. Generated $9 million over first 3 years.
- Devised strategy to strengthen long-term viability by transitioning company from a product reseller to a co-developer and marketer of vertical COBIS solutions (Microsoft award-winning document management, workflow automation and bank automation product).

President & CEO – Velasco S.A. – Ecuador (1989 to 1990)
Vice President for Corporate Administration & Development – Velasco S.A. – Ecuador (1987 to 1988)

High-profile executive assignment managing one of Ecuador's most successful and most profitable technology companies. Led a team of 200+ employees.

- Conceived and launched a corporate development strategy which transformed the organization from a hardware importer to an exporter of its own software.
- Spearheaded an aggressive business development initiative. Acquired software company, won exclusive marketing rights for Apple Computer in Ecuador, and negotiated numerous new distributorships with Oracle, NCR and other major technology organizations.
- Orchestrated a complex reorganization of corporate holdings and subsidiaries operations into a more efficient corporate holding structure with centralized finance, administrative and legal functions.
- Resolved a long history of collective bargaining issues through critical changes in personnel attitudes and corporate cultures/cooperation.
- Concurrently served as CFO with full financial responsibility. Led design and implementation of an automated, multi-currency, multi-company accounting system to better control operations in a highly inflationary environment.

MACOSA, S.A., Quito, Ecuador   1978 to 1987

(Velasco Group's 200-employee flagship company with $10 million in annual revenue. Developer/marketer of complete computer solutions and exclusive Ecuadorian distributor for NCR. COBIS, its banking automation software, earned a Microsoft product excellence award and is now Latin America's leading client-server banking system.)

General Manager (1986 to 1987)
Director – Financial & Administration (1985)
Manager – Customer Service (1984)
District Manager – Guayaquil Branch (1981 to 1982)
Manager – Management Information Systems (1980)
Systems Engineer (1978 to 1980)

Fast-track promotion from entry-level professional position to final assignment with full P&L responsibility for company operations throughout Ecuador. Honored with the 1986 NCR Corporation's "*Chairman's Award*" for outstanding performance. Excelled in systems/technology development, sales/marketing leadership, key account relationship development and operating/business management.

GERARD MONTEGUE

1650 Avenue de la Parc, Apt. 52
Montreal, Quebec H36 2R1

Phone (514) 231-6545   Fax (514) 231-6544

FOOD & BEVERAGE / HOSPITALITY / RESTAURANT MANAGEMENT

Fifteen years experience in Food & Beverage Management for exclusive hotels, restaurants and conference centers. Excellent qualifications in planning, marketing, budgeting, expense control, staffing, training and quality management. Contributed to significant revenue gains and cost reductions.

Multinational experience. Fluent in English, French and Arabic. Worldwide travel throughout the U.S., Canada, Turkey, Cyprus, Kuwait, United Arab Emirates (Dubai), Saudi Arabia, Bahrain, Egypt, Philippines and Switzerland. Permanent Resident of Canada.

Certified Food & Beverage Executive (CFBE), 1992
U.S. Educational Institute of American Hotel & Motel Association

PROFESSIONAL EXPERIENCE:

Conference Center Manager   1994 to 1996
BAHRAIN CONFERENCE CENTER / HYATT REGENCY HOTEL - Bahrain

Recruited to plan and direct the start-up of the country's first-ever conference center at this 5-star hotel complex. Managed all pre-opening activities (e.g., operations, equipment, staff recruitment, training) and a high-profile marketing and business development effort. Responsible for F&B operations, banquet and conference management, VIP relations, contract negotiations, event planning/logistics, kitchen operations, and all customer service functions.

- Built the Center from concept into a 22-employee operation generating over US$350,000 in revenues within first three months. Concurrently, managed 70 contract staff.
- Created policies, procedures, standards and performance goals.
- Designed budgeting, expense control and month-end reporting methods.
- Trained both permanent and contract staff in quality-based service.

NOTE: Resigned position in December 1996 to relocate to Canada.

Assistant Food & Beverage Manager   1990 to 1994
HASSAN HOTELS & RESORTS MANAGEMENT COMPANY - Dubai

Joined Hassan following their acquisition of the 5-star International Hotel of Dubai (previous employer). Working in cooperation with F&B Director, managed all operations for four on-site outlets, room service, and outside catering and banquets. Managed a permanent staff of 125 and up to 70 contract personnel. Authorized expenditures for US$3 million annual purchasing budget.

Held concurrent management responsibility for all on-site catering for the Head of State at the Dubai Royal Palace (Hassan held exclusive contract). Personally planned, staffed and managed events for worldwide political leaders and visiting dignitaries.

- Increased F&B revenues to US$750,000 per month. Expanded operations and service offerings, introduced operating/quality standards, and delivered consistently superior customer service.

*NOTE: Joined Hassan in 1990 after one year as **Restaurant Manager with International Hotel of Dubai** (acquired Hilton International in 1989).*

Acting Restaurant Manager   1986 to 1989
HILTON INTERNATIONAL - Abu Dabi
(5 star hotel with 406 rooms/suites, ballroom, 13 meeting rooms with 1150 guest capacity, 3 restaurants, tea lounge, 2 executive floors and complete sports/recreational facilities)

Full operating and P&L responsibility for management of La Palma Restaurant. Responsibility was diverse and included budgeting, staffing, training, kitchen operations, purchasing, inventory management, menu planning, customer service and quality control. Managed 20 employees.

- Built La Palma into the #1 restaurant in Abu Dabi with over 162,000 covers annually (approximately US$2.5 million).
- Achieved or surpassed all food, beverage and labor cost controls/budget goals.

Assistant Maitre D'Hotel   1985 to 1986
LE SOVERIEGN - Kuwait
(5 star hotel with 377 rooms/suites, 3 restaurants, tea lounge, 900 cover banquet operation, and sports facilities)

Second-in-command of all F&B operations throughout this metropolitan hotel. Focused efforts on improving service standards, designing operational and quality controls, and identifying/capturing cost reductions. Trained and supervised a staff of 24.

- Generated market's highest percentage of repeat clientele compared to similar F&B operations.

Previous Professional Experience (1979 to 1985) at exclusive, 5-star hotels including **Holiday Inn Pyramid** (Cairo), **Marriott Hotel** (Cairo) and **Massarah Intercontinental** (Saudia Arabia). Promoted rapidly through a series of increasingly responsible F&B service positions.

EDUCATION:

Graduate - Food & Beverage Management Program, 1993
Ecole Hotelier de la Societe Suisse des Hoteliers, Lausanne, Switzerland

Graduate - Hospitality Management Diploma, 1993
Educational Institute of American Hotel & Motel Association, Michigan, US

Graduate - Food & Beverage Management Specialization Program, 1989
Educational Institute of American Hotel & Motel Association, Michigan, US

CONTINUING PROFESSIONAL EDUCATION:

Completed extensive continuing professional education throughout career. Course highlights include:

- Time Management for Executives, 1994
- Sales & Marketing Promotions, 1993
- Managing Computers in the Hospitality Industry, 1992
- Hospitality Purchasing Management, 1992
- Action Centered Leadership, Kuwait Hotels Company, 1992
- Hospitality Human Resources Management, 1990
- Customer First Program, Bahrain Hotels Company, 1989
- Train the Trainers Course, Hilton International, 1989
- Organization & Administration, 1989

PROFESSIONAL AFFILIATIONS:

Associate Member, Hotel Catering & Institutional Management Association - U.K.
Chef de Table, Confrerie de la chaine des Rotisseurs - Kuwait

JONATHAN R. ANDRESS

PSC 144293, Box 1383833
APO, AE 09724
(381) 382-8873

SENIOR EXECUTIVE PROFILE
International Business, Economic Development & Government Affairs

Career Diplomat with outstanding leadership credentials, an in-depth knowledge of international trends and events, astute strategic planning and visioning skills, and the ability to build consensus across diverse political, social, cultural, economic and national lines. Maintain the highest level of personal and professional integrity. TS/SBI (top-level) US security clearance.

Successful in identifying emerging opportunities, initiating innovative programs and operations, negotiating public/private outsourcing agreements and partnerships, and delivering strong financial results. Top-notch turnaround, process redesign and productivity improvement performance. Keen problem solving, negotiating and decision-making skills. Committed team player, able to achieve cooperation and dedication.

MBA Degree
Graduate, US Foreign Service Leadership Program
Graduate, Sorbonne Executive Seminar Series

PROFESSIONAL EXPERIENCE:

DEPUTY ASSISTANT SECRETARY & CONTROLLER   1993 to Present
NATIONAL FOREIGN ALLIANCE AGENCY
Rio de Janeiro, Brazil

High-profile, high-impact, leadership position at NFAA Headquarters. Most Senior Executive responsible for the $2+ billion NFAA Infrastructure Design & Development Program (technology, communications, logistics, transportation and related support systems). Hold full strategic, operational, programming, financial and administrative responsibility, including world-class logistics and operations worldwide. Direct a staff of 55 senior professionals.

Chair the 12-nation NFAA Infrastructure Committee authorizing all capital investments. Serve as Assistant Secretary General in incumbent's absence with full responsibility for the division and all international liaison affairs.

- Orchestrated a complete turnaround and revitalization of the program. Professionalized business processes, streamlined operations, reduced staff 35% and saved more than $1.5 million annually.

- Led development of a structured system for program management to identify, cost, review and implement NFAA-funded investments. Expanded process to include all O&M, manpower and capital investment requirements.

- Redesigned the entire financial reporting system and supporting technologies to create a "real-world" financial tool understood in 19 different nations with 18 different ways of interpreting financial data.

- Structured and negotiated $500+ million in contracts with private business and industry worldwide to support NFAA operations.

PUBLIC INFORMATION OFFICER - AMERICAN EMBASSY – GHANA   1990 to 1993

U.S. Ambassador to this Third World African nation with 4 million citizens, virtually no economic infrastructure, epidemic health care problems, and tremendous political, social and religious unrest. Partnered with national government organizations to drive forward cooperative programs and initiatives in health care, energy development, environmental conservation,

- Created a culture of trust and cooperation with Ghana's newest government (following 1989 coup d'etat) and dramatically improved the image of the US.

- Negotiated an innovative partnership with Australian government officials to develop and fund a rural outreach program of primary health care nationwide. Institutionalized annual visits of US military health care teams to supplement in-country programming.

- Consulted with national government to initiate, negotiate and finalize restructuring of $140 million International Monetary Fund bank loan.

- Persuaded government opposition leaders that a violent insurrection was neither in their best interest nor in the best interest of the country. Outsourced embassy and development services to NGO and private sector.

AMBASSADOR DESIGNATE – US DEPARTMENT OF STATE   1989 to 1990
Washington, DC

Ambassador Designate working to develop an in-depth knowledge and expertise of Ghana, a small African nation, prior to appointment as that country's US Ambassador. Managed executive liaison affairs with US government departments and agencies, the International Monetary Fund, World Bank and non-governmental organizations. Concurrently, orchestrated the start-up and staffing of a new Presidential Commission on Bolivian-US immigration issues. Negotiated sophisticated outsourcing agreements with major universities nationwide to manage professional services in support of Commission operations.

EXECUTIVE DIRECTOR   1985 to 1988
BUREAU OF AFRICAN AFFAIRS, Washington, DC

Hand-selected for this significant leadership position with an organization managing bilateral relations between the US and major African nations. Established and maintained a highly-visible presence with US embassies and embassy leaders worldwide. Reported directly to the Assistant Secretary of the Bureau.

Supervised a staff of 39 providing planning, budgeting, personnel and administrative services for 88 overseas operations with 230 domestic and 5200 overseas employees. Challenged to initiate the strategies, programs and tactical actions to ensure fully-operational status of all Bureau operations during a period of intense negotiations for the INF Treaty.

- Restaffed American Embassy following the government's withdrawal of all national employees. Established outsourced sites in adjacent nations to support operations (e.g., warehousing, maintenance, transportation) and significantly reduced annual operating costs. Facilitated a dramatic improvement in cross-national cooperation.

Responded to the challenge of a dramatic reduction in operating funds and personnel to support operations after only six weeks in the position.

- Redesigned all critical operations, retrained and cross-trained staff, and delivered a measurable gain in the efficiency and productivity of operations. Trained and empowered staff to make decisions, rely on their judgment and move initiatives forward.

COUNSELOR FOR ADMINISTRATIVE AFFAIRS   1983 to 1985
AMERICAN EMBASSY – BOTSWANA

Orchestrated a complete turnaround and revitalization of all administrative operations (budgeting, warehousing, transportation, maintenance, general services) to support US operations throughout Botswana and surrounding region. Directed a staff of 41 Americans and 700 national employees. Operated within a politically-sensitive and volatile country. Introduced outsourcing and cut more than 15% from annual operating costs.

Joined U.S. State Department – Foreign Service Institute – in 1972. Promoted rapidly through a series of increasingly responsible management and leadership positions at posts worldwide. Notable highlights and achievements:

- US Representative on 14-nation RTET Program Committee responsible for strategic planning, funding and tactical execution of industrialization and development programs worldwide.

- Successfully maintained US Embassy operations and services during three political coups, numerous military uprisings and countless crisis situations.

- Launched an aggressive program to upgrade housing, transportation, maintenance, health care and other support services for US personnel stationed in Third World countries.

EDUCATION:

MBA – University of Miami Graduate School of Business – Miami, FL

BA – History, University of Mississippi – Hattiesburg, MS

Graduate – The Senior Seminar – Foreign Service Institute – Washington, DC

Certificate in Political-Military Studies – US Army War College – Carlisle, PA

Graduate – 500+ hours of continuing professional, management and leadership training

JAMES P. OSTEEN

5874 Youngstown Road
Oakland, California 94604

Phone: 510.258.3526
josteen@worldnet.att.net

GOVERNMENT RELATIONS PROFESSIONAL

CORPORATE PARTNERSHIPS & STRATEGIC ALLIANCES

Government Liaison to major corporations to facilitate the development and market introduction of advanced technologies, manage government-funded infrastructure and capital improvement projects, and direct a number of other public/private partnerships and joint ventures. Extensive experience consulting in the area of federal and state funding and procurement. Experience spans a broad range of industries and includes US, international and multinational corporations:

- DuPont Chemical
- Pfizer
- Drexel Heritage
- Ajinotmoto (Japan)
- Burlington Industries
- Harris Teeter
- Kelly Springfield
- Firestone
- Ford Motor Company

Delivered solid operating results to corporate partners through cooperative programs, including a 50%+ reduction in annual energy costs for aggregate savings of more than $42 million. Managed an average of 150 corporate partnerships and led 50-90 corporate training/government outreach programs each year. Outstanding performance in building consensus and cooperative participation.

Partnered with colleges and universities (North Carolina A&T University, UNC-Charlotte) as well as numerous local, state and federal government agencies to drive forward cooperative legislative, programming and funding initiatives. Extensive experience and a well-established network of contacts in both the EPA and Department of Energy.

LOBBYING & LEGISLATIVE PASSAGE

Successfully lobbied before the General Assembly more than 65 times for program approval and funding. Secured $4.7 million in FY97, won legislative approval to create a $2.5 million revolving corporate loan fund, and authored grants funded for over $1.8 million. Obtained special appropriation of $350,000 to fund start-up of new corporate venture (now a $3 million business with 40 employees).

Key member of management team credited with lobbying for and winning funding to save the state's Energy Division. Instrumental in facilitating a massive reorganization and turnaround. Introduced improved policies and processes spanning all core functions (e.g., government relations, corporate partnerships, technology, finance, staffing).

INFORMATION SYSTEMS & TECHNOLOGIES

Outstanding technical skills in systems design/development, software and applications development/customization and systems operations. Planned and directed installation of multi-user computer system and developed application software for project tracking, financial reporting and record management. Proficient in the use of the entire suite of Microsoft Office products – Excel, Access, Word and PowerPoint – and with Project, Lotus and WordPerfect.

ENERGY & ENVIRONMENTAL SYSTEMS & TECHNOLOGIES

Over 15 years' professional experience in energy and environmental services organizations with outstanding skills in the development, implementation and management of advanced systems and technologies. Extensive experience in developing quantitative methods, models and measurements to predict performance, resource requirements and financial implications.

BUDGETING & FINANCIAL MANAGEMENT

Managed annual operating and programs budgets of up to $750 million allocated for both internal government affairs and external corporate partnerships. Administered annual grant funds (up to $3.7 million annually) to corporate partners to finance infrastructure development, energy, environmental, capital improvement, equipment acquisition/retrofit. Outstanding analytical, financial analysis/reporting and financial planning skills.

PROFESSIONAL EXPERIENCE:

ABC LEARNING CENTER, LLC, Redding, California   1997 to Present

Co-Founder / Partner / Consultant

Launched entrepreneurial venture to deliver advanced technology for the diagnosis and treatment of sensory dysfunctions (e.g., ADD, ADHD, autism). Authored business plan, established business processes, created fee structure and internal accounting systems, and launched regional marketing campaign. Concurrently, manage R&D efforts to develop new technologies, new applications and new treatment methodologies.

- Reverse-engineered European medical device and converted to PC application for broad-based use.
- Partnered with five other facilities throughout the US to leverage technology and applications.
- Negotiated strategic partnership with health care provider to explain areas of practice specialization.

NORTH CALIFORNIA DEPARTMENT OF COMMERCE, Eureka, California   1980 to 1997

Manager – State Energy Program (1989 to 1997)
Assistant Section Chief – Technical Programs (1985 to 1988)
Manager – Institutional Conservation Program (1980 to 1987)

High-profile career developing, funding and managing cooperative public/private partnerships in emerging energy and environmental technologies. Managed up to 36 individual projects each year with total funding of approximately $5 million. Led a team of seven project managers (total of 435 employees).

Scope of management responsibility was extensive and included:

- Government & Corporate Relations
- Partnerships, Alliances & Joint Ventures
- Vendor Negotiations & Administration
- Capacity Planning & Analysis
- Performance & Quality Improvement
- Staff Planning & Resource Allocation
- Program Development & Management
- Project Planning, Funding & Field Management
- Grants & Contracts Administration
- Information Systems, Software & Technology
- Training & Public Speaking
- Organizational Planning & Leadership

Winner, 1989 EPA Administrator's Award for originating government/corporate program and partnerships that delivered $42 million in energy cost savings. Co-Winner, 1992 ASHRAE Technology Award for innovative energy development project.

DUKE UNIVERSITY, Durham, NC   1978 to 1980

Research Assistant – *Department of Mechanical Engineering & Materials Science*

EDUCATION:

CALIFORNIA POLYTECHNIC INSTITUTE AND STATE UNIVERSITY, Berkeley, California
Master of Architecture (1977). *Summa Cum Laude.*

NORTH CAROLINA STATE UNIVERSITY, Raleigh, NC
Bachelor of Environmental Design in Architecture (1975). *High Honors.*

NOREEN SWANSON, M.D.

239 Central Park West
New York, New York 10021
(212) 525-9878

HEALTH CARE ADMINISTRATOR / HOSPITAL DIRECTOR / BUSINESS MANAGER

Medical & Clinical Services / Finance & Budgeting / Regulatory Affairs / Training & Development
Policy Development / Physician Recruitment / Resources & Facilities Management / Public Affairs
Provider Relations / Patient Relations / Legislative Affairs / Insurance Administration

Health Care Administrator with 10+ years experience leading the development and delivery of profitable health care systems throughout the U.S., Canada and Europe. Combines strong business and financial management expertise with 16 years experience as a licensed medical doctor. PC proficient.

PROFESSIONAL EXPERIENCE:

Health Care Administrator - Policy, Quality of Care & Services Delivery   1992 to Present

Devoted the past four years to the planning, development, funding and implementation of improved health care delivery systems worldwide. Work in cooperation with hospital administrators, financial executives, government agencies, legislators, regulators, policymakers and public advocacy groups to drive forward innovative health care and managed care programs.

Care Foundation - South America (1994 to 1996)
Two-year position with an international charitable health care organization providing teams of health care administrators, primary care physicians, nurses, researchers and others throughout remote parts of the world. Held joint administrative and clinical responsibilities.

- Travelled throughout the jungles of South America introducing preventive medicine, nutrition and immunization programs.
- Conducted primary field research on medicinal properties and studied natural resistance to malaria and other tropical diseases.

Finland Ministry of Health (1994)
Twelve-month consulting assignment guiding the modernization and expansion of emergency management systems throughout all of Finland.

- Led management training programs on core health care issues (e.g., service delivery, quality of care, reimbursement, staffing, resource maximization, facilities management, technology, budgeting).
- Introduced several new management and administrative processes into existing health care operations and delivered average annual cost savings of 20%.

Nova Scotia, Canada Ministry of Health (1992 to 1993)
Thirteen-month *locum tenens* position guiding development of health care policy, establishing health care service programs and spearheading health care cost containment initiatives.

- Orchestrated preliminary planning and development for implementation of emergency medical response system throughout all of Nova Scotia.
- Introduced the "American" system of emergency room management and compensation structures into more than 150 hospitals.

Mississippi State Board of Health (1992)
Twelve-month *locum tenens* position providing policy, quality, planning and administrative leadership to the health care providers and provider organizations throughout the State of Mississippi. Focused efforts on expanding services and realigning cost structures.

- Accelerated the turnaround, service expansion and return to profitability of health clinic.

Medical Director - Emergency Department
1985 to 1991

WATKINS REGIONAL MEDICAL CENTER, Atlanta, Georgia

Senior Operating Executive directing all policy, business, financial, administrative, staffing and medical care operations for the Emergency Department of this 440-bed acute care hospital. Scope of responsibility was diverse and included:

Business Management

- Introduced state-of-the-art utilization review, quality assurance and internal audit programs to facilitate ongoing improvements in the delivery and cost of care.
- Directed physician recruitment, credentialing, scheduling and contract negotiations.
- Administered all insurance billing and collection programs with Medicaid, Medicare, Champus and major insurance companies nationwide.
- Designed/taught emergency training for field and hospital-based emergency response teams.
- Testified before the General Assembly on core health care issues (e.g., cost, reimbursement, Medicare, Medicaid, emergency care, delivery systems).

Financial Management

- Guided Board of Directors and executive team in the development of annual operating and capital budgets for the $32 million Emergency Department.
- Directed all general accounting, financial planning and reporting, budgeting, billing, collections and medical coding operations.
- Improved workflow/productivity through innovative training and process reengineering.
- Spearheaded several fundraising campaigns for new emergency department and capital improvement projects. Achieved total contributions of more than $11 million.

Senior Administrative & Medical Director
1981 to 1985

U.S. ARMY MEDICAL CORPS, Bamberg, Germany

Directed all operations for a large medical clinic servicing 15,000 military personnel, dependents and civilians. Responsible for care provider organization, all financial and budgeting affairs, purchasing, staffing, reporting, facilities, regulatory affairs and administration. Managed team of 500+ physicians, nurses, medical corpsman, technicians and support staff.

- Introduced chart review, peer review, utilization review and quality assurance programs throughout all departments.
- Pioneered an innovative preventive medicine program for troops worldwide.

Medical Intern
1980 to 1981

TRIPLER ARMY MEDICAL CENTER, Honolulu, Hawaii

One-year internship rotating through all primary care areas in this 1000-bed military hospital. Appointed Chairman of Internship Class, served on Utilization Review and Quality Assurance Committee, and managed several successful fundraising campaigns. Designed and taught emergency care training programs.

EDUCATION & PROFESSIONAL CREDENTIALS:

M.D., University of Mississippi School of Medicine, 1980
B.S., Biochemistry, Mississippi State University, 1976

Diplomate of the American Board of Emergency Medicine, 1988
Fellow of the American Academy of Family Physicians, 1987
Recertification in ACLS, BCLS and ATLS, 1996

PROFESSIONAL & CIVIC MEMBERSHIPS:

American Academy of Medical Directors, American Academy of Family Physicians, American College of Emergency Physicians, American Medical Association, Center for Battered Women & Abused Children (Volunteer)

LARRY M. VAN WINKEL

2587 Lumber Mill Road
Oklahoma City, Oklahoma 75347
Phone (803) 234-8647
Fax (803) 234-8623

HEALTH CARE INDUSTRY EXECUTIVE
Managed Care / Management Service Organizations / Physician Hospital Organizations
Health Care Systems Marketing / Physician Relations / Practice Management

Executive Director / Operations Manager / Marketing Director with expertise in the strategic planning, development and leadership of sophisticated health care practice organizations. Contributed to multi-million dollar revenue growth through advances in managed care concepts, contract services, market development, finance/accounting and human resources. Extensive MIS and PC technology skills. Integrated and standardized operating and administrative systems to deliver strong and sustainable cost reductions. MBA Degree.

PROFESSIONAL EXPERIENCE:

MIDWESTERN HEALTH ALLIANCE, Oklahoma City, Oklahoma   1994 to Present

EXECUTIVE DIRECTOR

Recruited as the Senior Operating Executive for this newly-created health care management company providing contract services to a 7-site, multi-hospital network. Challenged to reduce operating costs and improve market penetration through the strategic integration of management functions into one central- ized organization utilizing existing staff and facilities.

Scope of responsibility is diverse and includes accounting and finance, financial reporting, payroll administration, banking, credit, budgeting, program development/implementation, marketing and community outreach. Lead a team of 20 through a matrixed organization.

Achievements:

- Created a regional integrated delivery system with centralized strategic planning, administrative, recruitment, marketing, purchasing and contracting services.

- Established operating policies and procedures for new business venture, defined immediate and long- term operating goals, and realigned financial and personnel resources to provide comprehensive management services.

- Fully integrated all purchasing, vendor sourcing, and inventory planning and control functions for hospital group. Projections forecast a 5% reduction in pharmacy costs and a 50% reduction in medical/ surgical inventory carrying costs through implementation of JIT delivery system.

- Developed a regional health education network and coordinated resource allocation throughout the health care delivery system.

159

CONSOLIDATED MEDICAL CENTERS, Denver, Colorado   1989 to 1994

CORPORATE DIRECTOR / DIRECTOR OF MARKETING
ACTING OPERATIONS MANAGER

High-profile management position as one of two operating executives responsible for the dramatic growth of this ambulatory health care network (primary care, occupational medicine and rehabilitation). In cooperation with President/CEO, led the organization through a period of rapid expansion.

- Built CMC from two outpatient facilities with $3.3 million in annual revenues to six facilities with $10.4 million in annual revenues and 125 employees (including 15+ physicians and 25+ therapists).

- Delivered 214% revenue gain over five years (averaged 21% annually) and significantly improved customer service/satisfaction ratings.

- Established CMC as the largest occupational health care system in the metro Denver market.

- Linked CMC with specialty physician practices to create a pioneering managed care organization providing comprehensive administrative, sales/marketing, MIS, budgeting/financial and operating management expertise to the clinical care network.

- Negotiated "win-win" managed care contracts and joint ventures with specialty care physicians, employers, third party administrators and insurance companies.

Created strategic plans and objectives to build managed care network, drive revenue growth, integrate administrative infrastructure, and build a regional marketing and business development network. Recruited, trained and supervised marketing personnel, launched public relations initiatives and customer service programs, and designed a portfolio of marketing communications (e.g., brochures, print advertisements, satisfaction surveys).

Spearheaded computerization of the entire business organization. Automated operational forms, created computerized superbill and implemented leading edge case management system that significantly improved service levels and efficiencies. Established service delivery protocols, pricing systems and a comprehensive operating procedures manual.

Previous Professional Experience (1984 to 1989) as an Account Representative, Credit Analyst and Credit Manager. Acquired excellent experience in credit/financial analysis, commercial and consumer lending, portfolio administration ($18 million) and sales/marketing/new business development. Employers included:

US West Financial Services, Kansas City, Missouri (1987 to 1989)
The CIT Group / Equipment Financing, Inc., Overland Park, Kansas (1986 to 1987)
Norwest Financial Services, Springfield, Missouri (1984 to 1985)

EDUCATION:

Master of Business Administration, July 1988
UNIVERSITY OF MISSOURI, Kansas City, Missouri

Bachelor of Science (General Business), December 1984
SOUTHWEST MISSOURI STATE UNIVERSITY, Springfield, Missouri

CHRISTINE A. STANFORD, RN

2408 Springmont Drive – Miami, Florida 33101
Phone: (305) 432-2557 – Cell: (305) 435-9859

NURSING CAREER PROFILE

*Combining medical science and cutting-edge medical & diagnostic technology
with the humanistic side of patient care to provide holistic health care and whole body interventions.*

More than 15 years' primary nursing care and nursing management experience with several world-class institutions. Outstanding hands-on patient care and patient relationship management skills. Talented nurse educator and team leader. Knowledgeable across a wide range of nursing and medical specializations – ophthalmology, ER, oncology, gerontology, adult medicine, med/surg and cardiac care.

Strong "business" management skills in health care information systems/PC technology, office administration and the start-up of new health care facilities, programs and hospitals. Driven to succeed within challenging environments. Honest, capable, intuitive and creative. Able to make difficult decisions and effectively manage relationships between medical and surgical staffs, patients, nursing staffs and health care administrators. Conversational Spanish.

NURSING & HEALTH CARE EXPERIENCE:

UCLA – EYE INSTITUTE, Los Angeles, CA   1994 to 2000
(World-Renowned Ophthalmologic Surgical, Clinical Care & Research Center)

Registered Nurse – Medical Photography Department

Recruited to this prestigious health care institution based on previous clinical, administrative and managerial experience. Work hand-in-hand with an elite group of medical photographers conducting state-of-the-art ophthalmologic diagnostic assessments and surgical interventions. Manage a caseload of 50-100 patients daily. Concurrently, manage a diversity of administrative functions including supply management, database administration, payment processing and patient documentation.

- Developed and taught a 2-hour course on clinical ophthalmologic techniques to enhance staff competencies and technical proficiency.
- Designed and taught a course in emergency response and preparedness for administrative support team.
- Updated all policies and procedures to achieve OSHA certification.
- Personally manage nursing care for international VIP clientele.

USC – EYE INSTITUTE, Los Angeles, CA   1991 to 1994
(World-Class Ophthalmologic Research & Surgical Hospital)

Registered Nurse

Member of *Start-Up Nursing Team* responsible for the operational and clinical development of the Admissions and Information Center for the newly-opened Bascom Palmer Eye Institute at the University Of Miami School Of Medicine.

- Key player in the development of nursing policies, procedures and documentation requirements.
- Recruited, trained and supervised nursing staff.
- Clinical care responsibility for up to 30 patients.

LOURDES NURSES REGISTRY, Hialeah, FL   1985 to 1990

Registered Nurse – VIP Patient Division

Provided primary nursing care to national and international VIPs at the University of Miami Hospitals, Miami Heart Institute, Mount Sinai Hospital and in private homes. Independently managed patient scheduling, patient care, diagnostic assessments and expense budget. Extensive patient and family teaching responsibilities.

BOCA RATON COMMUNITY HOSPITAL, Boca Raton, FL   1981 to 1987

Registered Nurse – Orthopedics, Med/Surg, Oncology & Cardiac Care

Fast-paced primary care position in a high-volume community hospital. Rotated throughout all clinical care units to meet staffing shortages and patient care demands. Extensive ER and triage experience.

COLUMBIA-KENDALL MEDICAL CENTER in Miami, FL   1975 to 1980
Promoted from Staff Nurse to *Charge Nurse* within 11 months of hire.

<u>Previous Experience</u> includes an additional three years' hands-on clinical nursing experience with two prestigious medical institutions.

OTHER PROFESSIONAL EXPERIENCE:

Accepted opportunity with the National Park Service in 1998 to pursue lifelong personal interest in the environment, ecological preservation, and U.S. parks and game reserves. To date, have completed assignments at the Santa Monica Mountains National Recreation Area in California, Native American Culture Center in California, and Big Key National Preserve in the Florida Everglades.

Demonstrate outstanding communication, public presentation and public speaking skills. Plan to continue volunteer work with the National Park Service.

EDUCATION:

Registered Nurse	INTERFAITH MEDICAL CENTER, Brooklyn, NY (*Licensed to practice in Florida and California*)
BA – Psychology	FLORIDA INTERNATIONAL UNIVERSITY, Miami, FL
Certified	Advanced Cardiac Life Support (ACLS)
Certified	Basic Cardiac Life Support (BCLS)
Graduate	50+ hours of continuing professional education

JAMES R. NEWFIELD
723 Saxon Trail
Southlake, Texas 76092
(817) 416-8592

SENIOR HUMAN RESOURCES EXECUTIVE
Optimizing Performance Through Organizational Change & Proactive Business Leadership
Broad Industry Experience in US, European, Latin American & Far Eastern Markets
MBA Degree

Strategic HR Executive credited with building best-in-class organizations that have been consistently successful in achieving aggressive revenue and profit objectives. Catalyst for a series of innovative HR initiatives impacting 5000 employees. A creative thinker, problem solver and decision maker. Strong communications, interpersonal relations, mentoring, negotiation and mediation skills. Expertise:

- Organizational Culture & Vision
- HR Policy, Process & Systems Design
- Downsizing, Restructuring & Revitalization
- Union & Non-Union Employee Relations
- Training, Teaming & Leadership Development

- Merger & Acquisition Integration
- Benefits & Compensation Design
- HR Outsourcing Solutions
- HRIS Technology Solutions
- Long-Range Business Planning

PROFESSIONAL EXPERIENCE:

ABC MANAGEMENT, LLC (*DBA Ace Communities*), Dallas, TX   1996 to Present
(*National Real Estate Development/Golf Course Management Company with $1 billion in assets*)

Vice President - Human Resources
Recruited by the principals of King Investments following their 1996 acquisition of Prestige's Real Estate and Land Development Division. Assigned as the **Senior HR Executive for new corporation** – ABC Management – with complete responsibility for defining organizational culture, developing strategic HR plans, and positioning HR as a proactive partner to operations and business units nationwide. Total workforce now exceeds 1500.

- Created best-in-class HR organizations, systems, processes and practices as ABC has experienced dramatic growth and expansion over the past two years. Fully integrated 150 Prestige employees, 90 US General Life Insurance employees and others as the company has accelerated growth through acquisition.
- Introduced a focused, yet flexible, corporate culture to facilitate seamless integration of acquired business units, product lines and personnel.
- Led recruitment and selection for key positions throughout the organization, including the entire legal, finance, administrative and accounting organizations.
- Designed and implemented benefit programs, a performance-based appraisal and incentive compensation system, a system of staffing models and a complete HR infrastructure.

PRESTIGE CORPORATION   1980 to 1996

VP – Human Resources – Real Estate & Land Dev., New York, NY/Reston, VA (1989 to 1996)
Senior HR Executive for 1800-employee, $450 million division comprised of global corporate real estate services and domestic real estate development. Challenged to restructure and streamline the organization, reduce headcount, optimize productivity and positively impact bottom-line financial performance. Member of 6-person Divisional Leadership Team.

- Introduced industry-specific best practices benchmarking program as the catalyst for reorganization. Evaluated 237 different positions, redefined organizational staffing needs, introduced outsourcing and downsized workforce from 1800 to 450 employees.
- Orchestrated a massive corporate culture change initiative in response to organizational transition and implemented actions to optimize each business unit's performance.

- Conceived, developed and introduced a series of innovative HR programs, services and leadership initiatives (e.g., global TQM program, comprehensive Supervisory Training Program, performance-based incentive compensation program, succession planning).
- Spearheaded a successful union avoidance campaign to thwart organizing attempts throughout the land development and club operations portfolio.

Manager – Human Resources – U.S. Marketing, Fairfax, VA (1988 to 1989)
Member of 14-person Senior HR Leadership Team for Prestige's largest operating division (5000+ employees). Scope of responsibility encompasses the entire HR function with emphasis on compensation and benefits, HRIS, staffing, career development/succession planning, training, organizational development, EEO/Affirmative Action/diversity initiatives and relocation activities.

- Revitalized HR organization following five years of instability, internal change and restructuring. Designed grassroots HR programs to link field units with division HQ and provide a common organizational vision.
- Developed corporate model for "win-win" labor union contract negotiations.

Supervisor – Field Employee Relations Services, Los Angeles, CA (1986 to 1988)
Labor Relations Advisor, Chicago, IL (1983 to 1986)
Labor Relations Staff Assistant, Fairfax, VA (1980 to 1983)
Advanced rapidly through progressively responsible positions providing full service HR support to line and staff organizations of up to 3000 employees. Strong generalist experience in salary/compensation, EEO/Affirmative Action, training and workforce development.

- Transitioned HR from an administrative function into a strategic business partner working with senior management to drive key business and performance improvement initiatives.

Extensive experience in Labor Relations (e.g., contract negotiations, administration, disciplinary actions, arbitration). Chief Spokesperson & Negotiator for local and international contracts with both independent and international unions (previously, HQ function).

- Key participant in several successful union avoidance and union decertification programs at manufacturing sites and product distribution terminals nationwide.

FORD MOTOR COMPANY   1978 to 1980

Salary Administrator – Sales Operations, Detroit, MI (1980)
Personnel Representative – Sales Operations, Detroit, MI (1979 to 1980)
Employee Services Administrator – Parts & Services Division, Dearborn, MI (1978 to 1979)
Fast-track promotion through a series of increasingly responsible HR positions. Extensive experience in recruitment, benefits, compensation and employee relations.

UNITED STATES ARMY RESERVE   1973 to 1997

Four years active duty followed by 20-year personnel leadership career in reserve status. Advanced to final status as **Lieutenant Colonel & Joint Staff Officer**.

EDUCATION: **MBA Degree** (1978) / **BBA Degree** (1973) – RUTGERS UNIVERSITY

PERSONAL: Flight Instructor/Commercial Pilot ... Scuba Diver ... Eagle Scout

FLORENCE NEWMAN
flonewman22@aol.com

6733 Westbury Drive
Atlanta, Georgia 30327

Home: 407-584-2555
Office: 407-584-5457

SENIOR HUMAN RESOURCES & ORGANIZATION DEVELOPMENT EXECUTIVE
US & International Organizations ... High-Growth, Turnaround & Fortune 500
General Electric ... Acetel Communications ... Suburban HealthCare

Business Partner to senior operating and leadership executives to guide the development of performance-driven, customer-driven, market-driven organizations. Recognized for innovative leadership and counsel in transitioning under-performing organizations into top producers and guiding other organizations through accelerated growth and global market expansion. Decisive, energetic and focused. Talented team leader, team player and project manager.

Strategic HR Leader with expert qualifications in all generalist HR affairs. Particular success in:

- Recruitment & Employment Management
- Advanced HRIS Systems & Technologies
- Employee & Management Retention
- Benefits & Compensation Design
- Quality & Performance Improvement
- Consulting & Customer Service Delivery

- Training & Development Leadership
- Employee Reward & Recognition Programs
- Internal Change & Reorganization
- Merger & Acquisition Integration
- Organization Design & Development
- Vision, Mission & Shared Values Statements

Keen presentation, negotiation, problem solving and conflict management skills. Confidential Advisor to CEO.

PROFESSIONAL EXPERIENCE:

ACETEL COMMUNICATIONS, Atlanta, Georgia   1997 to Present

Vice President – Human Resources

Corporate Office and Senior HR Executive for a 10,000-employee, $1 billion, high-growth, global technology company in the digital wireless telecommunications industry. Company was faced with unique operating challenges resulting from rapid expansion including 150+ acquisitions over six years. Tasked with creating a formal HR infrastructure to support continued growth, standardize operations, create structure and control, and strengthen financial performance.

Hold complete strategic planning, leadership and operating management responsibility for all HR and OD affairs including employment/recruitment, compensation, benefits, employee relations, training & development, quality, organization effectiveness, payroll and HRIS. Lead a direct reporting staff of 40 with dotted line responsibility for 80 field HR personnel worldwide. Guide business and HR vision.

- Recruited 6400 employees in the first year, building total workforce to 9600. Conceived and implemented practices and programs to maximize human capital, drive performance improvement and achieve measurable business impacts.
- Redesigned benefit, salary and executive compensation programs. Introduced performance-driven incentives linked to individual and business unit contributions, expanded stock offerings and insurance options, and built a consistent structure to manage the delivery of employee services.
- Expanded internal training to include supervision and leadership, conflict management, teamwork and performance evaluation/improvement. Introduced numerous reward and recognition programs.
- Benchmarked GE programs to create Acetel's customer service and service excellence programs.
- Spearheaded quality improvement initiatives for product, service and employee performance.
- Counseled senior operating executives on relevant HR and organization issues resulted from six completed acquisitions.

ADVENTIST HOSPITAL HEALTHCARE SYSTEM, Bethesda, Maryland   1993 to 1997

Senior Vice President – Human Resources

Senior HR Executive recruited as part of a new management team challenged to upgrade operations, improve quality of care and strengthen financial performance of this 392-bed, community-based, not-for-profit hospital (1400 employees and $120 million in annual revenue). Led a 17-person staff and a $7.6 million budget. Reported to CEO. Member of Executive Personnel Committee of Board of Trustees.

- Initiated new assignment with a complete audit/analysis of the existing HR organization. Developed business plan to upgrade the entire HR infrastructure, all policies, procedures, services, programs and operations. Successfully transitioned the perception of HR from a bureaucratic function into a value-added service to the organization.
- In collaboration with the CEO, recruited 90% new executive team, including design of innovative executive compensation, incentive and retirement programs. Counseled CEO on HR and organization issues relative to proposed joint ventures and mergers.
- Restructured benefits programs, consolidated providers and saved $250,000+. Created a competency-based performance measurement system, established new salary structures, flattened the organization, expanded management responsibilities and delivered 15% cost savings.
- Introduced focus groups to develop a framework for the organization's vision, mission and shared values. Linked results to strategic business plan and translated into actionable programs.

GENERAL ELECTRIC COMPANY   1980 to 1993

High-profile 13-year career as one of the top 5 HR Executives in GE. Promoted rapidly through a series of increasingly responsible and complex HR and organizational leadership positions. Career highlights include:

Vice President – Human Resources (1990 to 1993)
GE ABC Division, Atlanta, Georgia

Recruited by the #1 HR Executive in GE to build and lead a state-of-the-art HR organization for a $100 million, 1200-employee information systems consulting business. Challenged to rebuild the organization's structure, create effective HR policies and systems, and support an aggressive business turnaround. Directed a staff of 13 and a budget of $1.5 million. Reported directly to the President.

- Built a best-in-class HR organization. Achieved 90% of objectives in less than one year.
- Orchestrated a complex business reorganization, removed two layers and downsized management by 50%. Results included significant gains in competitiveness, customer service and profitability.
- Executed a comprehensive redesign of all compensation and benefits programs, resulting in a better than 37% increase in workforce satisfaction.
- Restructured and automated the recruitment function. Introduced employee leasing programs, standardized operations and reduced workforce by 12% for $600,000 in annual cost savings.

Program Manager – Work-Out & Human Resource Development (1989 to 1990)
GE Corporate Management Training Facility, Rockville, Maryland

Selected as one of only six management personnel to lead the design and start-up of GE's Work-Out Program, an innovative, corporate-wide cultural transition from "top-down" management to "employee-empowered processes." Worked in collaboration with 13 Presidents and GE's Chairman to define new vision and create a program to lead GE's entire 453,000-person workforce through massive change..

- Honored by both management and peers for outstanding leadership performance in start-up efforts.
- Introduced the concepts and practices of risk taking, organization effectiveness, diversity, teamwork and other performance-driven processes, now mandatory management training at the GE Institute.
- Accompanied 50 executives to East Germany to evaluate joint venture, acquisition and other business development opportunities synergistic with GE's mission and values.
- Managed course design, content, faculty, facilities, registration, materials and platform implementation for GE's Corporate Entry Leadership Conference (2000+ participants annually).

Human Resources Manager (1986 to 1989)
GE Consumer Services Business, New York, New York

Member of 10-person management team of $750 million, 4000-employee business. Directed the complete HR function for 400+ employees in 15 locations worldwide (sales, marketing and operations). Full generalist HR and OD responsibilities with five-person professional/support staff.

- Orchestrated a successful downsizing that delivered $15 million in annual cost savings. Led subsequent reorganizations to flatten structure and enhance performance/productivity.
- Key driver in the design of a leading edge gainsharing program to retain key staff and management following GE's global reorganization.
- Won a Management Award for design, implementation and management of broadbanding compensation and bonus structure linking individual and team performance to business results.

Staffing Manager (1983 to 1985)
GE Appliances Business, Syracuse, New York

Fast-paced management position directing staffing for engineering and manufacturing operations at 40 sites nationwide (17,000+ total employees). Managed candidate sourcing (executive, professional, college), internal self-nomination program, minority recruitment campaigns, professional and managerial assessment, salary negotiations, succession planning/career counseling and policy interpretation.

- Successfully recruited and filled over 1100 professional and management positions in two years.
- Won a Managerial Award for development and project leadership of a fully-integrated, online job posting, self-nomination and applicant tracking system.
- Created prototype for GE's Student Leadership Conference for college recruitment.

Human Resources Manager – Central Europe (1982 to 1983)
GE Medical Systems Business, Frankfurt, Germany

Managed a complete international HR function including employment, compensation, benefits, training, policy administration, international labor relations, legal affairs and communications for 200+ sales and service employees in seven countries throughout Central Europe ($1+ billion in annual sales revenues).

- Directed a complex Hay Associates job analysis and evaluation study resulting in the development of uniform position levels and appropriate compensation systems.
- Introduced a career assessment/succession planning system integrating organization strengths with candidate pipeline to position the organization for sustained market growth.
- Customized US-based business training programs for specific European audiences.

Human Resource Management Program (1980 to 1982)
GE Medical Systems Business, Milwaukee, Wisconsin

One of only 20 MBA/MA graduates selected for GE's highly-competitive, corporate management development program consisting of rotational assignments, professional education and leadership opportunities. Positions as **Union Relations Specialist**, **Wage Management & Benefits Specialist** and **Employee Relations Representative**. Active in union negotiations with IAM and IBEW.

EDUCATION:

MA – Personnel Administration – Ohio State University – 1980

BS – Individual & Family Studies – The Pennsylvania State University – 1977

PAUL SCOTLAND

293 Walnut Avenue
Houston, Texas 77036

Phone: 832-544-1232   Email: pscotland@hotmail.com   Fax: 713-554-1777

TECHNOLOGY INDUSTRY EXECUTIVE / PROJECT MANAGER / DIRECTOR
Advanced Information, Data, Voice & Telecommunications Technologies

Expert in the design, development and global market introduction of advanced technologies to meet business, financial, competitive and customer demands. Combines strong general management qualifications with outstanding performance leading advanced technology organizations. Led the development of more than 30 new technologies, from concept, business case and feasibility analysis through the entire technology development cycle to penetration of consumer, commercial and military markets throughout the U.S. and abroad.

Leadership, management and business expertise includes:

- Mergers, Acquisitions, Strategic Alliances & Partnerships Worldwide
- Financial Planning/Analysis, Financial Modeling, Budgeting & Cost Management
- New Market Identification, Development & Expansion
- Worldwide Sales Management & Multi-Channel Product Distribution
- Quality, Performance & Productivity Improvement
- Training, Team Building & Competitive Performance

Technology expertise includes:

- Wireless & Wired Voice & Data Communications
- Data Systems Design, Engineering, Testing & Integration
- Mobile Data Application Architectures & Deployment
- Monitoring Satellites & Geographic Information Systems
- Multimedia, Video Conferencing, Voice Mail & Speech Synthesis
- Internet & Intranet Solutions

PROFESSIONAL EXPERIENCE:

NATIONAL MARINE SERVICE   1998 to Present

Project Manager – Monitoring, Control & Surveillance System

Currently leading the development of the organization's first-ever comprehensive surveillance system to monitor and control activities in commercial waters worldwide. Dual responsibility for leading both the technology development effort and creating the internal business and resource infrastructure to support development, implementation and ongoing operations.

ABC MOBILE NETWORKS   1997 to 1998

Business & Technology Consultant

Recruited by one of the world's largest multi-network satellite service providers to expand their technologies into the data communications market. Company already supplied major organizations (United Nations, Fortune 500 companies, international aid organizations) with advanced voice communications technologies.

- Successfully and profitably led ABC into new market with the development and commercialization of an entire portfolio of data communications products and services.
- Introduced five new products with tens of millions of dollars in revenue potential within both new and existing customer markets worldwide.
- Created business and organizational infrastructure for product development, packaging, manufacturing, marketing and distribution.
- Identified business partners and structured/negotiated global alliances to accelerate distribution.

MOBILE COMMUNICATIONS   1991 to 1997

Director of Business Development – Mobile Communications Division (1994 to 1997)

Senior Executive with full responsibility for a 250-person, $100 million organization. Challenged to lead the organization through a massive internal change initiative to profitably penetrate consumer and vertical commercial markets. Authored business cases to justify financial and resource investments and led technology teams in product development, redesign and market launch.

- Delivered $14 million in new revenues including a multi-year contract with the U.S. Air Force.
- Spearheaded redesign effort to integrate technologies into Internet-based messaging networks.
- Led development of five new product offerings with total market potential for $750 million.
- Negotiated and closed six strategic alliances with international partners and foreign governments.

Manager – Earth State Operations & Global Network (1993 to 1994)

Year-long project leadership responsibility for the global integration of Mobile's communication support services. Transitioned five independent sites worldwide into one cohesive business unit and technology organization. Led a multicultural technology and project management team. Achieved all operating, technology and financial objectives within first year.

Manager – Application Engineering (1992 to 1993)

Led a team of 15 engineers in design and development of advanced application engineering tools and products. Management responsibility for project leadership, resources, prioritization, cost/benefit and investment risk analysis, technology assessment, financial valuation and market viability. Redesigned business processes to improve project management capabilities and group productivity. Managed an average of 7-10 ongoing projects with total investment of more than $90 million.

Consultant – Applications Engineering Group (1991 to 1992)

Conceived, designed, developed, documented and tested remote satellite monitoring systems for commercial application. Hired by company after one year.

Technology Consultant   1987 to 1991

Treasury Department / U.S. Customs Service – Office of Security Enhancement
NASA / Goddard Space Flight Center – Laboratory for Terrestrial Physics
JHU / Applied Physics Laboratory – Digital Ground Systems Group
MIT / Lincoln Laboratory – Sensor Development Division

- Trained and led project teams of up to 20 technical and professional staff.
- Conducted feasibility assessments of various technologies and proposed projects to evaluate risk, complexity, cost, development time, interactivity and long-term financial value.
- Presented findings and recommendations to senior personnel including U.S. Secretary of Defense.
- Led the development of advanced technologies for both commercial and military applications (e.g., artificial intelligence, neural networks, expert systems, relational databases, bio-geophysical systems, satellite imagery, digital signal processing, acoustics, surveillance).

EDUCATION:

Post Graduate Studies in Electrical Engineering, Systems Engineering & Artificial Intelligence
RENSSELAER POLYTECHNIC INSTITUTE, Troy, New York (1984 to 1985)

Bachelor of Arts Degree in Physics, Math & Computer Science
FROSTBURG STATE UNIVERSITY, Frostburg, Maryland (1980 to 1984)
  Cum Laude Graduate ... Phi Eta Sigma ... Sigma Pi Sigma ... Kappa Mu Epsilon

Advanced Academic Project Experience with both Rensselaer and FSU in Robotics, Automation, Acoustics, Atomic & Plasma Radiation, Chemistry and Physics Departments.

RICHARD JACKSON

580 Hayman Court
Downers Grove, Illinois 60515
Email: dickjackson129@aol.com

Phone: 217-544-4777

Fax: 217-777-2487

SENIOR EXECUTIVE PROFILE
CHAIRMAN / CEO / MANAGING PARTNER
US & International Markets

Top-flight leadership career as Chairman / CEO building a $4 million company into a $60+ million global technology corporation. Achieved phenomenal growth and a strong competitive industry position through combined expertise in:

- Organizational Development & Leadership
- Team Building & Performance Optimization
- Strategic Planning & Business Development
- Sales, Marketing & Global Partnerships
- Acquisitions, Divestitures & Restructurings

- Sophisticated Manufacturing Operations
- Product Design, Development & Engineering
- Advanced Quality & Production Methods
- Continuous Process Improvement
- Corporate & Investment Finance

Graduate, Executive Leadership Training at Stanford University & University of California

---

PROFESSIONAL EXPERIENCE:

HIGHTECK   1985 to 1999
(*US semiconductor equipment manufacturer with sales & service worldwide. Formed by acquisition in 1985.*)

Chairman & CEO credited with transitioning a components/process module business with $4 million in sales into a state-of-the-art, systems-based solutions provider with $60+ million in annual sales worldwide. Customers include HP, IBM, Intel, TI, Motorola, Ericsson (Sweden) and Anam (Korea).

Business Leadership & Profitability

- Acquired HIGHTECK in 1985 through an LBO acquisition funded by private investor group. Personally managed all investor relations throughout 14-year tenure.
- Led the company through a dramatic reorganization, revitalization and market expansion. Drove revenue growth of 71% with profit margins up to 20% annually.
- Achieved and maintained solid profitability despite ongoing investments in R&D, infrastructure development, technology implementation and marketing.
- Created and implemented new corporate infrastructure encompassing all functional disciplines (e.g., sales, marketing, engineering, manufacturing, quality, process development lab, field service). Introduced performance benchmarks, measurable goals and business standards.
- Increased personnel to 525 (including 10 senior management reports) to keep pace with growth, market demand and organizational change.

Acquisitions, Divestitures, Restructurings & Investment Financings

- Structured and negotiated the $12 million sales of consumable quartz products business in 1990, after restoring the division to profitability. Invested $1 million profit in expanding core equipment manufacturing operations.
- Identified market opportunity and negotiated acquisition of Kodak components division in 1989 to compliment existing product lines and leverage market opportunities.
- Acquired technology company in Oregon providing software and automation capabilities for newly developed advanced cleaning system. Achieved ROI within less than 3 years.
- Led a major restructuring in 1987 in response to industry downturn. Consolidated two plants into one, eliminated unprofitable products, reduced personnel and lowered cost breakeven by 25%. Continued to increase market share despite recession and competition.
- Structured, negotiated and transacted more than $250 million in bank and venture capital financing to support initial company acquisition, working capital requirements, and subsequent acquisition and development efforts. Managed 1995 IPO through successful completion of road show.

R&D, Manufacturing & Total Quality Leadership

- Built a sophisticated manufacturing organization and continuous cross-functional product development program which strategically positioned Highteck as an industry leader. Introduced processes, systems, methods and technologies to optimize productivity and yield, reduce waste and virtually eliminate product failures.
- Consistently met/exceeded demanding customer technology and production requirements with 250+ systems installed in the past 3.5 years.
- Championed the development of a Quality Gain Share Program integrating the core concepts of Baldrige, Deming, Hoshin and ISO 9001. Introduced innovative performance measurements, metrics, tracking and employee participation initiatives.
- Received 15 equipment and process patents with 3 more in process. Successfully defended patent infringement and legal actions with no losses and substantial monetary awards.

ARTHUR YOUNG & COMPANY / ERNST & YOUNG

Fast-track promotion through a series of increasingly responsible positions to final promotion as **Managing Partner** of a 50-person consulting, tax, audit and financial services organization in Phoenix, Arizona. Broad industry experience with particular emphasis on public and private technology manufacturers, banks/financial institutions and construction/real estate developers.

- Led the organization through a period of sustained growth and expansion. Established a well-respected presence throughout the local business community and outstanding working relationships with top management of client companies.
- Key player in several significant IPO transactions.

EDUCATION:

Executive Development Program	STANFORD UNIVERSITY
Executive Development Program	UNIVERSITY OF CALIFORNIA AT IRVINE
Bachelor of Science Degree	UNIVERSITY OF CALIFORNIA LOS ANGELES (UCLA)

KENNETH W. LEE

333 Reston Drive
Eugene Oregon 30347

244.734.2888
kenlee@abc.com

SENIOR INFORMATION TECHNOLOGY & SYSTEMS EXECUTIVE
Architectures / Platforms / Software / Networks / Databases / Voice & Data Communications
Internet & Intranet Technologies / E-Commerce Technologies / Conversion & Migration

Chief Information Officer & Senior Board Executive successful in designing and optimizing technologies to drive business performance. Outstanding strategic planning, organizational development, team leadership and decision making skills. Astute negotiator and problem-solver. Successful in intense and demanding environments experiencing rapid change through internal growth, acquisition and revitalization. Strong finance and budget skills.

PROFESSIONAL EXPERIENCE:

Chief Information Officer (CIO)   ABC, LLC   1996 to Present

High-growth, $300+ million company with 35 locations in the U.S. and U.K. World's 2nd largest lighting company with events at the Super Bowl, Las Vegas and Broadway. Clients: Disney, MGM, Universal Studios, Nike, Mercedes & Toyota. Specialize in "themed entertainment" industries involving high transaction rentals, manufacturing, sales & design.

CIO, Vice President of Business Technology and member of 6-person Corporate Executive Board credited with transitioning this $35 million company into one of the nation's premier special events companies. Given full strategic planning, leadership and decision making authority for building the corporation's entire IT organization, infrastructure and operations. Led technology organization through $100 million public bond offering (Jamestown) and $65 million venture capital funding (XYZ Ventures).

Built the entire IT organization, from concept into a state-of-the-art centralized IT/IS model with distributed services worldwide. Recruited, trained and developed a staff of 37 technologists, including remote IT managers, a centralized network and operational team, and a matrix-managed finance/business team. Control over $100 million in annual operating and capital expense budgets.

Infrastructure Development:

- Partnered with MIT, Cisco and independent software company to develop high-speed **WAN technology**, one of the most critical drivers in the company's sustained and profitable growth. Developed a 20-node T1/T3 WAN within two years and achieved/maintained 99.9% uptime.
- Directed technology integration for **16 acquisitions** (30 sites) over 30 months. Built IT systems where none existed, replaced obsolete technology with legacy systems and achieved Y2K compliance for all operations. Introduced and achieved corporate-wide technology standardization.
- Built **data center** from start-up into a 24x7 operation supporting high-end SUN Unix systems and NT platform primarily hosting Oracle databases (ERP applications).
- Designed **LAN** models and standardized voice communications using a mix of open standard PBX's, voice mail and voice over IP. Built MCI back-up **ISDN** network and multiple secure Internet protocols.
- Centralized purchasing, payroll, budgeting and **help desk** operations for 1200 users.

Solutions & Applications:

- Revitalized fledgling **Oracle implementation** and took ABC "live" in less than 10 months. Modules included AP, AR, GL, Purchasing, Inventory, Project Management and HR.
- Designed "new" **Internet computing architecture** migrating Oracle applications onto a 3-tier web-based environment. Delivered 100% migration of 92 customizations within 60 days.
- Integrated 13 **email systems** (Lotus Notes, Eudora) into one system (Microsoft Exchange) to facilitate collaborative participation between all ABC companies and operating sites.
- Led selection and implementation of AT&T's VPN solution for direct access to ABC **private network**.
- Managed development, implementation and maintenance of two major **software systems** – rental asset management system and an equipment utilization program for $150+ million of assets.

Internet/Intranet Development:

- Led the design, development and execution of five major Internet/Intranet sites. Developed business and market strategies, financial plans, website interfaces and E-commerce transactional processes that supported successful launches, solid functionality and consistently strong performance.
  - intranet.abc.com (ABC Intranet deployed to 1000 users)
  - www.nightstar.com (independent LLC company)
  - www.industry.com (E-commerce site)
  - www.lite.poly.edu/html/milso_case.htm (sponsored research with Merrill Lynch)
  - www.abc-link.com (password-protected outsourced server – "Certnet" for ABC project management)

Commissioned Officer　　　　UNITED STATES MILITARY　　　　1986 to 1996

Fast-track promotion through a series of increasingly responsible leadership positions in Technology Deployment & Management, Search & Rescue, Immigration and Law Enforcement. Won numerous honors, awards and commendations for outstanding individual and team achievements.

Director – ABC Command Center – Santa Rosa (1994 to 1996)

Directed 24x7 command center and 30 personnel responsible for positioning and deploying all sea and air assets from Nova Scotia to Latin America (20,000 personnel and hundreds of vessels). Operated within an advanced IT environment with multiple databases and platforms (NT and Unisys). U.S. representative to International Search & Rescue & Law Enforcement exercises.

- Introduced leading edge databases, Internet communications and deployment systems to enhance the integrity of IT operations.
- Facilitated the seamless migration of operations, systems and technologies from New York to Virginia with virtually no interruption in workflow.

Commanding Officer – Jacksonville (1992 to 1994)

Selected from a competitive group of hundreds of candidates to "captain" one of the Military's newest vessels ($10 million ship with 17 crew). Led 300 search & rescue missions and law enforcement boardings.

- Orchestrated the successful beta site (including systems testing, debugging and failure analysis) for the first secure wireless data transfer at sea.

Naval Intelligence Officer – Republic of Country (1991 to 1992)

Head of Counter-Narcotics for Naval Intelligence in Central America. Managed sophisticated technologies, private networks and Government Intranet operations. Efforts contributed to 20 seizures valued in excess of $500 million. Technical advisor to the U.S. Embassy and Panamanian government. Top Secret Clearance.

- Tested and implemented the newest secure video and data transfer technology.
- Developed and managed the first multi-agency database (DB3) for cross-referencing, analysis and operational tracking of thousands of records weekly from numerous government agencies

Operations Department Head – Cape May (1986 to 1990)

Promoted from Communications & Operations Officer to Operations Department Head managing the start-up of a new 100-person search & rescue operations center. Designed operational and IT infrastructures. Managed secure satellite, wireless, ship-to-shore and data communications systems and technologies.

EDUCATION & PROFESSIONAL AFFILIATIONS:

MS – Information Management (*GPA – 4.0*), Polytechnic University of Brooklyn, 1995
BS – Mathematics & Computer Science – U.S. Military Academy of New London, CT, 1984
Board Advisor, Institute for Technology & Enterprise – **Board Member**, ABC Management Dept.

ANTHONY E. FRAZIER

387 E. Queens Road
Jackson, Mississippi 39010
Home: 601.587.5545 / Fax: 601.855.1445

SENIOR EXECUTIVE PROFILE
Leadership of Advanced Technology Companies – Start-Ups, High-Growth Ventures & Turnarounds
North America, Latin America, Europe, Far East, Middle East
MBA Degree

Technology Development & Commercialization
Technology Design, Engineering & Manufacturing
Technology Transfer & Commercialization
Integrated Systems & Technology Solutions
Advanced Telecommunications & Satellite Systems

International Marketing & Business Development
Strategic Market Planning & Competitive Positioning
New Product & New Technology Launch
Executive Negotiations, Presentations & Consultations
Partnership, Alliance & Joint Venture Management

Organizational Leadership & Operations Management
Multi-Site Operating & Profit/Loss Management
Performance, Productivity & Quality Improvement
World Class Manufacturing & Production Operations
Corporate Culture, Reengineering & Process Redesign

International Sales & Customer Management
Multinational Sales Force Development & Management
Sales Team Building & Team Leadership
Multinational Key Account Relationship Management
Customer & Marketing Multi-Media Communications

Canadian-American Business Achievement Award, 1998
Extensive Public Speaking, Teaching & Consulting Experience Worldwide

---

PROFESSIONAL EXPERIENCE:

ABC TECHNOLOGY, INTERNATIONAL, INC. , Toyko, Japan

Board Member / Senior Consultant (1998 to Present)
President & Chief Executive Officer (1990 to 1998)

Recruited by corporate joint venture partners to launch the start-up of new technology company to market remote radar systems technology and imagery worldwide. Given full leadership, negotiating and decision making responsibility for creating strategic business plan, negotiating complex government approvals and funding, developing market vision and tactical business development plans, staffing, establishing global distributor network and building operating infrastructure.

- Created and commercialized Japan's first radar satellite company (replacing less reliable optical/solar technology) requiring a massive initiative to educate the marketplace in the functionality of this pioneering technology. Far exceeded the financial, technological and operational objectives of investors, Japanese government and the industry.

- Devoted five years to obtaining government funding ($600 million), negotiating sales and distribution rights, establishing business operations and developing advanced technologies.

- Launched operations in 1996 and achieved profitability by end of first year. Built sales to $25 million with a staff of 150. Major clients included Georgia Pacific, BP, Lockheed Martin, Canadian Coast Guard, and Swedish and Norwegian government. Won business in Indonesia, Singapore and Colombia.

- Structured and negotiated a second round of government financing ($250 million) to fund development of second satellite system. Spurred further growth and expansion throughout new markets.

CDE INTERNATIONAL, Washington, DC

President (1998 to Present; 1988 to 1990)

Built a successful global consulting practice specializing in the transfer of advanced technologies throughout Europe, the Middle East, the Far East, North America and Latin America. Provided expertise in building worldwide sales distribution channels, negotiating international strategic alliances, creating innovative marketing programs, redesigning pricing structures, and driving strong sales and profit performance. Key engagements:

- Retained for exclusive 3-year contract with a French-based remote sensing technology company. Resolved market issues impacting performance, more than doubled revenues, and positioned the company as a strategic business partner. Negotiated new distribution agreements in the PRC, Japan, Thailand, Philippines, Singapore, Malaysia, Indonesia, Saudi Arabia, Ecuador and European countries.

- Retained for exclusive 3-year contract with ABC and Associates in Canada. Credited with profitably leading the company into the global advanced ground station technology market.

XXX TECHNOLOGY VENTURE, Washington, DC

Vice President – Marketing (1985 to 1987)

Recruited to provide executive marketing and business development leadership for an innovative RCA / Sony joint venture to commercialize satellite remote sensing technology from government to private sector. Created the entire marketing organization, established "for-profit" business culture and recruited talented sales professionals.

- Established worldwide sales and marketing division and built revenues from start-up to $22 million.

- Delivered phenomenal growth in international markets (60% of total company sales). Negotiated and profitable sales in China, Germany, UK, Spain, Israel, Japan and Brazil.

- Developed and directed an international distribution network to further expand market penetration.

- Personally structured and negotiated marketing agreements, partnerships and alliances with foreign governments, international sales agents and product/technology development firms worldwide.

- Built in-house software and applications development group to eliminate reliance on third-party vendors.

SOUTHERN REGIONAL TELEPHONE, Lexington, Kentucky

Vice President – Marketing (1983 to 1984)

Recruited following this AT&T company's deregulation in 1982, 15 months before the full AT&T divestiture. Challenged to transition the marketing organization from a bureaucratic infrastructure into a free enterprise corporation through dramatic changes in corporate culture, organization, staffing and operations. Focused efforts on the development and profitable market launch of value-added services (e.g., software, consulting) to create a distinctly competitive market position.

- Built a best-in-class marketing organization and drove revenues from $25 million to $100 million.

- Reduced workforce from 300 to 150, recruited 70+ professional staff, introduced field sales automation and restructured field sales teams. Rationalized and balanced technology offerings.

- Developed new advertising, sales promotion and trade show department. Honored with several distinguished industry awards for creativity and effectiveness of video and print campaigns.

ABC INDUSTRY APPLICATIONS, INC., Phoenix, Arizona

Vice President & Principal (1982 to 1983)

Launched new venture to introduce sophisticated computer applications software to the banking industry (using major IBM platforms). Defined, demonstrated and announced six new software packages within an intense 6-month time frame. Established immediate market recognition for innovation and functionality.

IBM CORPORATION – US, CANADIAN & INTERNATIONAL DIVISIONS

Director of Industry Marketing (1976 to 1981)
Manager – Market Requirements & Business Planning (1973 to 1976)

Key player in identifying market opportunity and launching a separate IBM International Division to market low-end computer products to the world's fastest growing markets. Instrumental in defining organizational strategy and objectives, recruiting/training sales team and managing the Division's growth and global expansion.

- Built new venture from $450 million to $2.1 billion in annual sales over first five years.

- Introduced the first-ever PC systems and distributed data processing technology into major international corporations. Delivered a 300% increase in sales over three years.

- Introduced industry's first third party software as a value-add to hardware. Reorganized application software development organization and reduced costs $50 million while improving customer deliverables.

- Chaired 10 management/executive task forces that launched new operating divisions, created specializing marketing units and drove major changes in corporate pricing policies.

- Created a portfolio of seminars to build international customer base and presented to 5000+ potential customers each year, 70% of whom ordered IBM product within 120 days. Ranked as the #1 sales tool by IBM's Country General Management Team.

Previous IBM experience in sales, sales management and systems/technology development.

- Led IBM's first industry-specific sales organization (versus traditional geographic or product segmentation).

- Created "balanced plans" concept integrating a cradle-to-grave product engineering, development, manufacturing, sales and support program. Introduced throughout the entire Systems Development Division.

EDUCATION:

MBA – Marketing – Indiana University

BA – Business Administration – University of Portland

Graduate – IMEDA International Product Marketing – Lausanne, Switzerland

EDWIN O. REIM

487 Riverbend Road, DesMoines, Iowa 50320

Office: 515.587.3256 / Cell: 515.422.9988 / Email: eoreim@hotmail.com

**Expert in Technology-Based E-Learning, Knowledge & Performance Improvement Systems
to Improve Human Performance, Optimize Employee Success & Drive Profit Growth**

World-class leader in the strategic development, design, technological development, marketing and delivery of advanced technologies to enable improved human, organization and financial performance. Successful corporate executive, consultant and entrepreneur with extensive experience in the Fortune 1000, Global 2000, IT, dot com, software and systems integration industries.

Thrive in challenging, high-energy start-up ventures, turnarounds and high-growth organizations worldwide. Characterized as a talented strategist, capital thought producer, communicator, project leader and customer relationship manager. Dedicated to innovative, technology-based solutions to complex business demands.

RECENT PUBLICATIONS:

- *"Learning and Organization Development in the New Economy"* – Business & Technology, May 2000
- *"e-Learning and Technology Systems"* – Strategy + Business, March 1999
- *"Ten Questions Every Executive Should Ask About Risk Management"* – CEO Magazine, June 1998
- *"Implementing Vision & Strategy"* – CEO Magazine, September 1997

PROFESSIONAL EXPERIENCE:

SENIOR DIRECTOR – GLOBAL SERVICES – ABC SOFTWARE   1999 to 2000

Member of 6-person Senior Executive Management Team leading this technology venture through organization development, market positioning and successful IPO (May 2000). Recruited to build consulting practice targeting CEO-level executives as the foundation for the "go-to-market" strategy to introduce enterprise-wide E-learning systems and technologies.

- Instrumental in the phenomenal growth of this new venture, from less than 30 to 100+ business and technology consultants and 6 to 50 customers throughout North America and Europe.
- Recruited experts in knowledge management and learning/training to guide product development/marketing/delivery for the Global 2000, education and government markets.
- Partnered with Anderson Consulting, PriceWaterhouseCoopers and other world class consultants to create a solutions-based selling strategy and facilitate product launch.
- Created internal coaching practice to support/guide efforts of executive and management teams throughout the corporation.

CONSULTANT & ENTREPRENEUR   1987 to 1999

Twelve-year track record of success pioneering innovations in Business Process Consulting, E-Learning, Knowledge Management, Human Performance & Organization Development.

- Led strategy, development and execution of 30+ consulting engagements with Global 2000 firms, start-ups, venture investment firms and the "Big 5". Created more than $20 million in opportunities.

177

- Launched several successful new technology ventures developing first-generation enterprise document management and spreadsheet applications software.
- Assembled/led technology, business, sales and marketing teams that introduced some of the world's most advanced E-learning and human performance improvement technologies.
- Built and managed successful client relationships with Andersen Consulting, Apple Computer, Bankers Trusts, Bell Atlantic, Caterpillar, Citibank, Entergy (now EMC), Ericsson, Federal Express, Gannett Publishing, GE Medical, GM/EDS, Holiday Inn, Johns Hopkins University Institute for Policy Studies, Merrill Lynch, Microsoft, NYNEX, Ogilvy & Mather, Sprint, USAA, Xerox and others.
- Consulted with leading venture capital firms (e.g., Oak, Alex Brown) to evaluate proposed technology acquisition and development projects.

Notable Projects, Ventures & Achievements:

Director – Intellectual Capital Development Strategy – ABC Bank. Retained by the Board of Directors to create and launch a massive effort to introduce sophisticated knowledge management practices into this $12 billion corporation (12,000 employees in 20+ locations worldwide).

- Created global strategy for program design/implementation and linked each individual component to improvements in organization efficiency and performance, management capability, client service and retention, and/or profitability.
- Launched several projects including ExpertShare, Lessons Learned Knowledge, Leadership Development Community, Desktop Knowledge Management, Product Knowledge, Risk Management Intellectual Property Protection and a Virtual University to enable tremendous performance results.

Director – CDE, Inc. Founding Board Member of internationally-recognized group of software engineers who consult and train global companies in improving their software development process. Full-time during company start-up with leadership responsibility for strategy, product/technology development, sales/marketing and delivery. Currently consult with management team to guide strategic development of technology-based learning and knowledge systems.

- Instrumental in positioning CDE as one of the world's most preeminent process improvement companies with a clientele including Ericsson, GE, GM, Kodak, Merrill-Lynch, Microsoft and Sprint.

Director – Advanced Technology Products – MNO Technologies. Long-term consulting engagement with redefining the strategy, marketing and products of MNO's systems integration division. Orchestrated development of embedded performance support technology to transfer learning from the human to computer-aided platform. Delivered multi-million dollar systems to Federal Express (customer service), GE Medical (sales), Holiday Inn (reservation) and other global corporations with sophisticated transaction-based applications.

- Negotiated and closed over $5 million in new client projects within two years. Positioned MNO as a world-class leader in E-learning and knowledge management.

Director – Energy Management Control Systems – RST. Full strategic, P&L, operating and leadership responsibility for new business venture including direct supervision of business unit CEO. Refocused business vision and strategy, designed organization infrastructure and introduced technology-based learning and knowledge systems. Technology Mentor to Corporate Vice Chairman.

- Worked in cooperation with Andersen Consulting to evaluate $100+ million opportunity for international product launch and several other strategic global initiatives.

MANAGER – CORPORATE EDUCATION MARKETING – XYZ   1982 to 1987

Aggressively recruited to lead nationwide launch into the education market. Challenged to create the strategy and business unit, secure the funding, build the organization, recruit/train the sales team and deliver the products to create a dominant presence throughout this rapidly-emerging market. Competed head-on with Apple Computer and Radio Shack.

- Built new venture from start-up to over $15 million in sales of learning and computation products.
- Partnered with higher education, K-12, education associations and government research laboratories (e.g., Harvard, MIT, Yale, USC) to create artificial intelligence workstations and other pioneering technology-based learning systems.
- Co-led the development and launch of the world's then-largest corporate distance learning program, the single most successful marketing program in XYZ's history. Effort impacted several hundred thousand people in education, government and business at thousands of sites throughout North America and Europe. Netted over $70 million in free press and media coverage.

VICE PRESIDENT – BANKAMERICA CORPORATION   1981 to 1982

Associate Director (Chief Operating Officer) and Secretary, Board of Directors for BankAmerica's Foundation. Controlled $9 million annual budget and $35 million in investment assets (principally grants to community service organizations, higher education institutions and public education facilities). Established strategy to guide corporate giving, created high-visibility community outreach campaign, built a fully-integrated internal IS function and funded/directed hundreds of programs.

EXECUTIVE DIRECTOR – ABC VOLUNTEER PROGRAM   1976 to 1981

Chief Executive Officer of start-up national non-profit association. Launched a massive PR effort that raised more than $2.5 million for program funding and included direct support from the White House, Congress, state legislators and labor unions nationwide. Leadership responsibility for budgeting, staffing, program development/delivery and marketing for a massive volunteer effort.

Previous Professional Experience in University Academic/Research and Government Policy Analysis.

EDUCATION:

Ph.D. – Statistics & Education – University of Illinois
M.A. – Education & Technology – Texas A&M University
B.A. – Education & Business – DePaul University

RAYMOND W. MITCHELL

12 Lamplighter Street
Kansas City, Kansas 66110
913-319-5544   raymitchell@yahoo.com

TECHNOLOGY INDUSTRY EXECUTIVE

Developing & Implementing Best-In-Class Software, Systems, Applications & Information Technologies
Certified Project Management Professional (PMP) – Project Management Institute
MBA – Computer Methodology

Business Case Development	Requirements Management	Contract Management
International Team Leadership	Technology Training	Test Management
Client Relationship Management	Risk Management	Capacity Maturity Modeling
Disaster Recover Planning	Client Server Applications	Systems Integration

Outstanding organizational, leadership, communication and team building competencies. Keen problem solving, analytical and negotiation skills. Consistently delivered multi-million dollar projects on-time and within budget.

TECHNOLOGY SKILLS & QUALIFICATIONS:

Hardware: RS6000, IBM Mainframe, Intel
Software: C, PLSQL, COBOL, PL1, CLIST, DBIII, Clipper, Lotus Notes, Word, MFS, Excel, PowerPoint, APS Excelerator, Excelerator Requirement Generator
Databases: Oracle, DB2, IMS
Op. Systems: AIX, MVS, OS2, NT
Data Transfer: Network Data Mover (NDM), File Transfer System (FTS)

PROFESSIONAL EXPERIENCE:

BELL SYSTEM – New York, New York   1985 to Present

Fast-track promotion through a series of increasingly responsible technology management positions. Advanced rapidly based on consistently strong performance in the planning, staffing, budgeting and leadership of multi-million dollar technology development and implementation projects.

Senior Manager – RapidRate Technology (2000 to Present)

Currently orchestrating the on-site implementation of a major systems conversion (order and billing) at 150-employee Kansas City location. Hand-selected for assignment to resolve critical productivity issues resulting from initial implementation. Full leadership responsibility for 30-person staff.

- Achieved/surpassed all performance improvement goals. Restored productivity from 15% to 50% within eight weeks while decreasing average customer contact time by 10%.
- Led user focus groups to identify and resolve key issues for IT, staffing and operations. Defined workflow processes and workstation deployment matrix, risk management plan and communication strategy.
- Managed technology team that provided up to 165 coaching sessions per day to internal users. Managed design, development, logistics and delivery of refresher classes for 780 students over three weeks.

Manager – ABC Program (1998 to 1999)

High-profile technology management position orchestrating the development, conversion and implementation of Oracle-based ABC order entry system (Carrier Access Billing System Automated Front End), a $390 million AT&T initiative. At peak, managed a staff of up to 26 employees and contractors and $1.8 million budget. Earned "President's Excellence Award" for project leadership.

- Created, designed and implemented a comprehensive ABC maintenance program. Established Steering Committee and IS Assessment Board, implemented 12-month rolling Resource Management Reporting System, designed Application Performance Measurements, and developed Release & Deployment Checklists to enhance quality and standardization. Developed formal business proposals for new technologies for long distance, E-commerce and new product development.
- Led a massive implementation of six ABC releases to support nationwide industry standard. Scope of responsibility was significant and included system and user requirements, system prioritization, project lifecycle, resource management, vendor contract administration and budgeting.
- Created standardized Product Manager's User Spec List, Product Manager's Status Report by Product, Systems Specification Guide, Release Capacity Model, online Centralized Specification Library & Tracking System, New Product Spec List Guide, formal Post-Installation Release Analysis Plan and Technical Review Board. Efforts resulted in double digit gains in productivity, significant reductions in project time and cost, and consistent achievement of all project objectives.
- Conducted ABC initial Capability Maturity Model (CMM) software assessment resulting in multiple process changes within the application. Implemented architectural changes to system which decreased cycle time for new product development from 6 months to 2 months.

Manager – ABC Implementation Program (1994 to 1997)

Technology Manager leading $950 million investment to develop ABC client server order entry system to service operations in 50 locations throughout six Northeastern states and support 1600 users processing 140,000 orders per year ($32 billion in revenue). Directed a staff of 73.

- Wrote and presented business case for $7.9 million in board-approved funding.
- Planned and orchestrated a successful technology development and implementation project, achieving all performance goals and objectives, and delivering project on-time and within budget. Most notably, increased billing accuracy from 80% to 91%.
- Coordinated integration of $1.2 million of capital equipment into existing data center.
- Delivered major cost reductions including 66% savings in development of technical specifications (through competitive RFP and subsequent negotiation of offshore development contract) and 15-person reduction in client staffing expense.
- Led Boston-based technology group responsibility for application development which decreased processing time from two weeks to two days.

Staff Director –Automated Front End Systems (1990 to 1994)
Senior Systems Analyst / Systems Analyst / Program Analyst (1985 to 1990)

Promoted rapidly during early professional career with Bell System. Most notable project was SAFE (SOP Automated Front End) development with a staff of 23. Reduced product cycle time from three months to one.

EDUCATION:

MBA – Computer Methodology – Baruch College – 1983
BBA – Operations Management – Baruch College – 1976
Executive Management & Leadership Training – University of Maryland – 1998
Bell System Leadership for the Millennium Development – 1998
Executive Management & Leadership Training – Hartford University – 1991

PROFESSIONAL AFFILIATIONS:

Project Management Institute – NYC Chapter
Bell System – Management/Union – Work & Family Corporate Committee
Kansas City School Board Subcommittee

GREGORY COSTELLO

2451 Avondale Avenue
Jacksonville, Florida 32205

Phone: 904-987-2145
gcostello@jaxrr.net

PROFESSIONAL QUALIFICATIONS:

INFORMATION TECHNOLOGY, SOFTWARE, SCIENCE, ENGINEERING & MATHEMATICS

Fifteen-year career integrating science, technology and applications development. Combines expert technical/engineering qualifications with outstanding performance in team building, team leadership and project management. Understand the interrelationship between science, technology and applications. Keen problem solving and decision making skills. Intensely accurate.

TECHNOLOGY SKILLS & QUALIFICATIONS:

Navigational: GPS & GIS Systems, Technologies & Applications

Software: Word, Excel, Access, Adobe Photoshop, Corel Draw, Paint Shop Pro

Languages: C++, FORTRAN, Assembler, Visual BASIC,

Operating Systems: Windows 95, Windows 98, Windows NT, IBM OS/2, UNIX, LINUX, LAN Networks

Extensive experience with digital imaging, electronic photographic imaging, optical imaging, image processing, harmonic analysis, signal processing and linear systems technologies. Excellent systems and software troubleshooting skills.

Experienced geophysicist in structurally complex geologic areas with responsibility for data acquisition, processing, interpretation, mapping and signal enhancement. Strong skills in oceanographic side-scan sonar and other advanced imaging technologies. Broad electrical and electronic engineering skills.

PROFESSIONAL EXPERIENCE:

AAA OCEANOGRAPHIC OFFICE, Jacksonville, Florida   1987 to Present

Physical Scientist, Mathematician & Oceanographer

Twelve-year professional career in the collection, analysis and reporting of sophisticated oceanographic data using advanced software, systems and technologies. Promoted through increasingly responsible projects, assignments and management positions to **Senior Project Manager** managing survey crews and ships traveling oceans worldwide. Concurrently, **Data/Technology Manager** and **Lead Oceanographer** (field data collection). Honored for performance and contributions with:

- Eight Job Performance Awards
- Two Quality of Service Awards
- One Special Act Award

Manage a diverse range of scientific, technical, technological, statistical and analytical projects for the detection and depiction (computer-generated models) of the ocean floor, and the prediction of currents on tidally-influenced land masses. Manage project teams and crews of up to 20. Significant technical writing and documentation, briefing/presentation and technology responsibilities.

MAJOR PROJECTS & ACHIEVEMENTS:

- Managed and/or participated in 24 at-sea field operations and data collection projects. Fully responsible for planning, staffing operations, technology, scientific experimentation, data collection, analysis and reporting. Most recent project involved a **$100,000 operating budget and $2+ million in advanced technology and instrumentation**.

- Designed and implemented **200+ software programs** over the past 12 years: **GPS** (Global Positioning System), Transponder Renavigation System (20 C++, FORTRAN and Visual BASIC programs driven by GUI), and the complete redesign of all IT software for the Biology Laboratory Division. Extensive experience in data collection, integration and digital imaging.

- Currently developing new **GIS applications** combining relational database with scanned imaging to digitize visual representation. Project requires extensive use of ARCVIEW, SQL and GMT.

- Designed the **only working software model** of tides and tidal current projections for the US Navy (includes harmonic analysis techniques).

- Presently servicing as **Acting Division Director** in supervisor's extended absence. Fully responsible for the entire organization, a staff of more than 250 and assets valued at $750 million.

AMOCO PRODUCTION COMPANY, Denver, Colorado   1984 to 1986

Geophysicist

Specialized in processing, graphic and visual representation, and presentation of seismic data indicating the location of oil deposits within the geologic layers of the earth. Designed sophisticated mathematical computations, computer data flow processes, structural maps and data reporting methodologies to guide exploration and drilling operations.

PREVIOUS PROFESSIONAL EXPERIENCE:

Mathematics Instructor employed with public school systems in Idaho and Oregon. Additional responsibilities as **Varsity Football Coach** and **Athletic Director**.

EDUCATION:

BS – Geophysics – #1 in Class – Boise State University – 1987

BS – Mathematics – Boise State University – 1979

Graduate Studies in Physics, Information Theory, Digital Filtering & Frequency Analysis

DWIGHT SARTORE

21 Badger Avenue
Bakersfield, California
Office (661) 587-1245

Home (661) 583-1414

Fax (661) 365-4877

INSURANCE INDUSTRY EXECUTIVE
Chief Executive Officer / President / Chief Operating Officer
Start-Up Ventures / Turnarounds & Revitalizations / High-Growth Companies

Forerunner in the strategic planning, research, design, development and market launch of innovative insurance products, programs and services to meet market demand. Equally successful in new market development despite intense competition. Delivered multi-million dollar growth in revenue, earnings and market share ratings.

Solid general management and leadership competencies with particular expertise in new business development, mergers and acquisitions, multi-site operations, performance/quality improvement, administration and long-term planning. Excellent background in development of innovative information and Internet technology systems to support industry growth and diversification. Keen troubleshooting and crisis management skills.

Strong executive presence with outstanding communication and negotiation skills. Excellent reputation throughout the insurance and financial services industries. Ethical with a high level of personal integrity and commitment.

Guest Speaker on Insurance, Economics of Rate, Cash Flow Underwriting & Loss Rating
at conferences, conventions, industry meetings and training programs nationwide.

PROFESSIONAL EXPERIENCE:

CHIEF EXECUTIVE OFFICER (CEO)   **LAM, INC.** - CA   1993 to Present

Recruited as the Senior Executive with full planning, administrative, operating, reinsurance and P&L responsibility for this disability planning corporation. Challenged to lead a targeted new product development program focused on the design/delivery of innovative disability products not covered by the managed care industry and focused on specific groups of insureds in need of new product coverage.

- Established Disability Benefit Trust Fund and built $3 million surplus while increasing beneficiary benefits 50%+ and reducing employer contribution costs 15%.

- Developed a self-administered, short-term, 26-week temporary disability benefits program that met all statutory requirements using a 501c(9) multiple employer trust. Project was initiated during tenure with Marlett; subsequently developed and launched in 1994 into one of the premier trusts in California.

- Championed development of a third-party health and disability product to provide protection to contractual recipient from the exposures of health and total disability to the contractual paying party to avoid an interruption, or total failure, of the paying party's ability to meet their financial obligations.

- Spearheaded development of a portfolio of other insurance products (e.g., breast cancer coverage, combined long-term care and disability product).

- Led technology team in the development of company website to leverage Internet e-commerce opportunities. Converted claims systems to a total proprietary software solution unique to the industry.

PRESIDENT	**MRLP GROUP, INC.** - CA (*Insurance Management Consulting Firm*)	1991 to 1993

High-profile executive consultant to carriers and intermediaries in the life, health and benefits and P&L insurance disciplines. Completed projects in London on behalf of a number of Lloyds' syndicates, and in the US for more than 65 clients. Scope of responsibility included all planning, operational and administrative processes in additional to full corporate P&L performance.

- Innovated the concept of a combined title company/P&C company as a next generation insurance product designed to lower exposure, reduce risk and cut costs by eliminating redundant operations.

CHIEF EXECUTIVE OFFICER (CEO)	**LANE INSURANCE COMPANY** - CA (*Specialty Insurance Company*)	1987 to 1991

CEO with full P&L and leadership responsibility for company recently acquired by Marlton Corporation (see below). Challenged to drive rapid growth and expansion through management of an aggressive new product development initiative. Concurrently, strengthened existing operations with implementation of new operating infrastructure and recruitment/training of quality personnel to support 42-state, multi-lines agency.

- Built Lane from virtual start-up to over $275 million in premium volume while maintaining below-industry loss ratings.

- Pioneered leading edge products including medical stop loss coverage (cross-over of medical/health and P&C) and a self-administered short-term disability product. Established a nationwide reputation for product innovation within the complex and changing health care industry.

CHIEF EXECUTIVE OFFICER (CEO)	**MARLTON CORPORATION** - CA (*National Managing General Agency*)	1984 to 1991

CEO & COO with strategic planning and operating responsibility for insurance product development and reinsurance agreements. Created and implemented underwriting, claims and administrative guidelines to lead this agency through a period of accelerated growth, expansion and diversification. Expertise in retrospective ratings and risk/loss management. Held full P&L responsibility.

- Led the acquisition of a national managing general agency in 1984. Transitioned from $25 million in revenues with a 380% loss ratio to $150 million in annual revenues with only an 80% loss ratio.

- Reconfigured portfolio from 3500 small to 1000 large policies and significantly reduced risk exposure.

- Conceived, built and directed a national distribution system of 150 locations.

- Orchestrated the acquisition of a 40-state multi-lines P&C company in 1987 (Lane Insurance Co.).

PREVIOUS PROFESSIONAL CAREER: Recruited by **Aetna Life & Casualty** immediately upon graduation. Achieved the highest level of performance in 37-person training class. Promoted to **Product R&D** Group. Subsequently joined **G.B. Parks & Co., Inc.**, later merged with **J.M. Bass Agency**, and rose to position of **Agency Partner** with full responsibility for insurance administration, underwriting, claims and finance. Built business into Top 30 in 100+ locations throughout the Northeastern US.

- Expanded personal lines firm into the commercial market and grew from $1 million to over $35 million in annual revenues (95% commercial). Ranked in the Top 30 agencies in the Northeastern US.

- Negotiated pioneering reinsurance partnerships and agreements with major insurance carriers.

EDUCATION: **BS, Business Administration, Dual Majors in Economics & Finance** – Babson College

CARLOS CAVALLO

Bragado 3061 5o
Campana, Argentina (1425)
Email: cavallo@cmfb.com.ar

Home Phone: 54-1-712-5487

Cell Phone: 54-1-542-4775

INTERNATIONAL BUSINESS EXECUTIVE
New Ventures / Market Revitalizations & Turnarounds / High-Growth Companies
Latin America, Eastern Europe, Asia & Africa

PROFESSIONAL PROFILE:

Sixteen-year career, building and leading successful new ventures throughout global business markets. Extensive PC qualifications including Windows 95, the complete suite of Microsoft Office applications, and numerous financial systems for planning, analysis, valuation and reporting. Bilingual in English & Spanish.

- Strategic Planning & Business Development
- New Venture Start-Up & Management
- Financial Planning, Analysis & Investment
- Organizational Development & Change

- International Marketing Leadership
- Field & Corporate Sales Leadership
- Administrative & Business Infrastructure
- Team Building & Performance Management

PROFESSIONAL EXPERIENCE:

AAA FINANCIAL FUND S.A., Buenos Aires, Argentina

1996 to Present

General Manager

Led the successful start-up of a new mutual fund company investing in mid-size growth companies throughout Argentina. Transitioned new venture from concept through all strategic planning and business planning functions, through market development and fund development to full-scale operation. Built critical partnerships with government agencies, local companies and international corporations.

- Succeeded against stiff market competition. Established the #1 money market fund in the country with a top-5 ranking in all other categories.
- Created all marketing and business development initiatives, designed advertising and direct mail campaigns, developed sales strategies, and launched country-wide market entry.
- Designed, issued and currently administer eight funds (closed end corporate loans fund, Timberland direct investment fund and six open end mutual funds).
- Appointed to Finance and Human Resources Leadership Teams of parent corporation.

JEANS INTERNATIONAL, San Francisco, California

1993 to 1996

New Venture Director / Finance & Administration Director - Argentina (1995 to 1996)

Led the "SWAT team" that successfully rebuilt Jean's market in Argentina as the first step in revitalizing the company's presence throughout Latin America. Challenged to resolve long-standing business issues resulting from the country's volatile economic and government market, introduced a US-based management style, and delivered $12 million in profitable revenue within the first year.

- Led project from concept through the entire start-up phase to market re-entry in just two months with the entire project completed in 10 months. Won Jean's highest performance distinction for this effort.
- Authored strategic business plan including mission, vision, objectives and critical issues.
- Orchestrated development of information systems and telecommunications support infrastructure including hardware and software selection, vendor selection, systems customization and installation.
- Guided development of a structured human resources function. Worked with consultants from Hay and Mercer to develop organizational charts, position descriptions, job grades and salary structures.

JEANS INTERNATIONAL (*Continued*):

Senior Financial Consultant (1993 to 1995)

International headquarters position providing financial leadership for a broad range of corporate projects (e.g., new ventures, strategic planning, feasibility assessment, financial analysis). Extensive experience in Eastern European, Asian, African and Latin American markets. Reported to VP of Finance.

- Project Leader for Latin American Headquarters relocation to Miami. Applied NPV, IRR and other forecasting/analysis methodologies to determine optimum location (e.g., shared resources, networking opportunities, international travel requirements, cost factors, budget).
- Project Manager for the design and execution of a business continuity strategy and revenue/profit revitalization plan for Brazil.
- Finance & Management Liaison between field teams and HQ to facilitate the profitable development of new ventures throughout Eastern Europe, Asia and Africa. Evaluated proposed joint ventures, partnerships, acquisitions and independent start-ups to determine most profitable entry strategies.
- Upgraded the corporation's Intercompany Profit Reporting & Performance Management System. Redesigned core processes for data collection, analysis, assimilation and reporting to enhance the quality and value of financial information.

FRANKLIN RESOURCES, San Mateo, California   1991 to 1992

Accountant / Portfolio Analyst

Fast-paced, time-sensitive position managing accounting and financial analysis functions for five mutual funds (total of $12 million in investment assets). Analyzed portfolios, determined cash positions, valued shares, and recommended specific buy and sell transactions.

UNIVERSITY OF CALIFORNIA SANTA BARBARA, California   1989 to 1990

Accountant / Financial Analyst

Only Financial Professional in the Program Department. Created new financial infrastructure integrating cost planning/analysis, operational and financial budgeting, financial analysis, cash flow management and long-term financial planning/forecasting. Provided tools for long-term growth and cost reduction.

Entrepreneur/Venture Projects Director (Publishing, Distribution, Restaurants), Argentina   1983 to 1987
Internal Auditor – Beloqui & Associates, Inc., Argentina   1983
External Auditor (Manufacturing, Financial Svc.) – Peat, Marwick, Main & Company, Argentina   1982

EDUCATION:

Master of Finance (Emphasis in Capital Markets), CEMA University – Argentina, 1997
Master of Arts in Economics (Emphasis in Finance), University of California Santa Barbara, 1992
Bachelor of Arts in Accounting, University of Belgrano – Argentina, 1987
Certified Public Accountant, 1984

Graduate of more than 200+ hours of continuing professional education in Management, Leadership, Marketing, Sales and Finance. Sponsored by Arthur Andersen, University of California, and the American Management Association.

CASTELO P. VARGAS

12 N. Arena Vista Avenue
Tucson, Arizona 85715
Email: cpvargas@aol.com

Residence: 520-574-2121

Business: 520-241-7412

INTERNATIONAL BUSINESS EXECUTIVE
Executive Vice President / Managing Director / COO / CEO
US, Latin America, Asia & Australia

Twenty-year leadership career building profitable international business organizations, including start-up ventures, acquisitions, turnarounds and high-growth organizations. Expert strategist, analyst, planner, team leader, negotiator and business driver who has delivered dramatic gains in revenues, profits and market share in both developed and emerging nations. Fluent in English, Portuguese and Spanish. Cross-functional management responsibility for:

- Profit & Loss Performance
- Multi-Site Operating Management
- Strategic Alliances & Partnerships
- Product Design & Development
- Multi-Channel Sales & Distribution

- Marketing & Business Development
- Infrastructure Development & Optimization
- Mergers, Acquisitions & Joint Ventures
- Information & Telecommunications Technology
- Customer Relationship Management

PROFESSIONAL EXPERIENCE:

GLOBAL EMERGING MARKETS LTD. – Arizona
1998 to Present

President & CEO

Recruited by shareholders of this start-up technology venture (collects and disseminates data on publicly traded companies in 62 emerging market countries) to redesign product development, sales and marketing strategies, build organizational infrastructure and competitively position for long-term, profitable growth. Selected from a competitive group of top-level executives based upon extensive experience in the planning and leadership of related technology and information provider organizations.

- Built infrastructure, reorganized management team, recruited staff and positioned company for $6 million in annual revenues by 2001 and $14 million by 2004.
- Accelerated product development cycle and managed database development through completion.
- Established and built a multi-tiered third party distribution network to expand market reach.
- Structured and negotiated $1 million in financings to support current cash requirements.

INVESTORS AMERICA INC. – New York
1993 to 1998

Executive Vice President / COO – Latin America (1996 to 1998)
Senior Vice President – Latin America (1993 to 1996)

High-profile leadership position as a member of Executive Management Committee and Investors America Holdings Executive Committee. Held full strategic planning, operating, marketing, business development and P&L responsibility for all Latin American operations. Scope of responsibility included regional managers, country managers, marketing directors, financial director, technical director, editor, HR manager and a staff of 400+.

Challenged to reinvent the Latin American business organization and create a market-driven acquisition program to capitalize upon emerging business opportunities. Clients included major US and international banking and capital markets institutions and local financial and media organizations.

- Achieved/surpassed all financial objectives. Increased revenue from $40 million to $85 million, profits from $4 million to $13 million and market penetration (terminals installed) by more than 200%.
- Relocated Latin American HQ to New York City to enhance the synergy between all Americas operations.
- Restructured the entire organization and its supporting infrastructure. Hired new management and marketing talent, shifted decision making responsibilities to the country level and repositioned market focus.
- Launched an aggressive new product development initiative to deliver market-specific products, services and technologies. Transitioned market perception from news information to financial services to broaden market reach and penetration. Resulted in a better than 50% growth in market share.
- Identified opportunity, structured and launched company's first commercial broadcast television venture, a 24-hour Spanish language news channel broadcasting in the US, Spain and Latin America.

INVESTORS AMERICA – AUSTRALIA – Sydney   1990 to 1992

Managing Director – Australia & New Zealand (1991 to 1992)
Regional Applications Manager – Southeast Asia (1990)

Promoted and given full responsibility for the marketing, development, operations and P&L performance of company's business organizations throughout Australia and New Zealand. Led through a multidisciplinary organization comprised of a wholly-owned subsidary, a company-owned subsidiary and a third-party distributorship. Challenged to strengthen and solidify distribution relationship, accelerate sales revenues, launch new product introductions and drive long-term profitability.

- Despite country-wide market instability, delivered 5% revenue and profit growth while strategically repositioning Investors America as the company of choice with all major accounts.
- Negotiated long-term contracts with Australia's four major banks, generating $24 million in annual sales.
- Appointed to the Board of Directors of a local software firm acquired by Investors America to create an internal channel for new software development.
- Facilitated the merger and integration of Sharp IP into Investors America Australian operations, eliminated unprofitable business lines and repositioned for continued market growth.
- Reconfigured core product mix, upgraded technology and expedited all customer conversions. Transitioned product focus to more advanced technology with lower volume, higher quality and improved profitability.
- Downsized operations in New Zealand and increased margins to 45% on $12 million in annual sales.

INVESTORS AMERICA – ASIA – Hong Kong   1988 to 1989

Marketing Manager

Recruited to Investors America to conceive, create and implement a completely new Information Management Systems strategy and business throughout the entire Asian market. Scope of responsibility extended from product planning, design and development to market launch and ongoing customer support.

CHASE MANHATTAN BANK – Hong Kong   1985 to 1987

Vice President – Asia/Pacific Operations & Systems – Global Trading & Treasury Division

Promoted to lead the design, engineering and execution of a new systems architecture, advanced technologies and a global LAN to support Chase operations throughout Asia Pacific (total of 72 branches and more than 350 employees). Delivered $5.1 million project on time and within budget. Surpassed all performance objectives.

CHASE MANHATTAN BANK – New York   1983 to 1985

Vice President / Group Project Manager – Global Trading & Treasury Division

High-profile HQ position leading the design, development and implementation of advanced technologies, networks and applications across all core financial, trading and treasury systems. Built technology infrastructure to support rapid growth and global expansion.

BANCO LAR / CHASE MANHATTAN BANK – Rio de Janeiro   1968 to 1983

Senior Vice President – Systems Planning & Development

Fast-track promotion through a series of increasingly responsible MIS management positions to final promotion as Senior Vice President (equivalent to Chief Information Officer) for one of Brazil's largest financial institutions.

EDUCATION:

UNIVERSITY OF MICHIGAN	Strategic Planning (1996)
NORTHWESTERN UNIVERSITY / KELLOGG	Executive Development Program (1986)
ESCOLA NACIONAL DE QUIMICA	Chemical Engineering (1970-72)

PERSONAL PROFILE:

Brazilian Citizen ... US Permanent Resident. Past Director, Brazilian American Chamber of Commerce

JAMES K. BLACKWELL

15 N Portal Drive NW
Washington, DC 20533

Office: 202-963-8565

jkblack@worldnet.att.net

SENIOR LEGAL, LEGISLATIVE, TAX & BUSINESS ADVISOR
Corporations, Partnerships, Associations, Coalitions, Special Interest Group & Government Agencies
US & International Interests, Projects, Programs, Issues & Opportunities

Expert Strategist & Legal Tactician promoting the development, funding, support and passage of policy and legislation favorable to represented parties. Successful in evaluating the political, economic, legal and government impact on specific policy and legislative action, garnering support and consensus between parties with vastly different agendas and objectives. A persuasive, educated and skilled negotiator with outstanding communication, client service and relationship management skills. Recognized for honor, integrity and loyalty. Advanced degrees.

PROFESSIONAL EXPERIENCE:

PRESIDENT & CEO – ZETNER CONSULTING, Washington, DC   1994 to Present

Launched entrepreneurial legal consulting practice at the request of White Stag and Bristol Corporation (past clients) to provide comprehensive leadership to favorably manage tax issues, laws, policies, regulations and legislative impacting their organizations. Created a unique attorney-client communications forum to provide comprehensive information on pending bills and activities on Capitol Hill. Established, and continue to build, a solid reputation for expertise in client relationship management within the legal community.

Specialize in the formulation and implementation of legislative strategies in the areas of tax, trade, appropriation, Native American issues and intellectual property. Key projects and legislation has included:

- **Legislative Proposal To Tax Indian Government**. Successfully defeated bill to tax tribal governments, halting an initiative with potential for a $5 billion negative economic impact.

- **National Gambling Impact Study Commission**. Senior Advisor and Lobbyist working to advance economic development by thwarting potential taxation. Extensive communications with *Time Magazine*, *Wall Street Journal*, *The Legislative Journal* and other major publications to educate the media and general public about the potential negative economic impacts.

- **Nantucket Glass Company Refinancing**. Crafted bill to give local Indian tribe tax exempt status allowing for $10 million in refinancing to support further development.

- **National Indian Gaming Association**. Advised Indian government political leaders and their vendors in defeating several anti-gambling appropriations supported by special interest groups.

- **Irish Affairs**. Promoted economic development, foreign investment and cross-border cooperation throughout Northern Ireland. Represented Irish political and business interests at the National Investment Conference, worked with Senator Howland to pass legislation, and contributed to numerous documentaries and news stories. Developed economic development funding sources.

- **Good Friday Trade & Investment Act / Irish Trade Legislation / Border Countries Free Trade Agreement**. Launched grassroots campaign and built broad coalition to support legislation favorable to US trade and investment in Northern Ireland. Prepared economic development package and negotiated privileged trade treatment with the full support of Parliament.

- **State of Virginia Business Development**. Partnered Virginia-based businesses with Northern Ireland counterparts to effectuate the entry of U.S. commercial interests in the European Union. Specialized in partnerships in the technology and medical services industries.

TAX COUNSEL – DEMPSEY, ALEXANDER, TEAL, ZIMMERMAN   1993 to 1994
Washington, D.C.

Recruited to this prestigious law firm ranked as the #1/#2 lobbyist in the U.S. and representing major U.S. corporations (e.g., American Airlines, Hess Corporation, A G Edwards). Provided expert strategic and tactical counsel to meet client needs in the areas of tax, trade and health care. Personally represented clients before congressional and Capitol Hill committee staffs to advance their positions and lobby for passage of favorable tax initiatives and incentives.

- Leveraged past relationship with White Stag developed while working in the U.S. Senate, and successfully brought them to the firm. Worked closely with their in-house counsel and executive team to promote corporate interests in capital gains and retirement security issues.

- Negotiated and closed business relationship to bring Intel Corporation to the firm, a major player in the technology industry. Provided legal expertise relative to intellectual property, trade and general appropriation issues.

TAX COUNSEL – UNITED STATES SENATE, Washington, D.C.   1990 to 1993

Tremendous professional opportunity working in cooperation with Senate Finance Committee member Max Baucus. Led a team of attorneys and support personnel working to enact legislative favorable state and federal tax proposals in the areas of Budgeting, Banking, Taxation and Foreign Tax Simplification. Notable projects and enacted legislation included:

- **Payroll Simplification Act of 1991** introduced to reduce the complexity of the corporate payroll tax deposit process. Consultations with Finance Committee, Treasury Committee and major payroll processing companies throughout the U.S.

- **Section 29 Fuel Source Credit**, Montana-specific legislation promoting economic development within the fuel and energy sectors. Extensive outreach and negotiations with other state senators to create a universal tax law.

- **Revenue Act of 1992** enacting economic, employment and tax legislation favorable to Native American Indian reservations. Worked in cooperation with Senator McCain's Chief of Staff to develop senatorial coalition and promote subsequent passage by President Bush.

- **Foreign Tax Simplification Act** designed to streamline the complete federal tax filing process. Created first generation proposal enacted six years later by the U.S. Senate.

TAX COUNSEL – TEDFORD & WILLIAMS, Dallas, Texas   1989 to 1990

Developed tax litigation strategies and analyzed income tax implications of international business transactions. Litigated issues relative to state, corporate, partnership and income taxation.

TAX COUNSEL – UNITED STATES TAX COURT, Washington, D.C.   1988 to 1989

Selected from a large group of competitive candidates to serve under the Honorable Henry Lee Dwight.

EDUCATION:

Executive M.B.A. Program – Georgetown University, Washington, D.C., 1997 to 1998

Masters of International Public Policy in Asian Studies – Major University, 1997
    A Famous School of Advanced International Studies

L.L.M. – Taxation – Loyola Marymount University-Los Angeles, 1988
Staff Member, California Tax Law Journal

Juris Doctorate – Loyola Marymount University-Los Angeles, 1986
Phi Delta Phi – International Legal Fraternity; Third Year Senator – Student Bar Association

B.A. – Political Science & Economics – Loyola Marymount University-Los Angeles, 1983
Dean's List; Hornbeck Scholar Award; Phi Gamma Mu – Undergraduate Honor Society

CONTINUING PROFESSIONAL EDUCATION:

Managing The Workplace: People, Strategy & Leadership, The Wharton School, Univ. of PA, 1999

Essentials of Decision Making, John F. Kennedy School of Government / Harvard University, 1999

Campaigns & Elections Training Seminar, Washington, D.C., 1999

Congressional Quarterly Media Relations Seminar, Washington, D.C., 1999

Strategies of Persuasion, John F. Kennedy School of Government / Harvard University, 1998

Program on Negotiation: Negotiations for Senior Executives, Harvard Law School, 1998

Principles & Practices of Conflict Management, Johns Hopkins University, 1998

Politics of Western Hemisphere Integration, Johns Hopkins University, 1998

Introductory Chinese, Georgetown University, 1998

Global Business Leadership Seminar, Georgetown University, 1995

Executive International Business Certificate Program, Georgetown University, 1995

PUBLICATIONS & PUBLIC SPEAKING ENGAGEMENTS:

- "Corporate Tax Developments," ABA *Tax Lawyer* (co-author)
- "Harvard's AAA Ruling: A Misnomer," *Newsletter of the Section on Taxation*, State Bar of Texas
- "Doing Business in Latin America" & "Doing Business in China" – International Trade Forum, Loyola Marymount University-Los Angeles

PROFESSIONAL AFFILIATIONS:

Washington International Trade Association
American Arbitration Association
American Red Cross – Board of Directors, Financial Development Committee
U.S. Tax Court – Federal Campaign Key Worker

CIVIC LEADERSHIP & AFFILIATIONS *(Select Listing)*:

Virginia Minority Supplier Member
Native American Rights Fund
Running Strong for American Indian Youth
National Museum of the American Indian
American Indian College Fund
National Indian Education Association
Indian Youth of America

Make-A-Wish Foundation
Japan-American Society
The Asia Society
Character Counts Advocate
College Bound
Food & Friends
American Ireland Fund

LYNETTE O. BORELLI, J.D.

97 Oakcrest Drive
Atlanta, Georgia 30307
Home: 678-963-5445 ... Office: 404-124-7485 ... LOBLAW@aol.com

LEGAL CAREER PROFILE:

CRIMINAL DEFENSE ATTORNEY with an outstanding record of performance in planning, preparing and managing high-profile criminal defense cases. Combines expert analytical, investigative, organizational, negotiation and courtroom litigation skills to prepare powerful defense for fraud, larceny, illegal drug, assault, and other felony and criminal cases.

Extensive experience in Family Law, Consumer Affairs, Bankruptcy, Insurance, Taxation, Torts and Estate Planning. Direct and decisive. Outstanding legal training, leadership and advocacy skills. PC proficient.

Admitted to practice in the District of Columbia and State of Georgia.
Member of the National State Bar Association and Military Bar Association.

PROFESSIONAL EXPERIENCE:

ATTORNEY – UNITED STATES NAVY – Office of the Staff Judge Advocate   1996 to Present

Distinguished legal career highlighted by rapid promotion through a series of increasingly responsible positions. Honored for outstanding performance, astute legal skills and the ability to effectively manage complex, sensitive legal affairs. Trusted advisor to senior-ranking military officials.

Defense Counsel – A Base, GA (1999 to Present)
Trial Counsel – A Base, NC (1998 to 1999)

High-profile, high-visibility criminal and contract law positions supporting top-level command personnel with worldwide responsibilities. Independently prosecuted criminal matters, from initial investigations through trial planning, pleadings, motions, memoranda, discovery , legal research and courtroom representation for court martial proceedings. Authored memoranda in response to Congressional and officer inquiries.

Notable Defense Cases & Legal Proceedings:

- Prosecuted a total of 150 cases with 148 convictions and only 2 acquittals. Managed 21 successful court martial proceedings, won acquittal in robbery court martial and production Article 32 evidence (preliminary hearing) to drop charges against enlisted soldier.
- Negotiated Chapter 10 (administrative discharge) after court martial and argued for release of soldier from active duty while pending administrative discharge.
- Lead Counsel in three highly-publicized economic crime cases involving conspiracy, fraud and larceny against the U.S. Government. Won all three cases.
- Successfully represented the U.S. Government in several adverse administrative proceedings.
- Prosecuted and obtained convictions in two child abuse cases.

NOTE: In current position, manage criminal defense and prosecution for ABC Base, ABC Base and ABC Base in Houston Texas (total of 28,000 military personnel assigned to these three installations).

Chief – Legal Assistance – A Base, KY (1997)

Managed Legal Assistance Office responsible for providing legal advice to soldiers, family members and military retirees in estate planning, consumer, divorce, child custody and support, paternity, tort and military administrative matters. Utilized negotiation skills to obtain relief for clients in unconscionable contracts, deceptive and fraudulent business matters, and illegal debt collection practices. Briefed personnel on core legal issues, including DOD policy on homosexuality. Trained and supervised a staff of six.

Notable Cases & Legal Proceedings:

- Promoted to Chief after only 10 months. Led office to win the 1997 Navy's Chief of Staff Award in Legal Assistance for consistently superior service and legal expertise.
- Instrumental in revitalizing the North Carolina Bar Association Legal Assistance for Military Personnel Committee's Continuing Education Program after years of inactivity. Coordinated seminar attended by 40+ military and civilian personnel.
- Appointed Co-Counsel in a successful civilian paternity and child support case.
- Successfully argued and won military administrative hearing banning a local business from advertising in the base newspaper to solicit soldier on the installation.

Legal Assistance Attorney – A Base, NY (1996 to 1997)

Assigned to the U.S. Navy's busiest Legal Assistance Office. Provided legal advice to 2000+ soldiers, family members and clients on family law, consumer issues and estate planning. Authored rebuttals to military administrative matters resulting in findings of non-liability, retention and removal of adverse matters from official personnel files.

Notable Cases & Legal Proceedings:

- Managed legal liaison affairs with the Federal Trade Commission, North Carolina Attorney General's Office, Better Business Bureau, and other government and civilian agencies. Demonstrated outstanding inter-agency coordination, communication and case management skills.
- Planned and led implementation of the installation's first Alternative Dispute Resolution (ADR) program.
- Drafted XVIII Airborne Corps New Officer Orientation Guide to indoctrinate newly-appointed officers to their legal responsibilities and code of conduct.
- Drafted 60+ estate planning documents for enlisted personnel and offices.

LEGAL AID SOCIETY OF DETROIT – Michigan   1995 to 1996

Attorney

Represented low income individuals in child custody and visitation matters. Coordinated placement of pro bono cases with private law firms and facilitated public/private liaison affairs.

COMMODITY FUTURES TRADING COMMISSION – Washington, D.C.   1994 to 1995
RESOLUTION TRUST CORPORATION – Washington, D.C.   Summers 1992 & 1993

Law Clerk / Legal Assistant

Conducted legal research and drafted memoranda on the Freedom of Information Act. For CFTC, revised annotations on Administrative Rules of Practice and computerized Brief projects for Enforcement Division. For RTC, authored appraiser liability guide and created defendant's computerized tracking system.

EDUCATION:

HOWARD UNIVERSITY SCHOOL OF LAW, Washington, D.C.
J.D. Degree – 1995 (*Jim Jones Award in Intellectual Property; Merit Scholarship*)

UNIVERSITY OF AKRON, Akron, Ohio
B.S., Computer Science & Business – 1992 (*Presidential Scholarship; Magna Cum Laude*)

Highlights of Continuing Professional Education:

- Judge Advocate General's Criminal Law Advocacy Course and Legal Assistance Course
- New Developments in Criminal Law
- U.S. Navy Trial Defense Service Spring & Fall Conferences

WAYNE FARRELL

34952 North Wind Drive
Topeka, Kansas 65229
(913) 528-2494

MANUFACTURING MANAGER / OPERATIONS MANAGER / PLANT MANAGER
Start-Up, Turnaround, Fast-Track Growth & Multinational Corporations

Results-driven Operating Executive with 15+ years management experience. Strong general management qualifications in strategic planning, manufacturing, fabrication and assembly, production scheduling and control, inventory/materials management, project management, warehousing, distribution, budgeting/finance, human resource affairs and capital improvement. Pioneer in MRP, TQM, SPC and other productivity/performance improvement initiatives.

Reduced manufacturing costs by more than $4.5 million while increasing operating profits in excess of $4.6 million.

PROFESSIONAL EXPERIENCE:

1001 PRODUCTS, INC., Topeka, Kansas   1993 to 1997
($27 million multi-product manufacturer and distributor)

PLANT MANAGER

Senior Operating Executive with full P&L responsibility for the strategic planning, development, operating management and turnaround of this 300-employee manufacturing organization. Established procedures, developed business plans and managed all production operations/control, scheduling, quality, testing, shipping/receiving, materials, inventory, staffing and financial reporting.

Introduced a series of productivity improvement, process reengineering, cost reduction and performance management programs that consistently improved production output, product quality and customer satisfaction. Innovated unique solutions to complex operating problems.

- Returned the company to profitability within first four months of hire. **Increased operating profit to over $1.6 million**.
- Realigned staffing patterns, restructured production scheduling, introduced improved materials planning procedures, and **reduced indirect labor costs by $380,000**.
- Reduced scrap by 2.5% weekly for an **annual cost savings of $187,000**.
- **Improved on-time delivery from 67% to 95%** and restored customer confidence.

ARCHITECTURAL PRODUCTS CORPORATION, York, Pennsylvania   1988 to 1993
($40 million manufacturer of commercial products and components)

PROJECT MANAGER (1992 to 1993)

Promoted by President to a special assignment targeting the collection of past due receivables that had been outstanding for three to five years. Managed complex communications and negotiations with customers nationwide, and coordinated with attorneys for cases in litigation.

- Closed contracts on 35 "open" projects and **recovered $6 million in cash** to the corporation.

PLANT MANAGER (1990 to 1992)

Full P&L responsibility for a 350-employee production operation, multi-million dollar annual operating budget, all capital expenditures, and an aggressive productivity, quality and performance improvement initiative.

ARCHITECTURAL PRODUCTS CORPORATION *(Continued):*

- Led successful turnaround from $200,000/month in losses to $200,000/month in profits. **Delivered full year profit contribution of $985,000**.
- **Decreased direct labor costs from 14.5% of total expenditures to 12.5%** through realignment of staffing, training and production scheduling programs.
- Orchestrated a dramatic consolidation and reduction in workforce in 1992.

SUPPORT PRODUCTION MANAGER (1988 to 1989)

Directed materials support for an 8-line, 400-employee operation. Responsible for receiving, raw materials processing, fabrication, paint operations, inventory control and warehousing. Managed 187 employees.

- Consolidated two shift operation into one which **reduced labor costs by $1.3 million annually** while sales revenues grew by $2.9 million over the previous year.
- **Increased productivity to 103% while reducing lost time accidents by 52%.**
- Reduced turnover to 1.19% annually, absenteeism to 3.1%, operating budgets by $331,000 and fabrication scrap by 40,000 pounds.
- Designed a completely new inventory control system, attained 98.2% accuracy and eliminated need for annual physical inventory.

KRESTMARK INDUSTRIES, Lewisville, Texas   1983 to 1987
($23 million finished products manufacturer and distributor)

PLANT MANAGER (1985 to 1987)
PRODUCTION MANAGER (1983 to 1985)

Full operating management responsibility for a 325-employee, high-volume production operation with 10-day lead time. Managed production planning and scheduling, materials management, inventory, manufacturing, assembly, test and packaging.

- Built production output to 2500 units/day to meet increased customer demand.

KAISER CORPORATION, Chalmette, Louisiana   1976 to 1982
(Largest U.S. aluminum manufacturer with $400 million in sales and 2600 employees)

PRODUCTION MANAGER - Louisiana

Promoted to Louisiana plant to facilitate a complete turnaround and return to profitability. Directed operations for 160 production cells with four supervisors and 60+ hourly personnel.

- Restructured the entire production operation and transitioned from $200,000/month loss to $200,000/month profit within two months. **Improved annual profitability by $2 million.**

PRODUCTION MANAGER - Washington

Fast-track promotion throughout a series of increasingly responsible plant operations, supervisory and management positions during 10-year career.

- Achieved record production and safety levels, won four corporate awards for performance improvement, and **cut lost time accident costs by $1.3 million annually**.

EDUCATION: **Business Administration**
LOUISIANA STATE UNIVERSITY / SOUTHEASTERN LOUISIANA UNIVERSITY

Continuing Professional Training in General Management, Management By Objectives, Communications, Computer Technology and Performance Management.

196

CHARLES H. TAYLOR

946 Cedar Court
Cary, North Carolina 27253
(910) 278-6547

SENIOR OPERATING, MANUFACTURING & MANAGEMENT EXECUTIVE

Delivered strong operating and financial results in challenging start-up, turnaround and high-growth operations through expertise in:

- Strategic Business & Market Planning
- Quality & Performance Improvement
- Cost Reduction & Revenue Gain
- Customer Relationship Management
- Production Processes & Standards

- Multi-Site Manufacturing Operations
- Technology & Engineering
- Product Rationalization & Diversification
- Purchasing & Materials Management
- Contract Negotiations

PROFESSIONAL EXPERIENCE:

WIP SYSTEMS, Raleigh, North Carolina   1988 to Present
($3.5 billion electronics technology manufacturer with 20 plants worldwide)

Vice President / Plant Manager, Raleigh, North Carolina (1994 to Present)
Senior Operating Executive with full P&L responsibility for a 140,000 sq. ft. contract manufacturing facility with 400 employees and revenues of more than $120 million annually. Challenged to plan and direct the turnaround and return to profitability of the operation. Lead a six-person management team responsible for operations, manufacturing engineering, materials, quality, technical programs, human resources, finance and marketing.

- Achieved/surpassed all turnaround objectives and returned the operation to profitability within less than 12 months. Delivered strong and sustainable operating gains:
  — 70% improvement in operating efficiency.
  — 250% reduction in cycle times.
  — 75% increase in product quality.
  — 100% on-time customer delivery.
- Launched regional market expansion to penetrate emerging customer markets and achieve product diversification. Increased sales revenues from $80 million to $120 million (30% growth).
- Identified, negotiated and closed two major new contracts (Fortune 500 technology OEMs).
- Restored credibility with one customer generating over $30 million in revenues to WIP. Resolved long-standing quality and delivery issues, implemented key account management strategy and revitalized business relationship.
- Achieved ISO 9002 and QS9000 quality certifications.

Plant Manager, Rochester, New York (1988 to 1994)
Recruited to WIP to direct the operating turnaround of a start-up contract manufacturing facility established through a strategic business partnership with IBM. Scope of responsibility included all planning, operating, staffing, budgeting, technology and customer management programs for a 150,000 sq. ft. manufacturing facility with 550 employees. Challenged to rebuild the manufacturing function and restore credibility with IBM.

- Achieved successful turnaround within first year and positioned for long-term growth. Increased sales by 35% and profit contributions by 20%.
- Delivered significant improvements in quality, productivity, cycle time and cost control through implementation of advanced operating processes, on-time delivery and quality standards.

AMERICAN DEFENSE SYSTEMS, Pittsburgh, Pennsylvania   1986 to 1988

Director of Operations

Full P&L responsibility for a 100,000 sq. ft. manufacturing facility with 400 employees and revenues of $65+ million. Developed operational strategies to improve productivity, efficiency, quality and delivery of sophisticated electronics technology. Directed manufacturing, quality assurance, test, material/production control, purchasing, manufacturing/plant engineering and industrial relations.

- Captured an average 10% reduction in annual material and labor costs to accelerate profit growth while maintaining constant sales pricing.
- Directed a $5 million technology investment to automate production line, implemented MRP II system, and drove forward several other critical technology installations.
- Achieved 100% on-time customer delivery and restored customer confidence.

MEDICAL DIAGNOSTIC INSTRUMENTS, Nashua, New Hampshire   1982 to 1986

Vice President / Co-Founder

General Manager of start-up medical instrument company funded through private investor financing and structured as a limited partnership. Designed business development, marketing and operating systems to transition from R&D to full-scale manufacturing. Created budget and performance objectives, directed implementation of accounting and inventory control systems, and created the entire operating and technical support infrastructures.

- Directed clinical trials at 15 hospitals and health care facilities nationwide to position company for full-scale market launch with five year projections at $25+ million.
- Recruited and led a highly creative technical staff toward the timely design completion of complex medical equipment and technology.

SMITHKLINE INSTRUMENTS, Boston, Massachusetts   1980 to 1982

Director of Operations

Directed operations of a 225-employee ultrasonic scanning equipment manufacturer. Planned, staffed, budgeted and managed production, system test, product assurance, material/production control, purchasing, manufacturing engineering, plant engineering and field service/technical support.

- Delivered annual operating cost reductions averaging 20%+ to accelerate profit gains.
- Installed disciplined manufacturing processes and stringent quality controls to standardize production methods, increase manufacturing output and improve product reliability.

MICRO-CONDUCTOR CORPORATION, Morristown, New Jersey   1972 to 1980

Manufacturing Manager

P&L responsibility for high-volume, 175-employee microwave amplifier/component manufacturer. Launched successful start-up of off-shore microwave component manufacturing facility.

Previous Professional Experience: Fast-track promotion through a series of manufacturing, engineering and operations management positions with Lockheed Electronics, RCA and Kearfott/Singer.

EDUCATION: **M.S., Management Science**, Stevens Institute of Technology
                    B.S., Industrial Engineering, Fairleigh Dickinson University

PUBLICATIONS:
- Co-Author, *"Computer Aided Design of Hybrid Microcircuits,"* National Electronic Packaging Conference.
- Author, *"Subtle Aspects of Micro-Packaging,"* Product Assurance Conference.

MILITARY SERVICE: Two-year tour of duty with the U.S. Navy.

ROBERT W. LEWIS

1093 St. Andrews Lane   Home   (513) 578-5735
Cleveland, Ohio 44052   Office   (513) 543-1169

CAREER PROFILE

Director of Operations / Director of Manufacturing / Plant & Production Manager
Start-Up, Turnaround, High-Growth & Multinational Operations

Top-Performing Business Manager with direct P&L responsibility for multi-site manufacturing, assembly and distribution operations. Delivered strong revenue and profit gains, multi-million dollar cost reductions and sustainable yield improvements. Expert in state-of-the-art manufacturing technologies and processes.

PROFESSIONAL EXPERIENCE:

THE DIAL CORPORATION, Cincinnati, Ohio   1995 to Present

Manufacturing Manager - Household Division
(Dial's fastest growing segment with $450 million in revenues)

Senior Manufacturing Director and Dial's only on-site management representative for five contract manufacturing facilities in Ohio, Illinois and Massachusetts. Hold full responsibility for the planning and management of all Dial business operations (e.g., inventory, materials, manufacturing, quality, logistics, packaging, distribution) for the Softsoap business line and for the administration of Dial/co-packer partnership contracts.

- Delivered 3.5% growth within a mature and highly competitive business market.
- Led integration of two new products into manufacturing operations, generating $7.5 million in new revenues within first year and poised for national launch into KMart and Wal-Mart. Facilitated product transition from Dial's product engineering teams into specific production, assembly and packaging operations in a tight, 16-week cycle.
- Spearheaded introduction of a series of continuous improvement initiatives that consistently strengthened productivity, product quality and customer satisfaction.

STORAGE SYSTEMS COMPANY, Cincinnati, Ohio   1994 to 1995

Business Unit Manager

Recruited by CEO to launch the start-up of a new business unit for this $5 million privately-owned distributor of material storage devices. Challenged to build new operation and establish market presence for introduction of ergonomically-designed material handling and logistics equipment.

- Successfully completed one-year contract. Brought business from initial planning through start-up and market launch. Negotiated preliminary relationships with manufacturers, assemblers and distributors throughout region and positioned company for strong market performance.

CAVU DISTRIBUTING, INC., Cincinnati, Ohio   1992 to 1994

Partner

Challenged to launch an entrepreneurial venture and capitalize upon core competencies in operations and distribution management. In cooperation with two other principals, directed start-up and initial management of new beverage distribution company.

- Transitioned company from concept through start-up to full-scale operations. Created all operating, business, financial, sales and service programs. Closed 100 accounts in first 60 days.
- Negotiated company sale to primary supplier and facilitated management transition.

REDKEN LABORATORIES, INC., Cincinnati, Ohio   1985 to 1992

Director of Manufacturing / General Manager of Eastern Operations

Senior Operating Executive (on-site) directing a sophisticated hair care products manufacturing and distribution facility. Held full P&L responsibility for the business unit. Directed a team of nine exempt and 100 non-exempt, non-union employees. Controlled assets valued in excess of $15 million. Administered $4 million in annual operating and capital budgets. Guided the annual strategic planning process.

Scope of responsibility was diverse and included materials planning, inventory, component manufacturing, process batch operations, industrial engineering, plant engineering, packaging, distribution, freight control, customer service, human resources, quality assurance and an aggressive continuous process improvement program.

- Produced 40 million units annually at 99.5% acceptance rate and 98% customer order accuracy.
- Led a $7 million construction program to expand facility from 35,000 to 150,000 sq. ft.
- Delivered over 35% ROI through implementation of vertical integration projects and bulk material purchasing programs.
- Appointed to numerous corporate task forces spearheading market integration programs, U.S./ international manufacturing analysis, bar coding technology implementation and distribution network consolidation. Efforts improved ROI to 40%.
- Saved $75,000 annually in material costs through employee-driven scrap reduction program.

AVON PRODUCTS, INC., Cincinnati, Ohio & New York, New York   1977 to 1985

Operations Manager (1984 to 1985)
Group Manager (1981 to 1984)
Packaging Manager (1980 to 1981)
Section Manager (1977 to 1980)

Fast-track promotion through a series of increasingly responsible operating and production management positions with the world's largest cosmetics company. As **Operations Manager**, directed a staff of 50 exempt and 550 non-exempt, non-union employees in the operation of a state-of-the-art, 1.3 million sq. ft. manufacturing complex (60 different production lines).

- Delivered strong and sustainable operating gains:
  - 20% reduction in cost of "non-conformance" through Crosby quality programs.
  - 15% reduction in undistributed labor costs for a 300-employee direct labor workforce.
  - 5% reduction in indirect labor costs through internal industrial engineering techniques.
  - 18% improvement in equipment reliability.

As **Group Manager for Manufacturing Operations** (corporate HQ position), served as corporate liaison between manufacturing, marketing, new product development and product cost. Guided U.S. and international operating locations in industrial engineering, equipment design, methods improvement, TQM and financial control.

- Captured over $1 million in operating cost reductions.

JOSEPH E. SEAGRAMS & SONS, Lawrenceburg, Indiana   1974 to 1977

Maintenance Supervisor for multi-million dollar bottling operation.

EDUCATION: **PURDUE UNIVERSITY**, Lafayette, Indiana
B.S., Industrial Management, 1974

Continuing Education in Leadership, Communications and Management Decision Making.

GARY R. JORDAN
547 Southbend
Queens, New York 19734
(212) 967-6984

SENIOR MARKETING & BUSINESS DEVELOPMENT EXECUTIVE
NationsBank, M&M Mars, Hershey

Dynamic management career spearheading successful marketing and business development programs nationwide. Combines expertise in strategic market planning, organizational leadership and project management with strong qualifications in campaign design, new product/service development and market launch. Participative leadership style with excellent skills in cross-functional team building, quality performance and productivity improvement.

Delivered the strategies and tactical development plans that drove
millions of dollars in revenue and profit growth.

PROFESSIONAL EXPERIENCE:

Corporate Marketing Consultant   1992 to Present
THE CONSULTING GROUP, Queens, New York

Executive Marketing Advisor to corporate clients in the publishing, health care and dairy industries throughout New York and Connecticut.

- **New England Dairy**. Long-term consulting assignment developing objectives, strategies and tactics to expand market penetration of specialty product. Contributed to solid 15% annual growth to over $70 million annually. Concurrent responsibility for advising CEO on product and company acquisitions. Reviewed more than 25 potential opportunities and currently in final due diligence review with several.

- **Futura Medical Publishing**. Defined marketing objectives, evaluated existing programs, and developed a series of targeted promotions and direct mail marketing campaigns.

Vice President / Marketing Director   1977 to 1992
NATIONSBANK, New York, New York

Spearheaded Nationsbank's successful and profitable entry into the nationwide Bankcard Insurance market to capitalize upon emerging market opportunity and exploit core competencies. Created innovative marketing programs targeted to key consumer markets throughout the U.S. and established Nationsbank as a major player within the industry.

- **Transitioned business unit from concept into a full-scale marketing and business development organization that grew to $100 million in annual volume within eight years.**

Built the entire marketing infrastructure, defined short-term marketing goals and long-term market development plans, and created high-profile, market-specific business development initiatives. Provided a decisive course of action to accelerate revenue/market growth. Recognized by corporate executives for expertise in market plan development, management and goal attainment.

NATIONSBANK *(Continued):*

- Conceived, developed, tested and introduced more than 20 new products and services to expedite market penetration, create strong revenue and profit streams, and gain a competitive market advantage.

    — Credit Insurance Product. $100 million in revenue in eight years.
    — Established Insurance Products. 20% annual growth.
    — Basic Life/Health Insurance Products. $1 million in two years.
    — "Buy By Mail" Savings Products. $500,000 in revenue in two years.
    — Airflight Insurance Product. Projected as second largest insurance revenue producer in Nationsbank's past 10 years.

- Revitalized Nationsbank's in-house insurance agency providing strategic and tactical marketing support for major consumer businesses (e.g., Bankcards, Choice Visa).

- Negotiated strategic partnerships and alliances across all business units to facilitate nationwide marketing and business development initiatives.

- Created innovative, distinctive and successful direct mail, telemarketing, advertising, promotion and business development campaigns.

- Led cross-functional project teams (e.g., strategic, financial, operating, creative design, production, marketing, sales).

- Built incremental revenue by 20% through expansion of third-party distribution network.

Product Manager - New Products   1975 to 1977
M&M/MARS, New York, New York

Spearheaded the development and market launch of a series of new products and line extensions for the Family Products Division.

- Led successful introduction of new brand which surpassed first year dollar and unit share objectives by 18%.

- Managed successful consumer research and testing to evaluate product potential.

Senior Brand Manager   1971 to 1975
HERSHEY COMPANY, INC., Hershey, Pennsylvania

Fast-track promotion through several brand management positions.

- Revised marketing campaign for "$100,000" bar and drove 250% increase in three years.

- Realigned marketing and brand management programs for Hershey's Syrup products, increasing revenues by up to 48% annually.

- Identified market opportunity and led the most profitable promotion in 12 years.

Assistant Account Executive   1969 to 1971
MATHEW BENDER & ASSOCIATES, New York, New York

Developed marketing strategy for "Payday" (#1 market position in 1971). Wrote marketing segments for Kelloggs' "Frosted Flakes" cereal (exceeded profit objectives by 12%). Directed successful test market launch of Kraft's "Macaroni & Cheese" line extension.

EDUCATION: BA, Yale University

THOMAS PAGNOTTI

241 Kingston Street
Little Rock Arkansas 72201
Home Phone: 501-541-5447   Email: tompagnotti@earthlink.net

SENIOR MARKETING, SALES & BUSINESS DEVELOPMENT EXECUTIVE
Executive Vice President / Senior Vice President / Director

Forerunner in identifying, leveraging and optimizing Internet & e-commerce marketing opportunities.

- Strategic & Tactical Marketing/Sales
- Sales Training, Team Building & Leadership
- Business Partners & Alliances
- Multi-Channel Distribution

- Competitive Market Intelligence
- Corporate & Investor Marketing
- Multi-Media Advertising Campaigns
- Corporate & Investment Finance & IPO's

PROFESSIONAL EXPERIENCE:

President / Chief Technology Marketing Executive   1995 to Present
AAA MARKETING, INC., Little Rock, Arkansas

Recruited by ownership of this exclusive marketing and public relations firm to:

- Expand and strengthen the delivery of its core investor relations service programs.
- Expand into emerging website and e-commerce market development opportunities.

Fully accountable for all executive/senior management functions, profit/loss performance, and all sales, marketing, business development and new product/service development operations. Heavy emphasis in personnel recruitment, training and leadership to build multi-faceted workforce able to manage technology requirements of both company ventures.

- Built new website development and e-commerce venture from concept to over $16 million in annual sales revenues. Penetrated diverse corporate markets including transportation, telecommunications, hospitality and financial services.

- Personally managed high-profile business development relationships with CEO's to promote AAA Marketing's emerging technology services and the value of Internet advertising/marketing.

- Strategized, built and directed a third business line focused on developing innovative Internet advertising websites to penetrate a larger and more diversified customer base. Brought to over $4 million in revenues within first year.

- Pioneered targeted email marketing during its early emergence. Generated a 25%+ response rate.

- Structured partnerships and alliances with ISP's and other technology provider companies, a critical initiative in increasing website traffic and generating client revenues.

- Introduced a telemarketing organization to further expand lead generation activities.

Joined the Executive Leadership Team of a 10,000-subscriber Internet Service Provider (ISP) during the proposed acquisition of AAA Marketing. Retained to plan and orchestrate critical acquisition analysis and dealmaking to support the company's aggressive growth strategy. Concurrently, designed economic model to increase customer base and led development of nationwide VAR network.

Senior Marketing & Business Development Executive   1989 to 1995
STAR MARKETING GROUP, Palo Alto, California

Consultant providing expert sales, marketing, business development, customer development and relationship management leadership across diverse industries and markets nationwide. Solidified reputation as a top revenue producer within highly competitive markets. Major projects included:

- **Marketing Consultant – Stock Brokerage Industry**. Launched innovative marketing and business development programs for firms seeking to expand their presence on Wall Street. Focused efforts on building relationships through cold prospecting, referrals and network development. Generated 15 new accounts, principally NASDAQ companies from $10 million to $100 million in size.

- **Marketing Consultant & Sales Trainer – Network Marketing Industry**. Identified market opportunity for sales training in multi-level marketing and merchandising. Developed seminars, negotiated product distribution rights and created a successful mail order venture that generated $1.5 million annually.

- **Business Development Consultant – Diabetes Consumer Care Company**. Evaluated the feasibility of expanding from California to nationwide market, including introduction of an expanded product portfolio (e.g., food, education, health care). Led start-up of mail order business, developed catalog and advertising materials, and generated $750,000 in revenues in first year.

Executive Vice President / Senior Vice President / Managing Director   1976 to 1989

High-profile business development, marketing and sales career with several Wall Street/NYC investment brokerages and securities firms. Advanced rapidly based on outstanding performance in revenue, customer and market growth. Succeeded against major competition. Notable achievements included:

LL Bean & Company (1988 to 1989)
- Conceived, designed, developed and launched an aggressive telemarketing and advertising campaign (including investing millions of dollars on the FNN cable television station) to drive the firm's growth and expansion. Personally generated 80% of total sales volume for the NYC office.

JT Moran & Company (1987 to 1988)
- Principal architect of the firm's phenomenal success in underwriting small cap IPO's. Built Moran to 1000+ brokers and dealers, 15 branches and $65 million in annualized revenue in first year. Instrumental in leading firm's IPO and secondary offering. Member of the Board of Directors.

MR Merrill & Company (1983 to 1987)
- Revitalized 17-year-old firm, increased sales force from 17 to 125 representatives and drove revenue from $1 million to $12+ million annually. Authored five articles on "*Telemarketing on Wall Street*."

Bear Stearns (1981 to 1983)
* Top revenue and client development performance with the nation's 8th largest securities firm.

RT Lorde Investors Corporation (1978 to 1981)
- Retail Sales & Marketing Director leading the entire sales, advertising and relationship/client development efforts for the firm. Personally ranked as the #1 revenue producer.

O'Neill & Feldman (1976 to 1978)
- #1 sales producer within first two months of hire.

EDUCATION: **BS – Business** – California State University – Bakersfield, CA – 1975

BRUCE GROSSMAN
3847 Outback Way
Dallas, Texas 83494-9713
(815) 834-9716

CORPORATE MARKETING & BUSINESS DEVELOPMENT EXECUTIVE
Expertise in Technology Development, Commercialization & Global Market Expansion

---

Dynamic management career leading start-up, turnaround and high-growth organizations through explosive market growth and unprecedented profitability. Combines extensive "hands-on" technical qualifications with consistent success in identifying opportunities for product launch, market penetration and accelerated growth. Strong general management, P&L management and HR leadership successes. MBA Degree.

PROFESSIONAL EXPERIENCE:

SOLVAY AMERICA, INC., Dallas, Texas   1983 to Present
(U.S. Division of Solvay S.A., Brussels, Belgium)

Solvay Enzymes, Inc., Indianapolis, Indiana
Vice President - International Business Development (1995 to Present)

Following an 11-year career with Solvay America, joined the Belgium parent corporation in April 1995 to spearhead development of a global marketing and business development initiative for the $100+ million Enzymes Division. Challenged to design strategy and implement systems/processes to create an integrated worldwide marketing function as part of the business group's aggressive turnaround program. Provide strategic and tactical marketing leadership to Group Presidents in North America, Germany, Australia, Argentina and the Far East.

- Positioned the Division to achieve its first profitable year since 1991. Currently projecting revenue growth of 20% in 1997.

- Launched a massive effort to globalize product development and commercialization throughout the R&D organization.

- Structured and negotiated cooperative ventures between Solvay operating divisions and product lines to leverage worldwide marketing capabilities.

- Investigated and managed preliminary negotiations for proposed joint venture in the PRC.

Solvay Interox, Dallas, Texas
Vice President - Marketing (1989 to 1995)
Vice President - Hydrogen Peroxide (1987 to 1989)
Marketing Director (1986 to 1987)
Technical Manager (1984 to 1986)
National Accounts Manager (1983 to 1984)

Recruited to Solvay America's Interox Division in 1983. During the next 11 years, built a global marketing organization that led the Division from revenues of less than $20 million to 1995 volume of $120+ million. Recruited and developed a talented team of marketing professionals that now serve as Solvay Interox's core marketing management team.

SOLVAY AMERICA, INC. *(Continued):*

- Established the initial marketing function, all long-range strategic and short-term tactical marketing plans, a comprehensive market research function, and a complete marketing communications program.

  RESULT: Delivered 100% revenue growth within two years.

- Promoted to Vice President in 1987. Developed "value-based" strategy to transition Division from commodity basis to product functionality to accelerate applications development and market expansion. Full marketing, technology development and technical service responsibility for the largest business group (Hydrogen Peroxide).

  RESULT: Increased annual revenues by more than 50% through a combined program of product development, applications development and market development.

- Promoted to Vice President of Marketing in 1989 with full P&L responsibility for Solvay Interox's entire marketing, field sales, technology and applications development, technical service and product distribution functions. Led a professional team of 50+, a $9 million annual operating budget and the entire North American field sales organization.

  RESULT: Built Division revenues from $45 million to $120 million annually, achieved #1 market position in North America, and surpassed all profit goals for six consecutive years. Implemented customer focus strategy to drive applications/ technology development.

HOOKER CHEMICALS & PLASTICS CORP., Niagara Falls, New York   1972 to 1983
(Currently Occidental Chemical Corporation)

Fast-track promotion through a series of increasingly responsible research, commercial development, sales and marketing positions. Career highlights included:

Marketing Manager - Chlorine & Caustic Soda (1982 to 1983)

Senior Marketing Executive for commodity chemicals throughout the North American market. Direct P&L responsibility for annual sales of $100 million.

Sales Manager - Technology Licensing (1979 to 1982)

Chief Technology Licensing Manager with global responsibility for technology and equipment marketing, licensing and contractual agreements. Operated worldwide.

- Negotiated, closed and directed projects valued up to $30 million each.

Project Manager - Technology Licensing (1976 to 1979)

Directed large-scale chemical plant construction projects that embodied licensed technology. Completed over $200 million in projects in the U.S., Europe, Asia and Latin America.

EDUCATION: **MBA**, State University of New York at Buffalo, 1975
BS / Chemical Engineering, Syracuse University, 1972

PATENTS: U.S. Patent No. 4,985,267 - "Versatile Process for Generating Chloric Acid"
U.S. Patent No. 4,854,753 - "Removal of Chlorate Electrolytes From Cells"

ELIZABETH FINLEY
1012 W. Kingfisher Drive
Savannah, Georgia 31410
lizfinley@aol.com

Phone: 912-574-5878

Fax: 912-874-4147

MARKETING, SALES & BUSINESS DEVELOPMENT EXECUTIVE

- Web & Broadcast Content Development
- New Product Launch & Positioning
- New Territory Development & Penetration
- Competitive Sales & Sales Management
- Public Relations, Branding & Recognition

- B2B & B2C Marketing
- Special Events & Meeting Planning
- Public Speaking & Seminar Presentations
- Sales Training & Team Leadership
- Customer Service, Retention & Management

Creative, confident and high-performance Executive with 15+ years' experience building new markets, driving revenue growth and improving competitive market positioning. Successful in start-up, turnaround and high-growth markets across diverse industries. Award-winning producer with outstanding presentation, communication, negotiation and closing skills. Dynamic presentation style. PC, Mac and Internet savvy.

Featured in "Two Thousand Notable American Women" & "Who's Who in Women"

PROFESSIONAL EXPERIENCE:

AAA RESOURCES, INC., Savannah, Georgia   1991 to Present

President

Launched entrepreneurial consulting venture specializing in content development for television broadcasts and Internet websites, sales, sales training, product marketing, project management, brand development and image management for markets nationwide.

- Built AAA Resources from concept into a well-respected consulting firm. Completed more than 450 projects across diverse consumer and business-to-business markets (e.g., radio and television broadcasting, real estate, legal, medical, hospitality).

- Launched over 125 new marketing campaigns for client companies and business professionals, including a multi-tiered business development and market expansion program that generated a 115% increase in customer base for a service organization.

- Designed innovative, high-performance marketing campaigns for a number of television stations throughout the region to penetrate non-traditional advertisers (e.g., agriculture, manufacturing, telecommunications). Personally closed over $6.8 million in sales.

- Created and hosted the "Women in Business" segment of the "Savannah Business Report" (half-hour weekly television broadcast). Negotiated business partnerships with corporate sponsor (Office Depot) to fund program development and production.

- Directed high-profile sales, marketing and advertiser development programs for the entire "Savannah Business Report" and other affiliated broadcasts. Personally generated over $3.1 million in sales.

- Spearheaded a massive marketing campaign for TriPlace, a $500 million, 11-block entertainment, retail and residential complex in Savannah. Instrumental in positioning TriPlace as one of the most upscale communities in the area, bringing top-name retailers and prominent homebuyers to the site.

- Orchestrated on-site sales training for corporate accounts throughout the State of Georgia. Consistently delivered value to sales teams, measured in increased revenues, number of new accounts and improved market share ratings.

BUSINESS UPDATE (*Division of AAA Resources, Inc.*), Savannah, Georgia   1997 to 1999

Founder & Executive Producer

Identified statewide market opportunity for the development, production and broadcasting of a new television show ("Business News You Can Use") to capitalize on tremendous success of national business magazine shows airing on CNBC, CNN and MSNBC. Independently created concept for fast-paced business broadcast, marketed to investors and business partners, and orchestrated the entire development and production process. Wrote copy, recruited on-air talent and secured paid advertisers.

- Transitioned new venture from idea to on-air production within 9 months. Achieved immediate and significant market penetration and reputation for quality and integrity of the broadcast.

- Won a 1988 Communicator's Award of Distinction and a 1992 Telly Award for Excellence in Broadcast Business News. Honored for ability to communicate above the best in the field, establishing Business Update as an industry benchmark for markets nationwide.

- Generated over $3 million in first-year sales revenues.

KDKA-TV (WESTINGHOUSE BROADCASTING), Pittsburgh, Pennsylvania   1982 to 1991

Sales Development Manager (1988 to 1991)
Account Executive (1982 to 1988)
Sales Trainee (1982)

Fast-track promotion through several increasingly responsible sales, new business development and account management positions. Specialized in the strategic planning and penetration of new business markets (e.g., retail, real estate, legal) of first-time television advertisers.

- Recruited and developed new sales team that closed over $1 million in first year sales.

- Personally closed over $10 million in sales over six years.

- Led an exhaustive analysis of the marketing objectives of hundreds of television advertisers and created an innovative niche marketing program and selling system subsequently adopted by all other Westinghouse-owned television stations.

EDUCATION & CONTINUING PROFESSIONAL STUDIES:

BA – Communications – Chatham College – Pittsburgh, Pennsylvania
Integrity Selling Systems Training Certificate (Certified Facilitator)
Sterling Institute Performance Management Training
Xerox Selling Systems

PROFESSIONAL & CIVIC AFFILIATIONS:

Association of Professional Women (Past President & Board of Directors)
American Seminar Leaders Association
Georgia Speakers Association
National Association of Women Business Owners
Florence Fuller Child Development Center (Board of Directors)

ALBERT BURNHAM

768 Hamline Place
Burbank, California 91503

Home: 818-547-5765

Office: 818-654-7412

BROADCAST INDUSTRY EXECUTIVE
Success in Creative Services, Marketing, Programming and Operations Leadership

Led the strategic development and profitable performance of local and network affiliate stations through phenomenal growth, expansion and financial success. Exceptional performance in identifying market/business opportunities and creating the programs, promotions, personnel and client relationships to outpace the competition and dominate the marketplace. Strong technology, negotiations, budgeting and leadership qualifications. Outstanding creative talents.

PROFESSIONAL AWARDS & DISTINCTIONS:

- ABC Gold Medallion for *Bay Area Olympians*, 1997
- NBC Gold Medallion for *Olympic Moments*, 1995
- CBS Merit for *Let Vanna Do It*, 1993
- MSN Merit for *Eyewitness Omnibus*, 1993
- Star Emmy for the KABC-TV documentary *A Soldier Returns*, 1989
- Top Award for *Olympic Moments*, 1985
- WOX Gold Medallion for *Battlestar*, 1977

PROFESSIONAL EXPERIENCE:

ABC BROADCASTING, San Francisco, California
1994 to Present

Vice President of Marketing & Programming – ABC (1996 to Present)
Vice President of Marketing & Programming – LMG San Francisco (1995 to 1996)
Director of Marketing & Programming – LMG San Francisco (1994 to 1995)

Recruited to plan and lead an aggressive turnaround and market repositioning of ABC Broadcasting and its 9 television stations throughout the Western US. Challenged to identify the critical factors impacting operating, creative and financial performance, and introduce a new image, new programming and new identity to foster profitable growth. Initially responsible for restructuring the company's largest operation (LMG); subsequently assumed responsibility for revitalization of the entire organization.

Scope of responsibility is significant and includes promotion, publicity, research, design, marketing and programming operations on a daily basis. Concurrently, provide long-term strategic direction to expand into new programming areas and new market audiences. Control $20 million in annual media budgets.

- Delivered substantial audience growth averaging 12% annually over the past four years. Achieved/ surpassed all objectives for market share, audience share, revenues and bottom-line profits.

- Conceived, created and directed production of high-profile marketing strategies and advertising campaigns for all Chronicle stations, *BayTV* (ABC's local cable channel) and *The Gate* (ABC's online news and information site).

- Negotiated win-win contracts with major syndicators throughout the region to advance programming opportunities and expand market reach. Conceived innovative partnership agreements to drive further growth and offer first-ever programming opportunities throughout local markets.

KOFP-TV, Los Angeles, California   1982 to 1995

Director of Creative Services (1989 to 1995)
Executive Producer (1987 to 1989)
Writer/Producer (1982 to 1987)

Thirteen-year career with the #1 ranked network affiliate in the Los Angeles broadcast market. Promoted based upon consistent contributions to innovative programming/production, promotions, advertising, publicity, design, animation, creative services and operations leadership. Planned and directed media budgets up to $9 million annually. Designed and produced innovative corporate presentations.

- Redesigned format, hired talent, launched a market-wide promotional campaign and transitioned news broadcasts into a high-profile segment to retain competitive market lead. Established a strong and recognizable corporate identity and news personality concept.
- Analyzed market position, developed strategic business plan, conceived and executed innovative promotional campaigns, and restored KORP to #1 market position following massive internal changes and increased network competition. Achieved/surpassed all turnaround objectives.
- Created and produced award-wining promotional programming for the 1989 Olympics.
- Instrumental in facilitating positive changes in management structure, business infrastructure, operations and creative services following ownership transition from ABC into privately-owned corporation.

Concurrent appointment as **Director of Video Design Group** for Capital Cities and the seven ABC-owned stations in Los Angeles (1991 to 1992). Planned and orchestrated a successful turnaround, restructuring and revitalization of the organization's internal graphics department. Consulted with station managers, programming and creative personnel to introduce advanced graphics design and production capabilities as a key foundation for competitive positioning, creative excellence and market dominance.

<u>Previous Professional Experience</u> included a series of increasingly responsible live on-air, creative, programming and production positions. Advanced through virtually all key positions within the radio and television broadcast industries. Highlights:

- **Producer/Director** – KORK San Francisco & Live Oakland A's Broadcasts (1980 to 1982)
- **Sports Anchor** – KIVW Sacramento (1978 to 1980)
- **Producer/Director** – KOMX Palm Springs (1978 to 1980)
- **Studio/Field Engineer** – KIH-TV San Francisco (1978)
- **On-Air Broadcaster** – KEBR-AM/FM Palm Springs (1976 to 1977)

EDUCATION:

BA – Political Science – Minors in Journalism & Communications, UCLA, 1976

Lead Role – Japanese Television Commercial – 1974
News Director – KLA-AM (UCLA Radio) – 1972 to 1973

JENNIFER BRISTOL
DIRECTOR / PRODUCER
FILM, VIDEO & TELEVISION

14 S. Sunburst Way
Anaheim, CA 92806
Phone (714) 857-9899
Fax (714) 544-2588

CAREER PROFILE

Over 15 years' experience in the conceptualization, creative design, scripting, casting, direction and production of film, video and television broadcasts. Successful in managing projects from initial development through the entire production process to completion. Excellent planning, organizational, communication and negotiation skills. Confident in managing large staffs, production crews and celebrity guests. Extensive public speaking and media interview/promotion experience. Professional experience in markets worldwide.

Winner of 12 Emmy Awards (10 as Producer & 2 as Director) for Alphabet Soup ("Best Children's Show")

PROFESSIONAL EXPERIENCE:

ALPHABET SOUP / CHILDREN'S TELEVISION WORKSHOP   1972 to 1998

> **Consulting Producer** (1997 to 1998)
> **Supervising Producer** (1992 to 1996)
> **Director** (1982 to 1996)
> **Producer** (1981 to 1992)
> **Associate Producer** (1976 to 1981)
> **Assistant to the Producer** (1975)
> **Stage Manager** (1974 to 1975)
> **Production Assistant** (1972 to 1974)

Member of a core team of film, video and television professionals credited with the development and global market success of Alphabet Soup (now broadcast in more than 450 markets worldwide). Pioneered innovative programming, casting, scripting and off-site production to create a show founded on intimacy with its viewership, a fervent commitment to education, and a comical, fun and enjoyable orientation.

Conceived and defined the concepts, formats, characters, themes and overall philosophy of Alphabet Soup productions. Recruited, trained and directed a team of 120 professionals and support personnel. Controlled an $11 million annual production budget.

- Produced 130 programs each year, 50+ shows per season and numerous video productions. Fully responsible for set design, puppet design, lighting, audio, camera work, costumes, make-up, hair, props and special effects.

- Consulted with coordinating producer on all film and animation projects, supervised directors and choreographers, managed writing and composing teams, chose and edited scripts and lyrics, developed new talent and selected field locations.

- Developed concepts and coordinated celebrity appearances with major film and television personalities (e.g., Whoopi Goldberg, Susan Sarandon, Tim Robbins, Itzhak Perlman, Lily Tomlin, Patti Labelle, Wynton Marsalis, Julia Roberts, Billy Crystal and Mel Gibson).

ALPHABET SOUP / CHILDREN'S TELEVISION WORKSHOP (*Continued*):

- Selected, acquired and implemented state-of-the-art, multimedia production technologies.

- Traveled worldwide to coordinate producers, directors, writers and researchers on joint venture projects in China, Russia, Mexico, Poland and Israel. Led on-site training in broadcast production and direction.

- Built relationships with subject matter experts to enhance the quality and effectiveness of all Alphabet Soup productions. Initiated market research studies and focus groups worldwide.

*NOTE: Currently consulting with Alphabet Soup / Children's Television Workshop on a freelance basis as **Producer/Director** (including Year 20 Season Premier and a number of Alphabet Soup Home Videos produced throughout a CIX/Sony Wonder joint venture).*

ABC PRODUCTIONS   1996 to Present

Director

Founded, marketed, funded and currently manage an independent film and video studio working with major corporate, film and video production companies nationwide. Provide full creative and film/stage direction for a number of projects. Credits include:

- *Car Safety For Children* (Ford Motor Company/CIX)
  (60-minute live staged production)

- *Don't Do This* (Sony Theaters/CIX)
  (30-second Muppet production shown in theaters prior to feature films)

- *Between The Lions* (Sirius Thinking Ltd./WGBH)
  (30-minute weekly literacy show currently in initial production)

- *Bear in the Big Blue House* (Jim Lanster Productions/WMMR)
  (30-minute preschool series broadcast on the Cartoon Channel)

- *Big Bag* (Children's Television Workshop – CIX /Cartoon Network)
  (30-minute preschool series broadcast on CIX)

- *NOW Nutrition Videos* (Prospect Associates)
  (Series of video presentations on health and nutrition)

- *Once Upon A Tree* (Tremendous Productions/Animal Planet)
  (30-minute preschool series broadcast on WMMR)

EDUCATION: **B.A., Communications**, Hunter College, 1973

AFFILIATIONS: National Academy of Television Arts and Sciences
                       Directors Guild of America
                       New York Women in Film

EMMETT A. MORALL

Phone: (212) 1478-8744
E-mail: emmorall@yahoo.com

36 Lafayette Street
New York, New York 10159

BROADCAST INDUSTRY EXECUTIVE
Building Top-Performing Radio & Television Broadcast Stations Within Intensely Competitive Markets

Dynamic leadership career developing and managing top-ranked network affiliates. Combines expert strategic planning, marketing and business development expertise with a solid commitment to employee development, customer development and market retention. Keen negotiation, decision making and problem solving skills.

PROFESSIONAL EXPERIENCE:

NEW YORK BROADCAST COMPANY, New York, New York   1991 to Present
Vice President (1997 to Present)   **General Manager** (1991 to 1997)

Senior Executive with full strategic planning, marketing, business development, operations, production, engineering/technology, human resources and P&L responsibility for five TV stations, two radio stations and a direct mail company housed within one facility. Lead a staff of 160 through 12 management reports.

KQIN TV (ABC Affiliate)	**KINF-TV** (FOX Affiliate)
KOOP-TV (FOX Affiliate)	**KEIE-FM** (Radio Station)
KCND-TV (Telemundo Affiliate)	**KOIY-AM** (Radio Station)
KLLO-TV (NBC Affiliate)	**New York Marketing** (direct mail company)

Conceived, developed and launched strategic master plan in 1992/3 to forge an aggressive expansion initiative. Greatest challenge has been to drive profitable growth while controlling operating costs, leveraging staff competencies, providing a common vision, and creating an energetic, motivated and customer-driven organization.

- **Revenue & Profit Growth**. Increased sales revenues from $4 million in 1991 to $17 million in 1999. Grew operating income from $770,000 to $4.3 million. Built production sales to $400,000+ annually from virtual start-up. Achieved/surpassed all revenue and income objectives.

- **Asset Value**. Dramatically increased the value of KONO-TV from $6 million to $19 million over four years. Currently valued at $40+ million (divested in 1995).

- **Market Ratings**. Transitioned Hispanic KIIM-FM from a virtual unknown into one of the top 2/3 radio stations in the market (23 rated stations). Consistently ranked #1 in the 18-34, 18-49 and 25-54 demographic ratings. Negotiated to remove New York based broadcast stations from New York City and replace with New York Broadcast properties as the only local FOX and WMIX stations in the market.

- **Acquisition Leadership**. Planned and directed complex negotiations for the acquisition of two radio stations in 1997. Structured and negotiated 10-year network franchising deal with Telemundo, requiring no upfront costs to New York Broadcast.

- **Industry Innovation**. Planned, structured and executed the first radio-to-television Local Market Agreement (LMA) in the US.

- **Customer Service**. Pioneered innovative customer (advertisers, viewers and listeners) development, service, loyalty and retention programs to foster team-wide commitment to customer satisfaction. Introduced TQM initiatives to further strengthen customer service and all other in-house operations.

- **Staffing & Performance Improvement**. Integrated acquisitions into existing operations, eliminated staff redundancies, and delivered double digit cost savings. Currently produce 23 hours of local news per week and 2.5 hours in Spanish with staff of only 45. Ranked #1 news department in the market.

- **Corporate Sponsorships & Community Outreach**. Positioned New York Broadcast as high-profile corporate citizens and sponsor of hundreds of community, health care and educational events.

THE INNOVATIVE GROUP, Albany, New York   1990 to 1991
Senior Account Executive

Joined regional advertising agency to orchestrate their expansion into the New York City market. Within 6 months, established a firm market presence, captured prominent local accounts and positioned Innovative for long-term growth/expansion.

- Within first two weeks, negotiated and closed a $600,000+ account for the Senior PGA Golf Tournament.

KILQ-TV, New York, New York   1987 to 1989
Sales Manager

Led sales department through two years of accelerated growth and expansion. Recruited, trained and directed sales team of seven. Consistently set new sales records on a monthly basis.

- Drove sales from $1.6 million to $3 million within just two years.

KIRV Radio, New York, New York   1995 to 1997
Operations Manager (1996 to 1997)
Sales Manager (1995 to 1996)
Sales Representative (1995)

Fast-track promotion through a series of increasingly responsible sales and operations management positions with one of the top broadcast stations in the market. Ranked as the #1 sales producer within three months of hire while assuming additional responsibility for promotions, marketing and operations.

- Led the station through a period of rapid change, reorganization and growth. Transitioned from #4 in the market with 6.8 share to #1 with 21.9 share. Achieved a better than 7 share competitive lead.

<u>Early Professional Experience</u> (1972 to 1995). Began radio career as an on-air broadcaster. Subsequently advanced through positions in sales, promotions, marketing, production and operations.

PROFESSIONAL & CIVIC AFFILIATIONS:

Board of Directors, New York Broadcast Association (1994 to Present)
Chairman, United Way (1996/97 & 1997/98). *Raised a record $1.4 million in final year.*
Board Appointment, New York Tramway Authority. *Managing $9 million renovation.*
Chairman, Governing Board, Shands Hospital (1997 to Present). *Managing $13 million expansion.*
Board of Directors, Shands Hospital (1994 to 1997)

PUBLICATIONS:

- "How To Establish A Local Market Agreement (LMA)," *Electronic Age*, 1999
- "A Television Balancing Act," *Electronic Age*, 1999
- *Aim Higher* (sales book), published in 1998
- "The Game We Played Like Tour Pros," *Golf News Magazine*, 1994

MAUREEN A. LESTER, RPh

42 School House Lane
Trenton, New Jersey 08332

Home: 124.369.4780
Email: MAL36@aol.com

CAREER PROFILE & QUALIFICATIONS

Fourteen years' progressively responsible experience in the development and leadership of high-volume specialty pharmaceutical dispensing operations. Expertise in creating operating processes, protocols, policies and technologies to support rapid growth, new drug introductions, regulatory approvals and patient quality of care (including acquisition, ongoing support and retention). Outstanding performance in building and managing working relationships with physicians, medical practices, health care institutions and insurance companies nationwide.

PROFESSIONAL EXPERIENCE:

KING PHARMACY, Trenton, NJ   1987 to Present

Director of Business Implementation – Sales & Marketing Division (1999 to Present)
Product Manager – Transplant & Infertility Business Unit (1997 to 1999)
Project Manager - Pharmacy Department (1995 to 1997)
Supervisor – Customer Service Call Center (1993 to 1995)
Supervisor – Pharmacist Phone Area (1990 to 1993)
Staff Pharmacist (1987 to 1990)

Fast-track promotion through a series of increasingly responsible management positions as Kings has transitioned from a retail pharmacy into one of the nation's leading specialty mail service pharmaceutical companies with more than 80 pharmacists nationwide, three wellness centers (SF, NY, LA) and over $500 million in annual revenues. Kings is currently the largest single transplant and HIV/AIDS pharmacy in the US with a strong presence in the infertility market.

Advanced through several newly-created positions in response to phenomenal growth. Challenged to develop new operations, systems, processes and business units to meet patient demand while enhancing quality of care and quality of patient support. Career highlights include:

NEW PROGRAM DEVELOPMENT

- *Acquisition Integration*. Member of 10-person management team orchestrating the integration of systems and operations following King's acquisition of ABC (leading pharmaceutical company).

- *Merck/Kings Lezxar Distribution Joint Venture*. Member of 10-person management team developing and directing the dispensing of a revolutionary new HIV/AIDS treatment under stringent FDA requirements. Built the entire dispensing protocol and system within three weeks. Led a staff of 5 supervisors and a team of 100+ as volume grew from 8000 to 60,000+ patients.

- *Serostim Distribution Program*. Developed dispensing protocol for an investigational new HIV/AIDS drug. Worked closely with insurance companies nationwide to establish reimbursement standards and schedules prior to FDA approval. Directed a team of 5 responsible for program design, implementation and operation.

- *Sales & Marketing Integration Program*. Currently facilitating development of cross-training programs to prepare the sales team (23 field representatives and management) to market all three lines of specialty pharmaceuticals (Transplant, AIDS, Infertility). In addition, coordinating implementation of managed care programs into the distribution process.

- *Patient Retention Program*. Spearheaded several initiatives to enhance patient retention. Decreased attrition to less than new patient acquisition for the first time in five years.

- *Patient Adherence Program*. Facilitated cooperative efforts between Clinical Pharmacy and Operations to ensure patient adherence to pharmaceutical regimens, identify non-compliant patients and introduce appropriate intervention methods.

ORGANIZATIONAL DEVELOPMENT & LEADERSHIP

- *Wellness Center Start-Up*. Lead Manager and Corporate Contact to the management team during the start-up and first year of operation of the LA and SF wellness centers.

- *Department Reorganization*. Key player in the integration and restructuring of key operating areas as the organization grew, expanded and redefined itself. Personally integrated Pharmacy Order Intake Area with Customer Service Area to create Pharmacy Services Business Group. Facilitated transition of New Patient Enrollment Group into the Sales & Marketing Department.

- *Acquisition Integration*. Member of 10-person management team orchestrating the integration of systems and operations following King's acquisition of ABC (leading pharmaceutical company).

- *Database Development & Statistical Analysis Projects*. Worked in cooperation with IT department to design and implement a number of statistical analysis and reporting methodologies. Designed successful new business models and coordinated associated IT development projects.

- *Policy & Procedure Development*. Established corporate policies for customer service, problem resolution, call monitoring and operations. Initiated a series of programs to integrate Operations Department with Sales Department to improve integrity of operations and quality of care.

Currently serve on the following corporate committees:

- Reimbursement Committee
- Reorder Card Committee
- Managed Care Implementation Committee

Previously served on 12 other corporate committees including:

- Dr. File Clean-Up Committee
- Compensation Committee
- Change Management Committee
- Customer Service Committee
- Call Monitoring Committee
- DSM Corporate Integration Committee
- Data Integrity Committee

GNC, INC., Pittsburgh, PA   1984 to 1987

Staff Pharmacist

Dispensed medications in a high-volume retail pharmacy. Counseled patients on a broad range of disease states, medication side effects and drug interactions.

EDUCATION:

BS – Pharmacy – Duquesne University – 1984

BS – Nutrition – Pennsylvania State University – 1980

JOHN P. MITCHELL

5378 Jefferson Avenue
Arlington, Virginia 22153
Email jmitchell@msn.com

Home (703) 351-5620   Work (202)267-5648

PUBLIC RELATIONS / MEDIA RELATIONS / COMMUNICATIONS / SPECIAL EVENTS

Talented Public Relations Strategist and Campaign Director with 10 years professional experience. Expertise in community/public outreach, multimedia communications, publications management and crisis management. Accomplished in managing relationships with major print and broadcast media nationwide. Skilled in large-scale event coordination/management. Consistently effective in meeting budget and schedule requirements.

PROFESSIONAL EXPERIENCE:

Public Relations Officer   1987 to 1995
UNITED STATES NAVY - Washington, D.C. / California / Virginia / Pennsylvania

Fast-track promotion through a series of increasingly responsible public relations / public affairs positions nationwide as one of only 200 designated spokespersons in the U.S. Navy. Won several distinguished commendations (2 Commendation Medals, Achievement Medal) for outstanding performance in the management of sensitive public relations programs and initiatives.

Public Relations / Public Affairs

- Rebuilt and revitalized non-active public relations function aboard the aircraft carrier USS Enterprise. Created innovative PR programs targeted to military and civilian personnel, re-established weekly newspaper and planned/hosted more than 10 special events.
- Developed course content and taught public relations training seminars to personnel throughout 12 Naval organizations.
- Publicized the Navy's assistance to victims of January 1994 earthquake in LA, winning positive media coverage and strengthening position of the Navy's response to domestic crises.
- Launched several high-profile public relations campaigns to recruit community board members and expand public information concerning two hazardous waste removal projects. Personally managed and responded to all public and local political inquiries.
- Wrote public relations guidelines for congressional visits emphasizing the management of high-profile events and strategies to leverage media exposure.
- Trained and supervised teams of up to 24, responsible for public relations, printing, graphic arts, photography, media relations, community outreach and administrative support.

Media / Press Relations

- Represented the Navy with major print and broadcast media nationwide including network affiliates, national and local correspondents, National Public Radio, Washington Post, New York Times, Los Angeles Times, Wall Street Journal, Time and Newsweek.
- Managed liaison affairs with local, national and international press, White House Press Office, Arlington National Cemetery and National Cathedral for national coverage of memorial services for the late Chief of Naval Operations and the late U.S. Commerce Secretary.
- Appointed spokesperson in regional and national media markets to handle high-visibility issues including base closures and related employee relocation issues, integration of women into combat assignments and emerging environmental concerns.
- Spearheaded communications with media nationwide to change negative reaction and media perception of large-scale environmental projects. Won positive coverage and support with major print and broadcast media.
- Responded to public and national media inquiries about the USS Iowa explosion at sea and operated the first "800" family information number (now standard in Navy crisis response).
- Coordinated media (including live segments on "Good Morning America") for the first U.S. port visit by Russian warships in 20 years. Managed affairs for 300+ media over a five-day period.

Public Relations Officer *(Continued)*:

Publications Management

- Editor of <u>Horizons</u>, a specialized publication with circulation of 9000+. Full responsibility for editorial content, story assignments, layout, design and outsourced printing contract.
- Editor and Sole Author of the only timely news service in the U.S. Navy. Wrote news and feature articles published weekly in Naval newspapers worldwide.

Multimedia Communications

- Designed and managed construction of renovated television and radio broadcast studio aboard the USS Enterprise. Directed programming, scheduling and transmission of broadcast services to 5000+ shipboard personnel.
- Led four-person editorial board responsible for content review and authorization of information posted on the USS Enterprise Internet Home Page.
- Authored press releases, news stories, articles, public outreach documents, correspondence, reports and other print communications.

Special Events

- Planned and directed educational tours aboard the USS Enterprise for thousands of U.S. and foreign visitors (e.g., general public, politicians, military personnel, visiting dignitaries, foreign attaches) during the vessel's travels throughout the U.S. and Latin America.
- Directed first-ever visits to Naval forces and a complete special events program for high-level government administrators and other noted dignitaries.
- Conceived, planned, staffed, publicized and directed 20+ special events throughout career.

Career Progression

Public Relations Officer - Naval District Washington Headquarters (1993 to 1995)
Public Relations Officer - USS Enterprise (1991 to 1993)
Asst Public Relations Officer - Naval District Washington Headquarters (1988 to 1991)
Asst Public Relations Officer - Pacific Fleet Headquarters (1985 to 1988)
Editor - Navy Internal Relations Activity (1983 to 1985)

EDUCATION:

B.S., Computer Science, Texas A&M University, 1983
(Distinguished Military Graduate - National Naval Officers Association)

Graduate, Public Affairs Officers Course, Defense Information School, 1983
(10-week, Graduate-Level Program Emphasizing Public Affairs/Communications)

References Provided Upon Request

PATRICK GODDARD

8765 E. Madison Avenue
Spokane, Washington 99012
Email: patgoddard@usa.net

Home: 877-258-5984   Office: 877-541-4544

GLOBAL SOURCING, PROCUREMENT & SUPPLY CHAIN MANAGEMENT
Engineering & Manufacturing Operations Worldwide
Fortune 50 Companies & Start-Up/Spin-Off Ventures
Cornell University Graduate

- Strategic Planning & Organizational Leadership
- Enterprise-Wide Supplier Chain Process Management
- Supplier Quality, Certification & Relationship Management
- Finance, Budgeting & Corporate Risk Management
- Team Building, Leadership & Performance Improvement
- Marketing & New Business Development

- US & International Manufacturing Operations
- Product Development & Commercialization
- Product & Process Engineering & Optimization
- Technical Call Center Operations & Customer Service
- Outsourcing (IT, HR, Mfg, Supply Chain)
- Import/Export & International Logistics

Excellent technology skills including proficiency with Oracle, SAP, Manugistics, PDM, MRP, BRP and ERP. Solid QA, TQM and ISO 9002 leadership qualifications. Extensive Y2K experience. Influential and persuasive with ability to build trust, rapport and profitable partnerships worldwide. Tolerant and flexible, yet assertive and determined.

PROFESSIONAL EXPERIENCE:

ABC CORPORATION, Spokane, Washington   1997 to Present
($2.3 billion leader in data storage and imaging applications technology. 6400 employees in 60 countries.)

Chief Procurement Officer

Recruited to build a professional global procurement function following the spin-off of five business units from 3M. Responsible for $1.2 billion in annual purchasing expenditures, $6.5 million annual direct budget, $7.5 million annual indirect budget, 44 direct reports (including 5 managers) and procurement activities of 275 employees at all 42 locations worldwide.

Created an entirely new business process and infrastructure to manage 100,000 annual transactions including procurement card, blanket orders, standard contracts, Internet/Intranet ordering, spend authorization, contract approval, 3-way matching, supplier qualifications/certification and supplier management process. Recruited and hired 20 procurement professionals and managers.

- Transitioned organization from its traditional, operational role into a strategic and integrated systems process for an immediate 25% SG&A expense reduction.
- Delivered $45 million in spend reduction and cost avoidance in 1998.
- Outsourced freight, logistics, IT, lab, facilities and business services for $10 million savings (12%).
- Consolidated supplier base from 10,000 to fewer than 100 who accounted for 80% of spending.
- Key sponsor of $100 million corporate-wide ERP Project. Led development and implementation of Oracle ERP system now operating across the entire scope of the company's worldwide supply chain operations (as well as Finance, HR, Sales and Marketing).
- Led strategy and project team in the implementation of SCOR methodology to optimize enterprise-wide supply chain processes.
- Directed completion of corporate-wide Y2K program including development of 400 contingency plans for 60 countries, 500+ product families, 50,000 software instances and 10,000 pieces of computer technology. Delivered project 25% below $6 billion budget.
- Led corporate risk management program to protect $200+ million of foreign currency transactions hedged via foreign currency forward and option contracts. Negated impact of currency and commodity price movements on income statement.

ABC CORPORATION, Chicago, Illinois   1977 to 1997
($25 billion conglomerate with 135 manufacturing facilities in 70 countries.)

Capital Sourcing Manager – Global Operations – Chicago (1996 to 1997)

Member of 8-person Senior Management Global Purchasing Team. Personally responsible for $1.7 million in annual purchasing turnover for new plants and expanded manufacturing capacity across 15 business units. Led a team of 34 direct reports plus five managers in Europe, Asia and South America. Controlled $3.5 million direct budget and $25 million indirect (contractor) budget. Reported to Director of Global Sourcing to VP of Sourcing & Logistics.

Challenged to deliver a 10% productivity improvement throughout the entire capital sourcing function. Provided strategic leadership and operating support to influence business managers to accept better practices and sourcing processes.   Concurrent responsibility for sourcing and logistics support for 500 design/engineering contract employees from Bechtel, Fluor Daniel, Brown & Root and others.

- Delivered $40 million in annual cost savings through expansion of 50 strategic supplier alliances. Guided development of future years' plans projected to double annual savings within three years.
- Co-led corporate capital improvement initiative resulting in $200+ million in cost avoidance (10%).

Procurement Manager – European Operations – The Netherlands (1995 to 1996)

Promoted to plan and direct the start-up of an integrated sourcing function across 25 manufacturing sites in eight countries. Managed an annual procurement volume of $800+ million in contracted services, engineering design and construction, engineered equipment, spare parts and MRO. Controlled a $6.5 million annual budget. Reported to Procurement Director for Europe.

- Developed and implemented best practices resulting in $23 million in annual cost savings in capital equipment, design and contracted services costs. Reduced MRO inventories $10 million.

Worldwide Equipment Sourcing Manager – Germany (1992 to 1995)

Promoted and transferred to Europe to direct an organization of 45 employees responsible for contract manufacturing at 50 supplier locations in 10 countries. Directed supplier selection, negotiations, contracts, QA and new product development. Reported to Director for Worldwide Operations.

- Led team through a period rapid change and restructuring. Achieved a $12 million reduction in variable cost and $4 million (60%) reduction in fixed cost.

Manufacturing Technical Manager – Illinois (1991 to 1992)
Quality Manager – Connecticut (1990 to 1991)
Engineering & Production Manager – Connecticut (1989 to 1990)
Equipment Development Supervisor – Connecticut (1984 to 1989)
National Customer Service Manager – Illinois (1981 to 1984)
Regional Service Supervisor – Illinois (1980 to 1981)
Technical Specialist/Development Engineer – Texas (1977 to 1980)

- Led team that developed and commercialized high-speed research centrifuge that broke through the traditional limits of technology. Co-inventor on underlying patent for new family of products.
- Expanded medical technology call and support center to 24x7 nationwide operations.
- Led three manufacturing facilities through successful ISO 9002 certification.

EDUCATION:

CORNELL UNIVERSITY, Ithaca, New York
BS – Electrical Engineering / BA – Biology (*Dual Degree Program*), 1980

JAMES L. BALDUFF

47 W. Oakcrest Lane
Elizabeth, New Jersey 07208
Email: jlbalduff@hotmail.com

Home: 908.587.3636

Office: 908.544.1147

QUALITY ASSURANCE MANAGER
Advanced Telecommunications Products, Systems & Technologies
Seventeen Years' Experience in Engineering, Manufacturing, Quality & Performance Improvement

Member of 10-person Senior Management Team leading one of the most profitable manufacturing facilities of a worldwide leader in the telecommunications industry. Delivered double-digit gains in product quality and yield through combined expertise in:

- QA Planning & Organizational Leadership
- Process Design & Automation
- Productivity, Efficiency & Yield Improvement
- Project Planning, Budgeting & Leadership
- Budgeting & Resource Allocation

- Product Manufacturability & Optimization
- Systems Integration & Simplification
- Professional & Technical Staffing
- Cross-Functional Team Leadership
- Supplier Quality Assurance

PROFESSIONAL EXPERIENCE:

ABC INC., Elizabeth, New Jersey   1993 to Present

Quality Assurance Manager – Mobile Systems Division (1998 to Present)
Senior Quality Engineer – Mobile Systems Division (1995 to 1998)
Quality Engineer – Private Radio Systems Division – Fixed-Site Technologies (1993 to 1995)

Quality Manager leading the entire Quality Assurance organization for the manufacturing group of ABC's $1 billion US Mobile Systems Division (IT cellular telecommunications equipment – transceivers, antenna systems and base stations). Manage a team of 10 direct reports and oversee 25 QA inspectors. Control a $1 million annual operating budget allocated for staffing, training, consulting and project delivery.

Manage within an intensely fast-paced, high-growth organization that has doubled revenues consistently year-over-year for the past three years. Member of the Worldwide Mobile Systems Quality Management Council working with 12-person international quality management team to drive corporate-wide QA initiatives to maintain world class manufacturing. Extensive travel within Sweden. Limited travel to Brazil.

Project Highlights, Achievements & Performance Improvements:

- Spearheaded initiative to expand quality commitment throughout the entire manufacturing organization, developed cross-functional quality teams, implemented real-time feedback for production operators and *reduced quality defects from 10% to less than 4%*.

- Led quality team that *reduced test failure rate from 25% to 15%* on the Division's largest transceiver product line (monthly production of 4000-6000 units).

- Led quality improvement team that introduced the Division's first fully-integrated product (LRO-2000 PCS base station). Consulted with customers, design engineers and manufacturing teams to facilitate product development, reliability and quality. *Delivered a 50%-75% increase in production yields*.

- Coordinated QA effort for industry-leading project integrating turnkey manufacturing for cellular base station transceivers. ***Integrated SMA, automated visual inspection, robotic cells and automated testing processes into one consolidated quality system***.

- ***Generated 20% system test yield improvement*** and ***50% throughput increase in systems audits*** for fixed-site telecommunications products within first year of hire.

- Designed, developed and directed introduction of a ***consolidated system for audit, inspection and measurement reporting***. Trained quality and manufacturing personnel, created standardized data formats, and implemented a paperless reporting system (Access).

- Developed and implemented an internal ***Auditor Certification Program*** for manufacturing inspectors.

- Hosted and passed several ***successful ISO 9000 audits*** in manufacturing, quality plans, product traceability and identification, and non-conforming material handling routines.

- Currently planning and coordinating resources for ***SPC implementation project*** and for ***transfer of all manufacturing documentation to Ericsson's proprietary Intranet***.

WESTINGHOUSE ELECTRONIC SYSTEMS GROUP, Baltimore, Maryland   1989 to 1993

Senior Quality Assurance Engineer

Planned and managed QA for incoming product components and IC devices. Advised test engineers on hardware/software quality issues and corrective actions. Significant project management responsibility.

- Designed and implemented an IC "Ship-to-Stock" program that ***reduced inspection costs 20%.***

MINCO TECHNOLOGY LABS / AUSTIN SEMICONDUCTOR, Austin, Texas   1983 to 1989

Test Department Manager (1985 to 1989)
Test Engineer (1983 to 1985)

Led a team of 30 engineers, technicians and operators. Managed budgeting, equipment acquisition, vendor relations and customer follow-up/support.

EDUCATION:

B.S., Electrical Engineering, University of Texas at Austin, 1983

Graduate, 100+ hours of continuing professional education in Quality Systems, Quality Management, Public Presentation, Communications, Leadership and Technology.

PROFESSIONAL AFFILIATIONS:

American Society for Quality (ASQ)
Volunteer, Habitat for Humanity (Ericsson Project)

JILL CLARKE

2514 Tree Line Drive
Cherry Hill, New Jersey 07896
(609) 654-8572

REAL ESTATE INDUSTRY PROFESSIONAL
Property Management / Leasing / Marketing / Tenant Relations

Twenty years experience in commercial and residential real estate. Consistently successful in increasing revenues, occupancy and income through expertise in building tenant relations and responding to tenant needs. Extensive qualifications in property/site renovation and construction, multi-year competitive leasing, multi-site property management and cost control/reduction. Outstanding communication and interpersonal relations skills.

PROFESSIONAL EXPERIENCE:

Broker of Record / Property Manager   1992 to Present
USI PROPERTY MANAGEMENT, INC., Clifton, New Jersey

> *Portfolio:* *163,000 square feet of prime office space in a 3-building complex on 9 acres with large parking lots and extensive landscaping. Asset value of $13.5 million.*

Recruited as the Senior Broker and Property Manager with full P&L responsibility for the entire portfolio. Scope of responsibility includes daily operations management, marketing, leasing, construction, renovation, tenant relations, tenant retention, collections, outsourcing, contract negotiations, purchasing, ADA compliance, monthly financial reporting and general office/administrative affairs.

- Increased occupancy from 29% to 73% in less than three years.
- Negotiated a 10-year contract with Linens & Things for corporate headquarters operation. Instrumental in negotiation of long-term (minimum of 5-year), high-yield leases with McGraw Hill/ Dodge, New York Life/Sanus, and numerous other corporations.
- Managed $1.5 million renovation with responsibility for the entire project cycle, from initial consultations with architects/designers through bid and contract award to project planning, scheduling, costing and on-site supervision. Delivered project on-time and within budget.
- Planned and directed implementation of fiber optic cables in partnership with New Jersey Bell to ensure the latest in telecommunications technology for tenant companies.
- Negotiated outsourcing contracts for facilities maintenance/repair, janitorial services and property security. Consistently reduced expenditures while increasing quality and tenant satisfaction.

Vice President / Broker of Record / Property Manager   1991 to 1992
THE KAMSON CORPORATION, Englewood Cliffs, New Jersey

> *Portfolio:* *230,000 square feet comprised of 3 office buildings and 11 luxury garden apartment complexes. Asset value of $200 million.*

Led the successful turnaround of the portfolio to meet investor and owner financial objectives. Held full responsibility for leasing, marketing, construction and renovation, tenant relations, cash flow management, financial reporting, ROI analysis and general administrative affairs. Spearheaded a high-profile marketing and public relations initiative to upgrade tenant quality. Directed staff of 30.

- Increased occupancy by 25% despite overall downward trend of real estate industry. Personally negotiated and closed over $750,000 in commercial leasing commitments within last six months.
- Managed a large-scale renovation to upgrade the facilities, properties and common areas of the portfolio as part of the initiative to increase tenant retention and improve market competitiveness.
- Negotiated and directed all maintenance and improvement work including electrical systems, HVAC conversions, elevators and grounds.

Association Manager   1988 to 1991
HILLS VILLAGE MASTER ASSOCIATION, Bedminster, New Jersey

Portfolio: *153-acre, 1492-unit Association with 4000+ residents. Asset value of $4.5 million.*

Managed a master community association for one of the largest planned urban developments (PUD) in the U.S. Established policies and procedures, developed organizational infrastructure and created cooperative working relationships between home owners, builders and investors.

- Launched a massive and successful public relations initiative (including Association TV channel) to expand communication between Association leadership and owners.
- Personally negotiated and resolved a number of issues negatively impacting the Association, the owners and the PUD. Created definitive documents to educate owners regarding Association rules and responsibilities to enhance quality of life.

President / Broker / Managing Partner / Property Manager   1979 to 1988
BERGER MANAGEMENT COMPANY, Montclair, New Jersey

As President of The Berger Group, represented sellers, buyers and investors in commercial real estate sales transactions totalling several million dollars. As President of Berger Management Company, held full P&L responsibility for the leasing, marketing and management of 2500 residential and commercial units at 12 properties throughout the region.

Broker / Residential Manager / Sales Representative   1971 to 1979
LEO, DIAZ AND PICA, Bloomfield, New Jersey

Brokered, marketed and leased residential and light commercial properties.

EDUCATION & PROFESSIONAL CERTIFICATIONS:

Certified Property Manager (CPM) Candidate, Institute of Real Estate Management, Current
Real Property Administrator (RPA), Building Owners and Managers Association, 1993
Registered Property Manager (RPM), International Real Estate Institute, 1993
Certified Real Estate Brokerage Manager (CRB), National Association of Realtors, 1985
Graduate Realtor Institute Designation (GRI), Bergen Community College, 1973
Licensed Real Estate Broker, State of New Jersey, Since 1975

PROFESSIONAL AFFILIATIONS:

National Association of Corporate Real Estate Executives (NACORE)
Building Owners and Managers Association International (BOMA)
Institute of Real Estate Management (IREM)
Industrial and Commercial Real Estate Women (ICREW)
International Real Estate Institute (IREI)
Community Association Institute (CAI)
Property Owners Association of New Jersey (POA)

GEORGE R. HAMMOND

98 Ben Franklin Drive
Orlando, Florida 32819

Home: 407.587.2588   Business/Fax: 407.654.9636   Email: ghammond42@aol.com

---

SENIOR RETAIL INDUSTRY EXECUTIVE
Building Profitable Start-Up, Turnaround & High-Growth Organizations
MBA Degree

Dynamic senior management career building high-profile retail corporations. Expertise in both specialty and big box formats. Consistently successful in driving revenue growth, improving operating efficiencies and increasing profitability. Success in:

- Strategic Planning / Development
- Operational Execution / Productivity
- Marketing / Branding
- Store Openings / Renovations

- Merchandising / Vendor Relations
- Logistics / Pipeline Management
- Systems Selection / Implementation
- Human Resources Development

PROFESSIONAL EXPERIENCE:

RELOCATION.COM, Mt. View, California   January 2000 to Present

Interim CEO

Leading the development of an Internet start-up to bring together retailers and relocating households, using quality online marketing programs, e-commerce initiatives and offers. Managing concept development / business plan, retailer sales / marketing, mover site / customer relations, site design, financial modeling and infrastructure.

THE ELECTRONIC STORE, Edison, New Jersey   1998 to 1999

President / CEO

Recruited to orchestrate an aggressive turnaround and return to profitability for this regional 40 store, 3,400 employee, and $600 million consumer electronics specialty retailer. Direct reports included EVP Merchandise and Marketing; EVP Finance/ CFO; SVP Store Operations; SVP Human Resources; VP Logistics; VP Loss Prevention; and, VP Legal/ Real Estate.

- Developed and executed a strategic plan increasing annual revenue by $100 million or 20% versus 1998 and successfully managed $40 million in capital expenditures for 18 store renovations, 3 new store openings, 2 prototype stores and implementation of new finance / retail systems.

- Significantly improved relations with over 50 key vendors, resulting in better product assortments, terms and pricing, generating 10% improvements in both gross margin and inventory turnover.

- Implemented store operating programs and merchandise presentation standards, resulting in a $500,000 annual expense savings and over a 20% improvement in customer service.

- Reduced logistics labor costs by over $125,000 while improving pick accuracy and on time delivery to stores and customers to 99%.

- Created and implemented a new marketing strategy and branding campaign, which repositioned the company, improved consumer awareness and increased store traffic by 15%-18%.

AAA APPLIANCES AND FURNITURE INC., Dallas, Texas   1995 to 1998

President / Co-Founder

Senior executive with full strategic planning, operations, merchandising, marketing, logistics, real estate and human resources responsibility for building a 13 store, $20 million chain selling name brand furniture, electronics and appliances.

- Developed and executed a unique retailing concept business plan and secured $20 million in equity funding and a $30 million senior debt line to support the business.

- Managed infrastructure development, created policies and procedures, selected retail systems, oversaw store design and site selection and built company to 130 employees.

- Developed a 115,00 square foot warehouse operation and supervised critical supply chain components including retail systems, product allocation, vendor relations, GMROI, in-stock, returns, repairs, receiving, stocking and customer service.

- Created a unique branding campaign consisting of television commercials and limited circulars focusing on price, brand names and service to differentiate us from "rent to own" competitors.

THE XYZ CONSULTING GROUP, Marietta, Georgia   1993 to 1995

Executive Consultant – Retail Industry – Bradlees, K*B Toys, Lowes & Others

- Oversaw a complete supply chain review for a big box discounter, identified $3.4 million in expense savings and created the processes and programs to secure those savings.

- Designed and implemented a store staffing and scheduling program for a specialty retailer resulting in a 10% cost reduction and improved merchandise in stock and presentation.

MONTGOMERY WARD, Chicago, Illinois   1989 to 1993

Vice President, Western Territory (1992 to 1993)
Vice President, Operations (1991 to 1992)
Vice President, Field Merchandising (1990 to 1992)
Vice President, Central Territory (1989 to 1990)

Fast track promotion through a series of increasingly responsible senior management positions. At peak had full P&L responsibility for 200 stores generating $3.2 billion in revenue and $93.5 million in pre-tax profit. Managed 6 regional directors, 29 market managers, 20 field merchandise managers and marketing, merchandising, human resources, operations, controller and loss prevention functions. Reported to the President of Store Operations.

- Developed and implemented a comprehensive marketing, merchandising and operations program for 30 store, $540 million Southern California market resulting in the reversal of 12-15% sales declines to 5% gains.

- Directed implementation of Electronics / Furniture marketing, merchandising, presentation and remodel program in 127 stores, resulting in an overall sales increase of 22% against trend.

- Developed and managed the implementation of a comprehensive " low cost " operator strategy, which generated annualized savings of $30 million or 15% of pre-tax profit.

ZAYRE CORPORATION, Framingham, Massachusetts   1975 to 1989

Thirteen years of progressive responsibility. Advanced from Budget and Planning Manager to Regional Vice President with full P&L responsibility for 91 discount stores.

EDUCATION: **MBA with Honors**, Babson College
                          B.S. Business Economics, University Of Rhode Island

JACQUELINE PREVATT

129 W. Crimson Drive
Santa Monica, CA 95404
Home: (310) 584-2588
Fax: (310) 655-2525

1741 S. Norwood Ave. #7
San Bernardino 92404
Home: (909) 587-8787
Fax: (909) 487-2557

SENIOR SALES REPRESENTATIVE & MARKETING MANAGER
Biotechnology / Pharmaceutical / Medical Instrumentation / Software
Delivering strong and sustainable revenue growth in highly-competitive domestic and international business markets.

SKILLS PROFILE:

- New Product Sales
- Distribution Sales Growth
- Competitive Product Positioning
- Large & Key Account Management
- Sales Team Training & Leadership
- Product Pricing & Promotions

- Relationship Sales
- Product Line Management
- New Product Launch
- Customer Training & Seminars
- New Market Development
- Business Planning & Forecasting

Expert in building top-producing business relationships with multinational customers and business partners worldwide. Strong Internet and technical qualifications. Extensive public speaking and customer presentation experience. High professional ethics.

PROFESSIONAL EXPERIENCE:

CONSULTANT – REGIONAL SALES MANAGEMENT, Western, U.S.   1995 to Present

Consultant to start-up ventures and high-growth companies to provide expertise in new market development, key account relationship management, new product/technology introduction, product pricing and positioning, strategic sales, competitive negotiations and revenue growth. Engagements:

BTE Science Products (*biotechnology equipment*) – 1998 to Present
High-profile sales, new business development and account management position expanding BTE's presence throughout Southern California and Arizona ($5 million potential revenue base). Developed/managed key account relationships at UCLA, USC, City of Hope, Cal Tech, UC Riverside, UC Irvine, Selectide and University of Arizona. Created and implemented key account program to enhance competitive market position and drive revenue growth. Liaison with local distributors.

Gencor, Inc. (*high-growth scientific equipment manufacturer*) – 1997 to 1998
Joined early-stage venture to guide product introduction of sophisticated new technology. Developed product positioning plan, created marketing collaterals and sales tools, established pricing structure, and launched promotional campaign. Led highly-complex presentations, product demonstrations and application-oriented seminars at major molecular biology centers, hospitals and biotech companies. Achieved significant growth in first years sales of new product and technology, including placements at the University of Washington, UC San Diego and University of Arizona.

SciMed/Dupont, Inc. (*biotechnology instrumentation*) – 1996 to 1997)
Spearheaded strategic development and national launch into biotechnology market for start-up research venture sponsored by DuPont. Realigned market focus to capture opportunities within the pharmaceutical, hospital, veterinary and food service industries. Prepared/presented strategic marketing plan to DuPont senior management and won approval for program implementation. Negotiated critical strategic alliances/relationships. Held concurrent responsibility for all sales, marketing and new business development efforts in a six-state Western region.

Sciweb (*start-up Internet software developer*) – 1995 to 1996
Authored formal marketing plan, coordinated site development/layout, and launched a full-scale marketing campaign to provide information, references, services and other links to the scientific and research community. Directed the entire sales cycle including development of marketing/collateral materials, client presentations, contract negotiations and project management.

BECKMAN INSTRUMENTS, Fullerton, California   1985 to 1995
(*$500 million worldwide leader in the biotechnology and medical instrumentation industries. Over 20 operating locations in the U.S., Europe, Latin America and the Pacific Rim.*)

Top-Producing Sales and Account Management Executive marketing sophisticated technologies and advanced products to pharmaceutical companies, research centers and biotechnology companies.

Account Manager - Northwest Sales District (1988 to 1995)
Bioanalytical Systems Group, Palo Alto, California

Planned, developed and managed all business development and customer management programs. Responsibility included market planning, competitive product positioning, account management, new product launch, and coordination of all technical support functions for key account base. Led a team of product technology and sales specialists in a matrix-managed organization.

- Promoted as the first Account Manager for $150 million U.S. Bioanalytical Systems Group. Delivered **200%+ revenue growth** in the biotechnology and pharmaceutical markets.
- Delivered the **"Highest Dollar Volume Sold in the World"** in 1995.
- Won numerous awards for outstanding revenue and profit performance. Ranked **#1 U.S. Sales Representative** in 1994.
- Served as **Chair of the U.S. Biotech Task Force** from 1991 through 1995.

Product Line Manager - Robotics Systems Group (1986 to 1988)
Spinco Division, Palo Alto, California

Participated in the strategic planning, development and management of the worldwide product introduction of new technology and associated product line. Traveled worldwide. Responsibility included market positioning, product sales, customer service, customer training, user group meetings, trade shows, sales forecasting and key account management. Developed pricing and marketing collaterals. Researched and identified emerging market and business opportunities worldwide.

- Built product line from **start-up to $6 million** in three years. Reengineered strategy following initial launch to enhance competitive positioning and increase market share.
- Led product training in the U.S. and Europe for key accounts (e.g., Glaxo, Institut Pasteur, Bayer).
- Created high-profile customer communications, follow-up and relationship management programs to improve future sales opportunities.

Senior Training Specialist - Technical Communications (1985 to 1986)
Spinco Division, Palo Alto, California

Recruited to design a series of training programs to support the $10 million molecular structure instrumentation product line. Served on the Molecular Structure Marketing staff, a six-person, multifunctional product marketing and management team.

EDUCATION: **M.S., Neurobiology & Molecular Biology**, University of Pittsburgh, 1985
B.S., Biological Sciences, University of California at Irvine, 1982

AFFILIATIONS: Former Chairman, Northern California Pharmaceutical Discussion Group
Member, Society for Neuroscience

JANET W. BECKSTROM

17 N. Pearl River Drive
Sunnyvale, CA 94086

Phone (650) 965-1447   Fax (650) 874-2554

SENIOR SALES & MARKETING EXECUTIVE
Domestic & International Business Development

Strategic Market Planning / Competitive Market Positioning / Multi-Channel Distribution
Sales Training & Team Leadership / New Product Launch / New Market Development

Dynamic sales and marketing management career delivering state-of-the-art technology worldwide. Achieved strong and sustainable revenue, market and profit contributions through expertise in business development, organizational development and performance management. Keen presentation, contract negotiation, communication and cross-cultural skills. Fluent in French (speaking, reading, writing). Understanding of Spanish and Italian.

PROFESSIONAL EXPERIENCE

Vice President - Latin America Operation
Vice President - Americas Operations – Crystal Software, Inc.
Sunnyvale, CA (1995 to 2000)

Recruited as the Vice President - Americas Operations for this $588 million NYSE company (ninth largest software provider in the world with customer base including 96% of the top 100 U.S. industrial corporations). Challenged to plan and orchestrate an aggressive turnaround and rejuvenation of the Americas sales organization. **Promoted to Vice President of Latin America Operation** (newly-created independent business unit). Held full P&L responsibility for the entire organization, strategic planning, financial performance, personnel, resources and daily business operations. Member of Sterling Software's 15-person senior executive management team.

Scope of responsibility included all sales, marketing, business development, channel development and customer management/retention operations throughout South America, Central America, Mexico and the Caribbean. Led a headquarters team of eight regional managers, product specialists, financial/accounting staff, marketing specialists and administrative support personnel. Managed a 30-person direct sales force in Brazil.

- Transitioned Americas organization from 44% of plan in 1995 to 112% of plan in 1996 ($7 million to $14+ million). Projected $20 million in total revenue by fiscal year end 1998.

- Expanded distributor base by more than 50% to increase market penetration and facilitate market launch of new product technologies and services.

- Provided strong organizational leadership and active participation in key account sales and business development. Resulted in a significant gain in employee morale, productivity and sales performance.

- Concurrent P&L responsibility for independent Brazilian-based sales and marketing company, Crystal Software do Brasil. Delivered 45% growth within less than one year through development of multinational customer base. Facilitated market introduction of EDI sales group with first year revenue at $1+ million.

Managing Partner
Software World Corporation
Sunnyvale, CA (1994 to 1995)

Founded international software distribution company focusing on distributed and systems software productivity tools (DB2, Oracle & Sybase systems). Created marketing strategies, communications, promotions, reseller channels and in-house sales programs. Developed partnership program for export/import of software services.

Director & General Manager - International Sales Operations
Landmark Systems Corporation
Washington, D.C. (1986 to 1994)

Fast-track promotion through four increasingly responsible international management assignments to final position as Senior Executive directing worldwide software sales and marketing operations for direct and reseller channels. Managed UK-based European operation and nine regional sales, marketing and technical support managers.

- Increased Landmark's international sales operation from a $3 million, six-country region to a $30 million, 50-country, worldwide sales organization representing 53% of corporate revenue.

- Established international reseller network to market distributed computing solutions for UNIX platforms including IBM AIX, HP-UX, Sun OS and Sun Solaris.

- Expanded and restructured sales networks in Western Europe, Eastern Europe, South America and the Pacific Rim through development of distributor channels for Landmark's Performance Series for MVS and VSE.

- Renegotiated software distribution agreement with European distributors, saving Landmark $5 million in contract dissolution compensation.

- Successfully renegotiated distribution agreements during product divestiture, resulting in a $9 million savings.

- Reviewed and approved multinational software sales contracts with Fortune 1000 companies.

- Honored for outstanding sales results and over-quota production for eight consecutive years.

Manager of Field Marketing - North American Sales Operations
Applied Data Research, Inc. (*Acquired by CA International*)
Washington, D.C. / Dallas, Texas (1979 to 1986)

Marketing Executive with full responsibility for the design, development and implementation of marketing programs for 15 U.S. offices and Canada on behalf of one of the world's largest independent software vendors. Liaison between North American Operations and International Division.

- Created innovative incentive programs and facilitated training programs for field sales and marketing teams. Coordinated week-long, annual worldwide sales and technical conference.

- Designed marketing collateral and promotional materials for use by North American sales offices.

- Expanded North American sales/marketing presence through participation in industry trade shows, conventions and exhibits targeted to both commercial and Federal sectors.

- Initiated nationwide seminar program to promote ADR's software products. Designed seminar materials, directed presentation programs and spearheaded implementation of computer-based lead tracking system.

Previous Professional Positions

Assistant to the Corporate Vice President of Public Relations, E-Systems, Inc.
Executive Assistant - International Department, Trammel Crow Company
Fundraising Director, Dallas-based civic and cultural organization

EDUCATION

B.A., San Francisco College for Women
Graduate Study/Psychology, University of Geneva - Switzerland
Graduate Study/MIS, University of Texas - Dallas

LINDA M. PRESCOTT
Sales & Marketing Executive – International Markets

3823 Gunther Drive
Salt Lake City, Utah 84121
Phone: (801) 548-3544   Email: lmprescott@yahoo.com

SALES & MARKETING EXPERTISE:

Twenty years' progressively responsible Sales, Marketing, Business Development and Product Development success in competitive business-to-business markets. Outstanding sales planning, sales training and team leadership skills. Top-flight sales negotiation and closing skills. Substantial experience in the Fortune 500 market including key account relationships with GE, Westinghouse, Sherwin Williams, Glidden Paints, Reliance Electric and other major corporations. Superb multi-cultural communication skills.

INTERNATIONAL EXPERIENCE:

Worldwide traveler with an excellent knowledge of languages, cultures, histories, economies and business trends in countries around the globe. Particularly knowledgeable of and comfortable in the Eastern countries including India, Nepal, Sri Lanka, Burma and Bangladesh. Extensive travel throughout European continent, Australia, New Zealand, Japan, Hong Kong, Singapore, Bangkok, Thailand, Malaysia, Indonesia, Bali and the Philippines. Honored to have met Mother Theresa, Sir Edmund Hillary and other noted world leaders.

Amateur explorer; scuba diving on the Great Barrier Reef, hot air ballooning with world renowned expert Charles Dollfus, mountain trekking in Nepal and the Himalayas, and other global adventures.

PROFESSIONAL EXPERIENCE:

Regional Sales Manager   1998 to 2000
Gemstar Communications, Salt Lake City, Utah

High-profile sales, business development and account management position with this $350 million communications company. Challenged to build US market presence for what had traditionally been a European-only publication (*Device Technology* magazine published in the UK). Managed a complex "turnaround" initiative to meet US market demand and establish a strong competitive position.

- Tripled previous years' revenues through aggressive and well-targeted business development program.
- Introduced several adjunct programs and services (e.g., trade show sales, professional roundtables) to strengthen customer relationships and drive annual revenues.

Executive Sales Consultant   1994 to 1998

Launched entrepreneurial venture providing sales, marketing, business development, product development and sales training/leadership expertise to client companies.

- **Grafik Design.** Guided company to 100% revenue growth. Introduced customer-focused selling processes, developed customer management and retention program, trained in-house sales team and designed marketing collaterals. Managed key account relationships and special presentations.
- **Putnam Publishing.** Developed and taught sales training seminar ("Philosophy of Selling") focused on market development, quality, negotiations, sales closings and long-term customer management. Consulted with Publisher/General Manager to identify and develop new product opportunities.
- **John H. Moore, Inc.** Retained on several exclusive contracts to accelerate new product launches and coordinate new market/new territory development initiatives. Personally negotiated and closed over $12.7 million in sales over four years.
- **US Postal Service.** Leveraged past experience in philately to create a soccer stamp album for sale/distribution to collectors worldwide. Identified immediate market potential for $375,000 in sales with global revenues conservatively projected at $1.5 million.

231

Vice President – National Sales   1992 to 1994
TechTrack, Provo, Utah

Recruited to start-up technology company specializing in the sale/distribution of municipal bond database information for use by major US companies in their competitive government bidding efforts. Given full autonomy for planning and executing national sales strategy, defining and capturing key accounts, establishing a competitive market position and facilitating product/service delivery.

- Penetrated major corporate accounts throughout the US in the paper manufacturing, automotive manufacturing and water treatment industries (e.g., Goodyear Tire, Scott Paper).
- Demonstrated outstanding sales presentation, negotiation and closing skills. Outpaced competition.

District Sales Manager   1990 to 1992
Golden Publications, Cleveland, Ohio

Challenged to restore market presence and customer-perceived quality of *Chemical Equipment*, Golden's flagship magazine publication (major competitor to leading McGraw-Hill product). Solely responsible for sales, customer development, customer management and revenue growth within a 5-state region.

- Launched a massive sales and marketing campaign to re-establish relationships with major customers and advertisers. Positioned Chemical Equipment as one of the primary marketing vehicles.
- Established a strong market presence in the chemical and petroleum plant industry and with leading industrial suppliers to these industries. Key accounts included Glidden Paints and Reliance Electric.
- Grew market share from 25% to 31% in first year despite four leading competitive publications. Closed $700,000+ in annual advertising sales revenues.

Regional Sales Manager   1984 to 1988
Chilton Publishing, Cleveland, Ohio

Sold/marketed *Industrial Maintenance & Plant Operations* (exclusive magazine publication) to leading US and international manufacturers. Full responsibility for revitalizing non-performing 4-state territory.

- Built regional sales volume from $450,000 to $650,000 despite intense market competition. Increased advertising revenues by better than 200%.
- Transitioned region from last in market to #1/#2 through personal efforts in restoring product credibility, building new customer relationships and training/motivating/supporting field sales teams.
- Sold/marketed to GE, Westinghouse, Reliance Electric, Sherwin Williams and other major US industrial manufacturers and suppliers.
- Recaptured and restored past account relationships, including negotiating a $90,000 exclusive contract.

National Account Sales Representative   1978 to 1983
Penton Publishing, Cleveland, Ohio

Recruited to join the field sales organization of one of the Top 10 business-to-business publishers in the US ($150+ million corporation). Challenged to build new sales territories and capture key corporate accounts in the industrial manufacturing market. Managed direct sales calls to CEOs, COOs, Senior Technical Executives and other top personnel at targeted customer accounts.

EDUCATION:

BS Degree – Geography – Western Michigan University – Kalamazoo, Michigan – 1977

MS. BOBBIE WESTON
bweston@bellatlantic.net

3894 E. Broadway Lane
Newark, New Jersey 07112

Home: 973-432-2021
Office: 973-411-6580

SENIOR SALES & MARKETING EXECUTIVE
Information Systems & Technology / Networking / Internet / E-Commerce / Systems Integration
MBA Degree in Marketing & Finance

Fifteen years' experience in the strategic planning, marketing, sale and support of advanced technologies, solutions and outsourced operations. High-energy with outstanding communications, general management, change management and process improvement skills. Cross-functional expertise in:

- Profit & Loss Management
- Strategic Sales & Account Planning
- New Product & Service Introduction
- Competitive Market Positioning
- Executive Sales Presentations

- Sales Training & Team Leadership
- Customer Relationship Management
- Management Training & Retention
- Competitive Sales Contracts & Bids
- Financial Negotiations & Transactions

PROFESSIONAL EXPERIENCE:

ISP SYSTEMS, Newark, New Jersey   1993 to Present
(World's leading distributor of PC products, network products & outsourcing services with annual sales of $4.5 billion. Formerly Lexon Information Services.)

Recruited to Lexon to provide high-level sales and marketing leadership during a period of rapid growth, including $4 million acquisition of ISP. Promoted rapidly through a series of increasingly responsible sales leadership positions based on consistently strong performance.

- *Corporate Sales Manager of the Year* – 1997
- *Sales Manager of the Year* – 1997
- *Eastern Region Sales Manager of the Year* – 1996, 1997, 1998

Area Vice President (1998 to Present)

Senior Executive with full strategic planning, market planning/analysis, new market/new business development, account relationship management, sales training, field team leadership and P&L responsibility for a 75-person, $400 million sales and technical support organization. Challenged to drive profitable growth through sale of computer products, networks and integrated service solutions for major accounts throughout Connecticut, New York and New Jersey.

- Realigned market plan and refocused sales team on the top 10 customers for integrated systems sales, solutions and support. Drove a **$45 million increase** in annual revenues.
- Built profitable account relationship with **MetLife** and sold over $3 million in outsourcing contracts (including placement of 100 ISP personnel at IBM sites nationwide. **Saved the client over $5+ million annually** in business operating costs.
- Captured key accounts for the corporation including **Morgan Stanley** and the **Gardner Group** while significantly increasing volume with existing customer base.
- Honored as **Top Regional Distributor for Compaq Computers** in 1997 and **Top Regional Distributor for IBM** in 1998.

Area Sales Director (1997 to 1998)

Led a 60-person (five teams) sales organization generating over $150 million in annual revenues. Key drive in reorganizing company into individual operating divisions following acquisition and integration of CompuCom.

- Launched an aggressive expansion into financial and banking sectors, **increasing sales 30%**.
- Led sales team selected by **American Express** as the Malcolm Baldrige Quality Award winner in both 1997 and 1998. **Saved the client over $1 million annually** through strategic project management, outsourcing and systems installation/administration.
- Won **five consecutive President's Club** awards for achieving annual sales and profit goals.

Corporate Sales Manager (1996 to 1997)

Revitalized non-performing corporate sales organization marketing large-dollar systems and solutions. Replaced 50% of field sales team within first year, introduced new sales process and account management systems, and refocused market/account penetration.

- **Increased sales from $12 million to $80 million** within three years, including a 50% gain in PC service revenues within first year.
- Negotiated, closed and directed a major POS terminal installation project for a large retail customer. Redesigned project management model and **saved the client $6 million** in cost.

AMDAHL CORPORATION, Newark, New Jersey   1989 to 1993
Global Sales Representative

Sold/marketed multi-million dollar computer systems and related services to Fortune 500 corporations and their subsidiaries worldwide. Emphasis on technical sales at the CIO level.

- **Achieved/surpassed all annual revenue and profit objectives**. Developed and negotiated unique sales contracts, pricing strategies and customer "financing proposals" to gain competitive market share and position Amdahl as a major industry player.
- Captured **Allied Signal** account from IBM and **sold $50+ million** in Amdahl technology.
- Personally negotiated and closed the largest computer sale in the history of the US Postal Service **($20 million competitive bid)**.

MERRILL LYNCH & CO., Atlanta, Georgia   1986 to 1988
Marketing Representative

Recruited following MBA degree and offered opportunity to learn the intricacies of the financial investment community and complex financial transactions. Traded equities and supported institutional accounts in Southeastern US. Used sophisticated computer analysis and modeling.

IBM CORPORATION, New York, New York   1980 to 1986
Marketing Representative / Systems Engineer

Sold IBM midsize and mainframe computers, storage, software and communications products to five national accounts. Largest project was design, installation and technical support of computer systems in customer travel office locations in 40 cities nationwide.

- **Increased annual sales from $1.1 million in 1982 to $3.1 million in 1985** (125% of quota each year). Honored with five President's Club awards for outstanding revenue production.

XEROX CORPORATION, New York, New York   1979 to 1980
A.M. INTERNATIONAL, New York, New York   1978 to 1979
Account Marketing Representative – Printing Equipment & Technology

EDUCATION:

MBA – Marketing & Finance – NEW YORK UNIVERSITY / STERN SCHOOL OF BUSINESS (1986)
BA – Economics – RUTGERS UNIVERSITY (1978)
Graduate – ISP Systems, IBM and Xerox Sales Training; Merrill Lynch MBA Training

MALCOLM WYMAN

48 Emerson Place
Boston, Massachusetts 02114

Home: 617-215-7845
Office: 617-986-3628

Email: malcolm@mwaii.com
Web Page: mwaii.com

SALES PROCESS, PRODUCTIVITY & PERFORMANCE IMPROVEMENT EXPERT
Armour, Chevron, Citibank, Coors, Dataserve, Frito-Lay, Nabisco, Pepsico, Wells Fargo
US & Global Customer Markets

Inventive and results-driven Executive credited with creating sales, sales management and organizational leadership processes that have enabled companies to work smarter and at less cost for dramatic revenue, market share and profit growth.

- Pioneered innovative and successful sales processes, feedback systems, team building processes, standards, growth mapping processes, consultative selling systems and sales management processes for organizations with up to 30,000 sales personnel worldwide.
- Architected and introduced integrated sales processes for all sales distribution channels (e.g., direct, distributor, retail outlet, wholesale outlet, contract business).
- Created more than 300 client-specific sales training and process improvement templates, customized to the specific operations of each sales and distribution channel.
- Coached, trained and led senior-level sales directors, vice presidents and general managers.

PROFESSIONAL EXPERIENCE:

MALCOLM WYMAN & ASSOCIATES INT'L, INC., Boston, Massachusetts   1989 to Present

President – Founded one of the most respected sales training, productivity improvement and performance management organizations in the US. Specialize in the creative, strategic and tactical design/implementation of sales processes to enhance productivity, improve customer service, and drive strong revenue, market share and profit growth.

Over the past nine years, completed 50+ engagements with major consumer products companies worldwide. Major clients have included American Olean Tile (division of Armstrong World Industries), Coors, Dataserv (Division of Bell South), Frito-Lay, Nabisco International and Pepsico Foods International. Retained for all engagements through direct client referrals.

- Partnered with newly appointed UK Sales Director of **Walkers Snack Foods** to redefine and reenergize field sales organization through process development/implementation.
  - Led one of the company's most successful sales team turnarounds, positioning Walkers as the #1 profit-producing unit in all of **Pepsico Foods International**.
  - Sales processes were implemented worldwide, contributing to PFI's position as the #1 Pepsico division.

- Currently leading **Nabisco's Frontline Sales Team**, a task force organized to study and enhance frontline sales processes of 17,000-person organization. Initiated pilot study in 450-person sales region to create new "sales organization" prototype for subsequent deployment worldwide.
  - Developed and introduced new hire, new account planning and new frontline sales management processes to strengthen sales growth, productivity and customer service performance.
  - Currently leading efforts to bring $10+ million project on line throughout 17,000-person sales organization.

- Currently engaged with **General Mills International** to recreate the sales and distribution processes of $50 million Caribbean business.
  - Restructured sales organization and sales territories, developed improved customer database, revised sales compensation, and initiated a series of customer service improvement and retention programs.
  - Currently leading implementation of growth mapping, gaining commitment and distributor database management processes.

DYNAMIC SYSTEMS, INC., Springfield, Massachusetts   1981 to 1989

Senior Vice President (1985 to 1989)
Vice President (1983 to 1985)
Senior Consultant / Manager of Management Consulting (1981 to 1983)

Instrumental in transitioning regional management consulting firm into an international firm with offices in NY, LA, Chicago, Atlanta, Dallas and Toronto, and serving 450+ clients in 30 countries. Major clients included Chevron, Frito-Lay, Pepsico, Swift, Square D, and major banking institutions in the US and Canada. Appointed to Executive Committee in 1984.

Principal responsibility for design/delivery of customer consulting and training programs across a broad range of industries,. Equally strong contributions in new venture development, new product development, business planning and business systems automation (resulting in dramatic cost reduction, significant gain in productivity and critical competitive advantage).

- Contributed to the highest gross margins and profit in the company's history with revenue growth from $1.2 million in 1982 to $7.8 million in 1989 (compounded rate of 38%).
- Orchestrated the development and marketing of five sales training systems for bank calling officers at Barclays, California Federal S&L, Citibank, Security Pacific, The Royal Bank of Canada and Wells Fargo. Created a strong and steady new revenue stream.
- Created and commercialized innovative training programs for the petroleum industry, successfully marketing and delivering to 400+ customers worldwide.

FRITO-LAY, INC., Dallas, Texas   1978 to 1981

Senior Vice President (1979 to 1981)
National Sales Training Coordinator (1978 to 1979)

Dual responsibility for the conceptualization, design, development, implementation and leadership of internal sales, operations and manufacturing training programs for Frito-Lay facilities and sales organizations nationwide. Identified and leveraged core competencies to drive productivity, quality and revenue/profit growth within an intensely competitive industry.

- Created, documented and led basic selling and route sales training programs for the company's 8000 route sales associates. Trained over 2000 individuals annually.
- Redesigned and shortened new hire sales training program.
- Designed and taught manufacturing training in 40 locations throughout the US, involving nearly 10,000 personnel in established and start-up production facilities. Established new standards for manufacturing training and developed internal trainer certification program.

ARMOUR FOODS COMPANY, Phoenix, Arizona   1971 to 1978

Manager of Sales Training (1976 to 1978)
District Sales Manager (1975 to 1976)
Product Department Manager (1973 to 1975)
Sales Representative (1971 to 1973)

- As Manager of Sales Training, designed, implemented and directed sales training programs for 1000+ sales representatives and sales managers nationwide.
- As District Sales Manager, led $50 million sales region and converted sales distribution system from store door to warehouse for $500,000 annual cost savings (union operation).
- As Department Manager, grew volume 20% and delivered $1.4 million net profit.
- As Sales Representative, increased sales revenue 500%. Won numerous sales awards.

EDUCATION: **BS – Mathematics** – Boston University - 1971

JOHN THOMPKINS

584 Stanford Court
Joliet, Illinois 60436

Phone: 815.873.2584   jthompkins@worldnet.att.net   Fax: 815.357.1598

SENIOR BUSINESS EXECUTIVE – US & INTERNATIONAL
Competitive Intelligence / Operations Security / Information & Internet Security / Corporate Security

Pioneer in the development and execution of advanced intelligence collection systems to guide strategic planning, market entry and competitive market positioning for major US and international companies. Expert in the protection and control of intellectual property, assets, trademarks and patents. Outstanding performance in identifying and negotiating opportunities for strategic alliances, joint ventures, acquisitions and business-to-business partnerships.

Senior Advisor to top corporate executives to provide intelligence and leadership in strengthening competitive positions worldwide. Keen negotiation, problem-solving, crisis management and relationship management skills. Powerful presentation and communications skills. Fluent in both written and oral Japanese.

Expert in the use of advanced technologies for research, reporting/documentation, financial analysis, customer tracking, competitive intelligence, information management and other applications. Thorough knowledge of Internet search methods, online data sources, Internet security and Public Key Encryption (PKE) methodologies.

- **Frequent Lecturer** on Business Intelligence, Economic Intelligence and Operations Security (OPSEC). Appeared on numerous television shows including *NBC Dateline* and quoted by Peter Schweizer in *Friendly Spies*, by Larry Kahaner in *Competitive Intelligence* and by Ira Winkler in *Corporate Espionage*.

- **Catalyst Award**, Society of Competitive Intelligence Professionals, 1998

- **Certificate of Appreciation**, National Counterintelligence Center (NACIC), 1995

PROFESSIONAL EXPERIENCE:

Managing Director   1992 to Present
THOMPKINS INTERNATIONAL, Joliet, Illinois

Launched entrepreneurial consulting venture to leverage knowledge, experience and relationships in competitive intelligence, advanced technologies and Japanese/Asian markets. Built company from concept into a thriving enterprise with major corporate clients throughout the US and Far East. Expanded practice beyond consulting to include the design/delivery of professional seminars and training programs on competitive intelligence, operations security and information/Internet security. Major clients and projects:

- **Leading US manufacturer of industrial equipment.** Provided market intelligence and identified acquisition opportunities to profitably enter the South Korean market.

- **Japanese subsidiary of major US electronics & communications manufacturer.** Guided company in defining competitive technology environment, interviewed subject matter and knowledge experts, evaluated competition and created strategic market development plan.

- **Major Japanese electronics manufacturer.** Advised principals in developing US office and forging strategic alliances with leading US technology firms to launch digital imaging and printing technologies.

- **Major US foods products manufacturer.** Researched and defined global market share, assessed competitive market activities, and delivered tactical plans to drive Asian market penetration.

- **Leading US pharmaceutical manufacturer.** Conducted patent search to support litigation and created a formal infrastructure to guide future patent filings, litigation and protection.

- **Big Six consulting firm.** Senior advisor on intellectual property protection, corporate operations security and competitive intelligence countermeasures.

237

Director – International Business Development   1990 to 1992
HI-TECH GROUP, Tokyo, Japan

Retained by CEO to orchestrate Hi-Tech's profitable entry into the Far Eastern commercial markets. Forged critical strategic alliances and provided a wealth of competitive intelligence to strategically map market penetration into the competitive technology industry.

Business Development Manager   1987 to 1989
IBM, Tokyo, Japan

Recruited for two-year assignment to facilitate IBM's entry into the Japanese marketplace and the delivery of leading edge systems integration solutions. Identified joint venture, strategic alliance and partnership opportunities to accelerate market penetration. Installed some of the first LAN technologies in Japan.

Managing Director   1985 to 1986
OZAWA INTERNATIONAL CORPORATION, Boston, Massachusetts

Founded specialized consulting practice providing business intelligence to major U.S. corporations with an emphasis on the Japanese and Far Eastern corporate markets.

Intelligence Officer   1977 to 1984
U.S. CENTRAL INTELLIGENCE AGENCY (CIA), Washington, D.C.

Undercover operations and surveillance in Japan, North Korea and Vietnam. Reported on political, economic and market activities impacting U.S. military and commercial presence.

EDUCATION:

International Business Management Program – Japan American Institute of Mgmt. Science, 1976
BA – Asian Studies – Sophia University, Tokyo, Japan, 1973

PROFESSIONAL PRESENTATIONS & PUBLIC SPEAKING ENGAGEMENTS:

Delivered over 150 presentations to corporate, government and association audiences over the past 10 years on Competitive Intelligence, Operations Security and Information Security. Highlights include:

- Society of Competitive Intelligence Professionals
- US Dept. of Commerce Technology Administration
- National Leadership Forum on Global Challenges
- International Security Systems Symposium
- Emory University
- Japan Center of Science & Technology
- American Society for Industrial Security
- Annual National OPSEC Conferences

PROFESSIONAL AFFILIATIONS:

President – Operations Security Professional Society (OPS)
Society of Competitive Intelligence Professionals (SCIP) – *SCIP/Japan Chapter*
Association of Former Intelligence Officers (AFIO)
National Military Intelligence Association (NMIA)
Business Espionage Controls & Countermeasures Association (BECCA)
Japan Society of Washington

HAROLD SUMPTER

84 Vermont Avenue
Berkeley, California 94707

Phone: (520) 546-1597
sumpter9@worldnet.att.net

SENIOR EXECUTIVE PROFILE
Global Supply Chain Management / Operations Management
Domestic & International
MBA Degree

Leader in the conceptualization, development, implementation and management of best-in-class business organizations. Consistently successful in strengthening enterprise equity value, reducing operating costs and improving bottom-line profitability through innovation, creativity and strategic organizational leadership. Dynamic management performance.

Strategic Planning	Customer Relationship Management	Competitive Contract Negotiations
Purchasing Strategies	Integrated Logistics Management	Strategic Alliances & Partnerships
Vendor Sourcing & Quality	Process & Performance Optimization	Program & Project Leadership

Published Author
Global Strategic Alliances, Global Supplier Development, Cost Reduction Strategies, Supply Chain Management

PROFESSIONAL EXPERIENCE

AAA SYSTEMS COMPANY, El Segundo, California   1997 to Present
(XYZ Aircraft spin off in 1997; one of only two AAA executives with full access to ABC purchase portfolio of $80+ billion.)

Senior Manager – Industrial Cooperation – International Programs

Hand-selected by AAA leadership to develop and direct an International Industrial Cooperation program with international electronics systems manufacturers. Challenged to create an organization committed to the operational and financial growth of these corporations by developing global partnerships and alliances for industrial cooperation within established and emerging markets. Immediate objective is to identify and enable $41 million in industrial offset for CY2000 contracts with an additional $200 million over the next seven years.

- Captured $32 million in cash and equity instruments through strategic alliance agreements for benefit of AAA engineering and manufacturing projects over the next seven years.
- Brought in $1.75 million in cash and $10.5 million in future cash from two ABC enterprise cost reduction agreements.
- Identified and established business opportunity agreements in excess of $17 billion over the next eight years.

ABC – XYZ HOLDINGS, Detroit, Michigan & Los Angeles, California   1978 to Present

Managing Executive – Strategic Initiatives – ABC (1994 to Present)

Selected by ABC President and CEO to design and implement strategic supplier business plans and manage supplier base throughout ABC Corporation and Delphi Automotive Systems. Collaborate with ABC executive management to identify and execute strategies that integrate advanced electronics design with ABC established technology projects. Manage a rolling $500 million purchasing portfolio of advanced planning, global sourcing and supplier programs to improve quality, service and technology while delivering significant annual cost savings.

- Directed in excess of 90 projects involving over 500 personnel across multiple functions. Delivered $420 million in earnings from 1994 to 1999 through aggressive cost reduction and program management/leadership efforts.
- Appointed Key Material Executive to the 1994 ABC XYZ operational redesign team facilitating complete reengineering of all operational aspects of $4.5 billion business segment in preparation for spin-off in 1997.
- Established commodity process for ABC XYZ through adaptation of the ABC worldwide purchasing process to reduce material costs, improve supplier quality and enhance supplier technology process. Effort impacted 1000+ personnel across eight functions and five business segments with annual purchasing expenditures of $1.2+ billion.

Business Executive – $1.8 Billion Business Unit – ABC XYZ Electronics (1991 to 1994)

High-profile management position orchestrating the development and implementation of Worldwide Purchasing™ methods throughout the entire business segment. Efforts impacted an organization of more than 325 employees and annual purchasing expenditures averaging $750 million. Led a direct reporting staff of 58.

- Negotiated strategic partnerships with domestic and international suppliers for $45 million in cost savings over three years. Met/exceeded all financial targets, enhanced customer satisfaction and improved competitive market position.
- Negotiated/executed 12 alliance agreements which contributed equity cost savings to nine programs and yielded savings of $121 million over three years.
- Solidified ABC's support to North American Operations, leveraging $70+ billion across 21 common suppliers.
- Invented the term and process known as Enterprise Cost Reduction which was validated by ABC Legal as meeting the standard for the Department of Justice Anti-Trust Codes. Launched the effort with cumulative savings of $351M.

Manager – Group Estimating – XYZ Aircraft Company (1988 to 1991)

Designed, staffed and directed an estimating systems organization of 80 professionals to develop/implement standardized costing and pricing methods for multi-million dollar engineering and manufacturing proposals.

- Successfully defended 75 government claims in excess of $375 million for defective pricing, fraud, false claims and false statements. Avoided costs and penalties of an additional $15 million through unique joint team-based approach.
- Improved estimating standards and efficacy of customer proposals, resulting in a 40% increase in cash flow, 65% reduction in errors and $145 million in new contract awards.

Manager – Group Contracts – XYZ Aerospace (1978 to 1988)

Fast-track promotion through increasingly responsible management positions directing logistics and contract negotiation. Interfaced with Department of Defense, engineering and contracting officers to manage pre/post award contracts and integrated logistics support activity for an international contract portfolio valued in excess of $150 million. Experienced in Manufacturing and Technology Licensing agreements with international governments and trade groups. Annual international portfolio under management was approximately $60 million with a 46-person staff.

EDUCATION

ABC INSTITUTE, Detroit, Michigan, 1999
Worldwide Purchasing / International Planning & Logistics

ABC / XYZ, Marina Del Ray, California, 1988
International Contracts / Supply Chain & Logistics Management

MBA / Organizational Management / CALIFORNIA STATE UNIVERSITY, Fullerton, 1998

CALIFORNIA STATE POLYTECHNICAL, Pomona, California, 1980
Certified Integrated Logistics Support Manager

BS / Finance & Public Administration / UNIVERSITY OF ARIZONA, Tucson, Arizona, 1978

PROFESSIONAL AFFILIATIONS

Executive Select:	1999 International Who's Who of Professionals
National Director:	National Contract Management Association – Southern Arizona
Faculty Chair:	Government Contracts Department – University of Phoenix
Faculty:	University of Colorado – International Strategic Business
Segment Executive:	XYZ Electronic Enterprise Re-Design Team
Industry Team Leader:	Department of Defense Federal Acquisition Regulation Assessment
Team Chair:	ABC XYZ – Advance Purchasing & Technology Transfer Group
Member:	International Society of Automotive Engineers; National Estimating Society

LAWRENCE BRITE

3525 S. Central Boulevard
New York, New York 14850
lbrite@yahoo.com

Phone: 321-487-3655
Fax: 324-214-3628
Cellular: 365-111-8412

TELECOMMUNICATIONS INDUSTRY EXECUTIVE
**Wireless, Local Telephone & Long Distance Communications – US & International Markets
Start-Up, Turnaround, High-Growth & Multinational Companies**

Pioneer in the development, funding, marketing, operations, revitalization and profitable leadership of leading edge telecommunications companies and ventures worldwide. Top record of performance in general business management, sales/marketing management and technical management. Decisive, strategic and performance-driven. Keen presentation, negotiation, communication and problem solving skills. Expert technical competencies in telecommunications systems, networks and technologies. Ph.D. and M.S. Degrees.

PROFESSIONAL EXPERIENCE:

ABC WIRELESS COMMUNICATIONS, INC. (ABC), New York, New York

Chief Operating Officer (1996 to 1998)
Executive Vice President – Operations (1994 to 1996)

Challenge: Recruited to venture company engaged in the development, operation and ownership (with strategic partners) of cellular, wireless local loop, mobile trunked radio and paging service companies in Asia and Latin America. Growth from 2 to 10 companies and 50,000+ subscribers.

Operated in a high-profile, fast-paced executive management position providing operating, financial, investment, strategic, marketing and government affairs leadership for subsidiary companies. Guided senior management teams of operating companies in raising capital, network planning, technology selection and construction, sales and marketing strategy, information technology, staffing, training, interconnect, regulatory approvals and licensing. Highlights:

XYZ – Kuala Lumpur, Malaysia (*wireless local loop company with national license*)
- **Board Director** leading six-month in-country effort which succeeded in reversing Malaysian cabinet decision to expropriate the company. Brought network to full operational status despite strong opposition from principal Malaysian telecommunications company. Market potential for 20 million subscribers at $1 billion.

Mirkom – Jakarta, Indonesia (*enhanced services mobile radio provider with national license*)
- **Board Director & Chairperson – Board Executive Committee** overseeing all technical, business and marketing operations for the start-up of a new network venture. Negotiated interconnect with Telkom Indonesia and won government approval to halt the issuance and renewal of private mobile radio licenses. Achieved #1 market position in first year.

Digitel Limited – Hong Kong, China (*analog cellular company with operations in China*)
- **Board Director & Senior Operations Executive** for six month engagement to launch the start-up of technology operations in China's richest province. Worked cooperatively with Chinese military leaders to commercialize their technology for mass market entry. Built subscriber base to 45,000 and raised $50 million in additional funding to support expansion.

AAA – Sao Paulo, Brazil (*trunked mobile radio provider with 1000+ channels throughout Brazil*)
- **Chairperson – Board Executive Committee** to launch operations in Sao Paulo and several other Brazilian cities (current subscriber base of 12,000).

IT-COMM – Wellington, New Zealand (*enhanced specialized mobile radio provider in NZ*)
- **Director & Chairman of the Board** leading the start-up of a new telecommunications company to service industrialized and remote regions throughout the country. Brought new venture to #2 in market share in the country.

241

ACE TELEMANAGEMENT, INC., Manhattan, New York

Senior Vice President – Sales & Service (1994)
Senior Vice President – Sales & Marketing (1993)
Senior Vice President & Chief Service Officer (1988 to 1993)

Challenge: Recruited to post-IPO company, a single point of contact, outsourcing provider of Centrex based telephone services, to provide strategic, technical, marketing, sales and customer service leadership. Company was founded in 1984 but was still operating as a virtual start-up as a result of regulatory requirements and competitive issues.

Scope of responsibility increased dramatically to encompass all technical, engineering, network management, sales, marketing and customer service operations as revenues grew from $35 million to $200 million over five years. Staffing responsibility for up to 400 employees. Operating budget responsibility for up to $32 million annually. Member of 6-person Senior Executive Committee.

- Created a fully-integrated, quality-based sales, marketing and customer service organization, the catalyst for the corporation's phenomenal growth cycle from 10 to 100 ACE centers.
- Improved gross margin by 22% despite product price reductions.
- Initiated corrective action to reverse high sales cancellations and sales staff turnover. Improved customer service and reduced cancellations by 50%. Upgraded hiring qualifications, inhouse training and incentive programs for a 40% reduction in staff turnover.
- Reduced an already low 1.7% customer churn per month by 18% over three years.
- Completed 40% of corporate restructuring and change management project to convert from field locations to business units when company was acquired in a hostile takeover. Consulted with new ownership and Board of Directors to facilitate a seamless transition and integration.

MAJOR COMMUNICATIONS COMPANY, Kansas City, Missouri

Corporate Vice President – Operations (1987 to 1988)
Vice President – Engineering & Operations – Pacific Division (1986 to 1987)

Challenge: Provided technical leadership for the strategic alliance and merger between ABC and DEF to create Major Communications. One of the few company executives with the organization throughout its entire infancy and challenging growth cycle to current position as the third largest long distance company in the US.

Credited with leading national telecommunications network through a period of dramatic technological change and enhancement. Held full strategic planning, financial, human resources, technical and operating management responsibility. Directed a staff of 1500. Managed a $153 million annual operating budget.

- Led successful conversion of the entire customer base from microwave technology and a switching network to new fiber network. Commissioned and put into service 20,000 route miles of digital fiber, 42 national switching centers and 2 international gateways.
- Delivered the best network/service performance ratings out of seven operating divisions for the Pacific region (Major's largest division with annual revenues of $540 million). Achieved "best in class" results despite 40% growth over first year.
- Consolidated seven regional division departments into one fully-integrated operating organization, reduced costs, enhanced team competencies and improved service quality.

GTE COMMUNICATIONS COMPANY, Burlingame, California

Director – Program Management & Engineering Administration (1985 to 1986)

Challenge: Retained by the senior management team of ABC (long distance communications company) following their acquisition of previous employer, North Central Communications. Challenged to provide strategic, technical and operational leadership for the turnaround and revitalization of non-performing Program Management & Engineering Administration Department.

- Recruited new management team and restored energy, drive and technical expertise.
- Returned $750 million national build-out construction project to on-time and within budget, and achieved all investment tax credit objectives.

SOUTHERN PACIFIC COMMUNICATIONS COMPANY (SPCC), Burlingame, California

Director – Operations Network Planning & Administration (1984 to 1985)
Director – Network Operations (1983 to 1984)
Manager – National Microwave (1982 to 1983)

Challenge: This start-up, facilities based, long distance communications company was not performing well despite rapid growth and expansion. Recruited to provide technical and operating management expertise to enhance performance, quality and service competencies.

- Reduced $400 million facilities access budget by $10 million while eliminating double digit access blocking in 120+ sales areas.
- Created an aggressive maintenance program and achieved over 99.9% network availability.
- Reduced toll fraud losses by over 50% through identification and prosecution of perpetrators.
- Led successful turnaround and return to peak performance of failing microwave department.

UNITED STATES MILITARY ACADEMY, West Point, New York

Deputy Head–Department of Electrical Engineering & Tenured Professor (1980 to 1985)

EDUCATION:

Ph.D. – Electrical Engineering, Purdue University, West Lafayette, Indiana
M.S. – Engineering, Purdue University, West Lafayette, Indiana
B.S., US Military Academy, West Point, New York

MARILYN CORTLAND
742 Riverside Road
Durham, North Carolina 27523

Home: 312-899-2475
Office: 316-587-3232

Pager: 800-587-6969 #25841
Email: mcortland@bellatlantic.net

TELECOMMUNICATIONS INDUSTRY EXECUTIVE

Combines 15+ Years General Management & Organizational/Operating Leadership Experience in:

- Business Strategy / Strategic Planning
- Financial Management / Risk Assessment
- Regional Sales & Customer Service Operations
- Multi-Channel Sales Support
- Budgeting & Cost Reduction/Avoidance
- Business Process Automation/Simplification

- Multi-Site Operations Management
- Multicultural Team Building & Leadership
- Strategic & Tactical Market Development
- Competitive Product & Service Positioning
- Call Center Operations Management
- Executive Negotiations & Presentations

Strong interpersonal, communications, analytical, negotiation, problem solving and project management performance. Flexible in dynamic, challenging and multicultural business organizations. Expert in building. mentoring, motivating and leading high-performance teams to achieve aggressive business opportunities and financial goals. Independent, creative and critical thinker with sound judgment and decision making competencies. Change agent, innovator and pioneer in quality management and performance improvement. Decisive, direct and results-driven to succeed.

MBA Degree in Finance & Economics
Extensive Leadership, Information Technology, Quality and Executive Development Training

---

PROFESSIONAL EXPERIENCE

ABC TELECOMMUNICATION CORPORATION   1982 to Present

Sixteen-year management career with one of the nation's largest and most diversified telecommunications corporations. Advanced rapidly through increasingly responsible positions in Customer Sales & Operations, Sales Channel Management, Quality, Regulatory, Finance, Network Services and Engineering/Installation. Career highlights include:

Director – NC Business Account Team Centers & ISDN Center (1995 to Present)
ABC Sales & Service Centers, Durham, North Carolina, Long Island & Manhattan, New York

Dynamic leadership position orchestrating the integration of 4 ½ director organizations into one multifunctional workforce (60+ managers and 340 associates) managing daily sales operations, order provisioning and billing for the top 15% revenue producing business customers throughout the New York metro region. Team services a cross-industry and multiple market-segmented customer base generating $560 million in total annual billed revenues to ABC. Manage a $30 million annual operating budget, all strategic business planning, service delivery, revenue growth, cost management and employee development/communications operations. Support multichannel direct and agent sales organizations.

- Built what is currently ranked as the #1 MegaCenter across the ABC New York/New England region.
- Met and/or exceeded all customer service, corporate, employee satisfaction, call center metrics and operational objectives in 1996 and 1997. Currently on target to again exceed all goals in 1998.

Director – Quality Services (1993 to 1995)
Director – Quality Services, Boston, Massachusetts

Led a team of six quality consultants supporting North Carolina and Strategic Business Unit Group Presidents and Vice Presidents in developing quality improvement plans and programs to accelerate revenue growth, improve customer service and facilitate aggressive cost reductions. Appointed Corporate Quality Spokesperson.

- Pioneered the successful implementation strategy for Malcolm Baldrige self-assessment analysis, subsequently adopted as a key strategic component of the ABC team award. Annual client performance earned 95%-110% team award.
- Conceived, created and introduced story boards, employee recognition/sharing rallies and open space technology sessions to facilitate proactive quality improvement initiatives.

ABC TELECOMMUNICATION CORPORATION – Continued

Staff Director – Authorized Sales Agents (1992 to 1993)
Sales Channel Management, Boston, Massachusetts

Corporate Sales Liaison to Authorized Sales Agents throughout Rhode Island and Eastern Massachusetts. Challenged to enhance business relationships, develop action-based business plans, strengthen competitive market positioning, improve product and service sales strategies, and drive profitable revenue growth. Direct report to Managing Director of Division.

- Transitioned lowest ranking agents to first-ever over quota performance. Closed 1992 at 158% of goal.
- Mentored two agents to win the 1993 *"Agent of the Year"* award and *"Top Agent of 1993 Sales Center"* award.
- Exceeded personal regional revenue budget by 28%.

Staff Director – Strategic Planning (1990 to 1992)
Interexchange Customer Service Center, Boston, Massachusetts

High-profile management position directing strategic planning functions for the $225 million ICSC Division. Concurrent responsibility for development and ongoing leadership of several core quality management and business process improvement teams. Team finalist for the 1991 and 1992 President's Award for *"Excellence Through Quality."*

Early Professional Career – ABC Telecommunications

Staff Director – Regulatory Issues (1989 to 1990) – Massachusetts State Rate Setting & Pricing Strategies
Associate Director – Finance (1987 to 1989) – Capital Structures, Bond Ratings, Rate of Return, Valuation
Loaned Executive – United Way of Central Massachusetts (1986) – Corporate Fundraising & Sponsorships
Associate Director & Office Manager – Operator Services (1985 to 1986) – System & Process Automation
Manager – Equipment Installation/Provisioning (1984 to 1985) – *Exceptional Performance Award*
Network Administration Supervisor (1982 to 1983) – Labor Relations

EDUCATION & PROFESSIONAL DEVELOPMENT

MBA – Finance & Economics (1995)	BABSON COLLEGE / F.W. OLIN GRADUATE SCHOOL
BS – Business Administration & Marketing (1984)	BOSTON UNIVERSITY SCHOOL OF MANAGEMENT
Information Technology & Data Markets (1992)	ALPHA III FORUM SEMINAR
Strategic Quality Management (1994)	UNIVERSITY OF MICHIGAN
Expatriate Leadership Training (1992)	WICE INTERNATIONAL TRAINING – Paris, France
Young Executive Development Program (1990)	ASPEN INSTITUTE / FUND FOR CORPORATE INITIATIVES

PROFESSIONAL HONORS & AWARDS

YMCA Black Achiever's Award (1997)	GREATER BOSTON YMCA
Diversity Recognition Award (1992)	ABC MARKETING & TECHNOLOGY
Fellow, Young Executives Program (1991 to Present)	FUND FOR CORPORATE INITIATIVES

PROFESSIONAL AFFILIATIONS & LEADERSHIP ACTIVITIES

BABSON COLLEGE CORPORATION (1994 to Present)
Trustee & Board Member / Vice Chair – Marketing & PR Committee / Committee on Corporation Members / Graduate Advisory Board / President's Society / Sir Isaac Newton Society / Volunteer – Career Services / MBA Reunion Committee

ABC TELECOMMUNICATIONS NORTH CAROLINA (1996 to Present)
Member / Speaker / Customer Advisory Board

THE ETHEL WALKER SCHOOL (1996)
Member – Alumnae Association & 1978 Graduate

YMCA TRAINING INCORPORATED (1994 to 1995)
Volunteer / Workshop Leader / Mentor / Liaison

GARY BLOCK

3154 Desert Sands
Reno, Nevada 64512
(644) 365-4321

TRANSPORTATION / LOGISTICS / DISTRIBUTION
Start-Up, Turnaround & Management of
Profitable, Multi-Site Dedicated Logistics Operations

Over 15 years experience in the Transportation Industry. Strong record of cost reduction, revenue improvement and quality/performance management. Excellent qualifications in operations planning/management, customer management, union negotiations and fleet management.

PROFESSIONAL EXPERIENCE:

RYDER DEDICATED LOGISTICS   1988 to Present
(Contracted Logistics, Distribution & Transportation Operations)

OPERATIONS MANAGER (1991 to Present)
OPERATIONS SUPERVISOR (1989 to 1990)
DISPATCHER (1988 to 1989)

Operations Manager responsible for the start-up, development, growth and management of RDL's contract services to Montgomery Ward throughout California and Nevada. Scope of responsibility includes the entire operation of each facility, including staffing, budgeting, financial reporting, cost control, dispatching, routing, scheduling, union relations/negotiations, DOT regulatory affairs, safety, training and customer management.

Transferred between three Ward logistics operations to coordinate the start-up of each and the subsequent turnaround following unsuccessful transition to other management teams. Assigned full P&L responsibility in 1994 for all three locations and a staff of 87.

- Built Montgomery Ward account from start-up to $5.5 million in annual revenues.

- Directed start-up of Las Vegas Home Delivery, San Diego Home Delivery and Garden Grove shuttle operations. Built each into a fully-staffed, full-service logistics facility operating at profitability within three months.

- Troubleshot and turned around poorly-performing operations. Delivered significant and sustainable financial gains through efforts in cost reduction, productivity improvement, service improvement and staff consolidation.

- Maintained competitive position against other dedicated logistics service contractors. RDL guaranteed a 20% reduction in operating costs to Ward following its take-over of Las Vegas facility. Delivered an actual 33% reduction in their costs while continuing to exceed RDL's profit objectives.

- Consulted with upper level management personnel to negotiate and resolve labor union problems.

RYDER DEDICATED LOGISTICS *(Continued):*

Since March 1995 have provided start-up expertise to numerous operations. Hold full responsibility for all logistics, distribution and transportation functions (e.g., budgeting, financial reporting, staffing, union relations, safety, training, dispatching, routing). Highlights include:

- Currently directing the turnaround of logistics and distribution operations for the Fletcher Challenge warehousing center in Los Angeles, California. Given full autonomy for this fast-paced, union operation managing incoming sea freight, warehousing and distribution to *The Los Angeles Times* and other major publishers, print shops and advertising agencies throughout the region. Supervise team of 25.

- Completed two-month special project as Operations Manager for the start-up of the Standard Brand Paints shuttle service facility in Torrance, California. Brought operation to profitability within two months with $1.1 million projected in first year revenues (10%-12% profit).

- Orchestrated the start-up of a complete logistics operation to service Homestead Home Delivery's customer base throughout the Western U.S. Held full P&L and operating management responsibility for this operation.

- Consulted with RDL management team in Toronto for the start-up of Canadian logistics operations for Consumer Gas and Sears Home Delivery.

Early career positions as a Dispatcher for RDL's fully-integrated logistics operations at Howard's Home Delivery, Circuit City Home Delivery and General Electric. Assisted in the shutdown of all three facilities, reassignment of personnel and reallocation of equipment.

EARLY LOGISTICS & TRANSPORTATION INDUSTRY EXPERIENCE as a Dispatcher and Driver with Wallace Transport and several other warehousing/distribution companies in the Western U.S.

EDUCATION:

RYDER DEDICATED LOGISTICS
Frontline Leadership Training
Logistics Management Training
Supervisory & Leadership Training

References Provided Upon Request

GILBERT T. WAINRIGHT

2942 Southern Drive
Savannah, Georgia 47652
(651) 496-8424

TRANSPORTATION INDUSTRY EXECUTIVE
Expertise in General Management and Sales/Marketing Leadership

Twenty years domestic and international experience in the shipping and freight consolidation industries. Combines expert qualifications in marketing, business development and key account management with equally strong operating unit and P&L management qualifications.

Delivered strong operating and financial gains within highly competitive markets worldwide.

PROFESSIONAL EXPERIENCE:

EAST LINE AMERICA, INC.   1991 to 1996

VICE PRESIDENT SALES - NORTH AMERICA
Recruited as the first new executive to join the existing management team following East Line's migration from agency to wholly-owned subsidiary. Challenged to rebuild and strengthen the corporation's sales, business development and account management organization to accelerate growth, solidify existing customer relationships and expand into new business markets. Directed a multinational staff of 140 sales and customer service personnel at 26 locations throughout North America. Devised innovative sales and business development programs to expand inbound and outbound lift from West Coast ports.

- Delivered strong financial gains despite capacity constraints and dissolution of all-water service. Increased total volume 46% and BCO Anera market share 220%.

- Built key account relationships with leading importers (e.g., Nike, Reebok, LA Gear, May Department Stores, Dollar General, Sears) and leading exporters (e.g., Sunkist, Haagen-Daaz, Union Carbide, IBP, Montfort).

- Led the start-up and managed five regional customer service departments to improve customer satisfaction, increase retention and relieve operating teams of direct customer contact. Established policies and procedures, defined service functions and recruited/trained a team of 42.

SEA-LAND SERVICE, INC.   1970 to 1990

General Manager - Sales (1987 to 1990)
Buyers & Shippers Enterprises, Inc. - Jacksonville, Florida
One of two senior operating executives with direct P&L for this worldwide freight consolidation company. Directed a 16-person sales and marketing organization, a 120,000 square foot West Coast freight consolidation facility, annual operating and capital expense budgeting, and long-range strategic planning. Executive-level responsibility for development and management of key account relationships throughout the U.S. and Canada.

- Instrumental in building volume from 25,000 to 45,000 containers (80%) from 175 customers within three years. Revitalized and strengthened relationships with key accounts (e.g., Reebok, Adidas, Meldisco, Avon, Kmart, The Limited, May Department Stores) to accelerate revenue growth and improve market position.

- Spearheaded start-up of ship direct programs for both U.S. and Asian operations, Asia-Europe freight consolidation service and West Coast deconsolidation and distribution operations.

- Successfully marketed ancillary product offerings including "Buy-Com," an innovative computer program designed for cargo tracking and reporting.

SEA-LAND SERVICE, INC. *(Continued):*

Country Manager - Bangkok, Thailand (1984 to 1987)
Full P&L responsibility for Sea-Land's Thailand operations, including sales, marketing, advertising, marine/terminal, intra-Asia pricing and U.S./Asia interport trade. Directed a staff of 35, a trucking/stevedoring operating agent and a large foreign labor pool. Executive-level responsibility for new business development and all international account sales.

- Delivered revenue growth averaging 20% to 30% annually within a competitive market.

- Maintained a highly visible position within Thailand's maritime community. Appointed Chairman of the Thailand/Pacific Freight Conference, Chairman of the American Chamber of Commerce Transportation Committee and Secretary of the Bangkok Shippers & Agencies Association.

- Launched the successful start-up of a new Sea-Land agency operation in Djakarta, Indonesia.

General Manager - Caribbean (1981 to 1984)
Senior Executive with full P&L responsibility for the leadership of Sea-Land operations throughout the entire Caribbean region (Dominican Republic, Jamaica, Haiti, Curacao, Aruba, Trinidad and the Leeward Islands). Responsible for strategic and tactical management of sales, marketing, advertising, operations, marine/terminal, human resources, labor relations and administration. Directed six agencies and two offshore corporate offices with 200+ employees (including a five-person expatriate management team).

- Increased annual revenues to $35 million (20% gain). Achieved 400% growth in reefer revenue production.

- Launched the start-up of Dominican Republic operations as primary linehaul and feeder hub for Central and South Caribbean to Florida operations.

Sales Manager - Seoul, Korea (1978 to 1981)
Import Sales Manager - Hong Kong (1978)
International Account Manager - Taipei, Taiwan (1976 to 1977)
Rapid promotion through several increasingly responsible sales management positions within the Pacific Rim. Managed North American import and export trade, inter-Asia and Asian-Middle East sales, marketing and advertising. Led teams of up to 20 sales professionals and personally managed key account relationships.

- Increased regional sales revenues to $30 million annually.

Early Sea-Land Career (1970 to 1976)
Promoted from Sales Representative (Philadelphia) to Account Executive (Baltimore) to Sales Manager (Houston).

EDUCATION: **Princeton University - BA Degree, 1969**
Graduate, 100+ hours of professional sales, management and leadership training.

AFFILIATIONS: National Freight Transportation Association
Board of Directors, Friends of Princeton University Ice Hockey

MICHAEL De LEON

9834 Avenida de Peces   Buenos Aires 6416, Argentina
011-64-4-713-8977

GLOBAL TRAVEL & TOURISM INDUSTRY EXECUTIVE

Sales & Marketing Management / Key Account Management / Customer Relationship Management
Travel Agency Operations / P&L Management / Information Technology / Professional Staffing
Public Relations & Promotions / Strategic Business Partnerships / Revenue & Income Growth

Well-respected Industry Executive with more than 15 years professional and managerial experience. Pioneer in the introduction of travel, tour and expedition programs throughout new regions worldwide. Established relationships with leading corporate, industry and embassy officials that have resulted in millions of dollars in travel revenues and a distinctive positioning within the highly competitive global market.

Fluent in English, Spanish, French and German. Dual citizenship in Argentina and France.

PROFESSIONAL EXPERIENCE:

Owner / Managing Director   1979 to Present
ASTRA TRAVEL, S.R.L., Buenos Aires, Argentina

Senior Operating Executive with full P&L responsibility for an exclusive travel agency specializing in adventure tours and expeditions worldwide (e.g., Antarctica, China, Easter Island, Galapagos, Tibet, Greenland, Vietnam). Hold full accountability for annual business/market planning, sales management, public relations and promotions, travel/tour design, corporate client development and management, supervision of accounting and finance functions, professional and support staffing, training, information technology and all administrative affairs. Negotiate and manage strategic partnerships with travel agencies and airlines (e.g., British Airways, Canadian Airlines) worldwide.

- Built revenues from **US$1.8 million to US$3 million**. Delivered consistent increases in sales performance with growth of up to 100% annually.

- Established global business relationships with embassies, companies, banks, international news agencies and other corporate accounts to plan and direct their travel and tour programs. Key accounts include Bank of America, Lloyds Bank, ICI Pharmaceutical and the British Embassy.

- Ranked as the **#1 agency in Argentina** for airline ticket sales between Argentina and Canada and the only travel agency in Argentina to exceed Canadian Airlines' sales quotas in 1993 and 1994. Earned the Airline's prestigious **"Sales Quota Achievement Award"** in 1994.

- Orchestrated the introduction of PC-based technologies to automate all reservation systems, accounting, reporting, database management and administration (Amadeus, Sabre, Galileo).

- Managed a key strategic partnership with Lindblad Travel, U.S.A. as their exclusive South American representative. Significantly expanded account revenues to the agency.

- Recognized worldwide by leading travel authorities and publications for innovative, upscale and high-quality tours and expeditions. Recommended in major travel guides including South American Handbook - The Travellers World Guide and Rand McNally's South American Handbook.

- Guest speaker at the University of El Salvador (Buenos Aires), American University Club, Argentine Travel Association, and other industry groups and symposia.

Agency won the German "Medal for Professional Tourism" for technical tours designed and sponsored in cooperation with Lufthansa, and the "Gold Medal" from the Argentine Association of Travel Agencies and Travel Agents as the first travel agency to open the Antarctic continent for tourism.

Manager - Cruise Department   1978
LINDBLAD TRAVEL, New York, New York

> Recruited to join this prestigious travel operator catering to an exclusive clientele (e.g., Prince Bernard of Holland, President of Shell International). Responsible for the sale/marketing of cruises and adventure expeditions to "new" destinations including Antarctica, Galapagos, South Pacific and the Arctic Region. Trained and supervised three travel agents.

Early Experience aboard the M.S. Lindblad travelling throughout the Antarctic region. Attended on-board lectures presented by Jacques-Yves Costeau, Roger Tory Peterson and Sir Peter Scott. Played a critical role in emergency rescue following the vessel's grounding and transfer of passengers to a Chilean Navy vessel.

EDUCATION:

ARGENTINE CATHOLIC UNIVERSITY, Buenos Aires, Argentina
Major in Political Science (1977)

UNIVERSITE DE SCIENCES POLITIQUES, Paris, France
Major in Political Science (1975)

LONDON UNIVERSITY, London, England
Certificate in Spanish Literature (1973)

UNIVERSITY OF CAMBRIDGE, Cambridge, England
Certificates in English, Spanish, Geography and Economics (1972)

Highlights of Management Training & Development:

- Management Training & Development, Lufthansa (1980 to 1981)
- Developing Management Skills, Pan American Airways (1979)
- Sales Dynamics, Pan American Airways (1978)
- Rates & Tariffs, Pan American Airways (1977)

PROFESSIONAL AFFILIATIONS:

Association of Tourism Industrial Professionals (SKaL)

- Appointed as the youngest member ever. Elected to the Board of Directors in 1982. Served as the Club Secretary in 1984 (honored as "Club of the Year" by the international association).

International Air Transport Association
American Society of Travel Agents
Argentine Association of Travel Agents
Association of Travel Agents of Buenos Aires
Argentine Chamber of Commerce for Tourism

Appendix A

Job Search, Career Management, Coaching, Counseling, Resume Writing & Other Career Resources

Following is a list of the professional members of the Career Masters Institute, a prestigious professional association whose members work with job seekers worldwide to help them plan and manage successful search campaigns. You will note that these individuals have earned a number of certifications and credentials. For your reference, the most common are referenced below:

CAC - Certified Accredited Consultant
CBC – Certified Behavioral Consultant
CCM – Credentialed Career Master
CEIP – Certified Employment Interview Professional
CHRE – Certified Human Resources Executive
CIPC – Certified International Personnel Consultant
CPC – Certified Personnel Consultant
CPRW – Certified Professional Resume Writer
IJCTC or JCTC – International Job & Career Transition Coach
LPC – Licensed Professional Counselor
NBCC – National Board Certified Counselor
NCC – National Certified Counselor
NCCC – National Certified Career Counselor
NCRW – National Certified Resume Writer
PCC – Professional Certified Coach

ALABAMA

Don Orlando, MBA, CPRW, JCTC, CCM
The McLean Group
640 South McDonough Street
Montgomery, AL 36104
334-264-2020
yourcareercoach@aol.com

Neal Parker
R.L. Stevens & Associates, Inc.
103 Aragorn Circle
Daphne, AL 36526
334-626-8235
nparker@rlstevens.com

Teresa Pearson, CPRW, JCTC
Pearson's Resume Output
16 Castle Way
Rucker, AL 36362
334-503-4314
pearsonresume@snowhill.com

ALASKA

Ann Flister, CPRW
Best Impression
360 E. International Airport Road, #6
Anchorage, AK 99518
907-561-9311
aflister@customcpu.com

ARIZONA

Kathryn Baker
American Career Executives
2400 E. Arizona Biltmore Circle, #2250
Phoenix, AZ 85016
602-381-1667
lbaugh@amcareer.com

Kathryn Bourne, CPRW, JCTC
CareerConnections
5210 E. Pima Street, Suite 200
Tucson, AZ 85712
520-323-2964
Ccmentor@aol.com
www.BestFitResumes.com

Patricia Cash, CPRW
Resumes For Results
PO Box 2806
Prescott, AZ 86302
520-778-1578
patticash@hotmail.com

Fred Coon
Arizona Career Marketing Group
14451 South 8th Street
Phoenix, AZ 85048-4440
480-283-6234
azcmg1@home.com
www.azcareermarketing.com

ARKANSAS

Stephanie Meehan
EdiType Business Services
623 W. Dickson Street
Fayetteville, AR 72701
501-442-9037
editype@dicksonstreet.com

Wanda McLaughlin, CPRW
Execuwrite
314 N. Los Feliz Drive
Chandler, AZ 85226
480-732-7966
wanda@execu-write.com
www.execuwrite.com

CALIFORNIA

Georgia Adamson CPRW, JCTC, CCM
Adept Business Services
180 W. Rincon Avenue
Campbell, CA 95008-2824
408-866-6859
georgiaa@bignet.net
www.ADynamicResume.com

Deborah Bates, MA, RPCC
JOB ONE
2545 Main Street
Susanville, CA 96130
530-257-2568
deborah@snowcrest.net

Julia Bauer, JCTC
eCoach2000
351 Staysail Court
Foster City, CA 94404
650-286-1460
julia@eCoach2000.com
www.eCoach2000.com

Kent Black
Kent Black & Associates
21 Lodge Lane
San Rafael, CA 94901
(800) 588-4145
kbconsult@aol.com

Randy Block, JCTC
Block & Associates
PO Box 5357
Larkspur, CA 94977
415-383-6471
randsrch@aol.com

Nita Busby, CPRW, CAC
Resumes, Etc.
438 E. Katella, Suite F
Orange, CA 92867
714-633-2783
resumes100@aol.com
www.resumesetc.net

Susan Luff Chritton
Pathways/Right Management Consultants
3227 Sweet Drive
Lafayette, CA 94549
510-283-8578
slc4pways@aol.com

Nancy Davis
Grossmont College
8800 Grossmont College Drive
El Cajun, CA 92020
619-644-7615
nancy.davis@gcccd.net

Christine Edick, CPRW, JCTC
Action Resumes
307 E. Chapman Avenue
Orange, CA 92866
714-639-0942
christine@actionresumes.com
actionresumes.com

Lynn Eischen CPRW
Eischen's Professional Resume Service
3258 W. Spruce
Fresno, CA 93711
(559) 435-3538
4resume@csufresno.edu
http://cvip.fresno.com/~ce082

Roleta Fowler Vasquez, CPRW
Wordbusters Word Processing, Resume & Writing Srvcs.
433 Quail Court, Fillmore, CA 93105
(805) 524-3493
resumes@jetlink.net
www.wbresumes.com

Darrell Gurney, CPC
Hunter Arts Publishing
12658 Washington Blvd., #104
Los Angeles, CA 90066
310-821-6303
publisher@hunterarts.com
www.hunterarts.com

Leatha Jones
Write Connection Career Services
PO Box 351, Vallejo
CA 94590
707-649-1400
Leatha@writeconnection.net
www.writeconnection.net

Shannon Jordan
Career Directions/UC San Diego
6925 Lusk Boulevard
San Diego, CA 92121
858-882-8014
shannonA@ucsd.edu
www.extension.ucsd.edu/careers

Nancy Karvonen, CPRW, IJCTC, CCM
A Better Word & Resume
771 Adare Way
Galt, CA 95632
209-744-8203
careers@aresumecoach.com
www.aresumecoach.com

Cindy King
King Business Services
505 West Olive Avenue, Suite 635
Sunnyvale, CA 94086
408-733-5163
ck@kingbservices.com

Dick Knowdell, NCCC, CCMF
Career Planning & Adult Dev Network
4965 Sierra Road
San Jose, CA 95132
408-441-9100
knowdell@best.com

Myriam-Rose Kohn, CPRW, JCTC, CCM
JEDA Enterprises
27201 Tourney Road, Suite 201
Valencia, CA 91355
661-253-0801
myriam-rose@jedaenterprises.com
www.jedaenterprises.com

Denise Larkin
ResumeRighter.com
1027 Clarendon Crescent
Oakland, CA 94610
510-834-9355
denise@resumerighter.com
www.resumerighter.com

Jenny Loveland
Rural Human Services, Inc.
286 "M" Street, Suite "A"
Crescent City, CA 95531
707-464-7441
jloveland@ncen.org

Laura Lyon
Executive Image Resumes
1185 Sandstone Lane
San Jose, CA 95132
408-926-2232
Laura@MyExecutiveImage.com
www.MyExecutiveImage.com

Carole Martin
The Interview Coach
1609 Fountain Springs Circle
Danville, CA 94526
925-933-6208
carole@interviewcoach.com

Dianne Millsap, JCTC
Executive Resume
3841 Carnegie Drive
Oceanside, CA 92056
888-344-7378
Di4Resume@aol.com
www.Di4Resume.com

Phil Mostovoy
Rural Human Services, Inc.
286 "M" Street, Suite "A"
Crescent City, CA 95531
707-464-7441
pmostovoy@ncen.org

Alicia Naiman
CareerProShop.com
4532 Olivegate Drive
Fair Oaks, CA 95628
916-966-5520
careerproinfo@onebox.com
www.CareerProShop.com

Ken Naas
Within Reach!
1060 Adlar Court
Chico, CA 95926
(530) 893-0867
withinreachkn@hotmail.com

Gloria Nelson, CPRW
Resume Works - EASS
333 N. Palm Canyon, Suite 208
Palm Springs, CA 92262
760-322-3465
gjnelson@eass.com
www.eass.com

Anita Radosevic,h CPRW, JCTC
Anita's Business & Career Services
315 W. Pine Street, Suite #5
Lodi, CA 95240
209-368-4444
abcservice@lodinet.com
www.abcresumes.com (in process)

Cricket Rubino
Claremont Executive Services
830 Claremont Drive
Morgan Hill, CA 95037
408-778-7211
crubino@ix.netcom.com
www.claremontservices.com

Walter Schuette, CPRW, JCTC, CEIP
Schuette & Associates, Inc.
931 South Mission Road, Suite B
Fallbrook, CA 92028
800-200-1884
tvwresume@aol.com
www.thevillagewordsmith.com

Katherine Simmons
NETSHARE.com
2 Commercial Boulevard, #200
Novato, CA 94949
415-883-1700
kathy@netshare.com
www.netshare.com

Makini Siwatu, CPRW, JCTC
Accent on Words
405 El Camino Real, #631
Menlo Park, CA 94025-5240
650-323-6823
accentwrds@aol.com

Rebecca Smith, JCTC
Rebecca Smith's eResumes & Resources
40087 Mission Blvd., Suite 306
Fremont, CA 94539
510-623-0768
rsmith@eresumes.com

Gina Snyder
RICS Associates
131 El Camino Real
Vallejo, CA 94590
707-643-8937
ginas@concentric.net

Sheryl Steinruck
Rural Human Services, Inc.
286 "M" Street, Suite "A"
Crescent City, CA 95531
707-464-7441
ssteinruck@ncen.org

Pauline Thaler, CPRW
Best Foot Forward
1218 Carlotta Avenue
Berkeley, CA 94707
510-528-5563
thaler@teleport.com

Dennis Turner
Rural Human Services, Inc.
286 "M Street, Suite "A"
Crescent City, CA 95531
707-464-7441
daturner@ncen.org

Vivian Van Lier, CPRW, JCTC
Advantage Resume & Career Services
6701 Murietta Avenue
Valley Glen, CA 91405
818-994-6655
vvanlier@aol.com

Susan Whitcomb, NCRW, CPRW
Alpha Omega Career Services
757 East Hampton Way
Fresno, CA 93704
559-2227474
susan@careerwriter.com
www.careerwriter.com

Barbara Woods
Rural Human Services, Inc.
286 "M" Street, Suite "A"
Crescent City, CA 95531
707-464-7441
bwoods@ncen.org

COLORADO

Kathy Black, MBA, JCTC
Career Recipes
1960 Denver West Drive, #611
Golden, CO 80401
303-679-1519
kathyjane@careerrecipes.com
www.careerrecipes.com

Nancy Valentine, JCTC
New Career Strategies
2404 Sheffield Circle, East
Fort Collins, CO 80526
970-472-8288
nancy@careerdesign.com

CONNECTICUT

Nancy Collamer
Jobsandmoms.com
29 Hassake Road
Old Greenwich, CT 06870
203-698-3160
ncollamer@aol.com
www.jobsandmoms.com

Catherine Eckert, CPRW
Creative Office Services
24 Timber Lane, PO Box 573
Windsor, CT 06095
860-688-6970
CCECPRW@aol.com

Elie Klachkin, MS, JCTC
Impex Services, Inc.
89 Tunxis Hill Road
Fairfield, CT 06432
203-335-5627
elie@resuMMe.com
www.resuMMe.com

Jan Melnik, CPRW
Absolute Advantage
PO Box 718
Durham, CT 06422
860-349-0256
CompSPJan@aol.com
www.janmelnik.com

Debra O'Reilly, CPRW, JCTC
ResumeWriter.com
16 Terryville Avenue
Bristol, CT 06010
860-583-7500
debra@resumewriter.com
www.resumewriter.com

DISTRICT OF COLUMBIA (WASHINGTON, DC)

Jay Gloede, JCTC
Environmental Protection Agency
401 M Street SW
Washington, DC 20460
202-260-5086
gloede.jay@epa.gov

FLORIDA

Anita Babcock, JCTC
B.O.S.S. Resumes & Career Focus Center
9500 Koger Blvd. N., Suite 222
St. Petersburg, FL 33702
727-577-1737
BOSS1FL@aol.com

Marva Creary
Business Operation Support Services
11985 N.W. 12 Street
Pembroke Pines, FL 33026
954-435-8492
marvelous@skybiz.com

Laura DeCarlo, CCM, CPRW, JCTC
A Competitive Edge Career Service
1665 Clover Circle
Melbourne, FL 32935
800-715-3442
getanedge@aol.com
www.acompetiveedge.com

Cathy Fahrman, CPRW
Heider's Resume Center
10014 North Dale Mabry Highway, #101
Tampa, FL 33618
813-262-0011
hssheider@aol.com
http://broswer.to/heidersresumecent

Art Frank, MBA
Resumes "R" Us
334 Eastlake Drive, Suite 200
Palm Harbor, FL 34685
727-787-6885
AF1134@aol.com

Gail Frank, NCRW, JCTC, MA, CEIP
Frankly Speaking: Resumes That Work!
10409 Greendale Drive
Tampa, FL 33626
813-926-1353
gailfrank@post.harvard.edu
www.callfranklyspeaking.com

Susan Garrett
Visual Media Technologies, Inc.
16332 Gulf Boulevard
Redington Beach, FL 33708
727-399-9838
vmti1@tampabay.rr.com
www.yourdigitaledge.com

Wayne Gonyea
Gonyea Career Marketing, Inc.
1810 Arturus Lane
New Port Richey, FL 34655-4930
800-532-9733
online@resumexpress.com
http://resumexpress.com

Rene' Hart, CPRW
Resumes For Success!
5537 N. Socrum Loop Road, #116
Lakeland, FL 33809
863-859-2439
renehart@resumesforsuccess.com
www.ResumesForSuccess.com

Beverly Harvey, CPRW, JCTC, CCM
Beverly Harvey Resume & Career Srvc
P.O. Box 750
Pierson, FL 32180
904-749-3111
beverly@harveycareers.com
www.harveycareers.com

Jim Kitt
EmployMax.com
2907 West Bay Drive
Bellaire Bluffs, FL 33770
727-499-9444
JTKITT@employmax.com
www.employmax.com

Cindy Kraft, CPRW, JCTC, CCM
Executive Essentials
PO Box 336
Valrico, FL 33595
813-655-0658
careermaster@exec-essentials.com
www.exec-essentials.com

Lisa LeVerrier Stein, MA, MS, CPRW, JCTC
Competitive Advantage Resumes & Career Coaching
433 Plaza Real, Suite 275
Boca Raton, FL 33432
954-571-7236
gethired@earthlink.net
www.jobcoaching.com, www.legalresumes.com

Diane McGoldrick, CPRW, JCTC
Business Services
2803 W. Busch Blvd., #103
Tampa, FL 33618
813-935-2700
mcgoldrk@ix.netcom.com

Shelley Nachum
Career Development Services
4801 S. University Drive, Suite 201
Fort Lauderdale, FL 33328
866-737-7767
Shelley@ExpertResumes.com
www.expertresumes.com

Jim O'Hara
Recourse Communications
1655 Palm Beach Lakes Blvd., #600
West Palm Beach, FL 33401
561-686-6800
johara@rcimedia.com
BestJobsUSA.com

Vito Santoro
Visual Media Technologies, Inc.
1059 Kingsway Lane
Tarpon Springs, FL 34689
727-938-1690
vms@yourdigitaledge.com
www.yourdigitaledge.com

Myra Solomon, IJCTC
Career Edge
260 Crandon Boulevard, #32-113
Key Biscayne, FL 33149-1540
305-606-4358
ACareerEdge@aol.com

Jean West, CPRW, JCTC
Impact Resume & Career Services
207 10th Avenue
Indian Rocks, FL 33785
727-596-2534
Resumes@TampaBay.RR.com
www.ImpactResumes.com

Lea Ann Williams
Executive Maker.com
9013 Deercress Court
Jacksonville, FL 32256
904-519-8516
LeaAnnW@aol.com
www.executivemaker.com

GEORGIA

Julianne Franke
Career Development & Resume Center
4055 Highway 29, Suite 475
Lilburn, GA 30047
770-381-9407
jfranke836@aol.com

Gwen Harrison, CPRW, NCRW
Advanced Resumes & Career Strategies
384 Bullsboro Drive, #344
Newnan, GA 30263
877-353-0025
cmi@advancedresumes.com
www.advancedresumes.com

Don Skipper, M.S., M.M.A.S., CCM
R.L. Stevens & Associates, Inc.
PO Box 49491
Atlanta, GA 30359
770-399-5757
dskipper@rlstevens.com
www.interviewing.com

IOWA

Elizabeth Axnix, CCM, CPRW, IJCTC
Quality Word Processing
329 E. Court Street
Iowa City, IA 52240-4914
800-359-7822
axnix@earthlink.net

Marcy Johnson, CPRW, CEIP
First Impression Resume & Job Readiness
11805 US Hwy. 69
Story City, IA 50248
515-733-4998
firstimpression@storycity.net
www.resume-job-readiness.com

ILLINOIS

Ann Brody
Career Solutions
1145 Franklin Avenue
River Forest, IL 60305
708-771-6848
ABHighland@aol.com

Jeff Brown, J.D.
Jeffrey Grant Brown, P.C.
105 W. Adams Street, #3000
Chicago, IL 60603
312-789-9700
brownlaw@primenet.com
www.jbrownlaw.com

Jack Chapman
Lucrative Careers, Inc.
511 Maple Avenue
Wilmette, IL 60091
847-251-4727
jkchapman@aol.com
members.aol.com/payraises

Siegfried Heck
All Word Services
924 E. Old Willow Road, Suite 102
Prospect Heights, IL 60070
847-215-7517
siegfried@ameritech.net

Cathleen Hunt, CPRW
Write Works
6630 North Northwest Highway
Chicago, IL 60631
773-774-4420
cmhunt@attglobal.net

Sally McIntosh, NCRW, CPRW, JCTC
McIntosh resumes.com / Advantage Resumes
35 Westfair Drive
Jacksonville, IL 62650
217-245-0752
sallysjm@aol.com
www.reswriter.com / www.mcintoshresumes.com

Jeff Williams
Bizstarters.com, LLC
415 E. Golf Road, Suite 110
Arlington Heights, IL 60005
847-593-5305
cms@postal.interaccess.com
www.bizstarters.com

INDIANA

Deloris Duff, CPRW, IJCTC
Document Developers
5030 Guion Road
Indianapolis, IN 46254
317-297-4661
deesdocs@earthlink.net

Mary Ann Finch Vandivier
Resume Counselor.com
40 S. 4th Street
Zionsville, IN 46077
317-873-3189
resumewriter@resumecounselor.com
www.resumecounselor.com

Linda Wood
Roche Diagnostics
9115 Hague Road, Bldg. A
Indianapolis, IN 46250
317-576-4990
linda.wood@roche.com
www.roche.com

KANSAS

Kristie Cook, CPRW, JCTC
Absolutely Write
913 N. Sumac
Olathe, KS 66061
913-269-3519
kriscook@absolutely-write.com
www.absolutely-write.com

Jacqui Barrett Dodson, CPRW
Career Trend
7501 College Blvd., Suite 175
Overland Park, KS 66210
913-451-1313
dodson@careertrend.net
www.careertrend.net

Leslie Griffen
CSG Partners, Inc.
7101 College Boulevard, Suite 740
Overland Park, KS 66210-1891
913-469-6660
Lgriffen@csgpartners.com

Patricia Miller, CPRW, JCTC
P.S. Agency, Inc.
250 N. Rock Road, #300C
Wichita, KS 67206
316-686-6529
patmiller@feist.com

Rudolph Smith, Jr.
Career Success
8814 W. 64th Place, #206
Merriam, KS 66202
913-722-1994
thaisun@swbell.net
www.webnow.com/careersuccess

James Walker, M.S.
Resource Consultants, Inc.
2919 Northwood Drive
Milford, KS 66514
785-239-2278
answergrape@hotmail.com

KENTUCKY

Debbie Ellis, CPRW
Career Concepts
103 Patrick Henry Court
Danville, KY 40422
859-236-4001
info@resumeprofessional.com
www.resumeprofessional.com

Amy Whitmer
Envision Resume Services
PO Box 7523
Louisville, KY 40257
502-473-1780
amy@envision-resumes.com
www.envision-resumes.com

LOUISIANA

Laurie Roy, CPRW, IJCTC
Just Your Type, Inc.
1006 E. St. Mary Blvd.
Lafayette, LA 70503
800-225-8688
laurie@justyourtype.com
www.justyourtype.com

MAINE

Trudy Haines, CPRW
HainesService/LetterPerfect
647 Main Street
Lewiston, ME 04240
207-783-8973
HainesSue@aol.com

Rolande LaPointe, CPC, CIPC, CPRW, IJCTC, CCM
RO-LAN Associates, Inc.
725 Sabattus Street
Lewiston, ME 04240
207-784-1010
RLapointe@aol.com

MARYLAND

Wendy Adams, B.S., CC
LearnShare
1000 Scott Street
Baltimore, MD 21230
410-728-2060
learnshare@aol.com
www.LearningShare.com

Diane Burns, CPRW, IJCTC, CCM
Career Marketing Techniques
5219 Thunder Hill Road
Columbia, MD 21045
410-884-0213
dianecprw@aol.com
www.polishedresumes.com

Vincent DeSanti
Pinnacle Career Resources, Inc.
10632 Little Patuxent Parkway, Suite 300B
Columbia, MD 21044
410-740-4111
PinnCareer@aol.com

Lisa Dolce, JCTC
Pinnacle Career Resources, Inc.
10632 Little Patuxent Pkwy., Suite 300B
Columbia, MD 21044
410-740-4111
PinnCareer@aol.com

Sherry Kolbe, Certified Job & Career Coach
Resume Consultants
212 Washington Avenue
Towson, MD 21204
410-823-9568
resumeconsult@hotmail.com

Dottie Perlman, NCC, PCC
Insight Associates, LLP
11611 LeHavre Drive
Potomac, MD 20854
301-294-0133
dottie@insight1.com
www.insight1.com

Marshall Wellisch
Job Searchers, Inc.
7676 New Hampshire Avenue
Silver Spring, MD 20783
301-445-2466
mwellis@toad.net

MASSACHUSETTS

Bernice Antifonario, M.A.
Antion Associates, Inc.
885 Main Street, #10A
Tewksbury, MA 01876
978-858-0637
Antion1@aol.com
www.antion-associates.com

Lea Cabeen
Corp. for Business Work & Learning
38 Broad Street
Newburyport, MA 01950
617-727-8158
lcabeen@mediaone.net

Pam Connolly, JCTC
A Fine Line
8 Pratt Street
Reading, MA 01867
781-944-5482
pamafl@aol.com

Joan Cousins, M.S.
CareerFocus
1480 West Street
Pittsfield, MA 01201
413-443-1154
jhcousins@aol.com

Beate Hait, CPRW, NCRW
Word Processing Plus
80 Wingate Road
Holliston, MA 01746
508-429-1813
beateh1@aol.com
www.ibssn.com/resumes

Larry Linden, Ph.D.
R.L. Stevens Inc.
115 Pine Street
Clinton, MA 01510
978-368-1458
llinden@rlstevens.com
www.interviewing.com

Bonnie Worthley
53 Howard Street
Haverhill, MA 01830
978-372-8125
Bszar@aol.com

Stephen Youd, MA, JCTC
Winning Percentage Careers
385 Court Street, Suite 311
Plymouth, MA 02360
508-746-3282
WPCareers@aol.com
www.career.baweb.com

MICHIGAN

Janet Beckstrom
Word Crafter
1717 Montclair Avenue
Flint, MI 48503
800-351-9818
wordcrafter@voyager.net

Leora Druckman
Facilitated Futures
1738 Waverly Road
Ann Arbor, MI 48103
734-369-2580
leorad@aol.com

Roberta Floyd
21395 Virginia Drive
Southfield, MI 48076
248-357-2426
rafloyd@earthlink.net

Joyce Fortier, MBA, CPRW, JCTC, CCM
Create Your Career
23871 W. Lebost
Novi, MI 48375
248-478-5662
careerist@aol.com
www.careerist.com

Maria Hebda, CPRW
Career Solutions, LLC
2216 Northfield, Trenton
MI 48183
734-676-9170
careers@writingresumes.com
www.writingresumes.com

Lorie Lebert, CPRW, JCTC
Resumes For Results, LLC
PO Box 267
Novi, MI 48376
248-380-6101
Lorie@DoMyResume.com
www.DoMyResume.com

Rich Porter
CareerWise Communications LLC
332 Magellan Court
Portage, MI 49002-7000
616-321-0183
rtporter@worldnet.att.net

Beverlee Rydel
TR Desktop Publishing
46813 Fox Run Drive
Macomb, MI 48044
810-228-8780
bevrydel@aol.com

Deborah Schuster, CPRW
The Lettersmith
PO Box 202
Newport, MI 48166
734-586-3335
lettersmith@foxberry.net
www.thelettersmith.com

Kathleen Tedsen
TR Desktop Publishing
46813 Fox Run Drive
Macomb, MI 48044
810-228-8780
trdesktop@cswebmail.com

Peggy Weeks
CompuPage
3914 W. Michigan Avenue
Battle Creek, MI 49017
616-964-7533
pweeks@voyager.net

Tammi Wheelock
Data Tamer Resume Service
9 Bonita Drive, Battle Creek
MI 49014-4315
616-964-6355
tammi@datatamer.net
www.datatamer.net

MINNESOTA

David Jones, CPC, CMF, MBA
Personnel Decisions, International
6600 France Avenue South, Suite 501
Minneapolis, MN 55435-1804
952-915-7602
davidj@pdi-corp.com

Mary Kay Kernan, M.A.
University of St. ,Thomas
1000 LaSalle Avenue
Minneapolis, MN 55403-2005
651-962-4763
mkkernan@stthomas.edu
www.stthomas.edu

Barb Poole, CPRW
Electronic Ink
1812 Red Fox Road
St. Cloud, MN 56301
320-253-0975
eink@astound.net

Linda Wunner, CPRW, IJCTC
A+ Career & Resume Design / Linda's PageWorks
4891 Miller Trunk Highway, #208
Duluth, MN 55811
218-723-1995
linda@successfulresumes.com
www.successfulresumes.com

MISSISSIPPI

John Stevens
Ghostwriter Editorial Services
6045 Ferncreek Drive
Jackson, MS 39211
601-957-1479
JJSTVNS@cs.com
www.ghostwriter-resume.com

MISSOURI

E. Robert Jones
University of Missouri - Columbia
W1025 EBE
Columbia, MO 65211
573-882-4487
JonesER@missouri.edu

Meg Montford, CCM, CPRW
Abilities Enhanced
PO Box 9667
Kansas City, MO 64134
816-767-1196
meg@abilitiesenhanced.com
www.abilitiesenhanced.com

Karen Silins
A+ Career & Office Pro
9719 Woodland Lane
Kansas City, MO 64131
816-942-3019
apluscareer@aol.com

Robin Smith
Family Support Center
750 Arnold Avenue
Whiteman AFB, MO 65305
660-687-7132
robin.smith2@whiteman.af.mil

Gina Taylor, CPRW
Gina Taylor & Associates, Inc.
1111 W. 77th Terrace
Kansas City, MO 64114
816-523-9100
GinaResume@aol.com
www.GinaTaylor.com

John David Walters, Ph.D.
Charter Institute of Training & Staff Development
1301 N.E. 74th Terrace
Gladstone, MO 64118
816-468-7276
careercrafters@hotmail.com

MONTANA

Laura West
Agape Career Services
20695 E. Mullan Road
Clinton, MT 59825
888-685-3507
agape@blackfoot.net
www.AgapeCareerServices.com

David West
Agape Career Services
20695 E. Mullan Road
Clinton, MT 59825
866-245-6248
agjob4u@blackfoot.net
www.agapecareerservices.com

NORTH CAROLINA

Douglas Allen
10309 John's Towne Drive
Charlotte, NC 28210
704-541-5370
doug@dougallen.com
www.dougallen.com

Alice Braxton, CPRW
Accutype Resume & Secretarial Services
635C Chapel Hill Road
Burlington, NC 27215
336-227-9091
accutype@netpath.net

Dayna Feist, CPRW, JCTC
Gatehouse Business Services
265 Charlotte Street
Asheville, NC 28801
828-254-7893
gatehous@aol.com

Doug Morrison, CPRW
Career Planners
2915 Providence Road, Suite 250
Charlotte, NC 28211
704-365-0773
pwresume@mindspring.com

John O'Connor
CareerPro Resumes
3344 Hillsborough Street, Suite 300B
Raleigh, NC 27607
919-821-2418
careerpro2@aol.com
www.careerproresumes.com

Vanessa Satterfield, CPRW
A Notable Resume
PO Box 37, Clayton
NC 27520-0037
919-550-8884
anotable1@aol.com

NEBRASKA

Renata Anderson
Typing Pro
4012 N. 94th Street
Omaha, NE 68134
402-573-1014
renata@radiks.net

Bridget Ann Weide
Image Building Communications
6818 Grover Street, Suite 302
Omaha, NE 68106
402-393-4600
RWDigest@aol.com
www.ResumeWritersDigest.com

NEVADA

Cindy Fass
Comprehensive Resume Srvcs.
5300 Spring Mtn. Road, 212-D
Las Vegas, NV 89146
702-222-9411
crsinvegas@aol.com

NEW HAMPSHIRE

Michelle Dumas, CPRW, NCRW
Distinctive Documents
146 Blackwater Road
Somersworth, NH 03878
603-742-3983
resumes@distinctiveweb.com
www.distinctiveweb.com

NEW JERSEY

Vivian Belen, NCRW, CPRW, JCTC
The Job Search Specialist
1102 Bellair Avenue
Fair Lawn, NJ 07410
201-797-2883
vivian@jobsearchspecialist.com
www.jobsearchspecialist.com

Neil Cunningham
ACT Associates
519 Fairfield Avenue
Ridgewood, NJ 07450
201-493-1316
neilc@nis.net
www.actresumes.com

Sally Dougan
Bert Davis Consultants
25 McCatharn Road, Lebanon, NJ 08833
212-838-4000
saldougan@aol.com

Nina Ebert
A Word's Worth Resume & Writing Srv
808 Lowell Avenue
Toms River, NJ 08753
732-349-2225
wrdswrth@gbsias.com

Penne Gabel
Business Training Institute
170 Hillman Avenue
Glen Rock, NJ 07452
201-447-9782
hrpenne@aol.com

Susan Guarneri, NCC, NCCC, LPC,
CPRW, IJCTC, CCM
Guarneri Associates/Resumagic
1101 Lawrence Road
Lawrenceville, NJ 08648
609-771-1669
Resumagic@aol.com
www.resume-magic.com

Fran Kelley
The Resume Works
71 Highwood Avenue
Waldwick, NJ 07463
201-670-9643
TwoFreeSpirits@worldnet.att.net
www.careermuse.com

Rhoda Kopy, CPRW
A Hire Image Resume & Writing Service
26 Main Street, Suite E
Toms River, NJ 08753
732-505-9515
ahi@infi.net
www.jobwinningresumes.com

Judith McLaughlin
ResumeWizards.com, Inc.
27 Lavern Street
Sayreville, NJ 08872
732-432-4000
2wizards@resumewizards.com
www.resumewizards.com

Igor Shpudejko, CPRW, JCTC, MBA
Career Focus
842 Juniper Way
Mahwah, NJ 07430
201-825-2865
ishpudejko@aol.com

Pat Traina
The Resume Writer
PO Box 351
Vallejo, CA 94590
732-239-8533
ptraina@aol.com
www.theresumewriter.com

Kathy Vandenburg
Prosperous Futures
16 Hill Hollow Road
Milford, NJ 08848
908-995-2193
jvandenburg@blast.net

NEW MEXICO

Tricia Miller, CPRW
Albuquerque T.V.I.
525 Buena Vista S.E., Albuquerque
NM 87106-4096
505-224-3069
tmiller@tvi.cc.nm.us

NEW YORK

Ann Baehr, CPRW
Best Resumes
122 Sheridan Street
Brentwood, NY 11717
631-435-1879
resumesbest@earthlink.net

Etta Barmann, CPRW, JCTC, MSW, CSW
Compu-Craft Business Services, Inc.
124 E. 40th Street, Suite 403
New York, NY 10016
212-697-4005
erbarmann@aol.com

Liz Benuscak
Bi-Coastal Resumes, Inc.
32 Old Schoolhouse Road
New City, NY 10956
914-708-9134
bi-coastal@prodigy.net

Mark Berkowitz, MS, NCC, NCCC, CPRW,
IJCTC, CEIP
Career Development Resources
1312 Walter Road
Yorktown Height, NY 10598
914-962-1548
cardevres@aol.com

Arnold Boldt, CPRW
Arnold-Smith Associates
625 Panorama TraIL Bldg. Two, Suite 200
Rochester, NY 14625
716-383-0350
arnoldsmth@aol.com

Kirsten Dixson, JCTC, CPRW
New Leaf Career Solutions
PO Box 991
Bronxville, NY 10708
888-887-7166
kdixson@newleafcareer.com
www.newleafcareer.com

Donna Farrise
Dynamic Resumes of Long Island, Inc.
300 Motor Parkway, Suite 200
Hauppauge, NY 11788
631-951-4120
donna@dynamicresumes.com
www.dynamicresumes.com

Judy Friedler, NCRW, CPRW, JCTC, CCM
CareerPro New York
56 Barrow Street, #G-1
New York, NY 10014
212-647-8726
judy@rezcoach.com
www.rezcoach.com

Margaret Lawson
Resume Processing & Career Services
PO Box 2664
New York, NY 10027
212-862-0053
Resumepr@aol.com

Ken Lawson
Partners in Human Resources International
9 East 37th Street, 7th Floor
New York, NY 10016
212-685-0400
klawson@partners-international.com
www.partners-international.com

Linsey Levine, MS, JCTC
CareerCounsel
11 Hillside Place
Chappaqua, NY 10514
914-238-1065
LinZlev@aol.com

Kim Little, JCTC
Fast Track Resumes
1281 Courtney Drive
Victor, NY 14564
716-742-2467
info@fast-trackresumes.com
www.fast-trackresumes.com

Jane Lockshin
YourMissingLink.com
60 Sutton Place South, #14BN
New York, NY 10022-4168
800-445-3557
jlockshin@yourmissinglink.com
www.yourmissinglink.com

Christine Magnus, CPRW
Business Services Plus
1346 E. Gun Hill Road
Bronx, NY 10469
718-519-0477
BizServ@aol.com

Linda Matias, JCTC, CEIP
CareerStrides
34 E. Main Street, #276
Smithtown, NY 11787
631-382-2425
careerstrides@worldnet.att.net
www.careerstrides.com

Michele Mattia
Philips Electronics
1251 Avenue of the Americas
New York, NY 10020
212-536-0573
michele.mattia@philips.com

Dorothy Mueller, Ph.D.
The Strickland Group
1420 York Avenue, #4B
New York, NY 10021
212-861-1623
dmueller@stricklandgroup.com
www.stricklandgroup.com

Peter Newfield
Career Resumes
PO Box 509
Goldens Bridge, NY 10526
800-800-1220
peter@career-resumes.com
www.career-resumes.com

Beth Stefani, MBA, Ed.M, JCTC
Orison Professional Services
265 Union Street, Suite 101
Hamburg, NY 14075
716-649-0094
info@orisonservices.com
www.orisonservices.com

Darby Townsend
257 W. 86th Street
New York, NY 10024
212-787-7757
dtowns5901@aol.com

Salome Tripi, CPRW
Careers TOO
3123 Moyer Road
Mount Morris, NY 14510
716-658-2480
srttoo@frontiernet.net
www.frontier.net/~srttoo

Marty Weitzman, NCRW, CPRW, JCTC
Gilbert Career Resumes Ltd.
275 Madison Avenue
New York, NY 10017
212-661-6878
gilcareer@aol.com
www.resumepro.com

Deborah Wile Dib, NCRW, CPRW, JCTC, CCM
Advantage Resumes of New York
77 Buffalo Avenue
Medford, NY 11763
631-475-8513
gethired@advantageresumes.com
www.advantageresumes.com

Martin Yate
Peregrine McCoy
PO Box 70
Sea Cliff, NY 11579
516-674-3329
mccoy007@earthlink.net

OHIO

Hanan Akra, CPRW
DocuMall,
4102 N. Main Street
Findlay, OH 45840
419-423-0259
documall@aol.com

Susan Anderson
US Air Force - Family Support Center
88 MSS/DFP, 2000 Allbrook Dr. #3
Wright Patterson AFB, OH 45433
937-656-0939
susan.anderson@wpafb.af.mil

Pierre Daunic, Ph.D.
R.L. Stevens & Associates, Inc.
1674 Quail Meadows Drive
Lancaster, OH 43130
740-689-8056
pdaunic@rlstevens.com

Richard Haid, Ph.D., PCC
Adult Mentor
157 E. Fairway Drive
Hamilton, OH 45013
513-868-1488
dickhaid@adultmentor.com
www.adultmentor.com

Alice-Kay Hilderbrand, JCTC
Ohio Northern University
Career Services Center
Ada, OH 45810
419-772-2145
a-hilderbrand@onu.edu
www.onu.ed/admin-offices/

Susan Hoopes
Cuyahoga Valley Career Center
8001 Brecksville Road
Brecksville, OH 44141
440-526-5200
cvccshoopes@netscape.net

Barrie Hubbard
Centennial, Inc.
1014 Vine Street, Suite 1525
Cincinnati, OH 45202
513-381-4411
barrie@centennial-inc.com

Deborah James
Leading Edge Resume & Career Services
1010 Schreier Road
Rossford, OH 43460
419-666-4518
OhioResGal@aol.com
www.leadingedgeresumes.com

Andrea Kay
PO Box 6834
Cincinnati, OH 45206
606-781-2228
AskAndrea@fuse.net

Louise Kursmark, CPRW, JCTC, CCM
Best Impression Career Services, Inc.
9847 Catalpa Woods Court
Cincinnati, OH 45242
513-792-0030
LK@yourbestimpression.com

Sue Montgomery, CPRW, IJCTC
Resume Plus
4140 Linden Avenue, #112
Dayton, OH 45432
937-254-5627
resumeplus@siscom.net
www.resumeplus.com

Jerry Tisovic
R.L. Stevens & Associates
5005 Rockside Road
Independence, OH 44131
216-642-1933
gtisovic@rlstevens.com

Caitlin Williams, M.Ed., Ph.D.
Successful Working Women, Inc.
24408 Westwood Road
Westlake, OH 44145-4838
440-716-0929
cpwms@aol.com

Janice Worthington-Loranca, MA, CPRW, JCTC
Fortune 500 Communications
6636 Belleshire Street
Columbus, OH 43229
614-890-1645
janice@fortune500resumes.com
www.fortune500resumes.com

PENNSYLVANIA

Jewel Bracy DeMaio, CPRW
A Perfect Resume.com
419 Valley Road
Elkins Park, PA 19027
800-227-5131
mail@aperfectresume.com
www.aperfectresume.com

Paula Brandt, CPRW
The Resume Lady
183 Valleyview Drive
Belle Vernon, PA 15012
724-872-9030
paula@resumelady.com
www.resumelady.com (in process)

Barbaraanne Breithaupt, IJCTC, CPRW, CO
Barbaraanne's Lasting Impressions
3202 Holyoke Road
Philadelphia, PA 19114-3522
215-676-7742
Tiger4PARW@aol.com

Bob Bronstein, MBA
Pro/File Research
548 Bethlehem Pike
Fort Washington, PA 19034
215-643-3411
bronsteinr@aol.com

Patricia Harrington, CPRW, JCTC
Accent Resume Design
567 Lenape Circle
Langhorne, PA 19047
215-860-5345
accentp@aol.com

Jeffrey Lewin
Bernard Haldane Associates
1150 First Avenue, #385
King of Prussia, PA 19401
610-491-9050
LewinJ@bhaldane.com

Jane Roqueplot, CBC
JaneCo's Sensible Solutions
194 North Oakland Avenue
Sharon, PA 16146
724-342-0100
janeir@janecos.com
www.janecos.com

Robert Wolk
Bernard Haldane Associates
5100 S. Convent Lane, #502
Philadephia, PA 19114
610-491-9050
perryxx@aol.com
www.jobhunting.com

PUERTO RICO

Myrna Muriel Gonzalez
Professional Office Support Srvcs.
Murcia #251
Vistamar, Carolina, PR 00983
787-750-4926
myrnaelena@hotmail.com

SOUTH CAROLINA

Kim Erwin
Clemson University
101 Barre Hall
Clemson, SC 29634
864-656-5727
kerwn@clemson.edu

Karen Swann, CPRW
TypeRight
384-4 College Avenue
Clemson, SC 29631
864-653-7901
karzim@carol.net

TENNESSEE

Carolyn Braden, CPRW
Braden Resume Solutions
108 La Plaza Drive
Hendersonville, TN 37075
615-822-3317
bradenresume@home.com

Marta Driesslein, CPRW
Cambridge Career Services, Inc.
300 Montvue Road, Suite A
Knoxville, TN 37919
865-539-9538
careerhope@aol.com
www.careerhope.com

Randall Howard
Randall Howard & Associates, Inc.
PO Box 382397
Memphis, TN 38183-2397
901-754-3333
RHAssociates@aol.com

Lynn Jackson
Russell, Montgomery & Associates/OI Worldwide
5050 Poplar Avenue, #328
Memphis, TN 38157
901-763-1818
Ljackson@oiworldwide.com
oiworldwide.com

Angela Majors
1137 Nelson Drive
Madison, TN 37115
615-868-8847
admajors@msn.com

TEXAS

Tracy Bumpus, CPRW, JCTC
RezAMAZE.com
1807 Slaughter Lane, #200, PMB 366
Austin, TX 78748
512-291-1404
tbumpus@rezamaze.com
www.rezamaze.com

Marsha Camp, CPRW, CCM
Accent on Success
711 N. Carancahua, Suite 700
Corpus Christi, TX 78475
361-884-7027
MarshaCamp@aol.com

Melinda Coker
6701 La Costa Drive
Tyler, TX 75703
903-561-5694
melinda_75703@yahoo.com

Mike Fernandes, CPRW
Resumes And More
13101 Preston Road, Suite 300, Dallas
TX 75240-5229
972-239-1991
MikeFernan@aol.com

Cheryl Harland, CPRW, JCTC
Resumes By Design
25227 Grogan's Mill Road, Suite 125
The Woodlands, TX 77380
888-213-1650
CAH@resumesbydesign.com

Lynn Hughes, MA
A Resume and Career Service, Inc.
PO Box 53932
Lubbock, TX 79453
806-785-9800
lynn@aresumeservice.com
www.aresumeservice.com

Shanna Kemp, M.Ed., IJCTC, CPRW
Kemp Career Services
2105 Via Del Norte
Carollton, TX 75006
972-416-9089
respro@aresumepro.com
www.aresumpro.com

Ann Klint, NCRW, CPRW
Ann's Professional Resume Service
1608 Cimmarron Trail
Tyler, TX 75703
903-509-8333
Resumes-Ann@tyler.net

Monique LaCour
Career Management Services
4800 Sugar Grove Blvd., #290
Stafford, TX 77477
713-270-6056
careermgt@usa.net

Peggy Mathias, CPRW, JCTC
Peggy's Paper Works
2525 Johnson, Suite A
San Angelo, TX 76904
915-224-2733
pege@wcc.net

Gerald Moore, CPRW
5536 Longview Circle
El Paso, TX 79924
915-821-1036
jmoore@dzn.com
www.thewritejob.com

William Murdock
The Employment Coach
7770 Meadow Road, Suite 109
Bedford, TX 76021
214-750-4781
bmurdock@swbell.net

Helen Newell
10101 South Gessner, #304
Houston, TX 77071
713-777-3715
helious21@aol.com

Joann Nix, CPRW, JCTC, CEIP
Beaumont Resume Service
7825 Fox Cove
Beaumont, TX 77713
409-899-1932
Info@agreatresume.com
www.agreatresume.com

Kelley Smith, CPRW
Advantage Resume Services
PO Box 391
Sugarland, TX 77487
281-494-3330
info@advantage-resume.com
www.advantage-resume.com

Ann Stewart, CPRW
Advantage Services
PO Box 535
Roanoke, TX 76262
817-424-1448
ASresume@aol.com

Kim Thompson, LPC, NBCC
New Avenues Career Management Programs
13811 Burgoyne
Houston, TX 77077
281-752-4015
kmathomp@aol.com

UTAH

Lynn Andenoro, CPRW, JCTC, CCM
My Career Resource
1214 Fenway
Salt Lake City, UT 84102
801-883-2011
Lynn@MyCareerResource.com
www.MyCareerResource.com

Diana LeGere
Executive Final Copy
PO Box 171311
Salt Lake City, UT 84117
801-277-6299
execfinalcopy@email.msn.com
www.executivefinalcopy.com

Tanya Civiero
Encore Resumes
19870 Horseshoe Hill Road
Calendon, Ontario, L0N 1C0
519-941-9887
tciviero@hotmail.com

Candace Davies, BBA, CPRW, FCI
Cando Career Coaching & Resume Writing
10710 90th Street
Grande Prairie, Alberta, T8X 1J8
780-513-0010
candoco@telusplanet.net
www.candocareer.com

Sandra Lim CPRW, CCM
A Better Impression
24 Wellesley Street W, Suite 2302
Toronto, Ontario, M4Y 2X6
416-961-8840
a_better_impression@myna.com

Leslie Lumsden
Richard Ivey School of Business/Univ. of Western
Ontario
1151 Richmond Street
London, Ontario, N6A 3K7
519-661-2111
Llumsden@ivey.uwo.ca

Ross MacPherson, MA, CPRW, JCTC, CEIP
Career Quest
1586 Major Oaks Road
Pickering, Ontario, L1X 2J6
905-426-8548
careerquest@primus.ca

Sylvia Mastromartino
Resume Excellence
643 16th Avenue
Richmond Hill, Ontario, L4C 7A8
905-709-8887
resumeexcellence@home.com

Nicole Miller
Mil-Roy Consultants
1729 Hunter's Run Drive
Orleans, Ontario, K1C 6W2
613-834-2160
resumesbymilroy@hotmail.com

INTERNATIONAL

Cristina Mejias
Career Managers S.A.
Talcahauano 833 7 A (1013)
Cap., Fed., Argentina
11-481-67500
consultores@careermanagers.com.ar
www.careermanagers.com.ar

Rick Browning
Rick Browning The Career Doctor
PO Box 523
Kings Cross NSW, 2010, Australia
coach@careerdoctor.com.au
www.careerdoctor.com.au

Gayle Howard, CPRW
Top Margin Resumes Online
7 Commerford Place
Chirnside Park, Melbourne, 3116, Australia
getinterviews@topmargin.com
www.topmargin.com

Paul Stevens
The Centre for Worklife Counselling
PO Box 407
Spit Junction, Sydney, 2088, Australia
worklife@ozemail.com.au
www.worklife.ozemail.com.au

Mohamed Sadik
Jolie Ville Hotels & Resorts
Sharm El-Sheikh
South Sinai, Egypt
206-260-0100
sadik1959@hotmail.com

Gilles Dagorn
Job Strategy
80 Avenue Charles de Gaulle
Neuilly, 92200, France
info@jobstrategy.fr
www.jobstrategy.fr

Paula Stenberg
CV Style
Level 5B, 9 Victoria St. East
Auckland, New Zealand
0064-9-377-3348
paula@cvstyle.co.nz
www.cvstyle.co.nz

Han Kwang, MBA, CCM
Personal Mastery Resources
196 Bishan Street 13 #03-559
Singapore, 570196
065-352-8756
haninc@magix.com.sg

John Read, JCTC
What Career Next!
Robinson Road, PO Box 1040
Singapore, 902040
065-354-3551
career@magix.com.sg
www.ecircles.com/magic/
j.cgi?IK=1750700C775@oem=ec

Christina Kuenzle
Coutts Career Consultants
Hauserstrasse 14
Zurich, 8006, Switzerland
411-268-8844
christine.kuenzle@coutts-consulting.ch

Appendix B

Resume Preparation Forms

Use the following forms to help you identify your core skills, knowledge and achievements, and then link them to your current career objectives. This information will serve as the foundation for your entire resume presentation. It will clearly outline the specific skills, qualifications, experiences and accomplishments that you offer that tie directly to the position(s) you are seeking. When you begin to write your resume (particularly your Objective, Career Summary and Professional Experience), remember these are the most important things to highlight in order to communicate that you have the "right stuff."

RESUME WRITING ACTIVITY #1

Identifying Your Skills & Knowledge

Make a complete list of the things that you do well. This list should include both professional functions (e.g., sales, product design, joint venture negotiations, technology implementation, strategic planning, budgeting) as well as more "general" skills (e.g., organization, project management, interpersonal relations, team building/leadership, oral and written communications, problem solving, decision making).

_____

_____

_____

_____

_____

_____

_____

_____

_____

_____

_____

_____

_____

_____

RESUME WRITING ACTIVITY #2

Identifying Your Career Achievements

Make a comprehensive list of the notable achievements, successes, project highlights, honors and awards of your career, with a focus on the past 10 years of employment. Whenever possible, use numbers or percentages to quantify results and substantiate your performance.

_____

_____

_____

_____

_____

_____

_____

_____

_____

_____

_____

_____

RESUME WRITING ACTIVITY #3

Identifying Your Career Objectives

List the industries and positions in which you are interested in career opportunities.

_____

_____

_____

_____

_____

_____

_____

_____

_____

_____

_____

_____

_____

_____

RESUME WRITING ACTIVITY #4

Linking Your Skills & Achievements With Your Objectives

Using your responses to Activity #3 (Career Objectives), select skills and accomplishments from your responses to Activity #1 and Activity #2 that relate to your objective(s). In doing so, you're making a connection between what you have to offer and what type of position you are interested in. For example, if your objective is a position in Technology Sales & Marketing Management, the fact that you have strong plastic products assembly skills is probably not relevant and therefore not necessary to include. However, the fact that you have excellent negotiation and account management skills is critical and should be at the forefront of your resume. The strategy is to select items from #1 and #2 that support #3.

OBJECTIVE #1:

RELATED SKILLS:

_____

_____

_____

RELATED ACCOMPLISHMENTS:

_____

_____

_____

OBJECTIVE #2:

RELATED SKILLS:

_____

_____

_____

RELATED ACCOMPLISHMENTS:

_____

_____

_____

_____

_____

_____

_____

Appendix C

Frequently Asked Questions

1. How long should a resume be?

The recommended length of a resume is 1-2 pages, realizing that in most instances an executive resume will be two pages long. It is virtually impossible to fit everything onto one page and have room for any substance or achievements.

There are, however, situations when a resume will be longer than 2 pages. If you are seeking a very senior-level (CEO, President, Chairman, Board Director) position. Consider this example: You are the CEO of a Fortune 50 company applying for a position as CEO of another Fortune 50. Although your professional work experience is critical, so are your professional affiliations, civic affiliations, non-profit affiliations, public speaking engagements, university teaching experience, and other professional activities. In a circumstance such as this, where the candidates are the top in the country, the search is quite selective and the stakes are high, a longer resume can be a more appropriate tool. The company is not just hiring the professional. Rather, the company is hiring the person, his network of contacts, and his reputation. Longer resumes are quite acceptable in this situation.

When you are writing a curriculum vitae (CV) and not a resume. If you are not familiar with CVs, these are career documents used most frequently in academic, research, medicine, science, and related fields. CVs are comprehensive documents that include *all* of an individual's experience, internships, externships, publications, affiliations, teaching experience, and more. Sections are not "highlighted" or summarized as in a resume. Rather, they are very detailed. It is not unusual to look at a CV that is 8, 10, or even 20 pages long. It has an entirely different "look and feel" than a resume.

2. Should you include dates of employment and education on a resume?

Ninety-five percent of the time the answer is a resounding *yes*. Dates give your readers a point of reference to understand how your career has progressed. Without dates, a reader cannot determine if you have been with your current employer 11 months or 11 years, and it makes the entire resume much more confusing.

It is also important to date your education (year you received your degree). Again, it is a good point of reference for your reader and clearly indicates the beginning of your career.

The exception to this rule is for over-50 job seekers. If you are in this employment market, refer to the section that follows on the particularities of resume writing for over-50 candidates.

3. Should you include months of employment?

The answer to this question is generally no. Most readers will not care if you started your current position in May 1994 or November 1994. Furthermore, at some point in the hiring process, you will most likely complete an application where you can share that specific information. The only time that months are recommended on resumes is for younger candidates with much less experience. If you are reading this book, you most likely do not fit into that category.

4. Are salary history and salary requirements the same thing?

No. Salary history is what you have made in past positions while salary requirements state your current compensation goals.

5. Should you include your salary history or salary requirements on a resume?

The resume is *not* the appropriate forum for a salary discussion. If, and only if, a prospective employer or recruiter asks for salary information should you provide it and then it is most appropriately addressed in your cover letter.

6. Must you always mail a cover letter with resume?

Yes, yes, yes. Consider this. When writing your resume you began with your entire career in your hands. You then consolidated everything onto 1-2 pages to create your resume. Now, to write a powerful cover letter, consolidate your resume into 1-2 hard-hitting paragraphs that address the *specfic* needs of the company to which you are writing.

Well-written cover letters complement your resume and draw the reader's attention to the key points of your career most related to that company's or recruiter's needs. They are an essential component of any job seeker's successful search campaign and can make the difference between an interview and no interview.

To learn to write expert cover letters, refer to *Best Cover Letters For $100,000+ Jobs* by Wendy S. Enelow (Impact Publications, 2001).

7. How should you present the fact that you are an "over-50" candidate?

My opinion is that you should NOT present this fact, at least not at the introductory resume stage of your job search. Why put something on your resume that may, in many instances, immediately exclude you from consideration? That is not the point of your resume. A resume is written to open doors and get interviews, not tell your entire life story.

Do not kid yourself for one minute. Prospective employers are often concerned about hiring the "older" worker, no matter how well qualified and successful. Therefore, you must be careful in your use of dates. When you write that you graduated from college in 1964, you are immediately communicating the fact that you are an older candidate. In this situation, your best strategy is to include your degree with no dates.

The same thing can be said about your employment experience. If you began your professional career in 1966 and include that date on your resume, again you have inadvertently communicated, "I'm 56 years old." That may not be the first thing that you want to share with a prospective employer, particularly as you are trying to get in the door for an interview! Sell your success, knowledge and expertise, and leave your age behind.

For more information about how to optimize the value of your older experience while omitting the dates to avoid "aging" yourself, read the following section.

8. Should you include ALL of your work experience on a resume?

The answer to this question is a definitive "it depends." If you are 42 years old, then yes, include all of your experience, although you will most likely only briefly summarize your earliest jobs in order to comfortably fit everything onto two pages. However, if you are 58 years old, you have to make some difficult decisions about how far back in your career to go on your resume and whether or not any of the older experience is related to your current objective. This is a one-on-one call that you will have to make depending on your own specific situation.

It may be that you can find real value in your older experience. Perhaps you worked for well-known and well-respected companies, were promoted rapidly, accomplished something great, developed a revolutionary new product, or did something else fantastic. If this is the case, you certainly will want to include this information on your resume. Here are a few sample strategies:

PREVIOUS PROFESSIONAL EXPERIENCE:

Promoted through a series of increasingly responsible management positions with Acceleron Technologies, a $200 million laser products R&D firm. (*focuses on fast-track career promotion*)

Previous professional experience includes several key management positions with IBM, Digital, and Hewlett-Packard. (*focuses on reputation of your employers*)

Reduced annual staffing costs by 28% in the first year and an additional 12% in the second year while HR Director for the Chase Manhattan Bank's International Division. (*focuses on your achievements*)

Note that there are no dates in any of the above examples. By using these strategies, you are able to highlight the important aspects of your early career without drawing attention to length of employment and age. What's more, you have been upfront in disclosing that you do have previous experience and therefore have been totally "above board" and not hidden anything. Using one of these strategies will get you off on the "right foot" with a prospective employer. There is nothing worse than having to defend something you wrote on your resume while you are in an interview!

Books by Wendy S. Enelow

1500+ Keywords for $100,000+ Jobs
Best Cover Letters for $100,000+ Jobs
Best Resumes for $100,000+ Jobs
Resume Winners From the Pros
Winning Interviews for $100,000+ Jobs

The Click and Easy™ Online Resource Centers –

Books, videos, software, training materials, articles, and advice for job seekers, employers, HR professionals, schools, and libraries

Visit us online for all your career and travel needs:

www.impactpublications.com
(career superstore and Impact Publications)

———————

www.winningthejob.com
(career articles and advice)

———————

www.contentforcareers.com
(syndicated career content for job seekers,
employees, and Intranets)

———————

www.greentogray.com
www.bluetogray.com
(military transition databases and content)

———————

www.ishoparoundtheworld.com
(unique international travel-shopping center)